Rick Steves

SPAIN &

PORTUGAL

2000

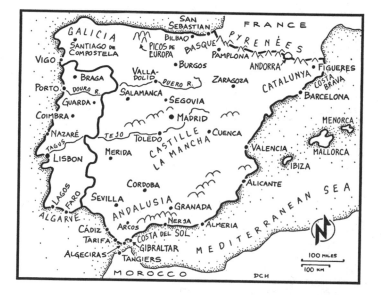

John Muir Publications
Santa Fe, New Mexico

Other JMP travel guidebooks by Rick Steves
Europe 101: History and Art for the Traveler (with Gene Openshaw)
Rick Steves' Postcards from Europe
Rick Steves' Europe Through the Back Door
Rick Steves' Mona Winks: Self-Guided Tours of Europe's Top Museums
 (with Gene Openshaw)
Rick Steves' Best of Europe
Rick Steves' France, Belgium & the Netherlands (with Steve Smith)
Rick Steves' Germany, Austria & Switzerland
Rick Steves' Great Britain & Ireland
Rick Steves' Italy
Rick Steves' London (with Gene Openshaw)
Rick Steves' Paris (with Steve Smith and Gene Openshaw)
Rick Steves' Rome (with Gene Openshaw)
Rick Steves' Scandinavia
Rick Steves' Phrase Books: German, Italian, French,
 Spanish/Portuguese, and French/Italian/German
Asia Through the Back Door (with Bob Effertz)

John Muir Publications, P.O. Box 613, Santa Fe, NM 87504
Copyright © 2000, 1999, 1998, 1997, 1996 by Rick Steves
Cover copyright © 2000, 1999, 1998 by John Muir Publications
All rights reserved.

Printed in the United States of America
First printing January 2000

For the latest on Rick Steves' lectures, guidebooks, tours, and public
television series, contact Europe Through the Back Door, Box 2009,
Edmonds, WA 98020, tel. 425/771-8303, fax 425/771-0833,
www.ricksteves.com, or e-mail: rick@ricksteves.com.

ISBN 1-56261-502-5
ISSN 1084-4414

Europe Through the Back Door Editor Risa Laib
John Muir Publications Editors Laurel Gladden Gillespie,
Krista Lyons-Gould
Research Assistance Brian Carr Smith
Production & Typesetting Kathleen Sparkes, White Hart Design
Design Linda Braun
Cover Design Janine Lehmann
Maps David C. Hoerlein
Printer Banta Company
Cover Photo Giralda Tower and Cathedral, Sevilla, Spain;
copyright © Blaine Harrington III

Distributed to the book trade by
Publishers Group West
Berkeley, California

*Although the author and publisher have made every effort to provide accurate,
up-to-date information, they accept no responsibility for loss, injury, loose stools, or
inconvenience sustained by any person using this book.*

CONTENTS

Introduction 1

*Planning Your Trip 2 • Trip Costs 2 • Exchange Rates 3 •
Prices, Times, and Discounts 3 • When to Go 4 •
Sightseeing Priorities 4 • Red Tape, Business Hours, and
Banking 4 • Language Barrier 5 • Travel Smart 5 • Tourist
Information 6 • Recommended Guidebooks 8 • Rick Steves'
Books and Videos 9 • Maps 10 • Transportation 10 •
Telephones, Mail, and E-mail 16 • Sleeping 17 • Eating in
Spain 20 • Eating in Portugal 22 • Stranger in a Strange
Land 22 • Back Door Manners 23 • Tours of Spain and
Portugal 23 • Send Me a Postcard, Drop Me a Line 23 •
Back Door Travel Philosophy 24*

Spain 25

   Barcelona 25

   Madrid 47

   Northwest of Madrid 69

   Toledo 86

   Granada 99

   Sevilla 119

   Andalucía's White Hill Towns 132

   Costa del Sol: Spain's South Coast 153

Morocco 173

Portugal 185

   Lisbon 185

   The Algarve 214

   Central Portugal: Coimbra and Nazaré 229

Appendix 252

*Iberian History 252 • Art 253 • Architecture 254 •
Bullfighting 255 • Fiestas 256 • Numbers and Stumblers 257 •
Let's Talk Telephones 257 • Metric Conversion 258 •
Climate 259 • Basic Spanish Survival Phrases 260 • Basic
Portuguese Survival Phrases 261 • Faxing Your Hotel
Reservation 262 • Road Scholar Feedback Form 263 •
Jubilee 2000 264*

Index 265

Top Destinations in Spain and Portugal

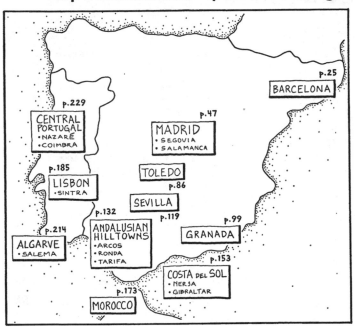

INTRODUCTION

Like a grandpa bouncing a baby on his knee, Iberia is a mix of old and new, modern and traditional. Spain and Portugal can fill your travel days with world-class art treasures, folk life, exotic foods, sunshine, friendly people, and castles where the winds of the past still howl. And, in spite of its recent economic boom, Iberia (particularly Portugal) remains Europe's bargain basement.

This book breaks Spain and Portugal into their top big-city, small-town, and rural destinations. It then gives you all the information and opinions necessary to wring the maximum value out of your limited time and money in each of these destinations. If you plan a month or less in Iberia, this lean and mean little book is all you need.

Experiencing Spain and Portugal's culture, people, and natural wonders economically and hassle-free has been my goal for 25 years of traveling, tour guiding, and writing. With this book, I pass on to you the lessons I've learned, updated for 2000.

Rick Steves' Spain & Portugal is a tour guide in your pocket, with a balanced, comfortable mix of exciting cities and cozy towns topped off with an exotic dollop of Morocco. It covers the predictable biggies and stirs in a healthy dose of Back Door intimacy. Along with seeing a bullfight, the Prado, and flamenco, you'll buy cookies from cloistered nuns in a sun-parched Andalusian town and recharge your solar cells in an Algarve fishing village. You'll eat barnacles with green wine in village Portugal and scramble the ramparts of an ancient Moorish castle. I've been selective, including only the most exciting sights and experiences. For example, there are countless whitewashed Andalusian hill towns; I recommend the best three.

The best is, of course, only my opinion. But after two busy decades of travel writing, lecturing, and tour guiding, I've developed a sixth sense of what tickles the traveler's fancy.

This Information Is Accurate and Up-to-Date

This book is updated every year. Most publishers of guidebooks that cover a region from top to bottom can afford an update only every two or three years, and then the research is often by letter. Since this book is selective, covering only the places I think make the best month or so in Iberia, it can be personally updated each summer. Even with annual updates, things change. But if you're traveling with the current edition of this book, I guarantee you're using the most up-to-date information available. Trust me, you'll regret trying to save a few bucks by traveling on old information. If you're packing an old book, you'll quickly learn the seriousness of your mistake... in Europe. Your trip costs about $10 per waking hour. Your time is valuable. This guidebook saves lots of time.

Planning Your Trip

This book is organized by destinations. Each destination is covered as a mini-vacation on its own, filled with exciting sights and homey, affordable places to stay. In each chapter, you'll find the following:

Planning Your Time, a suggested schedule with thoughts on how best to use your limited time.

Orientation, including tourist information, city transportation, and an easy-to-read map designed to make the text clear and your arrival smooth.

Sights with ratings: ▲▲▲—Don't miss; ▲▲—Try hard to see; ▲—Worthwhile if you can make it; no rating—Worth knowing about.

Sleeping and **Eating**, with addresses and phone numbers of my favorite budget hotels and restaurants.

Transportation Connections to nearby destinations by train, bus, or car, with recommended roadside attractions for drivers.

The **Appendix** is a traveler's tool kit, with telephone tips, a climate chart, a list of festivals, and cultural background.

Browse through this book, choose your favorite destinations, and link them up. Then have a great trip! You'll travel as a temporary local, getting the absolute most out of every mile, minute, and dollar. You won't waste time on mediocre sights because, unlike others, this guidebook covers only the best. Since your major financial pitfall is lousy, expensive hotels, I've worked hard to assemble the best accommodations values for each stop. And, as you travel the route I know and love, I'm happy you'll be meeting some of my favorite Spanish and Portuguese people.

Trip Costs

Five components make up your trip cost: airfare, surface transportation, room and board, sightseeing/entertainment, and shopping/miscellany.

Airfare: Don't try to sort through the mess yourself. Get and use a good travel agent. A basic round-trip flight from the United States to Madrid or Lisbon should cost $700 to $1,000, depending on where you fly from and when. Always consider saving time and money by flying "open-jaws" (into one city and out of another, e.g. into Barcelona and out of Lisbon).

Surface Transportation: For a three-week whirlwind trip linking all of my recommended destinations, allow $350 per person for second-class trains and buses ($500 for first-class trains) or $500 per person (based on two people sharing) for a three-week car rental, tolls, gas, and insurance. Car rental is cheapest to arrange from home in the United States. Train passes, easily purchased outside of Europe, are also available at some of the larger European train stations. You may save money, however, by simply buying tickets as you go (see "Transportation," below).

Room and Board: While most will spend more (because they've got it and it's fun), you can thrive in Iberia on $50 a day per person for room and board. A $50-a-day budget allows $5 for lunch, $15 for dinner, and $30 for lodging (based on two people splitting the cost of a $60 double room that includes breakfast). That's doable. Students and tightwads will do it on $30 ($15 per bed, $15 for meals and snacks). But budget sleeping and eating require the skills and information covered below (or more extensively in *Rick Steves' Europe Through the Back Door*).

Sightseeing and Entertainment: In big cities, figure $4 per major sight (Prado, Picasso Museum), $2 for minor ones (climbing church towers), and $25 for splurge experiences (flamenco, bullfights). An overall average of $10 a day works for most. Don't skimp here. After all, this category directly powers most of the experiences all the other expenses are designed to make possible.

Shopping and Miscellany: Figure $1 per coffee, beer, ice-cream cone, and postcard. Shopping can vary in cost from nearly nothing to a small fortune. Good budget travelers find that this category has little to do with assembling a trip full of lifelong and wonderful memories.

Exchange Rates
I list prices in pesetas and escudos throughout the book.

> 160 Spanish pesetas (ptas) = about $1;
> 100 ptas = about 65 cents.
> 190 Portuguese escudos = about $1;
> 100 escudos = about 55 cents.

The Portuguese use a dollar sign after the number of escudos (e.g., 180 escudos is 180$00 or 180$). To figure rough prices in dollars, think of pesetas and escudos as pennies and cut 33 percent in Spain (3,000 ptas = about $20) and cut about 50 percent in Portugal (5,000$00 = about $25).

Prices, Times, and Discounts
The prices, hours, and telephone numbers in this book are accurate as of mid-1999. Iberia is always changing, and I know you'll understand that this, like any other guidebook, starts to yellow even before it's printed.

In Europe—and in this book—you'll be using the 24-hour clock. After 12:00 noon, keep going—13:00, 14:00, and so on. For anything over 12, subtract 12 and add p.m. (14:00 is 2:00 p.m.).

This book lists peak-season hours for sightseeing attractions. Off-season, roughly October through April, expect shorter hours, more lunchtime breaks, and fewer activities. Confirm your sightseeing plans locally, especially when traveling off-season.

Portuguese time is usually one hour earlier than Spanish time (due to daylight saving time). Morocco can be up to two hours earlier than Spanish time.

While discounts for sightseeing and transportation are not listed in this book, seniors (60 and over), students (with International Student Identity Cards), and youths (under 18) often get discounts—but only by asking.

When to Go

Spring and fall offer the best combination of good weather, light crowds, long days, and plenty of tourist and cultural activities. Summer and winter travel both have their predictable pros and cons. July and August are most crowded and expensive in coastal areas, less crowded but uncomfortably hot and dusty in the interior. For weather specifics, see the climate chart in the Appendix. Whenever you anticipate crowds, particularly in July and August, call hotels in advance (call from one hotel to the next, with the help of your fluent receptionist) and try to arrive early in the day.

Sightseeing Priorities

Depending on the length of your trip, here are my recommended priorities.

3 days:	Madrid, Toledo
5 days, add:	Barcelona
7 days, add:	Lisbon
10 days, add:	Andalucía, Sevilla
14 days, add:	Granada, Algarve
17 days, add:	Costa del Sol, Morocco
20 days, add:	Coimbra, Nazaré
22 days, add:	Salamanca, Segovia

Red Tape, Business Hours, and Banking

You currently need a passport but no visa and no shots to travel in Spain, Portugal, and Morocco.

For visitors, Iberia is a land of strange and frustrating schedules. Most businesses respect the afternoon siesta. When it's 100 degrees in the shade, you'll understand why.

Generally shops are open from 9:00 to 13:00 and from 15:00 or 16:00 to 19:00 or 20:00, longer in touristy places. On Saturday, shops often open only in the morning and are closed Sunday. The biggest museums stay open all day. Smaller ones often close for a siesta.

Banking: Bring a Visa or MasterCard with a four-digit PIN so you can use the same card to withdraw cash from ATMs and to charge any expensive items. Both Spain and Portugal have easily available, easy-to-use 24-hour ATMs with English instructions. They'll save you time and money (on commission fees). I traveled painlessly throughout Spain and Portugal in 1999 with my Visa debit card. Get details at your bank and bring an extra copy of your card just in case it gets demagnetized or gobbled up by a machine. Bring some cash or a few traveler's checks as a backup. If you are planning on getting cash advances from your regular credit card, make sure to ask the card company about fees before you leave.

Banks are generally open Monday through Friday from 9:00 to 14:00 in Spain and 8:30 to 15:00 in Portugal (often with a lunch break).

Spanish banks charge acceptable commissions for changing traveler's checks. American Express offices (found only in big cities) have a slightly less favorable rate but change any type of traveler's check without a commission. Portugal's banks charge outrageous, unregulated commissions ($8–15). Shop around. Sometimes the hole-in-the-wall exchange offices offer better deals than the bank. Look for the rare American Express office. Better yet, have an ATM card handy.

Language Barrier

For me, nowhere in Europe is the language barrier more frustrating than in Iberia. Learn the key phrases. Here, more than in most places in Europe, a phrase book comes in handy, particularly if you want to interact with local people. You'll find that doors open quicker and with more smiles when you can speak a few words of the language.

Spanish is easier than Portuguese to learn and pronounce. Portuguese sounds like a French person speaking Spanish through a kazoo—while bouncing on a pogo stick. Try to learn the pleasantries. Fortunately, in Portugal's big cities and along the Algarve, people in the tourist business generally speak English. Otherwise, Spanish, French, or sign language come in handy.

My Spanish and Portuguese phrase book, which includes a traveler's dictionary, will help you soar over the language barrier. And look up the Survival Phrases in the Appendix of this book.

Travel Smart

Reread this book as you travel and visit local tourist information offices. Buy a phone card and use it for reservations and confirmations. Use taxis in the big cities, bring along a water bottle, and linger in the shade. Connect with the cultures. Set up your own quest for the best cream cake, cloister, fish soup, or whatever.

Enjoy the friendliness of the local people. Ask questions. Most locals are eager to point you in their idea of the right direction. Wear your money belt, pack a pocket-size notepad to organize your thoughts, and practice the virtue of simplicity. Those who expect to travel smart, do.

Design an itinerary that enables you to hit the festivals, bullfights, and museums on the right days. As you read this book,

Whirlwind Three-Week Tour

note the problem days: Mondays, when many museums are closed, and Sundays, when public transportation is meager. Treat Saturdays as weekdays.

Plan ahead for banking, laundry, post-office chores, and picnics. Maximize rootedness by minimizing one-night stands. Mix intense and relaxed periods. Every trip (and every traveler) needs at least a few slack days. Pace yourself. Assume you will return.

Warning: Tourists are targeted by thieves throughout Spain and Portugal, especially in Barcelona, Madrid, Sevilla, and Lisbon. While hotel rooms are generally safe and I've never heard of a tourist being mugged, cars are commonly broken into, purses are snatched, and pockets are picked. Be on guard, wear a money belt, and treat any commotion around you as a smoke screen for theft. Drivers should park carefully and leave nothing of value in the car; locals leave their cars empty and unlocked. When traveling by train, keep your rucksack in sight and get a *couchette* (bed in an attendant-monitored sleeping car) for safety on overnight trips.

Tourist Information
Your best first stop in a new city is the Turismo (tourist information office). Get a city map and advice on public transportation

Spain & Portugal's Best Three-Week Trip

Day	Plan	Sleep in
1	Arrive in Madrid	Madrid
2	Madrid	Madrid
3	El Escorial, Valley of Fallen, Segovia	Segovia
4	Segovia and Salamanca	Salamanca
5	Salamanca, Coimbra	Coimbra
6	Coimbra, Batalha, Fatima, Nazaré	Nazaré
7	Beach day in Nazaré, Alcobaça side trip	Nazaré
8	Nazaré, Lisbon	Lisbon
9	Lisbon	Lisbon
10	Lisbon side trip to Belém and Sintra	Lisbon
11	Lisbon to the Algarve	Salema
12	Free beach day, Sagres	Salema
13	Across Algarve, Sevilla	Sevilla
14	Sevilla	Sevilla
15	Andalucía's Route of White Villages	Arcos
16	Arcos, Jerez, Tarifa	Tarifa
17	A day in Morocco	Tarifa
18	Gibraltar, Costa del Sol	Nerja
19	Nerja to Granada	Granada
20	Granada	Granada
21	Through La Mancha to Toledo	Toledo
22	Toledo	Toledo/Madrid/fly

While this itinerary is designed to be done by car, it can be done by train and bus (seven to eight bus days and four to five train days). For three weeks without a car, I'd modify it to start in Barcelona and finish in Lisbon: From Barcelona, fly or take the night train to Madrid (see Toledo, Segovia, El Escorial); take the night train to Granada; bus along Costa del Sol to Tarifa (see Morocco); bus to Arcos, Sevilla, and Algarve; and take the train to Lisbon. This skips Coimbra and Salamanca and assumes you'll fly open-jaws into Barcelona and fly out of Lisbon. If you're catching the train from Lisbon back to Madrid, you can sightsee your way in three days (via Coimbra and Salamanca) or simply catch the night train to Madrid.

(including bus and train schedules), special events, and recommendations for nightlife. Many Turismos have information on the entire country. When you visit a Turismo (abbreviated TI in this book), try to pick up maps for towns you'll be visiting later in your trip.

While the TI has listings of all lodgings and is eager to book you a room, use their room-finding service only as a last resort (bloated prices, fees, no opinions, and they take a cut from your host). You'll get a far better value by using the listings in this book and going direct.

The national tourist offices in the United States are a wealth of information. Before your trip get their free general-information packet and request any specific information you want, such as city maps and schedules of upcoming festivals.

Spanish National Tourist Offices: For general info, call 888/OKSPAIN, www.okspain.org; 666 Fifth Ave., 35th floor, New York, NY 10022, tel. 212/265-8822, fax 212/265-8864; 845 N. Michigan Ave., Chicago, IL 60611, tel. 312/642-1992, fax 312/642-9817; 1221 Breckell Ave. #1850, Miami, FL 33131, tel. 305/358-1992, fax 305/358-8223; San Vicente Plaza Bldg., 8383 Wilshire Blvd. #960, Beverly Hills, CA 90211, tel. 323/658-7188, fax 323/658-1061.

Portuguese National Tourist Office: 590 Fifth Ave., Fourth floor, New York, NY 10036, tel. 800/PORTUGAL, tel. 212/354-4403, fax 212/764-6137, www.portugal.org.

Moroccan National Tourist Office: 20 E. 46th St. #1201, New York, NY 10017, tel. 212/557-2520, fax 212/949-8148, www.tourism-in-morocco.com.

Gibraltar Information Bureau: 1156 15th St. NW, Suite 1100, Washington, D.C. 20005, tel. 202/452-1108, fax 202/452-1109.

Recommended Guidebooks

You may want some supplemental travel guidebooks, especially if you are traveling beyond my recommended destinations. When you consider the improvement it will make in your $3,000 vacation, $25 or $35 for extra maps and books is money well spent. For several people traveling by car, the extra weight and expense of a small trip library are negligible.

Lonely Planet's guides to Spain and Portugal are thorough, well-researched, and packed with good maps and hotel recommendations for low- to moderate-budget travelers (but not updated annually). Students and vagabonds will like the hip *Rough Guide: Spain* and *Rough Guide: Portugal* (written by insightful British researchers, but not updated annually) and the highly opinionated *Let's Go: Spain and Portugal* (by Harvard students, thorough hostel listings, updated annually, includes Morocco). *Let's Go* is best for backpackers with a train pass interested in the youth and night scene. Older travelers enjoy Frommer's Spain/Morocco and Portugal guides even though they, like the Fodor guides, ignore alternatives that enable travelers to save money by dirtying their fingers in the local culture. The popular, skinny Michelin Green Guides to Spain and Portugal are excellent, especially if you're driving. They're known for their city and sightseeing maps, dry but concise and helpful information on all major sights, and good cultural and historical background. English editions are sold in Iberia. The well-written and thoughtful Cadogan guides to Spain and Portugal are excellent for "A" students on the road. The encyclopedic Blue Guides to Spain and Portugal are dry as the plains in Spain but just right for some.

The Eyewitness series has editions covering Spain, Barcelona, Sevilla/Andalucía, Portugal, and Lisbon (published by Dorling Kindersley, sold in the United States or Iberia). It's extremely popular for its fine graphics, 3-D cutaways of buildings, aerial-view maps of historic neighborhoods, and cultural background. I use and like them, but if you pull out the art, the print that's left is pretty skimpy.

Jan Morris' *Spain* provides a thoughtful warm-up for your sightseeing, and John Hopper's *The New Spaniards* provides an interesting look at Spain today. Juan Lalaguna's *Spain: A Traveler's History* provides a readable background on this country's tumultuous history.

Rick Steves' Books and Videos

Rick Steves' Europe Through the Back Door 2000 (John Muir Publications) gives you budget travel tips on minimizing jet lag, packing light, planning your itinerary, traveling by car or train, finding budget beds without reservations, changing money, outsmarting thieves, avoiding rip-offs, hurdling the language barrier, staying healthy, taking great photographs, using your bidet, and much more. The book also includes chapters on 34 of my favorite "Back Doors."

My **Country Guides**, a series of seven guidebooks including this book, cover the Best of Europe; Great Britain & Ireland; France, Belgium & the Netherlands; Italy; Scandinavia; and Germany, Austria & Switzerland. All are updated annually and come out in January.

My **City Guides** cover London, Paris, and Rome. Updated annually, they offer in-depth coverage of the sights, hotels, restaurants, and nightlife in these grand cities along with illustrated tours of the great museums.

Europe 101: History and Art for the Traveler (with Gene Openshaw, John Muir Publications, 1996) gives you the story of Europe's peoples, history, and art, offering you a good preparation for the sights of Iberia from Roman times through the Inquisition and up to the Spanish Civil War. Written for smart people who were sleeping in their history and art classes before they knew they were going to Europe, *101* really helps Europe's sights come alive.

Rick Steves' Mona Winks (with Gene Openshaw, John Muir Publications, 1998) provides fun, easy-to-follow, self-guided tours of Europe's top 20 museums in London, Paris, Rome, Venice, Florence, and Madrid. Madrid's Prado is the thickest tour in the book.

Rick Steves' Spanish & Portuguese Phrase Book (John Muir Publications, 1999) presents you with the words and survival phrases necessary to communicate your way through a smooth and inexpensive trip.

My television series, *Travels in Europe with Rick Steves*, includes six half-hour shows on Spain and Portugal. A new series of 13 shows, including one on Lisbon, airs in 2000, and 52 earlier shows are still airing on both public television and the Travel Channel. These are also available in information-packed home videos, along with my two-hour slide-show lecture on Spain and Portugal (call us at 425/771-8303 for our free newsletter/catalog).

Rick Steves' Postcards from Europe (John Muir Publications, 1999), my autobiographical book, packs 25 years of travel anecdotes and insights into the ultimate 3,000-mile European adventure. Through my guidebooks I share my favorite European discoveries with you. *Postcards* introduces you to my favorite European friends.

Maps

The maps in this book, drawn by Dave Hoerlein, are concise and simple. Dave, who is well-traveled in Spain and Portugal, has designed the maps to help you locate recommended places and get to the TIs, where you'll find more in-depth, free maps of the cities or regions.

Don't skimp on maps. Excellent Michelin maps are available (cheaper than in the United States) throughout Iberia in bookstores, newsstands, and gas stations. Train travelers can do fine with a simple rail map (such as the one that comes with your train pass) and city maps from the TIs. Drivers should invest in good 1:400,000 maps and learn the keys to maximize the sightseeing value.

Transportation

By Car or Train?

Cars are best for three or more traveling together (especially families with small kids), those packing heavy, and those scouring the countryside. Trains and buses are best for solo travelers, blitz tourists, and city-to-city travelers.

Traveling by Bus and Train

Public transportation in Spain is quickly becoming as slick, modern, and efficient as in northern Europe. Portugal is straggling in train service but offers excellent bus transportation. The best public-transportation option is to mix bus and train travel. Always verify

Cost of Public Transportation

2000 SPAIN FLEXIPASS

	1st class	2nd class
Any 3 days in 2 months ...	$200	$155
Extra rail days (max. 7)	35	30

Spain & Iberic Flexipass holders pay a supplement (included w/ reservation) for the fast Talgo and AVE trains. For $45 - $80 extra, your pass can get you from Madrid or Barcelona to Paris, Zurich, or Milan on a "Night Talgo" sleeper train.

1999 SPAIN RAIL & DRIVE PASS
(Prices may vary in 2000)

Any 3 rail days and 3 car days in 2 months.

	1st class	extra car day
Economy car	$240	$55
Compact car	257	75
Intermediate car	267	85
Compact automatic	267	85

Prices are approximate per person for 2 traveling together. Solo travelers pay about $80 extra. 3rd and 4th persons sharing car buy only the railpass. Extra rail days (5 max.) cost $45.

All passes: kids 4-11 half fare, under 4 free. For a railpass order form, or for Rick's complete Railpass Guide, visit www.ricksteves. com or call us at 425/771-8303. To order Rail & Drive passes, call DER at 800/549-3737 or Rail Europe at 800/438-7245.

IBERIC FLEXIPASS (SPAIN/ PORTUGAL)

1st class: Any 3 days in 2 months for $205.
Extra rail days (7 max.): $45.

PORTUGUESE FLEXIPASS

1st class: Any 4 days out of 15 for $105.

Iberia: Map shows approximate point-to-point one-way 2nd class rail fares in $US. Add up fares for your itinerary to see whether a railpass will save you money.

bus or train schedules before your departure. Never leave a bus or train station without your next day's schedule options in hand. To study ahead, see http://bahn.hafas.de/english.html.

Trains: While you could save money by purchasing point-to-point tickets as you go, you may find the convenience of a railpass worth the extra cost. Iberia, Spain, and Portugal offer "flexi" railpasses that allow travel for a given number of days over a longer period of time. Spain also offers a rail-and-drive pass, which, if used thoughtfully, gives you the ease of big-city train hops and the flexibility of a car for rural areas such as the Andalusian hill towns. Spain's train passes come with a fine-print extra that many travelers overlook: It's good on overnight Talgo trains from Madrid to Paris or Lisbon and from Barcelona to Paris, Milan, and Zurich (though a supplement is charged). A Eurailpass pays for itself only if you're traveling to Spain from the north (Paris to Madrid costs $135 second class). Remember, you'll be making a lot of connections by buses, which are not covered by Eurail. Travelers under age 26 can buy cheap tickets in Wasteels offices (in most major train stations).

If you're on a budget, avoid the pricey overnight hotel trains from France or Italy into Spain (cheaper options exist). If you can easily afford to take a hotel train, consider flying instead to save time.

Public Transportation Routes

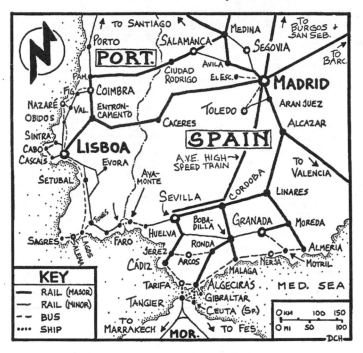

The long second-class train rides from Madrid to Barcelona, Lisbon, Sevilla, and Granada cost about $50 each. First class costs 50 percent more (often as much as a domestic flight).

Travelers with first-class reservations are entitled to the use of comfortable "Intercity" lounges in train stations in Spain's major cities.

Most overnight trains have berths and beds that you can rent (not included in the cost of your train ticket or railpass). Sleeping berths (*litera*) cost $15. A *coche-cama*, or bed in a classy quad compartment, costs $35; and a bed in a double costs $45. For long trips I go overnight on the train or fly (domestic shuttle flights are generally under $100). Even if you have a train pass, reservations (for 600 ptas) are required on long Spanish train rides (over three hours). Reserve a seat for your departure as soon as you arrive in a town, either at the train station or at a RENFE office in big city centers.

RENFE (the acronym for the Spanish national train system) used to be "Relatively Exasperating, and Not For Everyone," but it is getting better. Spain categorizes trains this way:

The high-speed train called the **AVE (Alta Velocidad Española)** whisks travelers between Madrid and Sevilla in less than three hours. AVE is now 85 percent covered by the Eurailpass (Madrid to Sevilla costs Eurailers about $9). Franco left Spain a train system that didn't fit Europe's gauge. AVE trains run on European-gauge tracks.

The **Talgo** is fast, air-conditioned, and expensive. Talgo 200 is a train designed to run on AVE rails. **Intercity** and **Electro** trains fall just behind Talgo in speed, comfort, and expense. **Rapido, Tranvia, Semi-directo,** and **Expreso** trains are generally slower. **Cercania** are commuter trains for big-city workers and small-town tourists. **Regional** and **Correo** trains are slow, small-town milk runs. Trains get more expensive as they pick up speed, but all are cheaper per mile than their northern European counterparts.

In Spain, *salidas* means "departures" and *llegadas* is "arrivals"; in Portugal, *partidas* and *chegadas* are departures and arrivals, respectively. To decipher Portuguese train schedules, *diario* means "daily," *mudanca de comboio* means "change trains," *so* means "only," and *não* means "not." This is a typical qualifier: *"Não se efectua aos sabados, domingos, e feriados oficiais"* (not effective on Saturdays, Sundays, and official holidays). Or *"So se efectua aos..."* ("only effective on...").

In Spain, long-distance trains are priced differently according to their time of departure. Peak hours (*punta*) are most expensive, followed by *llano* and *valle* (quietest and cheapest times). Overnight trains (and buses) are usually less expensive than the daytime rides. On Spanish train schedules, "LMXJVSD" are the days of the week, starting with Monday. A train that runs "LMXJV-D" doesn't run on Saturdays. *Laborables* can mean Monday through Friday or Monday through Saturday. In either Spain or Portugal, to ask for a schedule at a ticket or information window, say *"Horario para ____-____* [fill in names of cities], *por favor."* Most train stations have handy luggage lockers.

I'd buy my train tickets in Spain, but if you want to order from the States, RENFE does have a U.S. representative (Iberojet, $10 handling fee, credit cards accepted, U.S. tel. 800/222-8383).

Buses: Always make reservations for long-distance buses ahead of time. Bus service on holidays, Saturdays, and especially Sundays can be dismal. Ask at the tourist office about travel agencies that sell bus tickets (and reserve seats) to save you time if the bus station is not central. Don't leave a bus station to explore a city without checking your departure options and making reservations if necessary. In the countryside, stop buses by waving. You can always stow your luggage under the bus.

Portugal has mostly slow milk-run trains and an occasional Expreso. Off the main Lisbon–Porto–Coimbra train lines, buses are usually a better bet. In cases where buses and trains serve the same destination, the bus is often more efficient.

Bus schedules in Portugal are clearly posted at each major station. Look for "*Partidas*" (departures), not "*Chegadas*" (arrivals). They follow this standard format:

Destino	Partida	Chegada	Preço
Lisboa	14.15	16.35 (1)	1,200$

If you see this schedule in Coimbra, your bus leaves Coimbra at 14:15 and arrives in Lisboa at 16:35. The times are listed with periods instead of colons. Exceptions are noted with a numeral. For instance, the "(1)" means you should look for a list of definitions at the end of the schedule. (1) could be: "*Excepto sabados e domingos*" (Except Saturdays and Sundays). More key Portuguese "fine-print" words: Both *as* and *aos* mean "on." *De* means "from," as in "from this date to that date." *Feriado* means "holiday." *Directo* is "direct." *Ruta* buses make many stops. The posted schedules list most, but not all, destinations. If your intended destination isn't listed, check at the ticket/info window for the most complete schedule information. For longer trips your ticket may include an assigned seat.

Spain's bus system is more confusing than Portugal's because of its many different bus companies (though they're usually clustered within one building). The larger stations have an information desk with all the schedules. In smaller stations, check the destinations and schedules posted on each office window.

Iberian drivers and station personnel rarely speak English. Buses, even direct ones, often stop at stations for up to 30 minutes. In either Spain or Portugal, ask the driver "How many minutes here?" ("*¿Cuantos minutos aquí?*") so you can get out for a break. Some buses are entirely nonsmoking; others are nonsmoking only in the front. When you buy your ticket, ask for nonsmoking (*no fumadores* in Spanish, *não fumador* in Portuguese). It's usually pointless, since passengers ignore the signs, but it's a statement. Radios, taped music, and videos will accompany your ride. Bring earplugs for silence. Buses rarely have WCs but stop every two hours or so. Bus stations have WCs (rarely with TP) and cafés offering quick and cheap food.

Taxis

Most taxis are reliable and cheap. Drivers generally respond kindly to the request, "How much is it to ____, more or less?" (Spanish: "*¿Cuanto cuesta a ____, mas o menos?*" Portuguese: "*Quanto cuesta a ____, mais o menos?*"). Spanish taxis have more extra add-ons (luggage, nighttime, Sundays, train-station pickup, and so on). Rounding the fare up to the nearest 50 ptas or escudos is adequate for a tip. City rides cost $2 to $4. Keep a map in your hand so the cabby knows (or thinks) you know where you're going. All big cities have plenty of taxis. In many cases, couples travel by cab for little more than two bus or subway tickets.

Car Rental

It's cheapest to rent a car through your travel agent well before your departure. You'll want a weekly rate with unlimited mileage. Figure about $200 a week. For three weeks or longer, it's cheaper to lease; you'll save money on taxes and insurance.

Comparison shop through your agent. Beware of cheap weekly rates followed by very expensive daily costs. Remember you can turn in your car at any office on any day (normally with credit for early turn-in or extra charge for extension). Also remember that rental offices usually close midday Saturday until Monday.

I normally rent a small economy model. For peace of mind, I splurge for the CDW insurance (Collision Damage Waiver, about $14 a day). A few "gold" credit cards cover CDW insurance; quiz your credit-card company on the worst-case scenario. Travel Guard offers CDW for $6 a day (U.S. tel. 800/826-1300). With the luxury of CDW you'll enjoy Iberia's highways, knowing you can bring back the car in an unrecognizable shambles and just say, "S-s-s-sorry."

Driving

Driving in Iberia is great—sparse traffic and generally good roads. While the International Driver's License is officially required (cheap and easy to obtain from AAA; bring two photos and $10), I drive almost annually in Iberia with only my U.S. driver's license. (The Spanish version of AAA is the Real Automobil Club; Portugal's is the Automobil Clube de Portugal.)

Good maps are available and inexpensive throughout Iberia. Freeways in Spain and Portugal come with tolls (about $4 per hour) but save huge amounts of time. On freeways, navigate by direction (*norte, oeste, sur, este*). Also, since road numbers can be confusing and inconsistent, navigate by city names.

Drive defensively. If you're involved in an accident, you will be blamed and in for a monumental headache. Seat belts are required by law. Expect to be stopped for a routine check by the police (be sure your car-insurance form is up to date). There are plenty of speed traps. Tickets are issued and paid for on the spot. Portugal is statistically one of Europe's most dangerous places to drive. You'll see lots of ambulances on the road.

Gas and diesel prices are controlled and the same everywhere—around $3.50 a gallon for gas, less for diesel. *Gasolina* is either normal or super; unleaded is now widely available. Note that diesel is called *gasoleo*.

Get used to metric. A liter is about a quart, four to a gallon; a kilometer is six-tenths of a mile. Convert kilometers to miles by cutting them in half and adding back 10 percent of the original (120 km: 60 + 12 = about 72 miles; 300 km: 150 + 30 = about 180 miles).

If possible, make a copy of your key for safety and convenience. Choose parking places carefully. Leave valuables in the

Standard European Road Signs

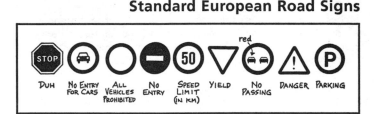

				red				
DUH	No Entry For Cars	All Vehicles Prohibited	No Entry	Speed Limit (in km)	Yield	No Passing	Danger	Parking

trunk during the day and leave nothing worth stealing in the car overnight. While you should avoid parking lots with twinkly asphalt, thieves break car windows anywhere, even at stop lights. Police recommend leaving the glove compartment open and your car unlocked at night. If it's a hatchback, take the trunk cover off at night so thieves can look in without breaking in. Parking attendants all over Spain holler, "*Nada en el coche*" ("Nothing in the car"). And they mean it. Ask at your hotel for advice on parking. In cities you can park safely but expensively in guarded lots.

Telephones, Mail, and E-mail

You cannot travel smartly in Iberia without using the telephones. A few tips will minimize frustration.

Coin-operated phones are rapidly being replaced by card-operated phones, making long-distance calling a breeze. Phone cards are normally purchased at a post office, newsstand, or tobacco (*tabaco*) shop. Upon entering Spain or Portugal, buy a phone card (*tarjeta telefónica* in Spanish, *cartão telefónico* in Portuguese). While the smaller-value card is usually enough, I buy the biggest and blow any remaining credit on a phone call home before leaving the country (about $1 per minute from any phone booth to the United States). Use your card to reserve hotels, confirm sightseeing plans, and call home. To use the card, simply insert it into the slot on the phone, wait for a dial tone and digital readout to show how much value remains on your card, and dial away—the cost of the call is automatically deducted from your card. Portuguese phone cards usually don't tell you your balance until after you dial, but they do thoughtfully beep for 15 seconds before dying. This gives you plenty of time to sign off or push the eject button (look at the directions on the phone beforehand) and slip in a new card.

Portuguese phones are even-tempered, but Spanish phones refuse to be rushed. After you "*inserta*" your "*tarjeta*" (phone card) into the Spanish phone, wait until the digital display says "*Marque numero*" and then dial. Dial slowly and deliberately. Push the square "R" button to get a dial tone for a new call.

Dialing Direct: All phone numbers in Spain and Portugal are nine-digit numbers (without area codes) that can be dialed direct throughout each country; for example, in Madrid you dial a nine-digit number whether you're calling Barcelona or across the street. To dial international calls direct, you'll need the international access codes and country codes (see the Appendix). European time is six/nine hours ahead of the east/west coast of the United States. Midnight in Seattle is breakfast in Madrid. Remember that if you're making hotel reservations from the United States.

USA Direct Services: Direct calls to the United States now cost about $1 a minute, significantly cheaper than rates charged by USA Direct Services such as AT&T, MCI, and Sprint. Still, calling the United States from any kind of phone is easy with a calling card. Each card company has a toll-free number in each European country that puts you in touch with an English-speaking operator who takes your card number and the number you want to call, puts you through, and bills your home phone number for the call (you'll pay about $2.50 for the first minute plus a $4.00 service charge and $1.50 per minute thereafter). Long calls are a reasonable value, but calling an answering machine is a $6.50 mistake. First use a small-value coin or a Spanish or Portuguese phone card to call home for five seconds—long enough to say, "call me," or to make sure an answering machine is off so you can call back, using your USA Direct number to connect with a person. For a list of AT&T, MCI, and Sprint calling-card operators, see the Appendix. I'd avoid using USA Direct (especially for calls between European countries), because it's much cheaper to call direct using coins or a Spanish or Portuguese phone card.

Mail: To arrange for mail delivery, reserve a few hotels along your route in advance and give their addresses to friends or use American Express Company's mail services (available to anyone who has at least one American Express traveler's check). Allow 10 days for a letter to arrive. Phoning is so easy that I've dispensed with mail stops all together.

E-mail: E-mail is still rare among Iberian hoteliers. I've listed e-mail addresses when possible, but they're few and far between. Cyber-cafés are becoming popular in most cities, giving you reasonably inexpensive and easy Internet access.

Sleeping

In the interest of smart use of your time, I favor hotels (and restaurants) handy to your sightseeing activities. Rather than list hotels scattered throughout a city, I describe my favorite couple of neighborhoods and recommend the best accommodations values in each, from $10 bunks to $180 doubles.

Spain and Portugal offer some of the best accommodations values in Europe. Most places are government-regulated, with posted prices. While prices are low, street noise is high (Spaniards are notorious night owls). Always ask to see your room first. Check the price

Sleep Code

To give maximum information in a minimum of space, I use this code to describe accommodations listed in this book. Prices listed are per room, not per person. When there is a range of prices in one category, the price will fluctuate with the season; these seasons are posted at the hotel desk. (Especially in resort areas, prices go way up in July and August.) A 6 or 7 percent tax (which is not included in listed prices) will often be added to your bill. Breakfast, while rarely included in Spain, is commonly included in Portugal.

S = Single room (or price for one person in a double).
D = Double or Twin. Double beds are usually big enough for nonromantic couples.
T = Triple (often a double bed with a single bed moved in).
Q = Quad (an extra child's bed is usually cheaper).
b = Private bathroom with toilet and shower or tub.
t = Private toilet only (the shower is down the hall).
s = Private shower or tub only (the toilet is down the hall).
CC = Accepts credit cards (Visa, MasterCard, American Express). If CC isn't mentioned, assume you'll need to pay cash.
SE = Speaks English. This code is used only when it seems predictable that you'll encounter English-speaking staff.
NSE = Does not speak English. Used only when it's unlikely you'll encounter English-speaking staff.

According to this code, a couple staying at a "Db-6,000 ptas, CC:V, SE" hotel would pay a total of 6,000 pesetas ($38) for a double room with a private bathroom. The hotel accepts Visa or Spanish cash in payment, and the staff speaks English.

posted on the door, consider potential night-noise problems, ask for another room, or bargain down the price. You can request either *con vista* (with view) or *tranquilo* (*calado* in Portuguese). In most cases the view comes with street noise. Breakfast may or may not be included in your room cost. It is often used as a bargaining chip. Ask before accepting a room. Most of the year, prices are soft.

All rooms have sinks with hot and cold water. Rooms with private bathrooms are often bigger and renovated, while the cheaper rooms without bathrooms often will be dingier and/or on the top floor. Any room without a bathroom has access to a bathroom on the corridor. Towels aren't routinely replaced every day, so you should drip-dry and conserve.

It's officially prohibited for hotels to use central heat before November 1 and after April 1 (unless it's unusually cold); prepare for cool evenings if you travel in spring and fall. Summer can be extremely hot. Consider air-conditioning, fans, and noise (since you'll want your window open), and don't be shy about asking for ice. Many rooms come with mini refrigerators.

Don't judge hotels by their bleak and dirty entryways. Landlords, stuck with rent control, often stand firmly in the way of hardworking hoteliers who'd like to brighten up their buildings.

Any regulated place will have a complaint book (*libro de reclamaciones* in Spanish and *livro de reclamações* in Portuguese). A request for this book will generally solve any problem you have in a jiffy.

Rooms in Private Homes: In both Spain and Portugal you'll find rooms in private homes, usually in touristy areas where locals decide to open up a spare room and make a little money on the side. Ask for a *cama, habitacion,* or *casa particulare* in Spain and a *quarto* in Portugal. They're cheap ($10–25 per bed without breakfast) and usually a good experience.

Historic Inns: Spain and Portugal also have luxurious, government-sponsored, historic inns. These *paradores* (Spain) and *pousadas* (Portugal) are often renovated castles, palaces, or monasteries, many with great views and stately atmospheres. While they can be a good value (doubles $80–200, reservations often necessary), I find many of them sterile, stuffy, and overly impressed with themselves, much like the tourists who stay there. I still list them where appropriate, as I enjoy wandering through them and having an occasional breakfast with real silver and too much service. But for a better value, sleep in what I call "poor-man's *paradores*"—elegant normal places that offer double the warmth and Old World intimacy for half the price.

Hostels and Campgrounds: Both Spain and Portugal have plenty of youth hostels and campgrounds, but considering the great bargains on other accommodations, I don't think they're worth the trouble and don't cover them in this book. Hotels and *pensiónes* are easy to find, inexpensive, and, when chosen properly, a fun part of the Spanish and Portuguese cultural experience. If you're on a starvation budget or just prefer camping or hosteling, plenty of information is available in the backpacker guidebooks, through the national tourist offices, and at local tourist information offices.

Making Reservations

Even though Easter, July, and August are often crowded, you can travel at any time of year without reservations. But given the high stakes, erratic accommodations values, and the quality of the gems I've found for this book, I'd highly recommend calling ahead for rooms. In peak times or for big cities, you can reserve long in advance. Otherwise, simply call several days in advance as you travel. For maximum flexibility, you might make a habit of calling between 9:00 and 10:00 on the day you plan to arrive, when the hotel knows who'll be checking out and just which rooms will be available. Use the telephone and the convenient phone cards. Most hotels listed are accustomed to English-only speakers. A hotel receptionist will trust you and hold a room until 16:00 without a deposit, though some will ask for a credit-card number. Honor (or cancel by phone) your reservations. Long distance is cheap and easy from public phone booths. Don't let these people down—I promised you'd call and cancel if for some reason you won't show up. Don't needlessly confirm rooms through the tourist office; they'll take a commission.

Those on a tight budget save piles of pesetas by traveling with no reservations and taking advantage of the discounted prices that hotels offer when it's clear they'll have empty rooms that day. Also, in the case of the numerous places offering a 10 percent discount to those booking direct with this guidebook (as noted in hotel listings), remember to negotiate your best deal and only then claim the discount.

If you know exactly which dates you need and really want a particular place, reserve a room well in advance before you leave home. To reserve from home, call, fax, write, or e-mail the hotel. Simple English usually works. To fax, use the handy form in the Appendix (online at www.ricksteves.com/reservation).

If you're writing, add the zip code and confirm the need and method for a deposit. A two-night stay in August would be "16/8/00 to 18/8/00" (Europeans write the date day/month/year, and hotel jargon uses your day of departure). You'll often receive a letter back requesting one night's deposit. A credit card will usually be accepted as a deposit, though you may need to send a signed traveler's check or a bank draft in the local currency. If your credit card is the deposit, you can pay with your card or cash when you arrive; if you don't show up, you'll be billed for one night. Reconfirm your reservations a day in advance for safety.

Eating in Spain

Spaniards eat to live, not vice versa. Their cuisine is hearty and served in big, inexpensive portions. You can get good $10 meals in restaurants.

Although not fancy, there is an endless variety of regional specialties. Two famous Spanish dishes are paella and gazpacho. Paella features saffron-flavored rice as a background for whatever the chef wants to mix in—seafood, sausage, chicken, peppers, and so on. Considered a heavy meal, it's usually served at midday rather than in the evening. Gazpacho, an Andalusian specialty, is a chilled soup of tomatoes, bread chunks, and spices—refreshing on a hot day and commonly available in the summer. Spanish cooks love garlic and olive oil.

Tipping is optional in Spanish restaurants, but many leave the coins or—if happy with the service, round the bill up to the next big bill (but not more than 5 percent).

The Spanish eating schedule frustrates many visitors. First off, many restaurants close during July or August. Secondly, when restaurants are open, they serve meals "late." Because most Spaniards work until 19:30, supper (*cena*) is usually served around 21:00 or 22:00. Lunch (*almuerzo*), also served late (13:00–16:00), is the largest meal of the day. Don't buck this system. Generally, no good restaurant serves meals at American hours.

The alternative to this late schedule, and my choice for a quick dinner, is to eat in tapas bars. Tapas are small portions, like appetizers, of all kinds of foods—seafood, salads, meat-filled pastries, deep-fried tasties, and on and on—normally displayed under glass at the bar (from about $1–10 for seafood). Confirm the price before you order (point and ask "*¿Quanto cuesta un tapa?*"). *Pinchos* are bite-size portions (not always available), tapas are snack-size, and *raciónes* are larger portions—a half of a meal. Common tapas include chorizo (spicy sausage), *gambas* (shrimp), *calamares fritos* (fried squid rings), *jamón serrano* (cured ham), *queso manchego* (sheep cheese), and *tortilla española* (potato omelet). *Bocadillos* (sandwiches) are cheap and basic. A ham sandwich is just that—ham on bread, period. A *montadito* is a tiny open-faced sandwich (common at tapas bars).

For a budget meal in a restaurant, try a *plato combinado* (combination plate), which usually includes portions of one or two main dishes, a vegetable, and bread for a reasonable price; or the *menu del dia* (menu of the day), a substantial three- to four-course meal that usually comes with a carafe of house wine. Flan (caramel custard) is the standard dessert. *Helado* (ice cream) is popular, as is *blanco y negro*, a vanilla-ice-cream-and-coffee float.

Eating and drinking at a bar is usually cheapest if you eat or drink at the counter (*barra*). You may pay a little more to eat sitting at a table (*mesa*) and still more for an outdoor table (*terraza*). Locate the price list (posted in fine type on a wall somewhere) to know the menu options and price tiers. In the right place, a quiet coffee break on the town square is well worth the extra charge. But the cheapest seats sometimes get the best show. Sit at the bar and study your bartender—he's an artist.

When searching for a good bar, I look for the noisy places with piles of napkins and food debris on the floor, lots of locals, and the TV blaring. Popular television shows include bullfights and soccer games, American sitcoms, and Spanish interpretations of soaps and silly game shows (you'll see Vanna Blanco).

Spain produces some excellent wine, both red (*tinto*) and white (*blanco*). Major wine regions include Valdepeñas, Penedès, Rioja, and Ribera del Duero. Sherry, a fortified wine from the Jerez region, ranges from dry (fino) to sweet (dulce). *Cava* is Spain's answer to champagne. Sangría (red wine mixed with fruit juice) is popular and refreshing. To get a small draft beer, ask for a *caña*. Spain has good, cheap, boxed orange juice (*zumo de naranja*). For something completely different, try *horchata de chufa*, a sweet, milky beverage made from earth almonds.

For a quick and substantial breakfast, order *tortilla española* (potato omelet) with your *café solo* (black) or *café con leche* (with milk) in any café. The town market hall always has a colorful café filled with locals eating cheap breakfasts.

Eating in Portugal

The Portuguese meal schedule, while still late, is less cruel than Spain's. Lunch (*almoço*) is the big meal, served between noon and 14:00, while supper (*jantar*) is from 20:00 to 22:00. Tapas, therefore, are not such a big deal. You'll eat well in restaurants for $8.

Eat seafood in Portugal. Fish soup (*sopa de peixe*) or shellfish soup (*sopa de mariscos*) is worth seeking out. *Caldo verde* is a popular vegetable soup. *Frango no churrasco* is roast chicken; ask for *piri-piri* sauce if you like it hot and spicy. *Porco a alentejana* is an interesting combination of pork and clams. As in Spain, garlic and olive oil are big. *Meia dose* means half portion, while *prato do dia* is the daily special. If appetizers (such as olives) are brought to your table before you order, they are not free; you will pay if you consume. If you don't want the unordered food, either ignore it or wave it off with a polite no.

For a quick snack, remember that cafés are usually cheaper than bars. *Sandes* (sandwiches) are everywhere. The Portuguese breakfast (*pequeno almoço*) is just *café com leite* and a sweet roll, but due to the large ex-pat English community, a full British "fry" is available in most touristy areas. A standard, wonderful local pastry is the cream cake, *pastel de Nata*.

Portuguese wines are cheap and decent. *Vinho da casa* is the house wine. *Vinho verde* is a young, light wine from the north that goes well with seafood. The Dão region produces the best red wines. And if you like port wine, what better place to sample it than its birthplace? Beer (*cerveja*) is also popular—for a small draft beer, ask for *uma imperial*. Freshly squeezed orange juice (*sumo de laranja*), mineral water (*agua mineral*), and soft drinks are widely available.

As in Spain, leaving the coins from your change is a nice touch. Rounding things up to the next big bill is considered generous.

Stranger in a Strange Land

We travel all the way to Europe to enjoy differences—to become temporary locals. You'll experience frustrations. Certain truths that we find "God-given" or "self-evident," like cold beer, ice in drinks, bottomless cups of coffee, hot showers, body odor smelling bad, and bigger being better, are suddenly not so true. One of the benefits of travel is the eye-opening realization that there are logical, civil, and even better alternatives. A willingness to go local ensures that you'll enjoy a full dose of European hospitality.

If there is a negative aspect to the European image of Americans, it is that we are big, loud, aggressive, impolite, rich, and a bit naive. While Europeans look bemusedly at some of our Yankee excesses—and worriedly at others—they nearly always afford us individual travelers all the warmth we deserve.

Back Door Manners

While updating this book, I heard over and over again that my readers are considerate and fun to have as guests. Thank you for traveling as temporary locals who are sensitive to the culture. It's fun to follow you in my travels.

Tours of Spain and Portugal

Your travel agent can tell you about all the normal tours, but they won't tell you about ours.

At Europe Through the Back Door, we offer 20-day tours of Spain and Portugal featuring most of the highlights in this book (departures April–October, 26 people on a big bus with lots of empty seats). For details, see www.ricksteves.com or call 425/711-8303.

Send Me a Postcard, Drop Me a Line

If you enjoy a successful trip with the help of this book and would like to share your discoveries, please fill out and send the survey at the end of this book to me at Europe Through the Back Door, Box 2009, Edmonds, WA 98020. I personally read and value all feedback.

For our latest travel information, visit www. ricksteves.com. For any updates to this book, check www.ricksteves.com/update. My e-mail address is rick@ricksteves.com. Anyone is welcome to request a free issue of our *Back Door* quarterly newsletter.

Judging from the happy postcards I receive from travelers, it's safe to assume you'll enjoy a great, affordable vacation—with the finesse of an independent, experienced traveler. Thanks, and *buen viaje!*

BACK DOOR TRAVEL PHILOSOPHY
As Taught in *Rick Steves' Europe Through the Back Door*

Travel is intensified living—maximum thrills per minute and one of the last great sources of legal adventure. Travel is freedom. It's recess, and we need it.

Experiencing the real Europe requires catching it by surprise, going casual... "Through the Back Door."

Affording travel is a matter of priorities. (Make do with the old car.) You can travel—simply, safely, and comfortably—anywhere in Europe for $70 a day plus transportation costs. In many ways, spending more money only builds a thicker wall between you and what you came to see. Europe is a cultural carnival, and, time after time, you'll find that its best acts are free and the best seats are the cheap ones.

A tight budget forces you to travel close to the ground, meeting and communicating with the people, not relying on service with a purchased smile. Never sacrifice sleep, nutrition, safety, or cleanliness in the name of budget. Simply enjoy the local-style alternatives to expensive hotels and restaurants.

Extroverts have more fun. If your trip is low on magic moments, kick yourself and make things happen. If you don't enjoy a place, maybe you don't know enough about it. Seek the truth. Recognize tourist traps. Give a culture the benefit of your open mind. See things as different but not better or worse. Any culture has much to share.

Of course, travel, like the world, is a series of hills and valleys. Be fanatically positive and militantly optimistic. If something's not to your liking, change your liking. Travel is addictive. It can make you a happier American as well as a citizen of the world. Our Earth is home to nearly 6 billion equally important people. It's humbling to travel and find that people don't envy Americans. They like us, but with all due respect, they wouldn't trade passports.

Globe-trotting destroys ethnocentricity. It helps you understand and appreciate different cultures. Travel changes people. It broadens perspectives and teaches new ways to measure quality of life. Many travelers toss aside their hometown blinders. Their prized souvenirs are the strands of different cultures they decide to knit into their own character. The world is a cultural yarn shop. And Back Door Travelers are weaving the ultimate tapestry. Come on, join in!

BARCELONA

Barcelona is Spain's second city and the capital of the proud and distinct region of Catalunya. With Franco's fascism now history, Catalunyan flags wave once again. Language and culture are on a roll in Spain's most cosmopolitan and European corner.

Barcelona bubbles with life in its narrow Gothic Quarter alleys, along the grand boulevards, and throughout the chic, grid-planned new town. While Barcelona had an illustrious past as a Roman colony, Visigothic capital, 14th-century maritime power, and, in more modern times, a top Mediterranean trading and manufacturing center, it's most enjoyable to throw out the history books and just drift through the city. If you're in the mood to surrender to a city's charms, let it be in Barcelona.

Planning Your Time

Sandwich Barcelona between flights or overnight train rides. There's little of earth-shaking importance within eight hours by train. It's as easy to fly into Barcelona as into Madrid, Lisbon, or Paris for most travelers from the United States. Those renting a car can cleverly start here, sleep on the train or fly to Madrid, see Madrid, and pick up the car there.

On the shortest visit Barcelona is worth one night, one day, and an overnight train out. The Ramblas is two different streets by day and by night. Stroll it from top to bottom at night and again the next morning, grabbing breakfast on a stool in a café in the market. Wander the Gothic Quarter, see the cathedral, and have lunch in Eixample (ay-SHAM-pla). The top two sights in town, Gaudí's Sacred Family Church and the Picasso Museum, are usually open until 20:00. The illuminated fountains (on Montjuïc, near Plaça Espanya) are a good finale for your day.

Barcelona

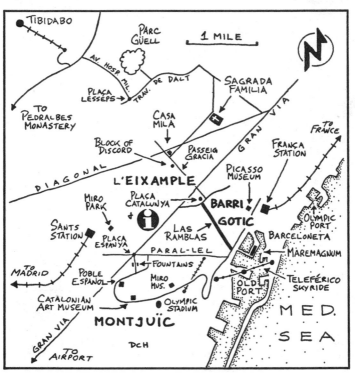

Of course, Barcelona in a day is a dash. To better appreciate the city's ample charm, spread your visit over two days.

Orientation

Orient yourself mentally by locating these essentials on the map: Barri Gòtic/Ramblas (Old Town), Eixample (fashionable modern town), Montjuïc (hill covered with sights and parks), and Sants Station (train to Madrid). The soul of Barcelona is in its compact core—the Barri Gòtic (Gothic Quarter) and the Ramblas (main boulevard). This is your strolling, shopping, and people-watching nucleus. The city's sights are widely scattered, but with a map and a willingness to figure out the sleek subway system, all is manageable.

Tourist Information

There are three useful TIs in Barcelona: at the airport, at the Sants train station (daily 8:00–20:00, off-season 8:00–14:00, at the access to platform 6), and on—actually under—Plaça de Catalunya, across from the El Corte Inglés store (daily 9:00–21:00, city walking tours in English Sat–Sun at 10:00, 950 ptas, 2 hrs, call to reserve, tel. 90-630-1282; fair rates at TI exchange desk, room-finding service worthwhile if you're desperate). Pick up the large city map and brochures on public transport, Gaudí, Miró, Dalí, Picasso, and the Barri Gòtic. Ask for the free quarterly Barcelona guide with practical information (museum hours, restaurants, transportation) and cultural information (history, festivals, and points of interest grouped by neighborhood).

Arrival in Barcelona

By Train: Although many international trains use the França Station, all domestic (and some international) trains use Sants Station. Both França and Sants have subway stations: França's is "Barceloneta" (two blocks away), and Sants' is "Sants Estacio" (under the station). Both stations have baggage lockers. Sants Station has a good TI, a world of handy shops and eateries, and a classy "Sala Euromed" lounge for travelers with first-class reservations (quiet, plush, TV, free drinks, study tables, coffee bar). There is nothing of interest within easy walking distance of either train station. Subway or taxi to your hotel.

  By Plane: Barcelona's El Prat de Llobregat Airport is 12 kilometers southwest of town and connected cheaply and quickly by Aerobus (immediately in front of arrivals lobby, 4/hrly, 20 min to Plaça de Catalunya, buy 485-ptas ticket from driver, tel. 93-412-0000) or by RENFE train (walk the tunnel overpass from airport to station, 2/hrly, 20 min to Sants Station and Plaça de Catalunya, 310 ptas). A taxi to or from the airport costs about 3,000 ptas.

Getting around Barcelona

Barcelona's subway (the Metro), among Europe's best, can be faster than a taxi and connects just about every place you'll visit. It has five color-coded lines (L1 is red, L2 is lilac, L3 is green, L4 is yellow, L5 is blue). Rides cost 145 ptas each. A T-1 Card gives you 10 tickets good for the bus or Metro for 795 ptas. Pick up the TI's guide to public transport.

  The handy Tourist Bus (Bus Turistic) shuttles tourists on a 24-stop circuit covering the must-sees, with stops at the funicular and *teleférico* to Montjuïc (Apr–Dec 9:00–21:30, buy tickets on bus). The one-day (1,800 ptas) and two-day (2,300 ptas) tickets include some serious discounts on the city's major sights. Buses run every 10 to 20 minutes and take three hours to do the entire circuit.

  Taxis are plentiful and honest (300 ptas drop charge, 100 ptas/km). You can go from the Ramblas to Sants Station for 600 ptas (100 ptas extra for each piece of luggage).

Helpful Hints

Theft Alert: Barcelona, after recently illuminating many of its seedier streets, is not the pickpocket paradise it was a few years back, but it's good to be alert—especially on the Ramblas.

American Express: AmEx offices are at Paseo de Gràcia 101 (Mon–Fri 9:30–18:00, Sat 10:00–12:00, tel. 93-415-2371, Metro: Diagonal) and on the Ramblas opposite the Liceu Metro station (daily 9:00–24:00, with a small TI, tel. 98-301-1166).

U.S. Consulate: Designed to be low profile, it's hard to find at Passeig Reina Elisenda 23 (tel. 93-280-2227).

Pharmacy: At the corner of Ramblas and Carrer de la Portaferrissa (daily 9:00–22:00).

Language: Although Spanish is understood here (and the basic survival words are the same), Barcelona speaks a different language—Catalan. (Most place-names in this chapter are listed in Catalan.) Here are the essential Catalunyan phrases:

Hello	*Hola*	(OH-lah)
Please	*Si us plau*	(see oos plow)
Thank you	*Gracies*	(GRAH-see-es)
Goodbye	*Adeu*	(ah-DAY-oo)
Exit	*Sordida*	(sor-DEE-dah)
Long live Catalunya!	*Visca Catalunya!*	(BEE-skah…)

Sights—The Ramblas

More than a Champs-Élysées, this grand boulevard takes you from rich at the top to rough at the port in a 20-minute walk. You'll find the grand opera house, ornate churches, plain prostitutes, pickpockets, con men, artists, street mimes, an outdoor bird market, elegant cafés, great shopping, and people willing to charge more for a shoeshine than you paid for the shoes. Take 15 minutes to sit on a white metal chair for 50 ptas and observe. When Hans Christian Andersen saw this street more than 100 years ago, he wrote that there could be no doubt that Barcelona was a great city.

Rambla means "stream" in Arabic. The Ramblas was a drainage ditch along the medieval wall that used to define what is now called the Gothic Quarter. It has five separately named segments, but addresses treat it as a mile-long boulevard.

Walking from Plaça de Catalunya downhill to the harbor, you'll see the following Ramblas highlights.

▲**Plaça de Catalunya**—This vast central square is the divider between old and new and the hub for the Metro, bus, and airport shuttle. The grass around its fountain is considered the best public place in town for serious necking. Overlooking the square, the huge El Corte Inglés department store offers everything from bonsai trees to a travel agency, plus one-hour photo developing, haircuts, and cheap souvenirs (Mon–Sat 10:00–21:30, closed Sun, supermarket in basement, 9th-floor terrace cafeteria with great city view—take elevator from west entrance, tel. 90-112-2122). Four great boulevards start here: the Ramblas, the fashionable Passeig de Gràcia, the cozier but still fashionable Rambla Catalunya, and the stubby, shop-filled, pedestrian-only Portal de L'Angel.

▲▲**La Boqueria**—This lively produce market (a.k.a. Mercat de Sant Josep) is an explosion of chicken legs, bags of live snails, stiff fish, delicious oranges, and sleeping dogs (Mon–Sat 8:00–20:00, best in the morning after 9:00, closed Sun). The Conserves shop sells 25 kinds of olives (go straight in; it's near the back on the right; 100-gram minimum, 40–70 ptas). Full legs of ham (*jamón serrano*) abound; *Paleta Iberica de Bellota* are best—strictly acorn-fed, about 15,000 ptas ($100) each. Beware: *Huevos de toro* are bull testicles—surprisingly inexpensive... but oh so good. Drop by Mario and Alex's Café Central for breakfast or an *espresso con leche* (far end of main aisle on left).

Café de L'Ópera—One of Barcelona's mainstays, this serves a good *café con leche* (daily 9:00–02:30, La Rambla 74, tel. 93-317-7585).

Gran Teatre del Liceu—Spain's only real opera house is luscious but closed for a few years for renovation because of a 1994 fire (tourable when it reopens).

Plaça Reial—This elegant neoclassical square comes complete with old-fashioned taverns, modern bars with patio seating, a Sunday coin and stamp market (10:00–14:00), and characters who don't need the palm trees to be shady. Escudellers, a street one block toward the water from the square, is lined with bars whose counters are strewn with vampy ladies. The area is well policed, but if you tried, you could get into trouble.

▲▲**Palau Güell**—The only look at a Gaudí Art Nouveau interior, and for me, it's the most enjoyable look at Barcelona's organic architect (300 ptas, combo ticket for 600 ptas covers a guided visit—beginning at Casa Lleo Morera, Paseo de Gràcia #35—to three Moderniste sights, 50 percent discount at three others, worthwhile for fans; usually open Mon–Fri 10:00–14:00, 16:00–20:00, Carrer Nou de la Rambla 3–5, tel. 93-317-3974). If you're tired and will see/have seen Casa Milà, skip the climb to the rooftop.

Chinatown (Barri Xines)—Farther downhill, on the right-hand side, is the world's only Chinatown with nothing even remotely Chinese in or near it. Named this for the prejudiced notion that Chinese immigrants go hand in hand with poverty, prostitution, and drug dealing, the actual inhabitants are poor Spanish, Arab, and Gypsy people down on their luck. At night the area is full of prostitutes, many of them transvestites, who cater to sailors wandering up from the port. Don't venture in at night.

Columbus Monument (Monument a Colóm)—Marking the point where the Ramblas hits the harbor, this 50-meter-tall monument built for an 1888 exposition offers an elevator-assisted view

from its top (250 ptas, daily 9:00–20:30; off-season 10:00–14:30,
15:30–19:30; skip the ascent if you plan on riding the harbor gondola to Montjuïc, which offers a far better view). It's interesting
that Barcelona would so honor the man whose discoveries ultimately led to its downfall as a great trading power. It was here in
Barcelona that Ferdinand and Isabel welcomed Columbus home
after his first trip to America.

Maritime Museum (Museo Maritim)—This museum covers the
salty history of ships and navigation from the 13th to 20th centuries.
Its 45-minute infrared headphone multimedia tour in English shows
off the Catalan role in the development of maritime technology
(e.g., the first submarine was Catalan). With fleets of seemingly
unimportant replicas of old boats explained in Catalan and Spanish,
landlubbers may find it dull (800 ptas, daily 10:00–19:00, closed
Mon in off-season).

Golondrinas—Little tourist boats at the foot of the Columbus
Monument make half-hour tours of the harbor every 20 to 30
minutes from 11:00 to 20:00 (285 ptas one way to other side of
harbor or 485 ptas round-trip). Consider this ride or the harbor
steps here for a picnic. They offer a glass-bottom, four-language,
90-minute port tour for 1,275 ptas.

Maremagnum—This modern Spanish monstrosity of a mall (with
a cinema, aquarium, and restaurants) offers fine city views. It's
connected to the waterfront by a slick wooden pedestrian draw-
bridge next to the *golondrina* boats.

Sights—Gothic Quarter (Barri Gòtic)

The Barri Gòtic is a bustling world of shops, bars, and nightlife
packed between hard-to-be-thrilled-about 14th- and 15th-century
buildings. Except for the part closest to the port, the area now
feels safe, thanks to police and countless streetlights. There is a
tangled grab bag of undiscovered courtyards, grand squares,
schoolyards, Art Nouveau storefronts, baby flea markets, musty
junk shops, classy antique shops, and balconies with domestic
jungles behind wrought-iron bars. Go on a cultural scavenger
hunt. Write a poem.

▲**Cathedral**—The colossal cathedral, a fine example of Catalan
Gothic, was started in about 1300 and took 600 years to complete.
Rather than stretching toward heaven, it makes a point to be simply
massive (similar to the Gothic churches of Italy). Under towering
arches, 28 richly ornamented chapels ring the finely carved 15th-
century choir (*coro*). While you can see the *coro* from the back for
free, paying the 125-ptas entry fee turns on the lights and lets you
get close up to the ornately carved stalls and the emblems representing the various Knights of the Golden Fleece who once sat here.
Don't miss the cloister, with its wispy garden, protective geese,
and WC, or the dark, barrel-vaulted Romanesque Chapel of Santa

Barcelona's Gothic Quarter

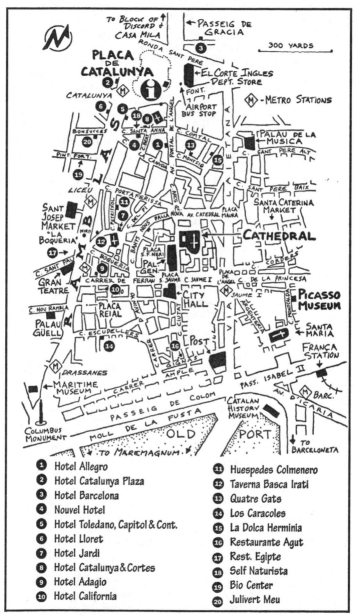

1. Hotel Allegro
2. Hotel Catalunya Plaza
3. Hotel Barcelona
4. Nouvel Hotel
5. Hotel Toledano, Capitol & Cont.
6. Hotel Lloret
7. Hotel Jardi
8. Hotel Catalunya & Cortes
9. Hotel Adagio
10. Hotel California
11. Huespedes Colmenero
12. Taverna Basca Irati
13. Quatre Gats
14. Los Caracoles
15. La Dolca Herminia
16. Restaurante Agut
17. Rest. Egipte
18. Self Naturista
19. Bio Center
20. Julivert Meu

Lucia, with its great old tombstone floor. The tiny 100-ptas museum is one plush room with a dozen old religious paintings (cathedral 8:00–13:30, 16:00–19:30; cloisters 9:00–13:00, 16:00–19:00; museum 10:00–13:00, 16:00–19:00; tel. 93-315-1554).

▲**Sardana Dances**—The stirring and patriotic Sardana dances are held at the cathedral (18:30 Sat, 12:00 Sun) and at Plaça de Sant Jaume (18:30 Sun). Locals of all ages seem to spontaneously appear. They gather in circles after putting their things in the center—symbolic of community and sharing. Then they raise and hold hands as they hop and sway gracefully to the band. The band (*cobla*) consists of a long flute, tenor and soprano oboes, strange-looking brass instruments, and a tiny bongolike drum (*tambari*). The rest of Spain mocks this lazy circle dance, but it is a stirring display of local pride and patriotism.

Shoe Museum (Museu del Calcat)—Shoe lovers enjoy this two-room shoe museum (with a we-try-harder attendant) on the delightful Plaça Sant Felip Neri (200 ptas, Tue–Sun 11:00–14:00, closed Mon, one block beyond the outside door of the cathedral cloister, behind Plaça de G. Bachs).

Royal Palace (Palau Reial)—Several museums are in the old Royal Palace complex next to the cathedral. The city history museum shows off Barcelona's Roman and medieval history along with piles of medieval documents in the Arxiu de la Corona d'Aragon (Archives of the Kingdom of Aragon). The Frederic Mares Museum combines a classy collection of medieval religious art with a quirky bundle of more modern artifacts—old pipes, pin-ups, toys, and so on (both museums open Tue–Sun 10:00–15:00, some nights until 18:00, closed Mon).

Plaça de Sant Juame—On this stately central square of the Gothic Quarter, two of the top governmental buildings in Catalan face each other: the Barcelona city hall (Ayuntamento) and the seat of the autonomous government of Catalan (Palau de la Generalitat). Sardana dances take place here Sunday at 18:30 (see "Sardana Dances," above).

▲▲**Picasso Museum**—Far and away the best collection of Picasso's (1881–1973) work in Spain, and the best collection of his early works anywhere, is scattered through two Gothic palaces a short walk from the cathedral. This is a great chance to see his earliest sketches and paintings and better understand his genius. You'll find no English information inside but if you follow the rooms in numerical order you can trace the evolution of his work. Picasso lived in Barcelona from 1895 to 1904. The first rooms show the 14-year-old hard at work. Room 13 holds a museum highlight: *Science and Charity*. Pablo painted this in 1897 at age 16. Note the tiny studies inside the door-way. The man in the painting is Pablo's first teacher—his dad. The baby was rented. From this point on, young Pablo Ruiz called him-self Picasso, moved to Paris in 1900, and sharpened the cutting edge.

The next rooms show Picasso romping through various styles and into his popular Blue Period (named for the tone and tint of his 1901–1904 works). After the Rose Period (1904–1905) we see Picasso the cubist (1917, room 21). In 1957 Picasso began a series of variations on Velázquez's famous *Las Meninas*. Study the copy of the realistic Velázquez original and the Velázquez/Picasso comparison chart. Then see if you can follow Picasso as he plays paddleball with perspective in the next few rooms. Before leaving, drop by the video room—opposite the café—to see Picasso at work. (700 ptas, Tue–Sat 10:00–20:00, Sun 10:00–15:00, closed Mon, Montcada 15–19, Metro: Jaume, tel. 93-319-6310.)

Textile and Garment Museum (Museu Textil i de la Indumentaria)—If fabrics from the 4th to 16th centuries leave you cold, have a *café con leche* on the museum's beautiful patio (museum, 400 ptas, Tue–Sat 10:00–20:00, Sun 10:00–15:00, closed Mon; patio is outside the museum but within the walls, 30 meters from Picasso Museum at Montcada 12–14).

▲**Catalana Concert Hall (Palau de la Música Catalana)**—This colorful hall is an extravagant burst of Modernisme, with a floral ceramic ceiling, colored-glass columns, and detailed mosaics. Admission is by tour only (1 hr, in English, 700 ptas, daily 10:00–15:30 through peak season, shorter hours off-season, call to reserve, tel. 93-268-1000). Ask about concerts.

Sights—Eixample

Uptown Barcelona is a unique variation on the common grid-plan city. Barcelona snipped off the building corners to create light and spacious eight-sided squares at every intersection. Wide sidewalks, hardy shade trees, chic shops, and plenty of Art Nouveau fun make the Eixample a refreshing break from the Old Town. For the best Eixample example, ramble Rambla Catalunya (unrelated to the more famous Ramblas) and pass through Passeig de Gràcia (described below, Metro: Passeig de Gràcia).

The 19th century was a boom time for Barcelona. By 1850 it was busting out of its medieval walls. A new town was planned to follow a gridlike layout. The intersection of three major thoroughfares—Gran Vía, Diagonal, and the Meridiana—would shift the city's focus uptown.

The Eixample, or "Enlargement," was a progressive plan in which everything was accessible to everyone. Each 20-block-square district would have its own hospital and large park, each 10-block-square area would have its own market and general services, and each five-block-square grid would house its own schools and day-care centers. The hollow space found inside each "block" of apartments would form a neighborhood park.

While much of that vision never quite panned out, the Eixample was an urban success. Rich and artsy bigshots bought plots along the grid. The richest landowners built as close to the center as possible. For this reason, the best buildings are near the Passeig de Gràcia. Adhering to the height, width, and depth limitations, they built as they pleased—often in the trendy new Moderniste style.

Sights—Gaudí's Art and Architecture

Barcelona is an architectural scrapbook of the galloping gables and organic curves of hometown boy Antonio Gaudí. A devoted Catalan and Catholic, he immersed himself in each project, often living on-site. He called Parc Güell, La Pedrera, and the Sagrada Familia all home.

▲▲Sagrada Familia (Sacred Family) Church—Gaudí's most famous and persistent work is this unfinished landmark. He worked on the church from 1891 to 1925; your 800 ptas admission helps pay for the ongoing construction (daily 9:00–20:00, off-season 9:00–18:00, Metro: Sagrada Familia, tel. 93-207-3031).

When finished, 12 100-meter spires (representing the Apostles) will stand in groups of four marking the three ends of the building. The center tower (honoring Jesus), reaching 170 meters up, will be flanked by 125-meter-tall towers of Mary and the four Evangelists. A unique exterior ambulatory will circle the building like a cloister turned inside out.

The nativity facade really shows the vision of Gaudí. It was finished in 1904, before Gaudí's death, and shows scenes from the birth and childhood of Jesus along with angels playing musical instruments. (Because of ongoing construction, you may need to access this area—opposite the entrance, viewed from outside—by walking through the museum. Don't miss it.)

The little on-site museum displays physical models used for the church's construction. Gaudí lived on the site for more than a decade and is buried in the crypt. When he died in 1926, only one spire stood. Judge for yourself how the controversial current work fits in with Gaudí's original formulation.

With the cranking cranes, rusty forests of rebar, and scaffolding requiring a powerful faith, the Sagrada Familia Church offers a fun look at a living, growing, bigger-than-life building. Take the lift (200 ptas) or the stairs (free but can be miserably congested) up to the dizzy lookout bridging two spires. You'll get a great view of the city and a gargoyle's-eye perspective of the loopy church. If there's any building on earth I'd like to see, it's the Sagrada Familia—finished.

▲Palau Güell—This is the best chance to enjoy a Gaudí interior (see above under "Sights—The Ramblas"). Curvy.

▲Casa Milà (La Pedrera)—This house and nearby Casa Battlo have Gaudí exteriors that laugh down on the crowds filling Passeig de Gràcia. Casa Milà, also called La Pedrera (The Quarry), has a

Modernisme

The Renaixenca (Catalan cultural revival) gave birth to Modernisme (Catalan Art Nouveau) at the end of the 19th century. Barcelona is the capital of Modernisme. Meaning "a taste for what is modern," it lasted from 1888 to 1906. This free-flowing organic style broke with tradition and experimented with glass, tile, iron, and brick. Decoration became structural.

Antonio Gaudí is the most famous Moderniste artist. From four generations of metalworkers, a lineage of which he was quite proud, he incorporated his ironwork into his architecture and came up with novel approaches to architectural structure and space.

Two other Moderniste architects famous for their unique style are Lluís Domènech i Muntaner and Josep Puig i Cadafalch. You'll see their work on "The Street of Discord" (see "Sights—Gaudí's Art and Architecture").

Barcelona's Eixample neighborhood shimmies with the colorful, leafy, flowing, blooming shapes of Modernisme in doorways, entrances, facades, and ceilings.

Modernisme fans appreciate the combo ticket that includes a guided visit to three Moderniste sights and a 50 percent discount to three others (600 ptas, buy at Casa Lleo Morera, Paseo de Gràcia #35, contact TI for tour times).

much-photographed roller coaster of melting-ice-cream eaves. This is Barcelona's quintessential Moderniste building. An elevator whisks you to the top, where you can wander under brick arches, frolic on the fanciful rooftop, and enjoy the fascinating *Espai Gaudí*, a multimedia exhibit of models, photos, and videos of Gaudí's works in English. Recently added, an apartment fully furnished from the Gaudí era contains a well-presented display on life in Barcelona in the early 1900s (600 ptas for museum/roof, 1,000 ptas includes apartment, daily 10:00–20:00; the 1,500-ptas fee for 21:30–24:00 viewing includes a glass of wine; Passeig de Gràcia 92, Metro: Diagonal, tel. 93-484-5995). At the ground level of Casa Milà is the original entrance courtyard for the Fundacio Caixa de Cataluyna, dreamily painted in pastels (free).

The Street of Discord—Four blocks from Casa Milà you can survey a noisy block of competing turn-of-the-century facades. Several of Barcelona's top Moderniste mansions line Passeig de Gràcia (Metro: Passeig de Gràcia). Because the structures look as though they are trying to outdo each other in creative twists, locals nicknamed the block between Consell de Cent and Arago, "The Street of Discord." First (at #43) and most famous is Gaudí's Casa Battlo, with skull-like balconies and a tile roof of cresting waves... or is it a dragon's back? (If you're tempted to frame your photos from the middle of the street, be careful—Gaudí died under a streetcar.) Next door, at Casa Amatller (#41), check out architect Puig i Cadafalch's creative mix of Moorish and Gothic and iron grillwork. On the corner (at #35), Casa Lleo Morera (by Lluís Domènechi Muntaner) offers more of a sense of a Moderniste interior; you can nose into the lobby and often climb to the first floor (combo ticket for 600 ptas covers a guided visit—beginning at Casa Lleo Morera, Passeig de Gràcia #35—to three Moderniste sights and a 50 percent discount at three others). The perfume shop halfway down the street has a free and interesting little perfume museum in the back.

Parc Güell—Gaudí fans find the artist's magic in this colorful park (free, daily 9:00–20:00) and small Gaudí Museum (200 ptas, daily 10:00–20:00, closes off-season at 18:00, Metro: Vallarca but easier by bus #24 from Plaça de Catalunya; 1,000 ptas by taxi). Gaudí intended this to be a planned garden city rather than a park. As a high-income housing project, it flopped. As a park... even after I reminded myself that Gaudí's work is a careful rhythm of color, shapes, and space, it was disappointing.

Modern Art Museum (Museu d'Art Modern)—East of the França train station in Parc de la Ciutadella, this manageable museum exhibits Catalan sculpture, painting, glass, and furniture by Gaudí, Casas, Llimona, and others (500 ptas, Tue–Sat 10:00–19:00, Sun 10:00–14:30, closed Mon).

Sights—Barcelona's Montjuïc

The Montjuïc (Mount of the Jews), overlooking Barcelona's hazy port, has always been a show-off. Ages ago it had the impressive fortress. In 1929 it hosted an international fair, from which most of today's sights originated. And in 1992 the Summer Olympics directed the world's attention to this pincushion of attractions.

There are many ways to reach Montjuïc: on the Bus Turistic (see "Getting around Barcelona," above); bus #50 from the corner of Gran Vía and Passeig de Gràcia (145 ptas, every 10 minutes); subway to Metro: Parallel and catch the funicular (250 ptas one way, 375 ptas round-trip, daily 11:00–22:00, shorter hours in winter); or taxi. The first three options leave you at the *teleférico*, which you can take to the Castle of Montjuïc (425 ptas one way, 625 ptas round-trip). Alternatively, from the same spot, you can walk uphill 20 minutes through the pleasant park. Only a taxi gets you doorstep delivery. From the port, the fastest and most scenic way to Montjuïc is via the 1929 Trasbordador Aereo (at the tower in the port, ride an elevator up to catch the dangling gondola, 1,200 ptas round-trip, 4/hrly, daily 10:30–20:00).

Castle of Montjuïc—This offers great city views and a military museum (200 ptas, Tue–Sun 9:30–19:30, closed Mon). The seemingly endless museum houses a dull collection of guns, swords, and toy soldiers. An interesting section on the Spanish-American War covers Spain's valiant fight against American aggression (from its perspective). Unfortunately, there are no English descriptions. Those interested in Jewish history will find a fascinating collection of ninth-century Jewish tombstones.

▲**Fountains (Fonts Lluminoses)**—Music, colored lights, and huge amounts of water make an artistic and coordinated splash on summer nights (Thu–Sun, 30-minute shows start on the half-hour, 21:30–24:00, from Metro: Plaça Espanya, walk toward the towering National Palace).

Spanish Village (Poble Espanyol)—This tacky five-acre model village uses fake traditional architecture from all over Spain as a shell to contain gift shops. Craftspeople do their clichéd thing only in the morning (9:00–19:30, not worth the time or the 950 ptas). After hours it becomes a popular local nightspot.

▲▲**Catalonian Art Museum (Museo Nacional d'Art de Catalunya)**—Often called "the Prado of Romanesque art," this is a rare, world-class collection of Romanesque art collected mostly from remote Catalan village churches in the Pyrenees (saved from unscrupulous art dealers).

The Romanesque wing features frescoes, painted wooden altar fronts, and ornate statuary. This classic Romanesque art— with flat 2-D scenes, each saint holding his symbol, and Jesus (easy to identify by the cross in his halo)—is now impressively displayed on replicas of the original church ceilings.

In the Gothic wing, fresco murals give way to vivid 14th-century paintings of Bible stories on wood. A roomful of paintings by the Catalan master Jaume Huguet (1412–1492) deserves a close look.

Before you leave, ice skate under the huge dome over to the air-conditioned cafeteria. This was the prime ceremony room and dance hall for the 1929 International Exposition (800 ptas, Tue–Sat 10:00–19:00, Thu until 21:00, Sun 10:00–14:30, closed Mon, tel. 93-423-7199). The museum is in the massive National Palace building above the fountains, near Plaça Espanya (Metro: Plaça Espanya, then hike up or ride the bus; the Bus Turistic and bus #50 stop close by).

▲**Fundació Joan Miró**—For something more up-to-date, this museum showcases the modern art talents of yet another Catalunyan artist and is considered the best collection of Joan Miró art anywhere. You'll also see works by other modern Spanish artists; don't miss the Mercury Fountain by Alexander Calder. This museum leaves those who don't like abstract art scratching their heads (800 ptas, Tue–Sat 10:00–20:00, Thu until 21:30, Sun 10:00–14:30, closed Mon, closes at 19:00 off-season).

Sleeping in Barcelona
(160 ptas = about $1)
Sleep Code: **S** = Single, **D** = Double/Twin, **T** = Triple, **Q** = Quad,
b = bathroom, **t** = toilet only, **s** = shower only, **CC** = Credit Card
(Visa, MasterCard, Amex), **SE** = Speaks English, **NSE** = No English.
Book ahead in July and August or run the risk of paying dearly
for a room nicer than you need. If you strike out, try the room-
finding service at the TI at Plaça de Catalunya.

Barcelona is Spain's most expensive city. Still, it has reasonable
rooms. A few places raise their rates in August and deal off-season.
Assume prices listed do not include the 7 percent tax or breakfast.
While many recommended places are on pedestrian streets, night
noise is a problem almost everywhere. Most places charge more for
a balcony overlooking a people-filled street. To save money and
gain sleep ask for "*tranquilo*" rather than "*con vista.*"

Sleeping near the Ramblas and in the Gothic Quarter
(zip code: 08002)
These accommodations are listed in roughly geographical order
downhill from Plaça de Catalunya. See map on page 31.

Hotel Allegro fills a renovated old palace with wide halls,
marble and hardwood floors, and elegant, modern rooms with all
the comforts. It overlooks a busy pedestrian boulevard (Db-25,000
ptas plus tax, extra bed-3,000 ptas, CC:VMA, family rooms, satel-
lite TV, air-con, elevator, a block down from Plaça de Catalunya
at Portal de l'Angel 17, tel. 93-318-4141, fax 93-301-2631, SE).

Catalunya Plaza, a business hotel, has all the air-conditioning
and minibar comforts (Sb-19,000 ptas, Db-22,000 ptas, includes
breakfast, CC:VMA, elevator, free nuts at the desk, on the square at
Plaça de Catalunya 7, tel. 93-317-7171, fax 93-317-7855, SE).

Hotel Barcelona is another big, American-style hotel
(Sb-17,000 ptas, Db-25,000 ptas, 32,000 ptas with a terrace,
CC:VMA, air-con, 1 block away at Caspe 1–13, tel. 93-302-5858,
fax 93-301-8674).

Nouvel Hotel, an elegant Victorian-style building on a fine
pedestrian street, has royal lounges and comfy rooms (Sb-12,125
ptas, Db without balcony-15,350 ptas, Db with balcony-18,000
ptas, includes breakfast, manager Gabriel promises 10 percent discount with this book; no balcony = quieter and cheaper; air-con,
hair dryers, CC:VMA, Carrer de Santa Ana 18, tel. 93-301-8274,
fax 93-301-8370, SE).

Hotel Toledano's elevator takes you high above the noise.
View balcony rooms overlook the Ramblas. Suitable for backpackers,
this small and folksy, and at times dumpy, hotel is run by the helpful
English-speaking owner Juan Sanz, his son Albert, and Jordi (Sb-
3,900 ptas, Db-6,900 ptas, Tb-8,600 ptas, Qb-9,600 ptas, cheaper
off-season, CC:VMA, Rambla de Canaletas 138, tel. 93-301-0872,

fax 93-412-3142, e-mail: Toledano@idgrup.ibernet.com). They run **Hostal Residencia Capitol** one floor above—quiet, plain, cheaper, and also appropriate for backpackers (S-2,900 ptas, D-4,600 ptas, Ds-5,200 ptas, cheap 5-bed room).

Hotel Continental has comfortable rooms, double-thick mattresses, wildly clashing carpets and wallpaper, an all-day complimentary coffee bar, and a good location at the top of the Ramblas (Db-10,000–13,000 ptas with breakfast, CC:VMA, fans in rooms, elevator, Las Ramblas 138, tel. 93-301-2570, fax 93-302-7360, www.hotelcontinental.com).

Hotel Lloret is a big, dark, Old World place on the Ramblas with plain, air-conditioned rooms—confirm prices first (Sb-6,000 ptas, Db-9,000 ptas, extra beds-1,000 ptas each up to quints, buffet breakfast-400 ptas, choose between a noisy Ramblas balcony or *tranquilo* in the back, CC:VMA, elevator dominates the stairwell, Rambla de Canaletas 125, tel. 93-317-3366, fax 93-301-9283, SE).

Hotel Jardi is a hardworking, clean, plain place on the happiest little square in the Gothic Quarter. Room prices vary with newness, views, and balconies (Sb-3,500–4,000 ptas, Db-7,000–8,000 ptas, Tb-7,800–9,500 ptas, breakfast-700 ptas, CC:VM if bill totals at least 15,000 ptas, no elevator, halfway between the Ramblas and cathedral on Plaça Sant Josep Oriol #1, tel. 93-301-5900, fax 93-318-3664, NSE). Rooms with balconies enjoy a classic plaza setting and minimal noise.

These sister hotels straddle a pedestrian street in buildings that reek of concrete. Run by the same company, they have good but plain rooms with mod bathrooms (Sb-7,000 ptas, Db-11,500 ptas includes tax and breakfast, CC:VMA, elevator): **Hotel Catalunya** (Carrer de Santa Ana 24, tel. 93-301-9120, fax 93-302-7870) and **Hotel Cortes** (Carrer de Santa Ana 25, tel. 93-317-9112, fax 93-302-7870).

Deeper in the Gothic Quarter, these two new, modern neighbors suffer from street noise but keep businesspeople happy with TV, telephone, and air-conditioning: **Hotel Adagio** (Sb-9,000 ptas, Db-11,000 ptas, Tb-13,000 ptas, saggy beds, includes breakfast, CC:VMA, elevator, Ferran 21, tel. 93-318-9061, fax 93-318-3724) and, across the street, the **Hotel California** (Sb-6,500 ptas, Db-10,000 ptas, Tb-13,500 ptas, includes breakfast, CC:VMA, Raurich 14, tel. 93-317-7766, fax 93-317-5474, email: hotel _california@seker.es, SE). The California lacks an elevator but has bigger and brighter halls and bathrooms. Hike halfway down the Ramblas (just past Metro: Liceu), then turn left at McDonald's.

Humble Places Buried in Gothic Quarter with Youth Hostel Prices

Pensio Vitoria has loose tile floors and 12 humble rooms, each with a tiny balcony. It's a fine line between homey and dumpy, but consider the price (D-3,000 ptas, Db-3,500 ptas, CC:VM, a block off the day-dreamy Plaça dei Pi at Carrer la Palla 8, tel. & fax 93-302-0834).

Hostal Campi, big, quiet, and ramshackle, is a few doors off the Ramblas (D-4,500 ptas, Db-5,500 ptas, no elevator, Canuda 4, tel. & fax 93-301-3545, NSE). **Huéspedes Santa Ana** is plain and claustrophobic, with head-to-toe twins (S-2,800 ptas, D-5,000 ptas, Db-6,000 ptas, T-7,000 ptas, Carrer de Santa Ana 23, tel. 93-301-2246). **Hostal Residencia Lausanne**, filled with backpackers, has only its location and price going for it (S-2,500 ptas, D-3,500 ptas, Ds-5,000 ptas, Db-6,500 ptas, TV room, Avenida Portal de l'Angel 24, tel. 93-302-1139, SE). **Hostal Residencia Rembrandt** keeps countless backpackers happy with simple rooms and a good location (S-2,800 ptas, Sb-3,800 ptas, D-4,500 ptas, Db-6,300 ptas, Tb-7,500 ptas, breakfast-400 ptas, Portaferrisa 23, tel. & fax 93-318-1011, SE). **Huéspedes Colmenero**, on a noisy pedestrian street, is a homey little place with five rooms, each with a tiny balcony (S-3,000–4,000 ptas, D-5,000–6,000 ptas, Db-6,000–7,000 ptas, less off-season, 2 streets toward the cathedral from the Ramblas at Petritxol 12, tel. 93-302-6634, fax: What's that?, Rosa NSE).

Sleeping in Eixample

For a more elegant and boulevardian neighborhood, sleep on or near Gran Vía de les Corts Catalanes in Eixample, a 10-minute walk from the Ramblas action.

Hotel Gran Vía, filling a palatial mansion built in the 1870s, offers Botticelli and chandeliers in the public rooms; a sprawling, peaceful sun garden; and spacious, comfy, air-conditioned rooms. It's an excellent value (Sb-10,000 ptas, Db-13,500 ptas, tax and breakfast extra, CC:VMA, book long in advance, elevator, Gran Vía de les Corts Catalanes 642, 08007 Barcelona, tel. 93-318-1900, fax 93-318-9997, SE).

Hotel Residencia Neutral, with a classic Eixample location, 35 cheery rooms, plush public rooms, and a passion for cleanliness, is the poor man's Hotel Gran Vía (tiny Sb-3,400 ptas, big Sb-6,000 ptas, Ds-5,000 ptas, Db-6,000 ptas, Ts-6,100 ptas, Tb-7,275 ptas, tax included, breakfast extra, CC:VM, elevator, elegantly located two blocks north of Gran Vía at Rambla Catalunya 42, 08007 Barcelona, tel. 93-487-6390, SE).

Eating in Barcelona

Barcelona, the capital of Catalunyan cuisine, offers a tremendous variety of colorful places to eat. The harbor area, especially Barceloneta, is famous for fish. Good tapas bars are all over the Gothic Quarter. Many restaurants are closed in August (or sometimes July), when the owners, like you, are on vacation.

Eating in the Gothic Quarter

Taverna Basca Irati serves 25 kinds of hot and cold Basque *pintxos* for 130 ptas each. These are open-face sandwiches—like Basque sushi but on bread. Muscle in through the hungry local crowd. Get an empty plate from the waiter, then help yourself. It's a Basque honors system: You'll be charged by the number of toothpicks left on your plate when you're done. Wash it down with a delicate glass of *sidra* (apple wine, 125 ptas) poured from on high to bring out the flavor (Tue–Sat 12:00–15:00, 19:00–23:00, Sun 12:00–15:00, closed Mon, a block off the Ramblas, behind the noisy amusement arcade at Calle Cardenal Casanyes 17, near Metro: Liceu, tel. 93-302-3084). **Juicy Jones**, next door, is a tutti-fruity vegetarian place with a hip menu (#7, great fresh juices).

Two popular but touristy places are side by side, just down from the Plaça Reial: **Los Caracoles** is a pricey Spanish wine cellar dripping in atmosphere (daily 13:00–24:00, Escudellers 14, a block toward the harbor from Plaça Reial in red-light bar country, Metro: Drassanes, tel. 93-302-3185). The neighboring **La Fonda** is brighter and more modern, with high-quality traditional cuisine at better prices and even more tourists. Arrive early or make a reservation to avoid the very long waits (Escudellers 10, daily 13:00–15:30, 20:30–23:30, tel. 93-301-7515).

The owner of the wildly successful La Fonda has opened **La Dolca Herminia** and **Les Quinze Nitz**—both serving good local food at good prices in a classy modern bistro setting. La Dolca Herminia, already popular but not yet touristy, is two blocks toward the Ramblas from the Palau de la Música at Magdalenes 27 (tel. 93-317-0676). Les Quinze Nitz is on the trendy La Plaça Reial at #6—you'll see the line (tel. 93-317-3075); after a late dinner here, head across the square (after midnight) to the speakeasy at the **Barcelona Pipa Club** at #3. Ring the bell to be let in and head upstairs to a world of velvet and jazz unknown to tourists and most locals. Dress appropriately and pay a 600-ptas-per-person cover charge with your drinks.

At **El Portalon**, a tapas bar at Banys Nous 20, locals clatter away evenings with dominoes, oblivious to the tourist mecca outside.

Restaurant Agut is a fine place for huge servings of local-style food in a local-style setting (inexpensive, closed in July or August, Calle Gignas 16, tel. 93-315-1709).

Egipte, with its late-19th-century ambience, attracts the opera crowd. Local stars' portraits are on the walls. Try the *pebrots amb bacalao*—red bell peppers stuffed with cod and served over rice (daily 13:00–16:00, 20:00–24:00, Rambla 79, downhill from the Boqueria, Metro: Liceu, tel. 93-317-7480).

Els Quatre Gats, Picasso's hangout, is famous but has become uppity and expensive. Before it was founded in 1897, the idea of a café for artists was mocked as a place where only *quatre* *gats* ("four cats," meaning nobody) would go (3,000 ptas meals, Mon–Sat 8:30–02:00, Sun 17:00–01:30, live piano nightly from 21:00, CC:VMA, Montsio 3, tel. 93-302-4140).

Eating near Plaça de Catalunya

Self Naturista is a bright and cheery buffet that will make vegetarians ánd health-food lovers feel right at home. Others may find a few unidentifiable plates and drinks. The food's already out— pick what you like and microwave it (Mon–Sat 11:30–22:00, closed Sun, near several recommended hotels, just off the top of Ramblas at Carrer de Santa Ana 11–17). Another vegetarian choice is **Bio Center** (Mon–Sat 9:00–17:00, closed Sun, Pintor Fortuny 25, Metro: Catalunya, tel. 93-301-4583).

Julivert Meu teams up regional specialties like *pan con tomate* (bread with tomato and olive oil), *jamón serrano* (cured ham), and *escalivadas* (grilled vegetables) in a rustic interior (Mon–Sat 13:00–01:00, Sun 13:00–17:00, 20:00–01:00, off the Ramblas at Bonsuccés 7, Metro: Catalunya, tel. 93-318-0343).

Eating Elsewhere in Barcelona

In the Eixample at **La Bodegueta**, have a *carajillos* (coffee with rum) and a *flauta* (sandwich on flute-thin baguette) in this authentic below-street-level bodega (Mon–Sat 8:00–2:00, Sun 19:00– 1:00, Rambla Catalunya 100, at intersection with Provenza, Metro: Diagonal, tel. 93-215-4894). Or slip into the classy **Quasi Quevi-ures** for upscale tapas, sandwiches, or the whole nine yards— classic food with modern decor (Passeig de Gràcia 24).

El Café de Internet provides an easy way to munch a sandwich while sending e-mail messages to Mom (600 ptas for a half-hour, Mon–Sat 9:00–24:00, closed Sun, Gran Vía 656, Metro: Passeig de Gràcia, tel. 93-412-1915, www.cafeinternet.es).

For a quick meal, pick up a healthy sandwich at **Pans & Company**. Its sister establishment, **Pastafiore**, dishes up salads and pasta at a fair price (500–800 ptas). Both are lifesavers on Sunday, when many restaurants are closed (daily 8:00–24:00, opens at 9:00 Sun, located on Plaça Urquinaona, Provenza, La Rambla, Portal de l'Angel, and just about everywhere else).

Eating in Barceloneta

This charming beach suburb of the big city has long been famous for its fresh-fish restaurants. Lately, the big money has shifted to new, more trendy locales, and Barceloneta has gone back to being a big, easygoing neighborhood. A grid plan of long, narrow, laundry-strewn streets surrounds the central Plaça Poeta Boscan. For an entertaining evening, start here (15-minute walk or Metro: Barcelo-neta). During the day a lively produce market fills one end of the square. At night kids play soccer and Ping-Pong.

Cova Fumada is the neighborhood eatery. Josep Maria and his family serve famously fresh fish (Mon–Fri 17:30–20:30, closed July, Carrer del Baluarte 56, on the corner at Carrer Sant Carles, tel. 93-221-4061). Their *sardinas a la plancha* (grilled sardines, 350 ptas) are fresh and tasty. *Bombas* (potato croquets with pork, 150 ptas) are the house specialty. It's macho to have it *picante* (spicy with chili sauce); gentler taste buds prefer it with garlic cream (all-i-oli). If you're not sure how you like it, get it *marica*. Catalunyan bruschetta is *pan tostado* (toast with oil and garlic, 140 ptas). Wash it down with *vino tinto* (house red wine, 80 ptas).

At **Bar Electricidad**, Arturo Jordana Barba is the neighborhood source for cheap wine. Drop in. It's 180 ptas per liter; the empty plastic water bottles are for take-away. Try a 75-ptas glass of Torroja Tinto, the best local red, or Priorato Dulce, a wonderfully sweet red (Mon–Sat 8:00–13:00, 15:00–19:00, across the square from Cova Fumada, Plaça del Poeta Bosca, #61, NSE).

Tapas in the Gothic Quarter

Tapas aren't as popular in Catalunya as they are in the rest of Spain, but Barcelona boasts great *tascas*—colorful local tapas bars. Get small plates (for maximum sampling) by asking for "*tapas*," not "*raciones*." For the most fun and flavorful route through the Gothic Quarter, go to Plaça de la Merce (Metro: Drassanes) then follow the small street that runs along the right side of the church (Carrer Merce), stopping at whichever *tascas* look fun.

La Jarra is known for its tender *jamón canario con patatas* (baked ham with salty potatoes). Across the street, **La Pulperia** serves up fried fish. A block down the street, **Tasca El Corral** makes one of the neighborhood's best chorizo *al diablo* (hell sausage), which you sauté yourself. It's great with the regional specialty *pan con tomate*. Across the street, **La Plata** keeps things wonderfully simple, serving extremely cheap plates of sardines and small glasses of keg wine. **La Socarrena** serves northern Spain mountain favorites (like *queso de cabrales*—very moldy cheese) with *sidra* (apple wine). You can smell **Las Campanas'** fragrant sausage a block away. Have a chat with the parrot at **Bar la Choza del Sopas**. At the end of Carrer Merce, **Bar Vendimia** serves up tasty clams and mussels. Carrer Ample, the street paralleling Carrer Merce, has more-refined bar-hopping possibilities.

La Cava del Palau, also in the Gothic Quarter, is a great wine bar, bubbling with Spain's sparkling wine (Verdaguer i Callis 10, near Palau de la Música Catalana).

Transportation Connections—Barcelona

By train to: Lisbon (1/day, 15 hrs with change in Madrid), **Madrid** (6/day, 7–9 hrs, $50 with *couchette*), **Paris** (3/day, 11–15 hrs, $70, night train, reservation required), **Sevilla** (4/day, 11 hrs), **Málaga**

(3/day, 14 hrs), **Nice** (1/day, 12 hrs, change in Cerbere). Train info: tel. 93-490-0202; international train info: tel. 93-490-1122.

By bus to: Madrid (6/day, 8 hrs, half the price of a train ticket).

By plane: To avoid 10-hour train trips, check the reasonable flights from Barcelona to Sevilla or Madrid. Iberia Air (tel. 93-412-5667) and Air Europe (tel. 90-224-0042) offer $80 flights to Madrid. Airport info: tel. 93-298-3838.

NEAR BARCELONA: FIGUERES, CADAQUES, AND MONTSERRAT

Three fine sights are day-trip temptations from Barcelona. For the ultimate in surrealism and a classy but sleepy port-town getaway, consider a day or two in Cadaques with a stop at the Dalí Museum in Figueres. Figueres is an hour from Cadaques and two hours from Barcelona. Pilgrims with hiking boots head 30 miles into the mountains for the most sacred spot in Catalunya, Montserrat.

Figueres

▲▲▲**Dalí Museum**—This is the essential Dalí sight. Inaugurated in 1974, the museum is a work of art in itself. Dalí personally conceptualized, designed, decorated, and painted it, intending to showcase his life's work. Highlights include the epic Palace of the Wind ceiling, the larger-than-life Mae West room (complete with fireplaces for nostrils), fun mechanical interactive art (Dalí was into action; bring lots of 25 and 100 ptas coins), and the famous squint-to-see Abraham Lincoln. Other major and fantastic works include the tiny *Le Spectre Du Sex-Appeal*, *Soft Self Portrait*, and the red-shoe riddle of *Zapato y Vaso de Leche*. The only real historical context provided is on the easy-to-miss and unlabeled earphone info boxes in the Mae West room (100 ptas). A bizarre video (near the exit) shows every half hour. While not in English, it's plenty entertaining (1,000 ptas, daily 9:00–20:00; off-season 10:30–18:00 and closed Mon; last entry 45 minutes before closing, free bag check has your bag waiting for you at the exit, tel. 97-251-1800). Dalí, who was born in Figueres in 1905, is buried in the museum. From the train station, follow "Museu Dalí" signs to the museum.

Connections: Figueres is an easy day trip from Barcelona or a stopover (trains from France stop in Figueres; lockers at the station). Trains from Barcelona depart Sants Station or the RENFE station at Metro: Passeig de Gràcia (hrly, 2 hrs).

Cadaques

Since the late 1800s, Cadaques has served as a haven for intellectuals and artists alike. Salvador Dalí, raised in nearby Figueres, brought international fame to this sleepy Catalan port in the 1920s. He and his wife, Gala, set up home and studio at the adjacent Port Lligat. Cadaques inspired surrealists such as Eluard, Magritte, Duchamp, Man Ray, Buñuel, and García Lorca. Even Picasso was drawn to this enchanting coastal *cala* (cove), painting some of his cubist works here.

In spite of its fame, Cadaques is laid-back and feels off the beaten path. If you want a peaceful beach-town escape near Barcelona, there's no better place. From the moment you descend into the town, taking in whitewashed buildings and deep blue waters, you're struck by the port's tranquillity and beauty. Have a glass of *vino tinto* or *cremat* (a traditional brandy and coffee drink served flambé style) at one of the seaside cafés and savor the lapping waves, brilliant sun, and gentle breeze.

The **Casa Museu Salvador Dalí**, once Dalí's home, gives fans a chance to explore his labyrinthine compound (1,300 ptas, Tue–Sun 10:30–20:10, closed Mon, closes spring and fall at 17:10, closed in winter, 15-minute walk over the hill from Cadaques to Port Lligat, limited visits, call to reserve a time, tel. 97-225-8063).

To see a few Dalís right in Cadaques, visit the small **Museu Perrot-Moore** (summer 10:30–13:30, 16:30–20:30, Calle Vigilant, tel. 97-225-8231). The **TI** is at Carrer Cotxe 2 (Mon–Sat 9:00–14:00, 16:00–21:00, Sun 10:00–13:00, tel. 97-225-8315).

Sleeping and Eating: Hotel La Residencia, owned by Dalí's first manager, Captain Moore, is a pleasant, pricey hotel strewn with art and sporting a sunny garden patio. One hundred and twenty original Dalí works—sculptures, prints, paintings, and photos (in addition to wall coverings and upholstery)—line the corridors and fill the rooms (Db-16,000 ptas, CC:VM, Avenida Caritat Serinyana 1, tel. 97-225-8312, fax 97-225-8013, e-mail: residencia@grn.es). These cheaper options are clean and conveniently located in the main plaza, around the corner from the TI and across from the beach: **Hostal Marina** (D-4,500 ptas, Ds-5,500 ptas, Db-8,000 ptas, breakfast-500 ptas, CC:VM, Riera 3, tel. & fax 97-225-8199) and **Hostal Cristina** (S-3,500 ptas, D-4,500 ptas, breakfast-500 ptas, La Riera s/n, tel. 97-225-8138).

For a fine dinner, try **Casa Anita**, down a narrow street from La Residencia. Sitting with others around a big table, you'll enjoy house specialties like *calamars a la plancha* (grilled squid) and homemade *helado* (ice cream). Muscatel from a glass *porron* finishes off the tasty meal (Juan and family, tel. 97-225-8471).

Connections: Cadaques is reached by Sarfa buses from Figueres (5/day, 80 min, 460 ptas) or from Barcelona (5/day, 2.5 hrs, 1,750 ptas, less frequent off-season, tel. 93-265-6508).

Montserrat

Montserrat, set amid spectacular mountains, is a popular day trip from Barcelona (53 km). This has been Catalunya's most important pilgrimage site for a thousand years. Hymns ascribe this "serrated mountain" to little angels who carved the rocks with golden saws. Geologists blame 10 million years of nature at work.

Montserrat's top attraction is **La Moreneta**, a basilica with the Black Virgin icon (daily 8:00–10:30, 12:00–18:30). The Moreneta is the patron saint and protector of Catalunya and is therefore the most revered religious symbol in the province.

The first hermit monks built huts at Montserrat around 900 A.D. By 1025 a monastery was founded. A choir school soon followed. The **Montserrat Escolania**, or choir school, is considered to be the oldest music school in Europe. Fifty young boys, who live and study in the monastery itself, make up the choir, which performs daily at 13:00 and 19:10 (choir on vacation in July).

Inside the basilica, be sure to see the Virgin close up (behind the altar). Pilgrims touch her orb; the rest is protected behind glass. Then descend into the prayer room for a view of the Moreneta from behind. Pilgrims dip a memento of their journey into the holy water or even leave a personal belonging here (like a motorcycle helmet for safety) to soak up more blessings.

In the summer watch a 15-minute video in English about the monastery (free, 2/day, ask at TI).

The **Museu de Montserrat** offers prehistoric tools, religious art, ancient artifacts, and a few paintings by masters such as El Greco, Caravaggio, Monet, Picasso, and Dalí (500 ptas, Mon–Fri 10:00–18:00, Sat–Sun 9:30–18:00, shorter hours in winter).

The Moreneta was originally located in the **Santa Cova** (holy cave), a 40-minute hike down from the monastery lined with statues depicting scenes from the life of Christ. While the original *Black Virgin* statue is now in the basilica, a replica sits in the cave.

The **Sant Joan funicular** (see below) continues another 250 meters beyond the monastery (560 ptas one way, 895 ptas round-trip) to the start of numerous hikes, described in the TI's "Six Itineraries from the Monastery" brochure.

Sleeping: You can sleep in the **old monks' cloister** far more comfortably than did its original inhabitants (twin-7,580 ptas, fine restaurant attached, tel. 93-877-7701).

Connections: Ferrocarriles Catalanes trains leave hourly for Montserrat from Barcelona's Plaça Espanya (1,855 ptas round-trip, cash only, no CC, Eurailpass not valid). From the Metro station, follow signs through several tunnels to the "FF de la Generalitat" underground station, then look for train line R5 (direction Manresa, departures 36 minutes past each hour, 1 hr). Get off at the Aeri de Montserrat stop at the base of the mountain, where the funicular awaits (the round-trip from Barcelona includes 4/hrly funicular ride). Returning, you'll find that top-of-the-hour funiculars connect with the hourly trains.

MADRID

Today's Madrid is upbeat and vibrant, still enjoying a post-Franco renaissance. You'll feel it. Even the statue-maker beggars have a twinkle in their eyes.

Madrid is the hub of Spain. This modern capital—Europe's highest, at more than 2,000 feet—has a population of more than 4 million and is young by European standards. Only 400 years ago, King Philip II decided to move the capital of his empire from Toledo to Madrid. One hundred years ago Madrid had only 400,000 people, so nine-tenths of the city is modern sprawl surrounding an intact, easy-to-navigate historic core.

Dive headlong into the grandeur and intimate charm of Madrid. The lavish Royal Palace, with its gilded rooms and frescoed ceilings, rivals Versailles. The Prado has Europe's top collection of paintings. The city's huge Retiro Park invites you for a shady siesta and a hopscotch through a mosaic of lovers, families, skateboarders, pets walking their masters, and expert bench sitters. Make time for Madrid's elegant shops and people-friendly pedestrian zones. Enjoy the shade in an arcade. On Sundays, cheer for the bull at a bullfight or bargain like mad at a mega–flea market. Lively Madrid has enough street singing, barhopping, and people-watching vitality to give any visitor a boost of youth.

Planning Your Time

Madrid's top two sights, the Prado and the palace, are worth a day. If you hit the city on a Sunday, allot extra time for a bullfight. Ideally, give Madrid two days and spend them this way:

Day 1: Breakfast of *churros* (see "Eating," below) before a brisk, good-morning-Madrid walk for 20 minutes from Puerta del Sol to the Prado; 9:00–12:00 at the Prado; afternoon siesta in Retiro

Park or modern art at the Centro Reina Sofia (*Guernica*) and/
or the Thyssen-Bornemisza Museum; Tapas for dinner around
Plaza Santa Ana.
Day 2: Follow this book's "Puerta del Sol to Royal Palace Walk"
(see below); tour the Royal Palace, lunch near Plaza Mayor; afternoon free for other sights, shopping, or side trip to El Escorial
(open until 19:00).

Note that the Prado, Thyssen-Bornemisza Museum, and
El Escorial are closed on Monday. For day-trip possibilities from
Madrid, see the next two chapters ("Northwest of Madrid" and
"Toledo").

Orientation

The historic center can easily be covered on foot. No major sight
is more than a 20-minute walk from the Puerta del Sol, Madrid's
central square. Your time will be divided between the city's two
major sights—the Royal Palace and the Prado—and its barhopping, car-honking, contemporary scene.

The Puerta del Sol is at the dead center of Madrid and of
Spain itself; notice the "kilometer zero" marker, from which all of
Spain is surveyed (southwest corner). The Royal Palace to the west
and the Prado Museum and Retiro Park to the east frame
Madrid's historic center.

Southwest of Puerta del Sol is a 17th-century district with the
slow-down-and-smell-the-cobbles Plaza Mayor and plenty of relics
from pre-industrial Spain.

North of Puerta del Sol runs the Gran Vía, and between the
two are lively pedestrian shopping streets. The Gran Vía, bubbling
with expensive shops and cinemas, leads to the modern Plaza de
España. North of Gran Vía is the gritty Malasana quarter, with its
colorful small houses, shoemakers' shops, sleazy-looking hombres,
milk vendors, bars, and hip night scene.

Tourist Information

Madrid has four Turismos (all closed on Sunday): one on the
Plaza Mayor at #3 (Mon–Fri 10:00–20:00, Sat 10:00–14:00, tel.
91-588-1636); another near the Prado Museum, behind the giant
Palace Hotel (Mon–Fri 9:00–19:00, Sat 9:00–13:00, Duque de
Medinaceli 2, tel. 91-429-4951); and smaller offices at the
Chamartin train station (Mon–Fri 8:00–20:00, Sat 9:00–13:00,
tel. 91-315-9976) and at the airport (same hours, tel. 91-305-
8343). During the summer you'll also find small temporary
stands with yellow umbrellas and yellow-shirted student guides
happy to help out lost tourists (there's a handy booth on Puerta
del Sol). Confirm your sightseeing plans and pick up a map and
Enjoy Madrid, the free monthly city guide. (The TI's free guide
to city events, *En Madrid,* is not as good as the easy-to-decipher

Madrid

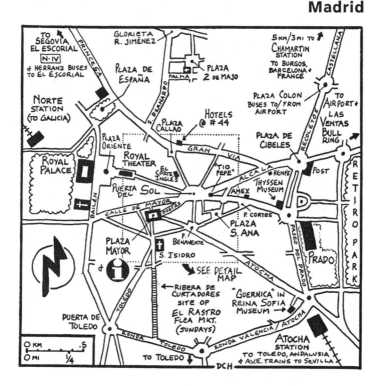

Spanish weekly entertainment guide, *Guía del Ocio*, on sale at street-side newsstands for 125 ptas.) If interested, ask at the TI about bullfights and Zarzuela (the local light opera). The free and amazingly informative *Mapa de Comunicaciones España* lists all the Turismos and highway SOS numbers with a road map of Spain. (If they're out, ask for the Paradores Hotel chain-sponsored route map.) If you're heading to other destinations in this book, see if the Madrid TI has free maps and brochures. Since many small-town TIs keep erratic hours and run out of these pamphlets, get what you can here. Get bus schedules, too, to avoid unnecessary trips to the various bus stations.

Arrival in Madrid

By Train: The two main rail stations, Atocha and Chamartin, are both on subway lines with easy access to downtown Madrid. Each station has all the services, though there is no TI at Atocha. In Spain, train rides longer than about three hours require reservations, even if you have a Eurailpass. To avoid needless running around, arrange your departure upon arrival.

Chamartin handles most international trains, and Atocha runs AVE trains to Sevilla. Both stations offer long-distance trains (*largo recorrido*) as well as local trains to nearby destinations (*cercanías*). Atocha is more clearly split into two halves (local and long-distance trains) with separate schedules; this can be confusing if you're in the wrong side of the building. Atocha also has two helpful (necessary) customer-service offices called Atención al Cliente (daily 7:00– 23:00)—one office for each half of the building. The Chamartin station is less confusing. Its customer-service office is beside the ticket windows, in the middle of the building, and the helpful TI is opposite track #20.

Club AVE in Atocha (upstairs) is a lounge reserved solely for AVE business or first-class ticketholders or Eurailers with a reservation (free drinks, newspapers, showers, info service, and so on). Club Intercity in Chamartin is less exclusive—you can get in if you have a first-class railpass and first-class seat or sleeper reservations.

Both train stations have Metro stops: Chamartin and Atocha RENFE. (Note that there are two Atocha Metro stops in Madrid; the train station's Metro station is "Atocha RENFE"). If you're traveling between Chamartin and Atocha, use the Cercanias trains (6/hrly, 12 min, free with railpass—show it at ticket window in the middle of all the turnstiles); they're far quicker than the subway. Trains depart from Atocha's track #2. At Chamartin, check the Salidas Immediatas board for the next departure.

At the downtown RENFE office you can get train information, reservations, and tickets (Mon–Fri 9:30–19:00, credit cards accepted, best to go in person, two blocks north of the Prado Museum at Calle Alcala 44, tel. 91-328-9020).

By Bus: Madrid's three key bus stations, all connected by Metro, are: Larrea (handles Segovia; Metro: Príncipe Pío), the brand-new Estación Sur Autobuses (covers Toledo, Ávila, and Granada; Metro: Méndez Alvaro), and Estación Herranz (serves El Escorial; in the Metro: Moncloa). For details, see "Transportation Connections" at the end of this chapter.

By Plane: Madrid's Barajas Airport, 10 miles east of downtown, comes well-equipped to help new arrivals. It has a 24-hour bank with fair rates, an ATM, a TI, a telephone office where you can buy a phone card, a RENFE desk for rail information, a pharmacy, on-the-spot car-rental agencies, and easy public transportation into town. Airport info: tel. 91-393-6000. By public transport, take the yellow bus from the airport to Madrid (to Plaza Colón, 4/hrly, 20 min, 385 ptas); then, from Plaza Colón, take a taxi or subway to your hotel (to get to the subway, walk up the stairs and face the blue "URBIS" sign high on a building—the subway stop, M. Serrano, is 50 yards to your right)

The airport' new Metro stop, Aeropuerto, provides a cheap (135 ptas) but time-consuming (45 min) way into town (access Metro at check-in level, transfer at Mar de Cristal to brown line #4—direction Arguelles, transfer at Goya to to red line #3 to Sol).

If you take a taxi (easily available from the airport bus station at Plaza Colón), insist on the meter; a ride through town should be less than 1,000 ptas. For a taxi to or from the airport, allow at least 3,000 ptas (5,000 ptas is a rip off). At the airport, get a rough idea of the price before you hop in. Ask "*¿Cuanto cuesta a Madrid, más o menos?*" ("How much is it to Madrid, more or less?")

Getting around Madrid

By Subway: Madrid's subway is simple, speedy (outside of rush hour), and cheap (135 ptas/ride). For 680 ptas, buy the 10-ride Metrobus ticket, which can be shared by several travelers and works on both the Metro and buses (available at kiosks or tobacco shops or in Metro). The city's broad streets can be hot and exhausting. A subway trip of even a stop or two can save time and energy. Pick up a free map (*Plano del Metro*) at most stations. Navigate by subway stops (shown on city maps). To transfer, follow signs to the next subway line (numbered and color-coded). End stops are used to indicate directions. Insert your ticket in the turnstile, then retrieve it as you pass through. Green *Salida* signs point to the exit. Use the neighborhood maps and street signs to exit smartly.

By Bus: City buses, while not as easy as the Metro, can be useful. If you're interested, get a bus map at the TI or the info booth on Puerta del Sol. Tickets are 135 ptas (buy on bus) or 680 ptas for a 10-ride Metrobus (buy at kiosks, in tobacco shops, or in the Metro). The Madrid Vision bus provides transportation and a tour (see "Tours of Madrid," below).

By Taxi: While taxis are easy to hail and reasonable (175 ptas drop, 85 ptas per km, late night 115 ptas per km; supplements for airport, train station, and bags), you'll go just as fast and a lot cheaper by subway.

Helpful Hints

Theft Alert: Be wary of pickpockets, anywhere, anytime, but particularly on Puerta del Sol (main square), the subway, and crowded streets. Wear your money belt. In crowds, keep your day bag in front of you. Some thieves "accidentally" spill something on your clothes, then pick your pocket as they help you clean up. The small streets north of Gran Vía are particularly dangerous even before nightfall. Fortunately, violent crime against tourists is very rare.

Museum Pass: If you plan to visit the Prado, Reina Sofia (*Guernica*), and Thyssen-Bornemisza museums, save 33 percent by buying the Paseo del Arte pass (1,200 ptas, available at all three museums).

Monday Plans: If you're in Madrid on a Monday (when the Prado is closed), you can visit the Royal Palace and Reina Sofia, rent a boat at Retiro Park, tour the nearby botanical gardens, shop, or café-hop.

Travel Agency and Free Maps: The grand department store, El Corte Inglés, has a travel agency (Mon–Sat 10:00–21:30, just off Puerta del Sol) and gives free Madrid maps (at the information desk, just inside the door at the northwest corner of the intersection of Preciados and Tetuan).

Telephones: The telephone office, centrally located at Gran Vía 30, has metered phones and accepts credit cards for charges over 500 ptas (daily 10:00–23:00).

American Express: The Amex office is at Plaza Cortes 2 (opposite Palace Hotel, six blocks from Metro: Sevilla, Mon–Fri 9:00–17:30, Sat 9:00–12:00, tel. 91-322-5455).

Embassies: The U.S. Embassy is at Serrano 75 (tel. 91-587-2200); the Canadian Embassy is at Nuñez de Balboa 35 (tel. 91-431-2350).

Laundromat: The self-service Lavamatique is funky but central (Mon–Fri 9:00–20:00, Sat 9:00–17:00, Cervantes 1).

Internet Access: Zahara is at the corner of Gran Vía and Mesoneros (Mon–Fri 9:00–0:30, Sat–Sun 9:00–01:30).

Tours of Madrid

Bus Tour—The Madrid Vision Bus takes tourists on a big hop-on hop-off sightseeing loop with a multilingual tape-recorded narration (2,200 ptas for all-day pass, departures from Gran Vía 32 every 45 minutes, 9:15–17:15, tel. 91-767-1743).

Walking Tour—British expatriate Stephen Drake-Jones gives entertaining, informative walks of historic old Madrid almost nightly (along with several other more specialized tours). A historian with a passion for the memory of Wellington (the man who stopped Napoleon), Stephen is the founder of the Wellington Society. For 2,500 ptas you become a member of the society for one year and get a free two-hour tour that includes stops at two bars for local drinks and tapas. Stephen, in his nearly eccentric style, takes you back in time to sort out the Habsburg and Bourbon history of this under-appreciated city. Stephen likes his drink—if you feel he's had too much, skip the tour. Tours start at the statue on Puerta del Sol (tel. 60-914-3203—a cell phone number that will cost you 200 ptas—to confirm tour and reserve a spot; Stephen also does inexpensive private tours for small groups; e-mail: sdrake_jones@hotmail.com).

Sights—From Madrid's Puerta del Sol to the Royal Palace

Connect the sights with the following walking tour. Allow an hour for this half-mile walk, not including your visit to the palace.

Heart of Madrid

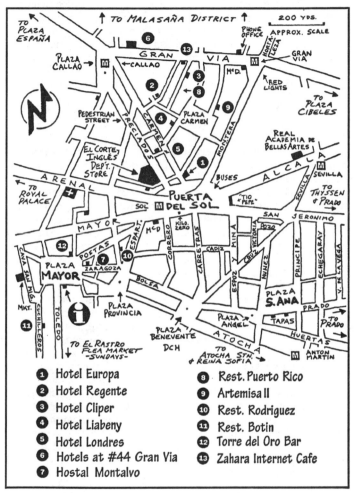

❶ Hotel Europa	❽ Rest. Puerto Rico
❷ Hotel Regente	❾ Artemisa II
❸ Hotel Cliper	❿ Rest. Rodriguez
❹ Hotel Liabeny	⓫ Rest. Botin
❺ Hotel Londres	⓬ Torre del Oro Bar
❻ Hotels at #44 Gran Via	⓭ Zahara Internet Cafe
❼ Hostal Montalvo	

▲▲**Puerta del Sol**—Even without its "kilometer zero" plaque, Puerta del Sol is ground zero for Madrid. Standing by the statue of Charles III, survey the square. Because of his enlightened urban policies, King Charles III (who ruled until 1788) is affectionately called the "best mayor of Madrid." He decorated the city squares with fine fountains, got the meddlesome Jesuits out of city government, established a public education system, made the Retiro a public park rather than a royal retreat, and generally cleaned up Madrid. The huge palace he faces was the first post office (which he established in the 1760s). Today the building is remembered for being a police headquarters during the reign of Franco. An amazing number of those detained and interrogated by the Franco police "tried to escape" by flying out the windows to their deaths. You'll see civil guardsmen at the entry. (It's said their hats have square backsides so they can lean against the wall while enjoying a cigarette.)

On New Year's Eve, crowds gather on this square, and, as the big clock atop the post office chimes 12 times, Madrillinos eat one grape for each ring to bring good luck through the coming year.

A plaque on the post office wall marks the spot where the war against Napoleon started. Napoleon wanted his brother to be king of Spain. Trying to finagle this, Napoleon brought nearly the entire Spanish royal family (the Bourbons) to Paris for negotiations. An anxious crowd gathered outside the post office awaiting word of the fate of their royal family. This was just after the French Revolution, and there was a general nervousness between France and Spain. The French guard appeared and the 2nd of May, 1808, massacre took place. Goya, who lived just up the street, observed the massacre and captured the tragedy in his paintings *2nd of May, 1808*, and *3rd of May, 1808*, which you'll see in the Prado.

Puerta del Sol is a hub for the Metro, buses, and pickpockets. Look up at the surveillance camera. In summer you'll see a yellow-umbrella TI booth with student tour guides helping visitors. The statue of the bear pawing the strawberry bush is the symbol of Madrid.

Walking from Puerta del Sol to Plaza Mayor: On the corner of Calle Mayor and Puerta del Sol, step into the busy Confiteria. It's famous for its savory, meat-filled *agujas* pastries (175 ptas); notice the racks with goodies hot out of the oven. Look back toward the entrance and notice the tile above the door with the 18th-century view of the Puerta del Sol. Compare this with the view out the door. This was before the square was widened, when a church stood where the Tío Pepe sign stands today. The French used this church to hold local patriots awaiting execution.

Continue down Calle Mayor. At McDonald's veer left up the pedestrian alley called Calle de Postas. The street sign shows the post coach heading for that famous first post office. Take a left up Calle San Cristobal. At the square notice the big brick 17th-century Ministry of Foreign Affairs building—originally a prison for rich prisoners who could afford the best cells. Look right and walk under the arch into...

Plaza Mayor—This square, built in 1619, is a vast, cobbled, traffic-free chunk of 17th-century Spain. Each side of the square is uniform, as if a grand palace were turned inside out. The statue is of

Plaza Mayor to Royal Palace

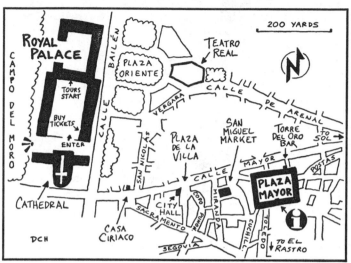

Philip III, who ordered the square's construction. Upon this stage, much Spanish history was played out: bullfights, fires, royal pageantry, and events of the gruesome Inquisition. Carved reliefs under the lampposts tell the story. During the Inquisition, many were tried here. The guilty would parade around the square (bleachers were built for bigger audiences) with billboards listing their many sins. They were then burned. Some were slowly strangled with a garrotte; they'd hold a crucifix and hear the reassuring words of a priest as this life was squeezed out of them. The square is painted a lovely shade of burgundy—the result of a city-wide vote. Since Franco's 1975 death, there has been a passion for voting here. Three different colors were painted as samples on the walls of this square, and the city voted for its favorite. Visit the subterranean museum of city exhibitions (free, hours depend on exhibition) under the fanciest facade (the Casa de la Panaderia—Royal Bakery).

Throughout Spain, lesser *plazas mayores* provide peaceful pools for the river of Spanish life. A stamp-and-coin market bustles here on Sundays from 10:00 to 14:00, and on any day it's a colorful and affordable place to enjoy a cup of coffee. The TI is at #3.

Finish your Plaza Mayor visit with a drink at the Torre del Oro Bar Andalu. This is Madrid's temple to bullfighting. You'll get a free tapa if Mariano is serving you between the hours of 11:00 and 13:00. Warning: They tend to order for tourists, serving them expensive dishes they didn't order; I ended up with a $10 plate I didn't want. To ask if the food is free, ask, "*¿Libero?*" The bar's ambience is "*Andalu*" ... Andalusian. Look under the stuffed head of "Barbero" the bull. At eye level you'll see a *puntilla*, the knife used to put a bull out of its misery at the arena. This was the knife used to kill Barbero.

Notice the incredible action caught in the bar's many photographs. Near Barbero, follow the photo series of a wanna-be bull-fighter who jumped into the ring and was killed by the bull. Below that is a series of photos showing the scandalous fight in which a banderillero (the guy who puts the arrows into the bull's back) was in trouble and his partners just stood by watching in horror as the man was killed. At the end of the bar in a glass case is the "suit of lights" El Cordobes wore in his ill-fated 1967 fight. With Franco in attendance, El Cordobes went on and on, long after he could have ended the fight, until finally the bull gored him. El Cordobes survived, the bull didn't. Find Franco with El Cordobes at the far end.

Walking from Plaza Mayor to the Royal Palace: Leave the Plaza Mayor on Calle Cuidad Rodrigo (left of Royal Bakery), passing a series of fine turn-of-the-century storefronts. From the archway you'll see Mercado de San Miguel, covered since 1900 (on left). Wander through this produce market, leaving on the downhill side and following the street left. At the corner, turn right, continuing downhill. A right on Calle de Punonrostro gives a feeling of medieval Madrid and eventually becomes Calle del Codo (where those in need of bits of armor shopped), before hitting Plaça de la Villa, the city hall square. Notice the Moorish arch where Calle del Codo hits the square. Ahead the flags of city, state, and nation grace the city hall. In the lovely garden there's a statue of Don Bazan—mastermind of the Christian victory over the Muslims at the naval battle of Lepanto in 1571. This pivotal battle ended the Muslim threat to Christian Europe.

From here Calle Mayor leads downhill a couple more blocks to the Royal Palace. Halfway down there's a tiny square opposite the recommended Casa Ciriaco restaurant (#84). The statue memorializes the 1906 anarchist bombing that killed about 50 people as the royal couple paraded by on their wedding day. While the crowd was throwing flowers, an anarchist threw a bomb from the top floor of #84 (which was a pension at the time). Amazing photos of the event are on the wall in the dining room of the restaurant.

▲▲▲**Royal Palace (Palacio Real)**—Europe's third-greatest palace (after Versailles and Vienna's Schonbrunn) is packed with tourists and royal antiques. After a fortress burned down on this site, King Phillip V commissioned this huge 18th-century palace as a replacement. How huge is it? Two thousand rooms with miles of lavish tapestries, a king's ransom of chandeliers, priceless porcelain, and paintings. Nowadays it's used only for formal state receptions and tourist's daydreams.

You can wander on your own or join an English tour (get time of next tour and decide as you buy your ticket; tours depart about every 20 minutes). The museum guidebook and the tour guides are equally dry, each showing a passion for meaningless data (850 ptas without a tour, 950 ptas with a tour, Mon–Sat 9:00–18:00, Sun 9:00–15:00; Oct–Mar Mon–Sat 9:30–17:00, Sun 9:00–14:00; Metro: Opera, tel. 91-542-0059). Your ticket includes the armory (most likely closed for restoration) and the pharmacy, both on the courtyard.

Sights—Madrid's Museum Neighborhood

These three worthwhile museums are in east Madrid. From Prado to the Thyssen-Bornemisza Museum is a five-minute walk; Prado to Reina Sofia is a 10-minute walk.

▲▲▲**Prado Museum**—The Prado is my favorite collection of paintings anywhere. With more than 3,000 canvases, including entire rooms of masterpieces by Velázquez, Goya, El Greco, and Bosch, it's overwhelming. Take a tour or buy a guidebook (or bring me along by ripping out and packing the Prado chapter from *Rick Steves' Mona Winks*). Focus on the Flemish and northern (Bosch, Dürer, Rubens), the Italian (Fra Angelico, Raphael, Botticelli, Titian), and the Spanish art (El Greco, Velázquez, Goya).

Follow Goya through his stages, from cheery (*The Parasol*), to political (*2nd of May, 1808* and *3rd of May, 1808*), to dark ("Negras de Goya": e.g., *Saturn Devouring His Children*). In each stage, Goya asserted his independence from artistic conventions. Even the standard court portraits from his "first" stage reflect his politically liberal viewpoint, subtly showing the vanity and stupidity of his royal subjects by the looks in their goony eyes. His political stage, with paintings like the *3rd of May, 1808*, depicting a massacre of Spaniards by Napoleon's troops, makes him one of the first artists with a social conscience. Finally, in his gloomy "dark stage," Goya probed the inner world of fears and nightmares, anticipating the 20th-century preoccupation with dreams. Also, seek out Bosch's *The Garden of Earthly Delights*. The art is constantly rearranged by the Prado's fidgety management, so even the Prado's own maps and guidebooks are out of date. Regardless of the latest location, most art is grouped by painter, and any guard can point you in the right direction if you say "*¿Dónde está...?*" and the painter's name as Españoled as you can (e.g., Titian is "Ticiano" and Bosch is "El Bosco"). Show up 30 minutes after it opens to avoid the initial flood (the Murillo entrance—at the end closest to Retiro Park—always has shorter line) or go at lunchtime, from 14:00 to 16:00, when the Prado is quietest (500 ptas, Tue–Sat 9:00–19:00, Sun 9:00–14:00, closed Mon; Paseo de Prado, Metro: Banco de España or Atocha—each a 15-minute walk from the museum, tel. 91-330-2800 or 91-420-2836).

▲▲**Thyssen-Bornemisza Museum**—This stunning museum displays the impressive collection that Baron Thyssen (a wealthy German married to a former Miss Spain) sold to Spain for $350 million. It's basically minor works by major artists and major works by minor artists (the real big guns are over at the Prado). But art lovers appreciate how the good baron's art complements the Prado's collection by filling in where the Prado is weak (Impressionism). For a fine walk through art history, ride the elevator to the top floor and do the rooms in numerical order. It's located across from the Prado at Paseo del Prado 8 in the Palacio de Villahermosa (700 ptas, Tue–Sun 10:00–19:00, closed Mon, Metro: Banco de España or Atocha, tel. 91-369-0151). Tired ones can hail a cab at the gate and zip straight to Centro Reina Sofia.

▲▲**Centro Reina Sofia**—This exceptional modern-art museum covers the art of our century. Ride the elevator to the second floor and follow the room numbers for art from 1900 to 1950. The fourth floor continues the collection from 1950 to 1980. The museum is most famous for Picasso's *Guernica*, a massive painting showing the horror of modern war. Guernica, a village in northern Spain, was the target of the world's first saturation-bombing raid, approved by Franco and carried out by Hitler. Notice the two rooms of studies for *Guernica* filled with iron-nail tears and screaming mouths. *Guernica* was exiled in America until Franco's death, and now it reigns as Spain's national piece of art. The museum also houses an easy-to-enjoy collection of other modern artists, including more of Picasso (three rooms divided among his pre-civil-war work, *Guernica*, and his post-civil-war art) and a mind-bending room full of Dalís. Enjoy a break in the shady courtyard before leaving (500 ptas, Mon and Wed–Sat 10:00–21:00, Sun 10:00–14:30, closed Tue, Santa Isabel 52, Metro: Atocha, across from Atocha train station, look for exterior glass elevators, tel. 91-467-5062).

More Sights—Madrid

Chapel San Antonio de la Florida—Goya's tomb stares up at a splendid cupola filled with his own frescoes (300 ptas, Tue–Fri 10:00–14:00, 16:00–20:00, Sat–Sun 10:00–14:00, closed Mon, Glorieta de San Antonio de la Florida, Metro: Príncipe Pío, tel. 91-547-0722).

▲**Royal Tapestry Factory (Real Fabrica de Tapices)**—Have a look at the traditional making of tapestries (250 ptas, Mon–Fri 9:00–12:30, closed Aug, cheap tours in Spanish only, Calle Fuenterrabia 2, Metro: Menendez Pelayo, take Gutenberg exit, tel. 91-551-3400).

▲▲**Retiro Park**—Siesta in this 350-acre green and breezy escape from the city. At midday on Saturday and Sunday the area around the lake becomes a street carnival, with jugglers, puppeteers, and lots of local color. These peaceful gardens offer great picnicking and

people watching. From the Retiro Metro stop, walk to the big lake (El Estanque), where you can rent a rowboat (450 ptas for 45 min). Past the lake, a grand boulevard of statues leads to the Prado. Charles III's Botanical Garden (Real Jardín Botánico) is a pleasant extension of Retiro Park (entry just opposite the Atocha end of the Prado). For 200 ptas you can escape all the commotion of Madrid and wander through a lush forest with trees from around the world (daily 10:00–19:00, Plaza de Murillo 2, Metro: Atocha or Retiro).
Parque de Atracciones—This colorful amusement park comes complete with Venetian canals, dancing, eating, games, free shows, and top-notch people watching (600 ptas admission, Super Napy all-inclusive ticket for rides-2,675 ptas, 1,500 ptas for kids, Jul–Aug daily 12:00–01:00, except Sat until 02:00, shorter hours off-season, Metro: Batan, tel. 91-463-2900 for exact times). This fair and Spain's best zoo (1,615 ptas entrance, daily 10:30–21:00, dolphin shows in good, new aquarium, tel. 91-512-3770) are in the vast Casa de Campo Park just west of the Royal Palace.

Shopping

Shoppers can focus on the colorful pedestrian area between Gran Vía and Puerta del Sol. The giant Spanish department store, El Corte Inglés, is a block off Puerta del Sol and a handy place to pick up just about anything you may need (Mon–Sat 10:00–21:30, closed Sun, free maps at info desk, supermarket in basement).
▲**El Rastro**—Europe's biggest flea market, held on Sundays and holidays, is a field day for shoppers, people watchers, and thieves (9:00–15:00, best before 12:00). Thousands of stalls titillate more than a million browsers with mostly new junk. If you brake for garage sales, you'll pull a U-turn for El Rastro. Start at the Plaza Mayor and head south or take the subway to Tirso de Molina. Hang on to your wallet. Munch on a *relleno* or *pepito* (meat-filled pastry). Europe's biggest stamp market thrives simultaneously on Plaza Mayor.

Nightlife

▲▲▲**Bullfight**—Madrid's Plaza de Toros hosts Spain's top bull-fights on most Sundays and holidays from Easter through October and nearly every day mid-May through early June. Top fights sell out in advance. Fights usually start punctually at 19:00. Tickets range from 500 to 10,000 ptas. There are no bad seats at Plaza de Toros; paying more gets you in the shade and/or closer to the gore (*filas* 8, 9, and 10 tend to be closest to the action). Booking offices add 20 percent and don't sell the cheap seats (Plaça del Carmen 1, tel. 91-531-2732). If you want to save money, buy your ticket at the bullring. Tickets go on sale the day of the fight at 10:00; 10 percent of the seats are kept available to be sold two hours before the fight

(Calle Alcala 237, Metro: Ventas, tel. 91-356-2200). The bullfighting museum (Museo Taurino) is next to the bullring (free, Sun and Tue–Fri 9:30–14:30, closed Sat and Mon, Calle Alcala 237, tel. 91-725-1857). See the Appendix for more on the "art" of bullfighting.

▲▲Zarzuela—For a delightful look at Spanish light opera that even English speakers can enjoy, try an evening of Zarzuela. Guitar-strumming Napoleons in red capes, buxom women with masks and fans, castanets and stomping feet, Spanish-speaking pharaohs, melodramatic spotlights, aficionados singing along from the cheap seats, where the acoustics are best—this is the people's opera. That's Zarzuela. Madrid's Theater Zarzuela is at Jovellanos 4 (Metro: Banco de Espana, tel. 91-524-5400). The TI's monthly guide has a special Zarzuela listing.

Flamenco—Save this for Sevilla if you can. In Madrid, Taberna Casa Patas is small, intimate, smoky, and powerful, with one drink included and no hassling after that (tickets around 3,000 ptas, shows at 22:00, Canizares 10, near Plaza Santa Ana, reservations tel. 91-369-0496). The Flamenco House is more touristy (Calle Torija 7, just off Plaza Mayor).

Sleeping in Madrid
(160 ptas = about $1)
Sleep Code: **S** = Single, **D** = Double/Twin, **T** = Triple, **Q** = Quad, **b** = bathroom, **t** = toilet only, **s** = shower only, **CC** = Credit Card (Visa, MasterCard, Amex), **SE** = Speaks English, **NSE** = No English. Breakfast is not included unless noted. In Madrid, the 7 percent IVA tax is generally, but not always, included in the price.

Madrid has plenty of centrally located budget hotels and *pensiónes*. You'll have no trouble finding a sleepable double for $30, a good double for $60, and a modern air-conditioned double with all the comforts for $100. Prices are the same throughout the year, and it's almost always easy to find a place. The accommodations I've listed are all within a few minutes' walk of Puerta del Sol. Competition is stiff. Those on a budget can bargain. Nighttime Madrid's economy is brisk. Even decent areas are littered with shady-looking people after dark. Just don't invite them in.

Sleeping in the Pedestrian Zone between Puerta del Sol and Gran Vía
(zip code: 28013)
Predictable and away from the seediness, these are good values for those wanting to spend a little more. Especially for these hotels, call first to see if the price is firm. Their formal prices may be inflated, and some offer weekend deals. Use Metro: Sol for these five hotels. See map on p. 53 for location.

Hotel Europa has red-carpet charm: a quiet courtyard, royal salon, plush halls with happy Muzak, polished wood floors, attentive staff, and 80 squeaky-clean rooms with balconies overlooking the pedestrian zone or an inner courtyard. All rooms have TVs (CNN) and big, modern bathrooms. Many rooms face an inner courtyard that amplifies voices and TV noise. Caution: Your words will travel. For a better night's sleep, feel free to remove their rubber-coated undersheets—then toss them into the hallway to make a statement (Sb-6,400 ptas, Db-8,500 ptas, Tb-12,000 ptas, Qb-14,000 ptas, breakfast-600 ptas, fine lounge on 2nd floor, elevator, fans in rooms, easy phone reservations with credit card, CC:VMA, Calle del Carmen 4, tel. 91-521-2900, fax 91-521-4696, e-mail: hoteleuropa @genio.infor.es, Sr. Garaban and his very helpful staff SE). The convenient Europa cafeteria/restaurant next door is a good value.

Hotel Regente is a big, traditional, and impersonal place with 145 plain but comfortable air-conditioned rooms and a great location (Sb-6,200 ptas, Db-9,500 ptas plus tax, CC:VMA, midway between Puerta del Sol and Plaza del Callao at Mesonero Romanos 9, tel. 91-521-2941, fax 91-532-3014).

Nearby, the **Hotel Cliper** is faded-elegant and bordering on rundown but has character and comfortable rooms on a fairly quiet street (Sb-5,800 ptas, Db-7,800 ptas, most rooms have air-con, elevator, CC:VMA, Chincilla 6, near Plaza Carmen, tel. 91-531-1700, fax 91-531-1707, SE).

The huge **Hotel Liabeny** feels classy and new, with 222 plush, spacious rooms and all the comforts. It's a business-class hotel that decided to lower its prices to get the tourist trade (Sb-11,900 ptas, Db-16,200 ptas, CC:VMA, air-con, if one room is smoky they can usually switch you to another, off Plaza Carmen at Salud 3, tel. 91-531-9000, fax 91-532-7421, www.apunte.es/liabeny, fax is better than Web access, SE).

Hotel Londres is a sad business-class hotel: dark, stark, and a little smoky and unfriendly (Db-10,100 ptas, renovated Db-11,700 ptas, ask for 15–20 percent off Jan–Mar and Jul–Aug, CC:VMA, elevator, air-con, don't trust their safes, Galdo 2, tel. 91-531-4105, fax 91-531-4101; e-mail: hotellondres@cempresarial.com).

Sleeping at Gran Vía #44
(zip code: 28013)
The pulse (and noise) of today's Madrid is best felt along the Gran Vía. This main drag in the heart of the city stays awake all night. Despite the dreary pile of prostitutes just a block north, there's a certain urban decency about it. My choices (all at Gran Vía #44) are across from Plaza del Callão, which is four colorful blocks (of pedestrian malls) from Puerta del Sol. Although many rooms are high above the traffic noise, cooler and quieter rooms are on the back side. The Café & Te next door provides a classy way to breakfast. The Callão Metro stop is at your doorstep, and the handy Gran Vía stop (direct to Atocha) is two blocks away.

Hostal Residencia Miami is clean and quiet, with lovely, well-lit rooms, padded doors, and plastic-flower decor throughout. It's like staying at your eccentric aunt's in Miami Beach. The bubbly landlady, Sra. Sanz, and her too-careful husband, who dresses up each day for work here, speak no English (S-2,500–3,000 ptas, D-3,500 ptas, Db-4,500 ptas; closed mid-July–August—if they take reservations then, they're booking you elsewhere; 8th floor, tel. 91-521-1464).

Across the hall, **Hostal Alibel**, like Miami with less sugar, rents seven big, airy, quiet rooms (D-4,000 ptas, Ds-4,500 ptas, Db-5,000 ptas, tel. 91-521-0051, grandmotherly Terese, NSE).

Hostal Residencia Valencia is run like a hotel with 32 big stark rooms. The friendly manager, Antonio Ramirez, speaks English (Sb-4,400 ptas, Ds-5,800 ptas, Db-6,200 ptas, Tb-8,200 ptas, Qb-9,200 ptas, CC:VMA, 5th floor, tel. 91-522-1115, fax 91-522-1113). Also a good value but a bit smoky and with less character is **Hostal Residencia Continental** (Sb-4,000 ptas, Db-5,200 ptas, CC:VMA, 3rd floor, tel. 91-521-4640, fax 91-521-4649, e-mail: continental@mundivia.es, SE).

Sleeping on or near Plaza Santa Ana
(zip code: 28012)

The Plaza Santa Ana area has plenty of small, cheap places. While well worn and noisy at night, it has a rough but charming ambience, with colorful bars and a central location (3 minutes from Puerta del Sol's "Tío Pepe" sign; walk down Calle San Jeronimo and turn right on Príncipe; Metro: Sol). At most of these hotels, fluent Spanish is spoken, bathrooms are usually down the hall, and there's no heat during winter. To locate hotels, see map on page 66.

Hopeless romantics might enjoy playing corkscrew around the rickety cut-glass elevator to the very simple yet homey **Pensión La Valenciana**'s old and funky rooms with springy beds. All rooms have balconies; three of them overlook the square (S-1,600 ptas, D-3,500 ptas, Príncipe 27, 4th floor, right on Plaza Santa Ana next to the theater with flags, tel. 91-429-6317, Esperanza NSE).

In the beautifully tiled building at **Plaza Santa Ana 15**, up a dark wooden staircase, are two good places. Unfortunately, a disco thumps Thursday through Saturday nights. **Hostal Filo** is squeaky clean and has a nervous but helpful management and 20 rooms hiding in a confusing floor plan (S-2,100 ptas, D-3,600 ptas, Ds-4,600 ptas, T-5,400 ptas, Ts-5,400 ptas, closed Aug, 2nd floor, tel. 91-522-4056). **Hostal Delvi** is simple, clean, and homey (S-1,800–2,000 ptas, D-3,200 ptas, Ds-3,700 ptas, Ts-4,700 ptas, 3rd floor, tel. 91-522-5998, Maria NSE). Maria offers these already-discounted prices to readers with this book.

The cheapest beds are across the street at **Hostal Lucense** (S-1,500 ptas, D-2,300 ptas, Ds-3,000 ptas, T-3,500 ptas, 200 ptas per shower, cheaper for 2 nights, Nuñez de Arce 15, tel. 91-522-4888, run by Sr. and Sra. Muñoz, both interesting characters, Sr. SE) and **Casa Huéspedes Poza** (same prices and owners, Nuñez de Arce 9, tel. 91-522-4871). Because of these two places, I list no Madrid youth hostels.

Hostal R. Veracruz II, between Plaza Santa Ana and Puerta del Sol, rents decent, quiet rooms (Sb-3,700 ptas, Db-5,200 ptas, Tb-6,900 ptas, CC:VM, elevator, air-con, Victoria 1, 3rd floor, 28012 Madrid, tel. 91-522-7635, fax 91-522-6749, NSE).

Splurges: To be on the same square and spend in a day what others spend in a week, luxuriate in **Hotel Reina Victoria** (Sb-21,000 ptas, Db-26,250 ptas, prices generally discounted to Db-18,000 in Jul–Aug, when this becomes a fine value, ask about "corporate rates," CC:VMA, Plaza Santa Ana 14, tel. 91-531-4500, fax 91-522-0307, SE). For a royal, air-conditioned breather and some cheap entertainment, spit out your gum, step into its lobby, grab a sofa, and watch the bellboys push the beggars back out of the revolving doors.

Suite Prado, two blocks toward the Prado from Plaza Santa Ana, is a better value, offering 18 sprawling, air-conditioned suites with a homier feel (Db suite-20,400 ptas, suites are modern and comfortable with fridges and sitting rooms, 2 extra kids sleep for free or 1 extra adult for 3,000 ptas, elevator, CC:VMA, Manuel Fernandez y Gonzalez 10, at the intersection with Venture de la Vega, 28014 Madrid, tel. 91-420-2318, fax 91-420-0559, Sylvia SE).

Sleeping Elsewhere in Central Madrid

Halfway between the Prado Museum and Plaza Santa Ana are two good places in the same building. At #34 Cervantes (28014 Madrid, Metro: Anton Martin) you'll find the spotless, friendly, and comfortable **Hotel Cervantes** (Sb-5,000 ptas, Db-6,000 ptas, CC:VMA, 2nd floor, tel. & fax 91-429-2745, NSE); and the equally polished and friendly **Hotel Gonzalo** (Sb-4,500 ptas, Db-5,700 ptas, CC:VMA, 3rd floor, tel. 91-429-2714, fax 91-420-2007, NSE).

Just off Plaza Mayor, **Hostal Montalvo** is sprawling; run by the Caraballo family; comfortable, with tons of extras; and just half a block east of the elegant Plaza Mayor on a quiet, traffic-free street (S-3,340 ptas, Sb-4,490 ptas, D-5,080 ptas, Db-5,750 ptas, Tb-8,490 ptas, elevator, CC:VM, Zaragoza 6, 28012 Madrid, 3rd floor, Metro: Sol, tel. 91-365-5910, fax 91-364-5260, SE).

Eating in Madrid

In Spain only Barcelona rivals Madrid for taste-bud thrills. You have three dining choices: an atmospheric sit-down meal in a well-chosen restaurant, an unmemorable basic sit-down meal, or a stand-up meal of tapas in a bar or (more likely) in several bars. Many restaurants are closed in August.

Eating near Puerta del Sol

Restaurante Puerto Rico has fine food, great prices, and few tourists (Mon–Sat 13:00–16:30, 20:30–24:00, closed Sun, Chinchilla 2, off Gran Vía, on same street as Hotel Cliper, tel. 91-532-2040).

Artemisia II is a hit with vegetarians who like good, healthy food in a smoke-free room (closed Aug, CC:VMA, Tres Cruces 4, just off Plaza Carmen, tel. 91-521-8721). **Artemisia I** is its sister (daily 13:30–16:00, 21:00–24:00, nonveggie options available, CC:VMA, Ventura de la Vega 4 off San Jeronimo, tel. 91-429-5092).

Eating near Plaza Mayor

At **Restaurante Rodriguez,** the food's not fancy but is hearty (closed July, San Cristobal 15, 1 block toward Puerta del Sol from Plaza Mayor, tel. 91-231-1136). Many Americans are drawn to Hemingway's favorite, **Sobrino del Botín** (daily 13:00–16:00, 20:00–24:00, Cuchilleros 17, a block downhill from Plaza Mayor, tel. 91-366-4217). It's touristy, pricey, and the last place he'd go now, but still, people love it, and the food is excellent. If phoning to make a reservation, ask for downstairs (for dark, medieval-cellar ambience) or upstairs (for a still-traditional but airier and lighter elegance). Those in need of a dirt-cheap but tasty *bocadillo* (sandwich) or *calamares* (squid) line up at the **Casa Rua** on Plaza Mayor's southwest corner (behind and to the right of the horse statue). Picnic shoppers forage at the **San Miguel market** (see "Picnics," below). For a great scene and reasonable prices, consider eating right on the Plaza Mayor.

For a fine meal with no tourists and locals who appreciate good local-style cooking, try **Casa Ciriaco** (2,000-ptas meals, Thu–Tue 13:30–16:00, 20:30–24:00, closed Wed, halfway between Puerta del Sol and the Royal Palace at Calle Mayor 84, tel. 91-548-0620). It was from this building in 1906 that an anarchist threw a bomb at the royal couple on their wedding day. Photos of the carnage are on the wall in the dining room.

Eating near the Prado

Each of the big three art museums has a decent cafeteria. After a long visit to the Prado, consider a meal on the tiny Plaza de Platarias de Matinez (directly across the busy highway from the Atocha end of the Prado), where two little eateries share the square and shade. **La Plateria** is a hardworking little café/wine bar with a good menu for light meals or a hearty salad. The chalkboard shows a list of items in three different sizes (daily 13:00–15:00, 17:00–24:00). The **Bar Museu**, a simpler place, serves tapas and sandwiches.

Tapas: The Madrid Pub Crawl Dinner

For maximum fun, people, and atmosphere, go mobile and do the "tapa tango," a local tradition of going from one bar to the next, munching, drinking, and socializing. Tapas are the toothpick appetizers, salads, and deep-fried foods served in most bars. Madrid is Spain's tapa capital—tapas just don't get any better. Grab a toothpick and stab something strange—but establish the prices first. Some items are very pricey, and most bars offer larger *raciónes* rather than smaller tapas. *Un pincho* is a bite-sized serving (not always available), *una tapa* is a snack, and *una ración* is half a meal. Say "*un bocadillo*," and it comes on bread as a sandwich. A *caña* is a small glass of draft beer.

Prowl the area between Puerta del Sol and Plaza Santa Ana. There's no ideal route, but the little streets (in this book's map) between Puerta del Sol, San Jeronimo, and Plaza Santa Ana hold tasty surprises. Below is an eight-stop tapa crawl. These places are good, but don't be blind to making discoveries on your own.

1. From Puerta del Sol, head east down Carrera de San Jeronimo to the corner of Victoria Street. Across from Museo del Jamón you'll find **La Tourina Cervecería**, a bullfighters' Planet Hollywood. Wander among trophies and historic photographs. Each stuffed bull's head is named, along with its farm, awards, and who killed him. Among the photos you can see Che Guevara, Orson Welles, and Salvador Dalí all enjoying a good fight. Find the Babe Ruth of bullfighters, El Cordobes, wounded in bed. The photo below shows him in action. Kick off your pub crawl with *rabo del toro* (bull-tail stew, 1,100 ptas) and a glass of red wine. Across the street at San Jeronimo 5 is...

2. Museo del Jamón (Museum of Ham), which is tastefully decorated, unless you're a pig. This frenetic, cheap, stand-up bar is an assembly-line of fast and deliciously simple *bocadillos* and *raciónes*. Options are shown in photographs with prices. For a small sandwich, ask for a *chiquito* (95 ptas). Just point and eat (daily 9:00–24:00, sit-down restaurant upstairs). Next, head halfway up Calle Victoria to the tiny...

3. La Casa del Abuelo, for shrimp lovers who savor sizzling plates of tasty little *gambas*. Try *gambas a la plancha* (grilled shrimp, 560 ptas) and *gambas al ajillo* (shrimp version of escargot, cooked in oil and garlic and ideal for bread dipping—700 ptas) and a 150-ptas glass of red wine (daily 11:30–15:30, 18:30–23:30, Calle Victoria 12). Continue uphill and around the corner to...

4. Casa Toni for refreshing bowls of gazpacho (200 ptas, closed mid-June–mid-July, Calle Cruz 14). This cold tomato-and-garlic soup is slurped by locals throughout the summer. Backtrack halfway down Calle Victoria and turn left, walking through an alley littered with dining tables to...

5. La Ria, a tapas bar that sells plates of 10 mussels—toss the shells on the floor as you smack your lips (19:00–23:00, Pasaje Matheu 5). *Mejillones picantes* is spicy (460 ptas). Wash each down with the crude, dry, white Ribeiro wine from Galicia. It's served in a ceramic

Plaza Santa Ana Area

1. Tourina Cerveceria
2. Museo del Jamon
3. Casa del Abuelo
4. Casa Toni
5. La Ria
6. Casa Alberto
7. Torre del Oro Bar
8. Chocolateria San Gines
9. Bar Vallidolid
10. Artemesia I
11. Pension Valenciana
12. Hostal Filo & Delvi
13. Hostal Lucense & Poza
14. Hostal R. Veracruz II
15. Hotel Reina Victoria
16. Suite Prado

bowl to disguise its lack of clarity. The place is draped in mussels. Notice the photo showing the floor filled with litter—a reminder that mussel bars have seen better days. In the 1970s they sold 14 tons a month. Now—with other, more trendy evening activities entertaining the cruising youth—it takes a year to sell 14 tons.

6. Jump to stop #7 or, for a classy side trip, follow Nuñez de Arce up to Plaza Santa Ana. Cross the square (past lots of trendy pubs) and continue one block down Calle Príncipe to the venerable **Casa Alberto**. It's been serving tasty tapas since 1827 (11:00–01:00, closed Sun evening, all day Mon, and most of Aug, Huertas 18, tel. 91-429-9356). It's hard to stop at just one *canape de salmon ahumado* (smoked salmon appetizer, 275 ptas). The popular dining room in the back has a different, pricier menu.

7. Head to Plaza Mayor for **La Torre del Oro Bar Andalu** (26 Plaza Mayor, tel. 91-366-5016). Bullfight aficionados hate the gimmicky Bull Bar across from Museo del Jamón (stop #1). This one has more soul. The walls are lined with grisly bullfight photos from annual photo competitions. Read the complete description above in the Plaza Mayor section. Be careful not to let the aggressive staff bully you into food you don't want.

8. The classy **Chocolatería San Ginés** is much loved locally for its *churros* (greasy cigar-shaped fritters) and chocolate. Open nightly from 22:00 to 7:00, it caters to the late-night crowd (mostly disco—the popular Joy disco is next door). Finish off your crawl with this sweet treat, dunking your *churros* into the pudding-like hot chocolate, as locals have done here for over 100 years (from Plaza Mayor, cross Calle Mayor and go down Calle P. de San Ginés to #5, off Calle Arenal, tel. 93-365-6546).

Fast Food, Picnics, and Breakfast

Fast Food: For an easy, light, cheap meal, try **Rodilla**—a popular sandwich bar on the northeast corner of Puerta del Sol at #13 (daily 8:30–20:30). **Pans & Company**, with shops throughout Spain, offers healthy, tasty sandwiches and great chef's salads (daily 9:00–24:00, on Puerta del Sol, Plaza Callão, Gran Vía 30, and many more).

Picnics: The department store **El Corte Inglés** has a well-stocked **deli**, but its produce is sold only in large quantities (Mon–Sat 10:00–21:00, closed Sun). A perfect place to assemble a cheap picnic is downtown Madrid's neighborhood market, **Mercado de San Miguel**. How about breakfast surrounded by early morning shoppers in the market's café? (Mon–Fri 9:00–14:00, 16:00–19:00, Sat 9:00–14:00, closed Sun; from Plaza Mayor, face the colorful building and exit from the upper left-hand corner.)

Churros con chocolate **for breakfast:** If you like hash browns and eggs in American greasy-spoon joints, you must try the Spanish equivalent: greasy *churros* dipped in thick, hot chocolate at **Bar Valladolid** (open from 7:00, closed Sun, 2 blocks off the Tío Pepe end of Puerta del Sol, south on Espoz y Mina, turn right on Calle de Cadiz). If you arrive early, it's *churros* and hookers. You'll see the changing of the guard, as workers of the night finish their day by downing a cognac and workers of the day start theirs by dipping *churros* or *porras* (simply fatter *churros*) into chocolate. (One serving is often plenty for two.) With luck, the *churros* machine in the back will be cooking. Throw your napkin on the floor like you own the place.

For something with less grease and more substance, ask for a *tortilla española* (potato omelet), *zumo de naranja* (orange juice), and *café con leche* (coffe with milk). Notice the expressive WC signs.

Transportation Connections—Madrid

By train to: **Toledo** (6/day, 1 hr, from Madrid's Atocha station), **Segovia** (8/day, 2 hrs, both Chamartin and Atocha stations), **Ávila** (6/day, 90 min, from Chamartin and Atocha), **Salamanca** (3/day, 2.5 hrs, from Chamartin), **Barcelona** (7/day, 8 hrs, mostly from Chamartin), **Granada** (6–9 hrs, a daily day train from Chamartin and a nightly train from Atocha), **Sevilla** (15/day, 2.5 hrs by AVE, 3.5 hrs by Talgo, from Atocha), **Córdoba** (16 AVE trains/day, 2 hrs, from Chamartin and Atocha), **Lisbon** (1/day, 10 hrs, overnight from Chamartin), **Paris** (4/day, 12–16 hrs, 1 direct overnight, from Chamartin). Train information: tel. 91-328-9020.

Spain's new AVE bullet train opens up some good itinerary options. Pick up the brochure at the station. Prices vary with times and class. The basic Madrid–Sevilla fare is 8,100 ptas (1,100 ptas less on the almost-as-fast Talgo). AVE is 85 percent covered by Eurail (so the Madrid–Sevilla–Madrid round-trip costs Eurailers about 2,400 ptas). So far AVE only covers Madrid–Córdoba–Sevilla. Consider this exciting day trip from Madrid: 7:00 depart, 8:45–12:40 in Córdoba, 13:30–21:00 in Sevilla, 23:30 back in Madrid. Reserve each AVE segment (tel. 91-328-9020).

By bus to: **Segovia** (2/hrly, 1.75 hrs, Larrea Lines, Paseo de la Florida 11, just past Hotel Florida Norte, Metro: Príncipe Pío); for **Ávila** (7/day, 2 hrs) and **Toledo** (2/hrly, 60 min), buses depart from Estación sur Autobuses (Metro: Méndez Alvaro, tel. 91-468-4200).

By bus, train, and car to El Escorial: Buses leave from the basement of Madrid's Metro stop Moncloa and drop you in the El Escorial center (4/hrly, 45 min, Autocares Herranz, tel. 91-890-4100). One bus a day (except for Mon) is designed to let travelers do the Valley of the Fallen as a side trip from El Escorial; the bus leaves El Escorial at 15:15 (15-min trip) and leaves Valley of the Fallen at 17:30. Trains run to El Escorial but let you off a 20-minute walk (or a shuttle-bus ride, 2/hrly) from the monastery and city center. By car, visiting El Escorial and Valley of the Fallen on the way to Segovia is easy (except on Mon, when both sights are closed).

Drivers' note: Avoid driving in Madrid. Rent your car when you leave. It's cheapest to make car-rental arrangements before you leave home. In Madrid try Europcar (San Leonardo 8, Chamartin station, tel. 91-323-1721, airport tel. 91-393-7235), Hertz (Gran Vía 88, tel. 91-542-5803, Chamartin station tel. 91-733-0400, airport tel. 91-393-7228), or Avis (Gran Vía 60, tel. 91-548-4205, airport tel. 91-393-7222). Ask about free delivery to your hotel. At the airport, most rental cars are returned at Terminal 1.

NORTHWEST OF MADRID:
EL ESCORIAL, VALLEY OF THE FALLEN, SEGOVIA, SALAMANCA

Before slipping out of Madrid by train, consider several fine side trips northwest of Spain's capital city.

Spain has a lavish, brutal, and complicated history. An hour from Madrid, tour the imposing and fascinating palace of Monasterio de San Lorenzo de El Escorial, headquarters of the Spanish Inquisition. Nearby, at the awesome Valley of the Fallen, pay tribute to the countless victims of Spain's bloody civil war.

Segovia, with its remarkable Roman aqueduct and romantic castle, is also an easy side trip from Madrid. Farther out, you can walk the perfectly preserved medieval walls of Ávila. And at Salamanca, enjoy Spain's best town square, caffeinated with a frisky college-town ambience.

Planning Your Time

See El Escorial and the Valley of the Fallen together in less than a day (but not Mon, when sights are closed). By car, do them en route to Segovia; by bus, make it a day trip from Madrid.

Segovia is worth a half-day of sightseeing and is a joy at night. Ávila, while not without charm, merits only a quick stop to marvel at its medieval walls, if you're driving in the neighborhood.

Salamanca, with its art, university, and Spain's greatest Plaza Mayor, is worth a day and a night but is stuck out in the boonies. On a three-week Barcelona–Lisbon "open-jaws" itinerary, I'd hook south from Madrid and skip Salamanca. If you're doing a circular trip, Salamanca is a natural stop halfway between Portugal and Madrid.

In total, these sights are worth a maximum of three days if you're in Iberia for less than a month. If you're in Spain for just a week, I'd still squeeze in a look at El Escorial and the Valley of the Fallen.

Sights near Madrid

EL ESCORIAL

The Monasterio de San Lorenzo de El Escorial is a symbol of power rather than elegance. This 16th-century palace, 30 miles northwest of Madrid, gives us a better feel for the Counter-Reformation and the Inquisition than any other building. Built at a time when Catholic Spain felt threatened by Protestant "heretics," its construction dominated the Spanish economy for 20 years (1563–1584). Because of this bully in the national budget, Spain has almost nothing else to show from this most powerful period of her history.

The giant, gloomy building looks more like a prison than a palace (gray-black stone, 200 yards long, 150 yards wide, over 100 miles of passages, 2,600 windows, 1,200 doors, 1,600 overwhelmed tourists). Four hundred years ago, the enigmatic, introverted, and extremely Catholic King Philip II ruled his bulky empire and directed the Inquisition from here. To 16th-century followers of Luther, this place epitomized the evil of Catholicism. Today it's a time capsule of Spain's "Golden Age," packed with history, art, and Inquisition ghosts.

The Monasterio looks confusing at first, but you simply follow the arrows and signs in one continuous walk-through. Guides in each room can answer basic questions. The entrance (off Grimaldi, a minute's walk from TI) is the best place to start. This is the general order you'll follow (though some rooms are sure to be closed for renovation). The small **Museo de Arquitectura** has easy-to-appreciate models of the palace and the machinery used to construct it. The **Museo de Pintura**, packed with big paintings in small rooms, features works by Titian, Veronese, Rubens, Bosch, van Dyck, and van der Weyden. The **king's apartments** are notable for their austerity, with a bed that's barely queen-size. The king made sure his quarters came with a view... of the church's high altar. Stairs take you down into the **Panteón Real**, the gilded resting place of 26 kings and queens, four centuries' worth of Spanish monarchy. The lazy Susan–like **Panteón de los Infantes** holds the remains of various royal children and relatives. Paintings by Ribera, El Greco, Titian, and Velázquez elegantly decorate the *salas capitulares* (chapter rooms). The **cloister** (which may be partially closed) glows with bright, newly restored paintings by Tibaldi.

Follow the signs to the **church**. The altar is spectacular when illuminated (put 100 ptas in the small box near the church entrance, just before the gated doors), but the highlight is Cellini's marble sculpture *The Crucifixion* (to the left as you enter).

Last comes the *biblioteca*, or the library (have your ticket handy). Savor this room. The ceiling is a burst of color, and the meshed bookcases feature illustrated books. At the far end of the room, the elaborate model of the solar system looks like a giant gyroscope, revolving unmistakably around the earth. Notice the misshapen North America.

Admission to the palace is 850 ptas (Tue–Sun 10:00–19:00, enter before ticket office closes at 16:00, closed Mon; Oct–Mar closes at 18:00; tel. 91-890-5904). A tour is included if you pay 950 ptas for admission, but the tour (available 10:00–18:00) is limited to the apartments and mausoleum only, and English tours occur only if there is an English-speaking guide available and in the mood. You'll find scanty but sufficient captions in English within the palace. For more information, skip the tour and get the *Visitor's Guide: Monastery of San Lorenzo El Real de El Escorial* (900 ptas, available at any of several shops in the palace). It follows the general route you'll take and is better than the cheaper but overly comprehensive book-length *Official Guide* (600 ptas).

If you arrive by bus at the town of San Lorenzo de El Escorial, walk from the bus station to the TI (by heading down Juan de Toledo, angling to the right across the plaza onto Avenida Juan de Borbón de Battenberg). The TI (Mon–Thu 11:00–18:00, Fri–Sun 10:00–19:00, tel. 91-890-5313) is on the corner of Grimaldi in front of the entrance of the Monasterio.

Up the hill from the TI on Grimaldi are two pleasant,

stair-stepped plazas (Jacinto Benavente and San Lorenzo), dotted with trees and cafés. Nearby is the pedestrian-friendly Calle Juan de Leyra.

The town is worth a browse. To shop for a picnic, stop by the Mercado Publico on Calle del Rey 9, a four-minute walk from the palace (Mon–Fri 9:00–14:00, 17:00–20:00, Sat 10:00–14:00, closed Sun). For a change from Spanish fare, consider pizza at Tavolata Reale (near Monasterio entrance, tel. 91-809-4591) or Restaurante China Hong Kong (Calle San Anton 6, tel. 91-896-1894).

Transportation Connections—El Escorial

From Madrid: Buses leave from the basement level of Madrid's Metro stop Moncloa and drop you in the town center of San Lorenzo de El Escorial, near the Monasterio (4/hrly, 45 min, Autocares Herranz, tel. 91-890-4100).

The **train** is less convenient. Although trains leave twice hourly from Madrid's Atocha station, you're dropped a 20-minute walk (or shuttle-bus ride, 2/hrly) from San Lorenzo de El Escorial town center and Monasterio.

Consider combining a day trip to El Escorial and the Valley of the Fallen. The bus company Autocares Herranz offers one round-trip bus connection every afternoon (except Mon, when sights are closed) from El Escorial to the Valley of the Fallen (see below).

VALLEY OF THE FALLEN (EL VALLE DE LOS CAÍDOS)

Eight kilometers from El Escorial, high in the Guadarrama Mountains, a 150-yard-tall granite cross marks an immense and powerful underground monument to the victims of Spain's 20th-century nightmare—its civil war (1936–1939).

The stairs that lead to the imposing monument are grouped in sets of 10s, meant to symbolize the Ten Commandments (including "Thou shalt not kill"—hmm). The emotional pièta draped over the entrance was sculpted by Juan de Avalos, the same artist who created the dramatic figures of the four evangelists at the base of the cross.

A solemn silence and a stony chill fill the "basilica"—larger (860 feet long) than St. Peter's—as Spaniards pass under the huge, forbidding angels of fascism to visit the grave of General Franco. The term *basilica* normally designates a church built over the remains of a saint, not a fascist dictator. Franco's prisoners, the enemies of the right, dug this memorial out of solid rock.

The sides of the monument are lined with 16th-century Brussels tapestries of the Apocalypse and side chapels containing alabaster copies of Spain's most famous statues of the Virgin Mary.

Interred behind the high altar and side chapels are the remains of the approximately 50,000 people, both Republicanos and Franco's Nacionalistas, who lost their lives in the war. Regrettably the urns are not visible, so it is Franco who takes center stage. His grave, strewn with flowers, lies behind the high altar. In front of the altar is the grave of José Antonio, the founder of Spanish fascism. Between these fascists' graves is the statue of a crucified Christ. The seeping stones seem to weep.

On your way out, stare into the eyes of those angels with swords and two right wings and think about all the "heroes" who keep dying "for God and country," at the request of the latter (650 ptas, Tue–Sun 9:30–19:00, closed Mon).

The expansive view from the monument's terrace includes the peaceful, forested valley and sometimes snow-streaked mountains. A funicular climbs to the base of the cross and a better view (350 ptas round-trip, 10:30–19:00, tel. 91-890-5611). Near the parking lot (and bus stop) are a small snack bar and picnic tables.

Without a car, the easiest way to get to the Valley of the Fallen is from El Escorial by an Autocares Herranz bus (1/daily except Mon, 15 min, leaves El Escorial at 15:15, leaves the Valley of the Fallen at 17:30, 970-pta round-trip includes admission to the site). Buy your ticket in El Escorial at the bar on Calle del Rey, just around the corner from the bus stop (the bus driver will point the way).

SEGOVIA

Fifty miles from Madrid, this town of 55,000 boasts a great Roman aqueduct, a cathedral, and a castle. Segovia is a medieval "ship" ready for your inspection. Start at the stern—the aqueduct—and stroll up Calle de Cervantes to the prickly Gothic masts of the cathedral. Explore the tangle of narrow streets around Plaza Mayor and then descend to the Alcázar at the bow.

Orientation

Tourist Information: The two TIs are helpful. One is on Plaza del Azoguejo, under the aqueduct (daily 10:00–20:00, tel. 92-146-2914); the other at Plaza Mayor 10 (daily 10:00–14:00, 17:00–20:00, tel. 92-146-0334). Both have shorter hours off-season.

Arrival in Segovia: The train station is a 30-minute walk from the center. Take a city bus from the station to get to Calle de Colón near Plaza Mayor (2/hrly, 100 ptas, leaving from the same side of the street as the station—confirm by asking, "*¿Para Plaza Mayor?*"). Taxis are a reasonable option (600 ptas). If you arrive by bus, it's a 15-minute walk to the center (turn left out of the bus station and continue straight across the roundabout onto Calle Ladrera). Day-trippers can store luggage at the train station but not at the bus station. Drivers can park their cars overnight for free in the park facing the Alcázar (gate closes at about 19:00).

Helpful Hints: The Telefónica phone office has handy

metered phone booths (Mon–Sat 10:00–14:00, 17:00–21:30, closed
Sun, accepts credit cards for charges over 500 ptas, on Plaza de los
Huertos). If you buy handicrafts such as tablecloths from street
vendors, make sure the item you're buying is the one you actually
get; some unscrupulous vendors substitute inferior goods at the
last minute. Internet cafés are plentiful but inconveniently located
in the new town; ask at the TI for the latest and closest.

Sights—Segovia

▲**Roman Aqueduct**—Built by the Romans, who ruled Spain for
more than 500 years, this 2,000-year-old *acueducto Romano* is 2,500
feet long and 100 feet high, has 118 arches, was made without any
mortar, and still works. It's considered Segovia's backup plumbing.
From underneath the aqueduct, climb the steps off Plaza Azoguejo
for an overhead view.

▲**Cathedral**—Segovia's cathedral was Spain's last major Gothic
building. Embellished to the hilt with pinnacles and flying buttresses, the exterior is a great example of the final overripe stage
of Gothic, called "Flamboyant." The dark, spacious, and elegantly
simple interior provides a delightful contrast. In the chapel to
the immediate left of the entry, notice the the dramatic gilded "Car-
roza de la Custadia." (If it's not here, look in the cathedral museum.)
The Holy Communion is placed in the top of this templelike cart
and paraded through town each year during the Corpus Christi
festival. The *Tree of Life*, by Ignacio Ries, is also worth finding (in
the rear left as you face the front). It shows hedonistic mortals dancing atop the tree of life. Look closely to see a skeletal Grim Reaper
preparing to receive them into hell and Jesus ringing a bell implor-
ing them to wake up before it's too late. The cathedral is free—just
walk by the ticket counter unless you want to see the small but interesting museum and cloister (museum admission 300 ptas, tour of
church and museum included—ask if an English-speaking guide is
available, daily 9:00–19:00, off-season 9:30–18:00).

▲**Alcázar**—This Disneyesque rebuild, an exaggeration of an old
castle that burned down here in 1862, is fun to explore and worthwhile for the view of Segovia. While it's said that Isabel first met
Ferdinand here and that Columbus came here to get his fantasy
financed, the tower is of little importance historically. Only a
portion of the keep, which you'll pass through as you enter, is
from the original castle (400 ptas, daily 10:00–19:00, off-season
until 18:00, get the 25-pta English brochure).

Strolling—Roman and Romanesque Segovia was made for roamin'.
Rub shoulders with Segovian yuppies parading up and down Calle
Juan Bravo. For subtler charm, wander the back streets, away from
the trinket shops and ladies selling lace. Segovia has a wealth of
12th- and 13th-century Romanesque churches (usually open during
Mass, often around 8:00 and 19:30, ask at TI). Look Catholic and

Segovia

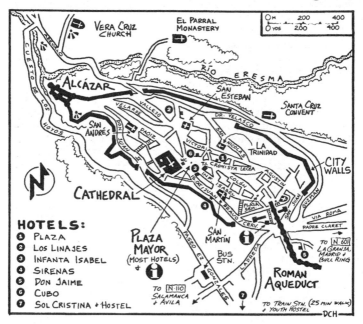

drop in. The San Justo church has well-preserved 13th-century frescoes (free, daily 10:45–13:45, 15:00–19:30, off-season until 18:00; near base of aqueduct, a couple of blocks from Plaza Azoguejo, in the newer side of town). The caretaker, Rafael, might invite you to climb the bell tower for "the best view of Segovia."

▲**Vera Cruz Church**—This 12-sided 13th-century Romanesque church was built by the Knights Templar and used to house a piece of the "true cross" (200 ptas, Tue–Sun 10:30–13:30, 15:30–19:00, closed Mon, off-season until 18:00, closed Nov, outside of town beyond the castle, a 20-minute walk from main square). There's a postcard view of the city from here, and more views follow as you continue around Segovia on the small road below the castle labeled *ruta turistica panoramica*.

▲**La Granja Palace**—This "Little Versailles," 10 kilometers south of Segovia, is much smaller and happier than El Escorial. The palace and gardens were built by the homesick French King Philip V, grandson of Louis XIV. It's a must for tapestry lovers. Fountain displays send local crowds into a frenzy at 17:30 on most summer Wednesdays, Saturdays, Sundays, and holidays; July 25th and August 25th have the best shows of the year (confirm schedule at

Segovia TI). Entry to the palace includes a required 45-minute
guided tour, usually in Spanish (650 ptas, Tue–Sun 10:00–18:00,
closed Mon; off-season Tue–Sat 10:00–13:30, 15:00–17:00, Sun
10:00–14:00; tel. 92-147-0019). Eight buses a day make the 30-
minute trip from Segovia.

Sleeping in Segovia
(160 ptas = about $1, zip code 40001)
Sleep Code: **S** = Single, **D** = Double/Twin, **T** = Triple, **Q** = Quad,
b = bathroom, **t** = toilet only, **s** = shower only, **CC** = Credit Card
(Visa, MasterCard, Amex), **SE** = Speaks English, **NSE** = No English.

The best places are on or near the central Plaza Mayor. This
is where the city action is: the cheapest and best bars, most touristic and *típico* eateries, and the tourist office. Segovia is crowded on
weekends and in July and August, so arrive early or call ahead.
The 7 percent IVA tax and breakfast are rarely included.

Hostal Plaza is just off Plaza Mayor toward the aqueduct.
You'll find *serioso* management and long, snaky corridors, but the
rooms are clean and cozy (S-3,100 ptas, 1 Sb-5,000 ptas, D-4,500
ptas, Db-5,800 ptas, Tb-7,830 ptas, CC:VM, Cronista Lecea 11,
tel. 92-146-0303, fax 92-146-0305, SE).

Hotel Los Linajes is ultra-classy, with rusticity mixed into its
newly poured concrete. This poor-man's parador is a few blocks
beyond the Plaza Mayor, with commanding views and modern,
air-conditioned niceties (Sb-8,750 ptas, Db-12,500–16,000 ptas,
depending on room size, Tb-14,500 ptas, cheaper off-season, break-
fast-900 ptas, parking-1,000 ptas, CC:VMA, air-con, elevator, Dr.
Velasco 9, tel. 92-146-0475, fax 92-146-0479). From Plaza Mayor,
take Escuderos downhill; at the five-way intersection, angle right
on Dr. Velasco. Drivers, follow brown signs from aqueduct.

Hotel Infanta Isabel, right on Plaza Mayor, is the ritziest hotel
in the old town. It's friendly, elegant, and pricey, but 20 percent
cheaper off-season (Sb-8,000 ptas, Db-12,000–14,000 ptas depending on room size, some rooms with plaza views, CC:VMA, elevator,
tel. 92-146-1300, fax 92-146-2217, SE).

A place I don't like that fills a void in Segovia is the big,
stuffy, hotelesque **Hotel Sirenas** (Sb-6,000 ptas, Db-8,500 ptas,
cheaper off-season, air-con, elevator, CC:VMA, 3 blocks down
from the Plaza Mayor at Calle Juan Bravo 30, tel. 92-146-2663
fax 92-146-2657, NSE).

Hostal Don Jaime, near the base of the aqueduct, is shiny-
new, well maintained, and friendly (S-3,000 ptas, Db-5,500 ptas,
Tb-6,800 ptas, Qb-7,000 ptas, CC:VM, Ochoa Ondategui 8; from
TI at aqueduct, cross under the aqueduct, go right, angle left, then
snake uphill for two blocks; tel. 92-144-4787, SE).

Right on Plaza Mayor at #4 is a tiny and dark but clean-
enough place (look hard for the "Hospedaje Habitaciones" sign).

The **Hospedaje Cubo** has five simple, sinkless but tidy rooms; ask for a room *con ventana* to avoid the windowless room (S-1,500 ptas, D-3,000 ptas, T-4,500 ptas, ask at the ground-level La Oja Blanca Bar if rooms are available before climbing up, Plaza Mayor 4, tel. 92-146-0318, Maria Jesus Cubo NSE). **Pensión Ferri,** around the corner, is a last resort (S-1,500 ptas, D-2,500 ptas, shower-350 ptas, Escuderos 10, half block off Plaza Mayor, tel. 92-146-0957, NSE).

Across from the train station is **Hostal Sol Cristina** (S-2,500 ptas, D-4,200 ptas, Db-5,500 ptas, T-5,600 ptas, Tb-6,800 ptas, Calle Obispo Quesada 40, tel. 92-142-7513, NSE) and its nearby twin, **Hostal Residencia Sol Cristina-Dos** (same prices, same phone number).

The **Segovia Youth Hostel** is a great hostel—easygoing, comfortable, clean, friendly, and very cheap (1,000-ptas beds, open Jul–Aug only, Paseo Conde de Sepulveda 4, between the train and bus stations, tel. 92-144-1111).

Eating in Segovia

Look for Segovia's culinary claim to fame, roast suckling pig (*cochinillo asado*: 21 days of mother's milk, into the oven, and onto your plate—oh, Babe). It's worth a splurge here or in Toledo or Salamanca. While you're at it, try *sopa Castellana*, soup mixed with eggs, ham, and garlic bread.

Mesón de Candido, one of the top restaurants in Castile, is the place to spend 4,000 ptas on a memorable dinner (daily 12:30–16:30, 20:00–23:00, Plaza Azoguejo 5, under the aqueduct, tel. 92-142-8103 for reservations, the gracious Don Alberto SE).

Narizotas, a more modern place, attracts locals and tourists with 2,000-pta *platos combinados* (daily 12:30–16:00, 20:00–24:00, CC:VM, Plaza de Medina del Campo 1, tel. 92-146-2679).

The cheapest bars and eateries line Calle de Infanta Isabel, just off Plaza Mayor. For nightlife, the bars on Plaza Mayor, Calle de Infanta Isabel, and Calle Isabel la Católica are packed. And there are a number of discos along the aqueduct.

Have breakfast at the cafeteria bar **Korppus** (Plaza del Corpus 1, a block down Calle Isabel la Católica from the Plaza Mayor, look for blue awnings). There's a **supermarket** in the old town (at Traviesa Dr. Laguna, near Telefónica office). An **outdoor produce market** thrives on Plaza de los Huertos (Thu 8:00–14:00).

Transportation Connections—Segovia

By train to: Madrid (9/day, 2 hrs, both Chamartin and Atocha stations). If day-tripping from Madrid, look for the Cercanías (commuter train) ticket window and departure board in either of Madrid's train stations and get a return schedule. Train information: tel. 92-142-0774.

By bus to: La Granja Palace (8/day, 30 min), **Ávila** (3/day, 45 min), **Salamanca** (3/day, 3–4 hrs, transfer in Labajos; consider busing from Segovia to Ávila for a visit then continuing to Salamanca by bus or train), **Madrid** (hrly, 1.75 hr, Madrid's Larrea bus station, Metro: Príncipe Pío, just past Hotel Florida Norte at Paseo de la Florida 11, tel. 92-142-7707).

ÁVILA

A popular side trip from Madrid, the birthplace of St. Teresa is famous only for its perfectly preserved medieval walls. You can climb onto them through the gardens of the parador. Ávila's old town is charming, with several fine churches and monasteries. Pick up a box of the famous local sweets called *yemas*—like a soft-boiled egg yolk cooled and sugared.

Ávila is well connected to **Segovia** (3 buses/day, 45 min), **Madrid** (1 train/hrly, 2 hrs, both Chamartin and Atocha stations), and **Salamanca** (3 trains/day, 2 hrs; 3 buses/day, 2 hrs). While there are no lockers at the bus station, you can leave bags at the train station—a 10-minute walk away. By car, it's easy and worth a look if you're driving from Segovia or Madrid to Salamanca. Train information: tel. 92-022-0998.

SALAMANCA

This sunny sandstone city boasts Spain's grandest plaza, its oldest university, and a fascinating history, all swaddled in a strolling, college-town ambience.

Salamanca is a youthful and untouristy Toledo. The city is a series of monuments and clusters of cloisters. The many students help keep prices down. Take a paseo with the local crowd down Rua Mayor and through Plaza Mayor. The young people congregate until late in the night, chanting and cheering, talking and singing. When I asked a local woman why young men all alone on the Plaza Mayor suddenly break into song, she said, "Doesn't it happen where you live?"

Orientation

Tourist Information: The more convenient Turismo is on Plaza Mayor (under the arch, on your right as you face the clock; Mon–Sat 9:00–14:00, 16:30–18:30, Sun from 10:00, tel. 92-321-8342). The other TI, covering Salamanca and the Castile region, is in the Casa de las Conchas on Rua Mayor (daily 10:00–14:00, 17:00–20:00, tel. 92-326-8571). Summertime-only TIs also spring up at the train and bus stations.

Arrival in Salamanca: From Salamanca's train and bus stations it's a 20-minute walk or an easy bus ride (80 ptas) to Plaza Mayor. From the train station, turn left out of the station and walk down to the ring road, cross it at Plaza España, then angle slightly left up Calle Azafranal. Or you can take bus #1 from the train station, which lets you off at Plaza Mercado (the market), next to Plaza Mayor.

From the bus station, turn right and walk down Avenue Filiberto Villalobos; take a left on the ring road and the first right on Ramon y Cajal. Or take bus #4 from the station to the city center; the closest stop is on Gran Vía, about four blocks from Plaza Mayor (ask a fellow passenger, "*¿Para Plaza Mayor?* "). Taxis to the center cost around 400 ptas.

Helpful Hints

The RENFE office, near Plaza Mayor, sells long-distance train tickets and *couchette* reservations (Mon–Fri 9:00–14:00, 17:00–20:00, Plaza de Libertad 10, tel. 92-326-3333, NSE but helpful). Some travel agencies, such as Viajes Salamanca next to the Turismo on Plaza Mayor, sell city-to-city bus tickets. A handy underground parking lot is at Plaza Santa Eulalia; some hotels give you a discount stamp on your parking receipt.

Maria Cruz is a good local guide (2-hr tour/8,000 ptas for small group, tel. 92-319-3166, cellular tel. 90-922-0757).

Campus Cibermatico offers Internet access for 400 ptas per half hour (Mon–Fri 10:00–14:00, 17:00–21:00, Sat 10:00–14:00, Plaza Mayor 10, first floor, tel. 92-327-1131).

Sights—Salamanca

▲**Plaza Mayor**—Built in 1755, this ultimate Spanish plaza is a fine place to nurse a cup of coffee and watch the world go by. The town hall, with the clock, grandly overlooks the square. The Arch of the Toro (built into the eastern wall) leads to the covered market. Imagine the excitement of the days, just 100 years ago, when bullfights were held in the square. How about coffee at the town's oldest café, Café Novelty?

▲▲**Cathedrals, Old and New**—These cool-on-a-hot-day cathedrals share buttresses and are both richly ornamented. You get to the old through the new. Before entering the new church, check out the ornate Plateresque facade (Spain's version of Flamboyant Gothic). At the side door of the facade, look for the astronaut added by a capricious restorer in 1993. This caused an outrage in town, but now locals shrug their shoulders and say, "He's the person closest to God."

The "new" cathedral, built from 1513 to 1733, is a mix of Gothic, Renaissance, and Baroque (free and lackluster). The recorded music helps. The *coro*, or choir, blocks up half of the church, but its wood carving is sumptuous; look up to see the elaborate organ.

The entrance to the old cathedral (12th-century Romanesque) is near the rear of the new one (300 ptas, daily 10:00–13:30,

Salamanca

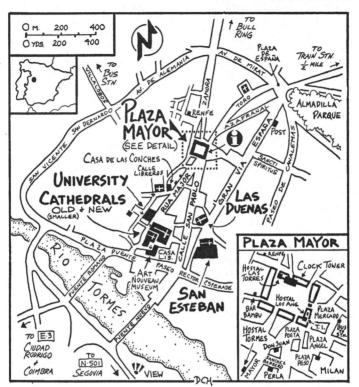

16:00–19:30). Sit in a front pew to study the 53 altarpiece scenes from Mary's life (by the Italian Florentino, 1445) and the dramatic Last Judgment fresco above it—notice Jesus sending condemned souls into the literal jaws of hell.

Then head into the cloister and explore the chapels, notable for their unusual tombs, ornate altarpieces, and ceilings with leering faces. Capilla San Bartolome de Los Anajas has a gorgeously carved 16th-century alabaster tomb and wooden Moorish organ.

▲▲**University**—Salamanca University, the oldest in Spain (est. 1230), was one of Europe's leading centers of learning for 400 years. Columbus came here for travel tips. Today many Americans enjoy its excellent summer program. The old lecture halls around the cloister, where many of Spain's Golden Age heroes studied, are open to the public (300 ptas, Mon–Sat 9:30–13:00, 16:00–19:00, Sun 10:00–13:00, the free English info sheet is full of details; enter from

Patio de Escuela, off Calle Libreros). Some of the rooms are still used by the university for prestigious academic ceremonies.

In the Hall of Fray Luis de León, the tables and benches are made of narrow wooden beams, whittled down by centuries of studious doodling. Professors spoke from the church-threatening *catedra*, or pulpit. It was here that free-thinking Fray Luis de León, after the Inquisition jailed and tortured him for four years, returned to his place and started his first post-imprisonment lecture with, "As we were saying..."

The altarpiece in the chapel depicts professors swearing to Mary's virginity (how did they know?), and the library upstairs is definitely worth the climb. Check out the cloister's ceiling outside the library for home-decorating ideas.

The entrance portal of the university is a great example of Spain's Plateresque style—masonry so intricate it looks like silver work. The people studying the facade aren't art fans. They're trying to find a tiny frog on a skull that students looked to for good luck.

As you leave the university, you'll see the statue of Fray Luis de León. Behind him, to your left (his right), is the entrance to a peaceful courtyard containing the Museum of the University, notable for Gallego's fanciful 16th-century *Sky of Salamanca* (included in university admission).

▲**Museo Art Nouveau y Art Deco**—Located in the Casa Lis, this museum is a refreshing change of pace, with its beautifully displayed collection of stained glass, jewelry, and statues (300 ptas, Tue–Fri 11:00–14:00, 17:00–21:00, Sat–Sun 10:00–21:00, closed Mon, Calle Gibraltar 14, between the cathedrals and the river, tel. 92-312-1425).

Casa de las Conchas—The aptly named "House of Shells," dating from 1503, is a landmark on Rua Mayor (free, patio open Mon–Fri 9:00–21:00, Sat–Sun 9:00–14:00, 16:00–19:00). If you s shells broken off or missing, it's because long ago people believe there were pearls beneath each shell. Go upstairs for a close-up view of the powerful towers of the 17th-century Clerecia churc The church, worth a look, is open sporadic afternoons.

Church of San Esteban—Dedicated to St. Stephen (Esteban) th martyr, this complex contains a cloister, a pantheon of tombs, a r seum, a sacristy, and a church. Before you enter, notice the Plate esque facade and its bas-relief of the stoning of St. Stephen. The crucifixion above is by Cellini. Once inside, follow the free Engl pamphlet and arrows. Upstairs you'll find the museum (with illu trated 16th-century choir books at the far end) and the entranc the choir. The church is overwhelmed by a Churriguera altarpi textbook example of the style named after him. Quietly ponder gold-plated cottage cheese, as tourists retch and say "too much their mother tongue (200 ptas, daily 9:00–13:30, 16:00–20:00).

Convento de las Dueñas—Next door, the much simpler *co*

is a joy. It consists of a double-decker cloister with a small museum of religious art. Check out the stone meanies exuberantly decorating the capitals on the cloister's upper deck (200 ptas, daily 10:30–13:00, 16:30–19:00). The nuns sell sweets daily except Sunday (375 ptas for a box).

Honorable Mention—Romantics will enjoy the low-slung Roman bridge, much of it original, spanning the Rio Tormes. The ancient (pre-Roman) headless bull, blindly guarding the entrance to the bridge, is a symbol of the city. Nearby, at the Parque Fluvial, you can rent rowboats.

Sleeping in Salamanca
(160 ptas = about $1)

Sleep Code: **S** = Single, **D** = Double/Twin, **T** = Triple, **Q** = Quad, **b** = bathroom, **t** = toilet only, **s** = shower only, **CC** = Credit Card (Visa, MasterCard, Amex), **SE** = Speaks English, **NSE** = No English.

Salamanca, being a student town, has plenty of good eating and sleeping values. All my listings are on or within a three-minute walk of the Plaza Mayor; directions are given from the Plaza Mayor, assuming you are facing the building with the clock (e.g., 3 o'clock is 90 degrees to your right as you face the clock). The 7 percent IVA tax is included only in the prices charged by the cheaper hotels.

Hostal Los Angeles, at about three o'clock, has simple but cared-for rooms, with a few overlooking the square. Stand on the balcony and inhale the essence of Spain (S-1,800 ptas, D-3,000 ptas, Db-4,500 ptas, T-4,500 ptas, Tb-6,500 ptas, all rooms with plaza views have full bathrooms, Plaza Mayor 10, 37002 Salamanca, tel. 92-321-8166, Luis and Sabina NSE). To try for a view, request, "*Con vista, por favor.*" If that fails, avoid the windowless room by requesting, "*Con ventana*" (window).

Hotel Las Torres, another on-the-square option, has modern, spacious rooms with all the amenities (Sb-8,500 ptas, Db-11,200 ptas, CC:VMA, avoid their restaurant, entrance just off square at Consejo #4, Plaza Mayor 47, under the clock, 37002 Salamanca, tel. 92-321-2100, fax 92-321-2101, SE). Rooms with views cost the same as rooms without views.

Hotel Don Juan, just off Plaza Mayor, has classy, comfy rooms and an attached restaurant (Sb-6,500 ptas, Db-9,000 ptas, Tb-12,000 ptas, cheaper off-season, elevator, air-con, double-paned windows, CC:VMA; exit Plaza Mayor at about 5 o'clock and turn right to Quintana 6, 37001 Salamanca; tel. 92-326-1473, fax 92-326-2475, SE).

Hotel Milan, your best normal-hotel-budget bet, is a tired but classic old Spanish hotel. It has a friendly yet professional atmosphere and quiet rooms (Sb-3,800 ptas, Db-5,900 ptas, elevator, CC:VM, leave the Plaza Mayor about 5 o'clock and go left

around fancy hotel to Plaza del Angel 5, 37001 Salamanca, tel. 92-321-7518, fax 92-321-9697, NSE).

The homey **Hostal La Perla Salmantina** is sleepable and in a quiet location but will be closed part of 2000 for remodeling (D-3,500 ptas, Ds-4,000 ptas, Db-5,000 ptas; exit Plaza Mayor at about 6 o'clock and walk down Rua Mayor, then left to Sánchez Barbero 7, 37001 Salamanca; tel. & fax 92-321-7656, NSE).

The handy **Hostal Tormes** is a student-type residence with clean but spartan rooms on the pedestrian street connecting Plaza Mayor and the university (S-2,700 ptas, D-4,500 ptas, Db-5,100 ptas, Rua Mayor 20, 37008 Salamanca, tel. & fax 92-321-9683, NSE).

Hostal Plaza Mayor has 19 small but welcoming rooms and a good location just southwest of Plaza Mayor—exit the plaza at seven o'clock (Sb-4,500 ptas, Db-7,500 ptas, Plaza del Corrillo 20, attached restaurant, tel. 92-326-2020, fax 92-321-7548).

Eating in Salamanca

There are plenty of good, inexpensive restaurants between Plaza Mayor and Gran Vía and as you leave the Plaza Mayor toward Rua Mayor. Just wander and eat at your own discovery or try **Café Novelty** (Plaza Mayor's oldest coffee shop) or any of several places on Calle Bermejeros, such as **Taberna de Pilatos** (at #5, Mon–Sat 13:00–15:00, 21:00–03:00, closed Sun).

Restaurante Isidro has a super assortment of seafood and meat dishes (menu of the day 1,200 ptas, daily 13:00–16:00, 20:00–23:00, Pozo Amarillo 19, about a block north of the covered market, close to Plaza Mayor, tel. 92-326-2848). **Restaurante Dulcinea** is a classier, pricier version of the Isidro (menu of the day-1,400–1,950 ptas, Pozo Amarillo 5, tel. 92-321-7843).

Mandala is popular with the younger crowd for its tasty tapas, attractive setting, and good prices (daily 8:00–24:00, Calle Serranos 9–11; from Casa de las Conchas follow Rua Antigua alongside Clerecia church for two blocks, tel. 92-312-3342). Wash down your tapas or *plato combinado* with a *batido* (milkshake).

Tops for tapas in Salamanca is the **Café Chinitas**, one of several tapas bars lining Calle Van Dyck. It's a 15-minute walk from Plaza Mayor, but its prices and selection are great. On a hot day the iced gazpacho hits the spot. It's offered daily in summer; otherwise, hope for the "*Hay Gazpacho*" sign (daily 8:00–01:00, Van Dyck 14–16; from Plaza Mayor, follow Toro north as it changes its name to Maria Auxiliadora; after you cross Avenida de Portugal, take the 3rd left; tel. 92-325-0293). Runner-up, and far more central, is **Bar Bambu**, offering cheap, good tapas just off the southwest corner of Plaza Mayor (daily 9:00–01:30, Calle Prior 4, pass the Burger King and immediately head downstairs). Overlooking Plaza Mayor, the **Cervantes Bar** (next to the TI) serves great tapas, salads, and meals to a mainly local crowd of all ages.

Salamanca's high student population supports a vast array of trendy hangouts. The best way to locate current hot spots is to find the touts handing out fliers and coupons at the clock tower around 23:00. Popular places include **Country**, with great music, a student vibe, and dice-for-free-drinks games (Juan de Almeida 5); **Cum Laude** (across from Bar Bambu); and the tacky **De Laval Genoves Submarino**, with its submarine-like interior (Calle San Justo 27–31, 5-minute walk east of Plaza Mayor). Other good, centrally-located tapas bars can be found at **El Candil** (on Ventura Ruiz Aguilera) and **La Covachuela**, where the waiter will amaze you with coin tricks (in the Portales de San Antonio; establish prices before ordering).

The covered *mercado* (market) on Plaza Mercado (Mon–Sat 8:00–14:00, closed Sun) is ideal for picnic gatherers. And if you always wanted seconds at Communion, buy a bag of giant Communion wafers, a local specialty called *obleas*.

Transportation Connections—Salamanca

By train to: Madrid (3/day, 2.5–3.5 hrs, new and fast Finnish-made TRD trains require 200-ptas reservation, Chamartin station), **Ávila** (3/day, 1 hr; also 3 buses/day), **Barcelona** (1/day, 10 hrs; also 1 bus/day), **Coimbra** (1/day, 6 hrs, departs from Salamanca station at about 4:30); taxis to the station are available at any hour at Plaza Mercado for about 400 ptas. Train information: tel. 92-312-0202.

By bus to: Segovia (3/day, 4 hrs, transfer in Labajos or Ávila; consider a brief visit to Ávila en route), **Ciudad Rodrigo** (7/day, 1 hr). Bus info: tel. 92-323-2266.

CIUDAD RODRIGO

(Worth a visit only if you're traveling from Salamanca to Coimbra.) This rough-and-tumble old town of 16,000 people caps a hill overlooking the Río Agueda. Spend an hour wandering among the Renaissance mansions that line its streets and exploring its cathedral and Plaza Mayor. Have lunch or a snack at El Sanatorio (Plaza Mayor 14). The tapas are cheap, the crowd is local, and the walls are a Ciudad Rodrigo scrapbook, including some bullfighting that makes the Three Stooges look demure.

Ciudad Rodrigo's cathedral—pockmarked with scars from Napoleonic cannon balls—has some entertaining carvings in the choir and some pretty racy work in its cloisters. Who said, "When you've seen one Gothic church, you've seen 'em all"?

The TI (tel. 92-346-0561) is just inside the old wall near the cathedral and can recommend a good hotel such as Hotel Conde Rodrigo. The Plaza Mayor is a two-block walk from the TI.

Ciudad Rodrigo is a convenient stop on the Salamanca-to-Coimbra drive. Buses connect Salamanca and Ciudad Rodrigo with surprising efficiency in about an hour. From there you can connect (with less ease) to Coimbra.

Route Tips for Drivers

Madrid to El Escorial to the Valley of the Fallen to Segovia (50 miles): Taxi to your car-rental office (or ask if they'll deliver the car to your hotel). Pick up the car by 8:30 and ask directions to highway A6. Follow "A6-Valladolid" signs to the clearly marked exit on M505 to El Escorial. Get to El Escorial by 9:30 to beat the crowds. The nearby **Silla de Felipe** (Philip's Seat) is a rocky view-point where the king would come to admire his palace being built.

From El Escorial, follow "C600-Valle de los Caídos" signs to the Valley of the Fallen. You'll see the huge cross marking it in the distance. After the tollbooth, follow "Basilica" signs to the parking place (toilets, tacky souvenirs, and cafeteria). As you leave, turn left to Guadarrama on C600, go under the highway, and follow signs to Puerto de Navacerrada. From there, you climb past flocks of sheep, over a 6,000-foot-high mountain pass (Pto. de Navacerrada) into old Castile, and through La Granja to Segovia. (Segovia is much more important than La Granja, but garden lovers enjoy a quick La Granja stop.)

At the Segovia aqueduct, turn into the old town (the side where the aqueduct adjoins the crenellated fortress walls) and park on or as close to the Plaza Mayor as possible. To be legal—and they do issue expensive tickets—buy a ticket from the nearby machine to park in areas marked by blue stripes; place the ticket on your dashboard (45 ptas/30 min, 90-min maximum 9:00–20:00; free parking 20:00–9:00, Sat afternoon, and all day Sun). You should be safe on the square.

Segovia to Salamanca (100 miles): Leave Segovia by driving around the town's circular road, which offers good views from below the Alcázar. Then follow signs for Ávila (road N110). Notice the fine Segovia view from the three crosses at the crest of the first hill. Just after the abandoned ghost church at Villacastin, turn onto N501 at the huge Puerta de San Vicente (cathedral and TI are just inside). The Salamanca road leads around the famous Ávila walls to the right. The best wall view is from the signposted Cuatro Postes, a mile northwest of town. Salamanca (N501) is clearly marked, about an hour's drive away.

A few miles before Salamanca, you might want to stop at the huge bull on the left of the road. There's a little dirt path leading right up to it. The closer you get, the more you realize it isn't real. Bad boys climb it for a goofy photo, but I wouldn't. For a great photo op of Salamanca, complete with river reflection, stop at the edge of the city (at the light before the first bridge).

Parking in Salamanca is terrible. You can park dangerously over the river or along the Paseo de Canaliejas for free. I found a meter near my hotel (along Calle Palominos) and kept it fed (100 ptas for 90 min, 9:00–14:00, 16:00–20:00, free Sat and Sun afternoon). Leave nothing of value in your car. The only safe parking is in a garage.

TOLEDO

An hour south of Madrid, Toledo teems with tourists, souvenirs, and great art by day, delicious roast suckling pig, echoes of El Greco, and medieval magic by night. Incredibly well preserved and full of cultural wonder, the entire city has been declared a national historical monument.

Spain's historic capital is 2,000 years of tangled history—Roman, Visigothic, Moorish, and Christian—crowded onto a high, rocky perch protected on three sides by the Tejo River. It's so well preserved that the Spanish government has forbidden any modern exteriors. The rich mix of Jewish, Moorish, and Christian heritages makes it one of Europe's art capitals.

Toledo was a Visigothic capital back in 554 and—after a period of Moorish rule—Spain's political capital until 1561, when it reached its natural limits of growth as defined by the Tejo River Gorge. Though the king moved to more spacious Madrid, Toledo remains the historic, artistic, and spiritual center of Spain. In spite of tremendous tourist crowds, Toledo just sits on its history and remains much as it was when El Greco called it home and painted it 400 years ago. If you like El Greco, you'll love Toledo.

Planning Your Time

To properly see Toledo's museums (great El Greco), cathedral (best in Spain), and medieval atmosphere (best after dark), you'll need two nights and a day (but not Mon, when most sights are closed).

Toledo is just 60 minutes away from Madrid by bus (2/hrly) or train (6/day). A car is useless in Toledo. See the town outside of car-rental time (or drop your car here).

Toledo

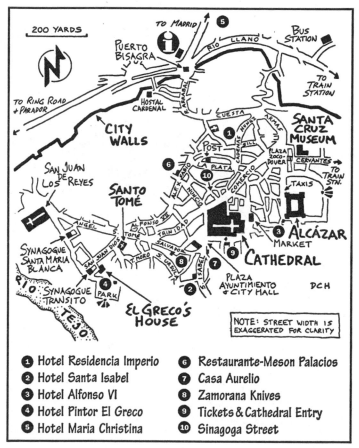

200 YARDS

N

TO MADRID ⑤

PUERTO BISAGRA

BUS STATION

RIO LLANO

TO RING ROAD & PARADOR

TO TRAIN STATION

HOSTAL CARDENAL

CITY WALLS

ARRABAL

CUESTA

NUÑEZ

ARMAS

SANTA CRUZ MUSEUM

①

POST

CADENAS

GILL

PLAZA 2000-DOVER

CERVANTES

TO TRAIN STN.

SAN JUAN DE REYES

⑥

LA PLATA

ALEX. ZANO

⑩

COMERCIO

TAXIS

SANTO TOMÉ

NUÑEZ

ALFONSO XII

TRINIDAD

ALCÁZAR

③ MARKET

SYNAGOGUE SANTA MARIA BLANCA

ANGEL

S. TOMÉ

SALVADOR

ⓈAN JUAN DIOS

MORO

S. URSULA

⑧

S. ISABEL

⑦

⑨ CATHEDRAL

DCH

RIO

SYNAGOGUE TRANSITO

④ PARK

②

PLAZA AYUNTIMIENTO & CITY HALL

TEJO

EL GRECO'S HOUSE

NOTE: STREET WIDTH IS EXAGGERATED FOR CLARITY

① Hotel Residencia Imperio
② Hotel Santa Isabel
③ Hotel Alfonso VI
④ Hotel Pintor El Greco
⑤ Hotel Maria Christina

⑥ Restaurante-Meson Palacios
⑦ Casa Aurelio
⑧ Zamorana Knives
⑨ Tickets & Cathedral Entry
⑩ Sinagoga Street

Orientation

Lassoed into a tight tangle of streets by the sharp bend of the Tejo River (called the Tagus where it hits the Atlantic, in Lisbon), Toledo has the most confusing medieval street plan in Spain. But it's a small town of 65,000, major sights are well signposted, and most locals will politely point you in the right direction.

Look at the map and take a mental orientation walk past Toledo's main sights. Starting in the central Plaza Zocódover, go southwest along the Calle de Comércio. After passing the cathedral on your left, follow the signs to Santo Tomé and the cluster of other sights. The visitor's city lies basically along one small but

Toledo's Plaza Zocódover

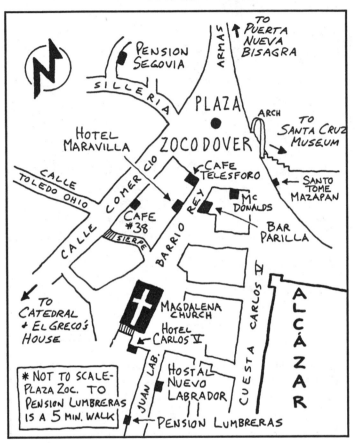

central street. Still, I routinely get completely turned around. Knowing that the town is bounded by the river on three sides and is very small, I wander happily lost. When it's time to get somewhere, I pull out the map or ask, "*¿Dónde está Plaza Zocódover?*"

Tourist Information

The TI is just outside the Bisagra Gate at the train and bus station end of town (Mon–Sat 9:00–19:00, Sun 9:00–15:00; Oct–Jun Mon–Fri 9:00–18:00, Sat 9:00–19:00, Sun 9:00–15:00; can recommend local guides, tel. 92-522-0843). The readable local guide, *Toledo, Its Art and Its History* (small version 700 ptas, sold all over town), explains all the sights (which generally provide no on-site information) and gives you a photo to point at and say, "*¿Dónde está... ?*"

Arrival in Toledo

"Arriving" in Toledo means getting to Plaza Zocódover. From the train station, that's a 20-minute hike, taxi ride (400 ptas), or easy bus ride (#5 or #6, 115 ptas, pay on bus, confirm by asking, "*Para Plaza Zocódover?*"). If you're walking, turn right as you leave the station, cross the bridge, pass the bus station, go straight through the roundabout, and continue uphill to the TI and north gate (Puerta Bisagra is the last surviving gate of the 10th-century fortifications). From the bus station, Plaza Zocódover is a 15-minute walk or short bus ride (#5, see directions from train station, above).

Sights—Toledo

▲▲**El Greco's Art**—Born on Crete and trained in Venice, Domenikos Theotocopoulos (tongue-tied friends just called him "The Greek") came to Spain to get a job decorating El Escorial. He failed there but succeeded in Toledo, where he spent the last 37 years of his life. He mixed all three regional influences into his palette. From his Greek homeland, he absorbed the solemn, abstract style of icons. In Venice he learned the bold use of color and dramatic style of the later Renaissance. These styles were then fused in the fires of fanatic Spanish-Catholic devotion.

Not bound by the realism so important to his 16th-century contemporaries, El Greco painted dramatic visions of striking colors and figures—bodies unnatural and elongated as though stretched between heaven and earth. He painted souls, not faces. His work is on display at nearly every sight in Toledo. Thoroughly modern in its disregard of realism, it seems as fresh as contemporary art.

▲▲▲**Cathedral**—Holy Toledo! Spain's leading Catholic city has a magnificent cathedral. Shoehorned into the old center, its exterior is hard to appreciate. But the interior is so lofty, rich, and vast that it grabs you by the vocal cords, and all you can do is whisper, "Wow."

While the basic cathedral is free, seeing the great art—in five separate places within the cathedral—requires a ticket for 500 ptas (well worthwhile, sold in shop opposite church entrance, Mon–Sat 10:30–18:30, Sun 14:00–18:00).

Holy redwood forest, Batman. Wander among the pillars. Sit under one and imagine when the light bulbs were candles and the tourists were pilgrims—before the "No Photo" signs, when every window provided spiritual as well as physical light. The cathedral is primarily Gothic, but since it took more than 200 years to build (1226–1493), you'll see a mix of styles—Gothic, Renaissance, and Baroque. Enjoy the elaborate wrought-iron work, lavish wood carvings, window after colorful window of 500-year-old stained

Toledo Cathedral

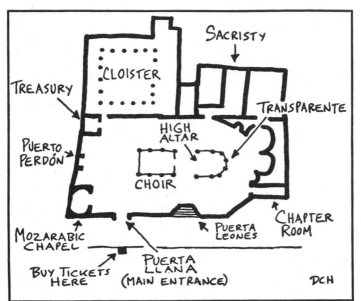

glass, and a sacristy with a collection of paintings that would put any museum on the map.

This confusing collage of great Spanish art deserves a guided tour. Try to hire a private guide (or freeload) or at least follow a local guidebook. Here's a framework for your visit.

First, walk to the center to marvel through the iron grill at one of the most stunning high altars in Spain—and one of the country's best pieces of Gothic art.

The **choir** faces the high altar and requires a piece of your five-part ticket. It's famous for its fine carving. The lower wooden stalls are decorated with scenes from the Christian victory over the Muslims at Granada. The upper stalls feature New Testament figures carved out of alabaster. The iron grill of the choir is notable for the dedication of the man who built it. Domingo de Cespedes, a Toledo ironworker, accepted the commission to build the grill for 6,000 ducats. The project, which took from 1541 to 1548, was far more costly than he anticipated. The medieval Church didn't accept cost overruns, so, to finish it, he sold everything he owned and went into debt. He died a poor—but honorable—man.

The *transparente*, behind the high altar, is a unique feature of the cathedral. In the 1700s a hole was cut into the ceiling to let a sunbeam brighten the Mass. Melding this big hole into the Gothic church presented a challenge that resulted in a Baroque masterpiece. Gape up at this riot of angels doing flip-flops, babies breathing thin air, bottoms of feet, and gilded sunbursts. It makes you hope no one falls down. I like it, as did, I guess, the long-dead cardinal whose hat hangs from the edge of the hole. (A perk that only cardinals enjoy is choosing the place in the cathedral in which their hat will hang till it rots.)

The cathedral's **sacristy** has 20 El Grecos and masterpieces by Goya, Titian, Rubens, Velázquez, and Bellini. First, look at the fine perspective work on the ceiling. Then walk to the most important painting in the collection. El Greco's first masterpiece, from 1579, *The Spoiliation* (a.k.a. *The Denuding of Christ*) hangs above the marble altar. This was one of El Greco's first Toledo commissions after arriving from Venice. Notice the parallel contrasts: Jesus' delicate hand before a flaming red tunic and Jesus' noble face among the sinister mob. On the right is a rare religious painting by Goya, the *Betrayal of Christ*, which shows Judas preparing to kiss Jesus, identifying him to the Roman soldiers. Among the many other El Greco paintings, you'll find a lifelike 17th-century carving of St. Francis by Pedro de Mena.

The *sala capitular*, or chapter house (also requiring a part of your ticket), has a rich gilded ceiling, interesting Bible-story-telling frescoes, and a pictorial review of hundreds of years of Toledo archbishops. Imagine sitting down to church business surrounded by all this tradition and theology. As you leave, notice the iron-pumping cupids carved into the panels lining the walls.

The **treasury** (*tesoro*) has plenty to see. The highlight is the 10-foot-high, 430-pound monstrance—the tower designed to hold the Holy Communion bread (the Host) during the festival of Corpus Christi (body of Christ) as it parades through the city. Built in 1517 (by a man named Arfe), it's made of 5,000 individual pieces held together by 12,500 screws. There are diamonds, emeralds, rubies, and 400 pounds of gold-plated silver. The inner part is 35 pounds of solid gold. Yeow. The base is a later addition, from the Baroque period. Traditionally, it's thought that much of this gold and silver arrived on Columbus' first load home. To the right of the monstrance find the fancy sword of Franco. Next to that is a 700-year-old Bible printed and beautifully illustrated by French monks. Imagine the exquisite experience of reading this with its lavish illustrations through medieval eyes. The finely painted crucifix on the opposite side is by the great Gothic Florentine painter Fra Angelico. Notice how it depicts Jesus alive on the back and dead on the front. This was a gift from Mussolini to Franco. Hmmmm.

If you're at the cathedral between 9:30 and 9:45, you can peek into the otherwise-locked **Mozarabic Chapel** (Capilla Mozarabe) to witness the Visigothic Mass, the oldest surviving Christian ritual in Western Europe. You're welcome to partake in this stirring example of peaceful coexistence of faiths—but once the door closes, you're a Visigoth for 30 minutes.

▲▲Santa Cruz Museum—This great Renaissance building was an orphanage, built from money left by Cardinal Mendoza when he died in 1495. It's in the form of a Greek cross under a Moorish dome. The arms of the building—formerly wards—are filled with 16th-century art, tapestries, furniture, armor, and documents. It's a stately, classical, music-filled setting with a cruel lack of English information.

Eighteen El Grecos gather in one wing upstairs, including the impressive *Assumption of Mary*—a spiritual poem on canvas (notice old Toledo on the bottom). Painted one year before his death in 1614, this is considered the culmination of El Greco's artistic development.

An enormous blue banner hangs like a long, skinny tooth opposite the entry. This flew from the flagship of Don Juan of Austria and recalls the pivotal naval victory over the Muslims at the Battle of Lepanto in 1571. Lepanto was a key victory in the centuries-long Muslim threat to Christian Europe (200 ptas, Mon 10:00–18:30, Tue–Sat 10:00–18:30, Sun 10:00–14:00, Cervantes 3).

▲Alcázar—This huge former imperial residence—built on the site of Roman, Visagothic, and Moorish fortresses—dominates the Toledo skyline. The Alcázar became a kind of right-wing Alamo during Spain's civil war when a force of Franco's Nationalists (and hundreds of hostages) were besieged for two months. Finally, after many fierce but futile Republican attacks, Franco sent in an army that took Toledo and freed the Alcázar. The place was rebuilt and glorified under Franco. Today you can see its civil war exhibits, giving you an interesting—and right-wing—look at the horrors of Spain's recent past (200 ptas, Tue–Sun 9:30–14:30, closed Mon, may be open afternoons).

▲Santo Tomé—A simple chapel holds El Greco's most loved painting. *The Burial of the Count of Orgaz* couples heaven and earth in a way only The Greek could. It feels so right to see a painting left where the artist put it 400 years ago. Take this slow. Stay awhile—let it perform. It's 1323. You're at the burial of the good count. After a pious and generous life, he left his estate to the Church. Saints Augustine and Steven have even come down for the burial—to usher him directly to heaven. "Such is the reward for those who serve God and his saints."

More than 250 years later, in 1586, when the count's descendents reneged on their payments, the Church went to court and won. To celebrate the victory, a priest hired El Greco to make a painting of the burial to hang over the count's tomb.

The painting has two halves divided by a serene—but not

sad—line of noble faces. The physical world ends with the line of nobles. Above them a spiritual wind blows as colors change and shapes stretch. Notice the angel, robe caught up in that wind, "birthing" the soul of the count through the neck of a celestial womb into Heaven—the soul abandoning the physical body to join Christ the Judge. Mary and John the Baptist both intervene on behalf of the arriving soul. Each face is a detailed portrait. El Greco himself (eyeballing you, seventh figure in from the left) is the only one not involved in the burial. The boy in the foreground is El Greco's son (200 ptas, daily 10:00–18:45, until 17:45 in off-season).

▲▲**Museo El Greco**—This old house, often wrongly called El Greco's, gives you a good look at the interior of a traditionally furnished Renaissance home. You'll see El Greco's masterful View of Toledo and portraits of the Apostles (400 ptas, Tue–Sat 10:00–14:00, 16:00–18:00, Sun 10:00–14:00, closed Mon, Samuel Levi 3).

Sinagoga del Transito (Museo Sefardi)—Built in 1366, this is the best surviving slice of Toledo's Jewish past (same price and hours as El Greco Museum, on Calle de los Reyes Católicos, next to El Greco Museum).

Sinagoga del Santa Maria Blanca—This synagogue-turned-church with Moorish arches is an eclectic but harmonious gem (200 ptas, daily 10:00–14:00, 15:30–19:00, closes off-season at 18:00, Reyes Católicos 2-4).

Shopping

Toledo probably sells as many souvenirs as any city in Spain. This is the place to buy medieval-looking swords, armor, maces, three-legged stools, and other Nouveau antiques. It's also Spain's damascene center, where for centuries craftspeople have inlaid black steel with gold, silver, and copper wire. At Calle Ciudad 19, near the cathedral and Plaza Ayuntamiento, you can see swords and knives being made in the workshop of English-speaking Mariano Zamorano. Judging by what's left of his hand, his knives are among the best. El Martes, Toledo's colorful outdoor flea market, bustles on Paseo del Carmen (below the Alcazar) Tuesday from 9:00 to 14:00.

Sleeping in Toledo
(160 ptas = about $1)

Sleep Code: **S** = Single, **D** = Double/Twin, **T** = Triple, **Q** = Quad, **b** = bathroom, **t** = toilet only, **s** = shower only, **CC** = Credit Card (Visa, MasterCard, Amex), **SE** = Speaks English, **NSE** = No English. Breakfast and the 7 percent IVA tax aren't included unless noted.

Madrid day-trippers darken the sunlit cobbles, but few stay to see Toledo's medieval moonrise. Spend the night. Spring and fall are high season; November through March and July and August are low. There are no private rooms for rent.

Hotel Residencia Imperio is a well-run place offering 21 rooms with solid air-conditioned comfort in a handy old-town location (Sb-4,280 ptas, Db-6,200 ptas, Tb-8,380 ptas, includes tax, 5 percent discount with this book, CC:VMA, elevator, Calle de las Cadenas 5, tel. 92-522-7650, fax 92-525-3183, e-mail: himperio @teleline.es, SE).

Hotel Maravilla is wonderfully central, quiet (unless you get a room on the street), and convenient. Despite its claustrophobic halls and simple rooms, it offers a decent midrange value in the old center (Sb-4,300 ptas, Db-7,000 ptas, Tb-9,500 ptas, Qb-11,700 ptas, includes breakfast and tax, CC:VMA, air-con, a block behind Plaza Zocódover at Plaza de Barrio Rey 7, 45001 Toledo, tel. 92-522-8317, fax 92-522-8155, Ana and Felisa Maria speak some English).

Hotel Carlos V is well located, overlooking the cathedral, between the Alcázar and Plaza Zocódover. It suffers from the obligatory stuffiness of a correct hotel but has bright, pleasant rooms and bathrooms you could make love in (Sb-9,500 ptas, Db-14,000 ptas, Tb-18,000 ptas, breakfast-1,100 ptas, less off-season, CC:VMA, air-con, elevator, Plaza Horno Magdalena 3, 45001 Toledo, tel. 92-522-2100, fax 92-522-2105, SE). Ask for a view room overlooking the cathedral.

Around the corner, the quiet, modern **Hostal Nuevo Labrador** is just as nice, with clean, shiny and spacious rooms for about half the price (Sb-3,800 ptas, Db-6,400 ptas, Tb-8,500 ptas, Qb-10,000 ptas, includes tax, CC:VMA, Juan Labrador 10, 45001 Toledo, tel. 92-522-2620, fax 92-522-9399, NSE). The new **Hostal Cento**, run by the same family, offers a similar value (Db-6,500 ptas, just off Plaza Zocódover at Calle Nueva 13, tel. 92-525-7091).

Down the same street, the smaller, family-run **Pensión Lumbreras** has a tranquil courtyard and 12 rooms, some with views—such as room #6 (1 S-1,700 ptas, D-3,000 ptas, T-4,200 ptas; their huge, view Q for 5,600 ptas can sleep up to six; includes tax, breakfast 225 ptas, Juan Labrador 9, 45001 Toledo, tel. 92-522-1571, Gonzalez family NSE).

Hotel Santa Isabel, in a 15th-century building two blocks from the cathedral, has 23 clean, modern, and comfortable rooms and squeaky tile hallways. Avoid only the few "*atico*" rooms that have only a skylight (Sb-4,200 ptas, Db-6,500 ptas, Tb-8,000 ptas, includes tax, breakfast-600 ptas, parking-900 ptas, CC:VMA, air-con, elevator, buried deep in old town so take a taxi not the bus, Calle Santa Isabel 24, 45002 Toledo, tel. 92-525-3120, fax 92-525-3136, www.santa-isabel.com).

Pensión Segovia is cheap and very central, with some night noise. It's also old, rickety, and dingy, with questionable beds and memorable balconies. Duck your head; the ancient ceilings are low (D-3,000 ptas, T-4,500 ptas; from Plaza Zocódover go down Calle de la Sillería and take the 2nd right to a tiny square, Calle de Recoletos 2, 45001 Toledo, tel. 92-521-1124, NSE but friendly).

Across from the Alcázar is **Hotel Alfonso VI**, a big, touristy establishment with large, airy rooms, tour groups, and souvenirs for sale all over the lobby. I hate to steer anyone there, but in central Toledo you take what you can get (Sb-10,000 ptas, Db-14,000 ptas, Tb-18,000 ptas, breakfast-1,200 ptas, includes tax, CC:VMA, some air-con, General Moscardo 2, 45001 Toledo, tel. 92-522-2600, fax 92-521-4458, e-mail: alfonsovi@macom.es, SE). Ask for a view room.

The best splurge in town is **Hostal de Cardenal**, a 17th-century cardinal's palace built into Toledo's wall. It's quiet and elegant, with a cool garden and a fine restaurant. This poor-man's parador is at the dusty old gate of Toledo, closest to the station but a hike below the old-town action (Sb-7,800 ptas, Db-12,600 ptas, Tb-16,350 ptas, 5 percent discount with this book, CC:VMA, air-con, near Puerta Bisagra, Paseo de Recaredo 24, 45004 Toledo, tel. 92-522-4900, fax 92-522-2991, e-mail: cardenal@macom.es, stuffy staff SE).

Hotel Pintor El Greco is similar to Hostal de Cardenal but at the far end of the old town. It's plush and modern-feeling, with all the comforts, yet in a historic 17th-century building. A block from Santo Tomé in a Jewish Quarter garden, it's very quiet (Sb-12,600 ptas, Db-16,400 ptas, plus tax, includes breakfast, CC:VMA, air-con, elevator, Alamillos del Transito 13, tel. 92-521-4250, fax 92-521-5819, e-mail: info@estancias.com, SE).

Sleeping outside of Town

On the road to Madrid (near bullring): Hostal Gavilánes II is bright and modern, with 15 comfortable rooms and easy parking, a 15-minute walk from Plaza Zocódover (Sb-6,000 ptas, Db-8,000 ptas, Db suite-8,600 ptas, Tb-8,000 ptas, Qb-9,600 ptas, breakfast-350 ptas, sporadic air-con, CC:VM, Marqués de Mendigorría 14, 45003 Toledo, tel. 92-521-1628, NSE). There are two "Gavilánes" hotels; this one's at the bullring, Plaza de Toros.

Cheaper, though not as good a value for the money, is the neighboring **Hostal Madrid**, which has clean, simple rooms (Sb-3,500 ptas, Db-5,200 ptas, Tb-7,020 ptas, CC:VM, air-con, Calle Marqués de Mendigorría 7, 45003 Toledo, tel. 92-522-1114, NSE). This *hostal* spreads its rooms through two buildings on either side of the street; the best rooms and reception area are in the building on the bullring side of the street. The annex has plain Db-5,000 rooms without air-conditioning or breakfast.

Hotel Maria Cristina is a sprawling modern hotel with all the comforts under a thin layer of pre-fab tradition (Db-11,600 ptas, plus tax, CC:VMA, Marques de Mendigorria 1, next to bull-ring, tel. 92-521-3202, fax 92-521-2650, SE).

For the view: For those who want it all and will leave the town center and pay anything to get it, Toledo's **Parador Nacional Conde de Orgaz** is one of Spain's most famous, enjoying the same Toledo view El Greco made famous from across the Tejo Canyon (Db-21,000 ptas, CC:VMA, 2 windy miles from town at Cerro del Emperador, 45002 Toledo, tel. 92-522-1850, fax 92-522-5166, www.parador.es, SE). Take a cab here just to see the sunset from the terrace (700 ptas one way).

Near train station: The youth hostel **Albergue Juvenil San Servando**, closed the first half of 2000 for remodeling, is lavish but cheap, with small rooms, a swimming pool, views, and good management (1,300 ptas per bed, San Servando castle near train station, over Puente Viejo outside town, tel. 92-522-4554, NSE).

Eating in Toledo

A day full of El Greco and the romance of Toledo after dark puts me in the mood for suckling pigs—roasted. For a splurge, the palatial **Hostal de Cardenal Restaurante** serves wonderfully prepared local specialties, including pigs and *perdiz* (partridge). Call to reserve (lunch from 13:00, dinner from 20:30, near Puerta Bisagra, Paseo de Recaredo 24, tel. 92-522-0862).

Toledo's three **Casa Aurelio** restaurants each offer reasonably priced food and a classy atmosphere (2,500-ptas menu, closed Sun and Tue, CC:VA, at Plaza Ayuntamiento 8 near the cathedral, tel. 92-522-7716, other branches at Sinagoga 1 and at Sinagoga 6).

Restaurante-Meson Palacios serves good food at cheap prices (lunch from 13:00, dinner from 19:30, on Alfonso X, near Plaza de San Vicente). **Rincón de Eloy** is a more elegant alternative (1,500-ptas menu, Juan Labrador 16, near the Alcazar).

Restaurant Plaza is on a tiny square behind Plaza Zocódover (take the alley from Plaza Zocódover past Café Casa Telesforo to Plaza de Barrio Rey). The bars and cafés on Plaza Zocódover are reasonable, seasoned with some fine people watching.

For breakfast, **Comercio 38** serves croissants and *churros* (between Plaza Zocódover and the cathedral at Comércio 38). Their *churros*, as good as any, rival lutefisk as the leading European national dish of penitence. For hearty eaters, they serve a huge tortilla McMuffin.

For a sweet and romantic evening moment, get a pastry and head down to the cathedral. Sit on the Plaza del Ayuntamiento (there's a comfortable perch 10 yards down the lane from the huge granite bowling ball). The fountain is on your right, Spain's best-looking city hall is behind you, and her top cathedral, built back when Toledo was Spain's capital, shines brightly against the black night sky before you.

For Toledo's famous almond-fruity-sweet *mazapan*, try **Casa Telesforo** at Plaza Zocódover 17 (125 ptas each, or a mix of nine kinds in a 1,000-ptas box, daily 9:00–24:00), or try the slicker and less expensive **Santo Tomé** on the opposite side of Plaza Zocódover (good *tolenadas*).

Picnics are best assembled at the **Mercado Municipal** on Plaza Mayor (on the Alcázar side of the cathedral, open until 14:00, closed Sun). This is a fun market to prowl, even if you don't need food. If you feel like munching a giant Communion wafer, one of the stalls sells crispy bags of *obleas* (a great gift for your favorite pastor).

Transportation Connections—Toledo
Far more buses than trains connect Toledo with Madrid.

To Madrid by bus (2/hrly, 60 min, Madrid's Estación sur Autobuses, Metro: Méndez Alvaro), **by train** (6/day, 60 min, Madrid's Atocha station), **by car** (40 miles, 1 hr). Toledo bus info: tel. 92-521-5850; train info: tel. 92-522-3099.

Car Rental: Avis is within Toledo's city walls at Galeria Comercial 107, Paseo del Miradero (tel. 92-521-4535), and Hertz is across from the train station at Paseo Rosa 40 (tel. 92-525-3890).

LA MANCHA
(Visit only if you're driving between Toledo and Granada.)
Nowhere else is Spain so vast, flat, and radically monotonous. La Mancha, Arabic for "parched earth," makes you feel small—lost in rough seas of olive-green polka dots. Random buildings look like houses and hotels hurled off some heavenly Monopoly board. It's a rough land where roadkill is left to rot, where bugs ricochet off the windshield and keep on flying, and where hitchhikers wear red dresses and aim to take you for the ride.

This is the setting of Cervantes' *Don Quixote*, published in the 17th century, after England sank the Armada and the Spanish Empire began its decline. Cervantes' star character fought doggedly for good, for justice, and against the fall of Spain and its traditional old-regime empire. Ignoring reality, Don Quixote was a hero fighting a hopeless battle. Stark La Mancha was the perfect stage.

The epitome of Don Quixote country, the town of **Consuegra** must be the La Mancha Cervantes had in mind. Drive up to the ruined 12th-century castle and joust with a windmill. It's hot and buggy here, but the powerful view overlooking the village, with its sun-bleached, light-red roofs; modern concrete reality; and harsh, windy silence makes for a profound picnic (a 1-hour drive south of Toledo). The castle belonged to the Knights of St. John (12th and 13th centuries) and is associated with their trip to Jerusalem during the Crusades. Originally built from the ruins of a nearby Roman circus, it has been newly restored (200 ptas). Sorry, the windmills are post-Cervantes, only 200 to 300 years old.

If you've seen windmills, the next castle north (above Almonacid, 12 kilometers from Toledo) is more interesting than the Consuegra castle and free. Follow the ruined lane past the ruined church up to the ruined castle. The jovial locals hike up with kids and kites.

Route Tips for Drivers

Granada to Toledo (250 miles, 5 hrs): The Granada–Toledo drive is long, hot, and boring (see "La Mancha," above). Start early to minimize the heat and make the best time you can. Follow signs for Madrid/Jaen/N323 into what some call the Spanish Nebraska—La Mancha. After Puerto Lapice, you'll see the Toledo exit.

View the city from many angles along the Circumvalación road across the Tejo Gorge. Drive to Parador Conde de Orgaz just south of town for the view (from the balcony) El Greco made famous in his portrait of Toledo.

Enter Toledo by the north gate and park in the open-air guarded lot (cheap but not safe overnight) or in one of two garages. The garage just past the Alcázar is easy and as central as you need (1,200 ptas/24 hrs). You can usually park free in the lot just down the street from the garage or in the huge dirt lot below and behind the Santa Cruz Museum.

Toledo to Madrid (40 miles, 1 hr): It's a speedy *autovía* north, past one last bullboard, to Madrid. The highways converge into M30, which circles Madrid. Follow it to the left ("*Nor y Oeste*") and take the Plaza de España exit to get back to Gran Vía. If you're airport bound, keep heading into Madrid until you see the airplane symbol (N-II). Turn in your rental car at terminal T-1.

GRANADA

For a time, Granada was the grandest city in Spain; but in the end, it was left in the historic dust. Today it's a provincial town with more than its share of history and bumper stickers reading "Life is short. Don't run." We'll keep things fun and simple, settling down in the old center and exploring monuments of the Moorish civilization and monuments of its conquest. And we'll taste the treats of an African-flavored culture that survives today.

Granada's magnificent Alhambra fortress was the last stronghold of the Moorish kingdom in Spain. The city's exotically tangled Moorish quarter bustles under the grand Alhambra, which glows red in the evening while locals stroll, enjoying the city's cool late-night charms.

There is an old saying: "Give him a coin, woman, for there is nothing worse in this life than to be blind in Granada." This city has much to see, yet it reveals itself in unpredictable ways. It takes a poet to sort through the jigsaw-puzzle pieces of Granada. Peer through the intricate lattice of a Moorish window. Hear water burbling, sight unseen, among the labyrinthine hedges of the Generalife garden. Listen to a flute trilling deep in the swirl of alleys around the cathedral. Don't be blind in Granada—open your senses.

Planning Your Time
Granada is worth one day and two nights. Consider the night train connection with Madrid (or Barcelona), giving the city a night and a day. The Costa del Sol's best beach town, Nerja, is just two quick hours away (by bus), postcard-perfect white hill towns like Ronda are three hours (bus or train), and Sevilla is an easy four-hour train ride.

In the morning, tour the cathedral and Royal Chapel (both closed roughly 13:00–16:00) and stroll the pedestrian-zone shopping scene. Do the Alhambra in the early evening (during peak season, reserve ahead; see "Sights—Granada's Alhambra," below). Be at the Albaicín viewpoint for sunset and then wander the Moorish Quarter (Albaicín) until you find the right place for a suitably late dinner.

Orientation

While modern Granada sprawls (300,000 people), its sights are all within a 20-minute walk of Plaza Nueva, where dogs wag their tails to the rhythm of the street musicians. Nearly all my recommended hotels are within a few blocks of Plaza Nueva. Make this the hub of your Granada.

Plaza Nueva was a main square back when kings called Granada home. This historic center is in the Darro River Valley, which separates two hills: one with the great Moorish palace, the Alhambra; and the other with the best-preserved Moorish quarter in Spain, the Albaicín. To the southeast are the cathedral, Royal Chapel, and Alcaicería (Moorish market), where the city's two main drags, Gran Vía de Colón and Calle Reyes Católicos, come together. Calle Reyes Católicos leads into the modern city.

Tourist Information

There are three TIs. The handiest—in the courtyard of what was a Moorish hotel 500 years ago—is at Corral del Carbon (Mon–Sat 9:00–19:00, Sun 10:00–14:00; from Plaza Isabel la Católica, take Reyes Católicos in the opposite direction from Alhambra, take first left, walk through keyhole arch, tel. 95-822-5990). Another TI is near Puerta Real on Plaza de Mariana Pineda (Mon–Fri 9:30–19:00, Sat 10:00–14:00, tel. 95-822-6688). Both of these TIs have shorter hours off-season. Get the free Granada map and verify your Alhambra plans. Check the posted bus and train schedules. The other TI is at the Alhambra.

Arrival in Granada

By Train: Granada's train station is connected to the center by frequent buses or a 20-minute walk down Avenida Constitución and Gran Vía de Colón. Taxis are cheap (500 ptas to the center). The train station has lockers.

Exiting the train station, walk straight ahead down the tree-lined road. At the first major intersection (Avenida de la Constitución), you'll see the bus stop on your right. Take buses #9 or #11 and confirm by asking the driver, "*¿Catedral?*" (kat-ay-dral; the nearest stop to Plaza Nueva). Buy your ticket (120 ptas) from the driver. Get off when you see the fountain of Plaza Isabel la Católica in front of the bus at the stop near the cathedral; cross the busy Gran Vía and walk two blocks to Plaza Nueva.

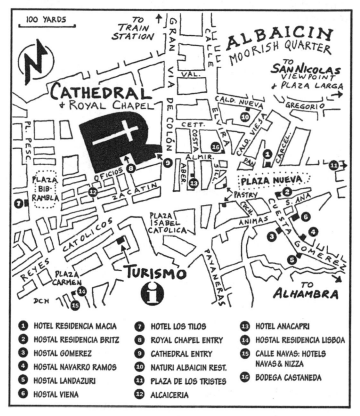

By Bus: Granada's main bus station, where all long-distance buses stop, is a bus or taxi ride from the center (station tel. 95-818-5010). To get to the city center, take bus #3 (120 ptas) and get off just after turning right through the Plaza Isabel la Católica (with the fountain) at the stop opposite the cathedral. Plaza Nueva is two blocks east.

By Car: Driving in Granada's historic center is restricted to buses, taxis, and tourists with hotel reservations (tell the police officer). The *autovía* (freeway) circles the city with a *circumvalación* road. To reach Plaza Nueva, take exit #132, direction "*Centro, Recogidas.*" Calle Recogidas leads directly into the heart of town. There will probably be a police block at Puerta Real (Victoria Hotel). Ask here for Plaza Nueva. Double-park at Plaza Nueva long enough to get directions to a parking garage near your hotel (but, considering the risk of both police and thieves, don't leave your car unattended).

Getting around Granada

With such cheap taxis and nearly all points of interest an easy walk from Plaza Nueva, you may not even need the buses. You'd be most likely to hop a bus to/from the train or bus stations, to/from the Alhambra, and for the circuit around Albaicín. You buy bus tickets (120 ptas) from the driver. Sharable *bonobus* strips of 15 tickets costs 1,000 ptas (buy at tobacco shop or on bus).

Helpful Hints

When you see women wanting to give you leaves or flowers, avoid them like the plague.

Bus/Train Tickets: To save yourself a trip to the train station or bus station, get schedule information from the TI or a travel agency. Most travel agencies sell long-distance bus or train tickets (generally open Mon–Fri 9:30–13:30, 17:00–20:00, Sat 9:00–13:30, closed Sun; Viajes Bonanza is handy at Reyes Católicos 30, tel. 95-822-9777).

Post Office: The PO is on Puerta Real (Mon–Fri 8:30–20:30, Sat 9:00–13:00, tel. 95-822-2000).

American Express: Amex is across from the main TI (Reyes Católicos 31, tel. 95-822-4512).

Internet Access: Madar Internet is at Calderia Nueva 12, amid *teterias* (tea shops) and two blocks off the Plaza Nueva (400 ptas/hr, Mon–Sat 10:00–24:00, Sun 12:00–24:00).

Festivals: From late June to mid-July the International Festival of Music and Dance offers some of the world's best classical music in the Alhambra at reasonable prices.

Local Guide: Margarita Landazuri is a local guide who speaks English, knows how to teach, and has reasonable rates (tel. 95-822-1406). If she's busy, her partner, Miguel Angel, is also good.

Sights—Granada's Alhambra

This last and greatest Moorish palace is one of Europe's top sights. Attracting up to 8,000 visitors a day, it's the reason most tourists come to Granada. Nowhere else does the splendor of Moorish civilization shine so brightly.

The last Moorish stronghold in Europe is, with all due respect, really a symbol of retreat. Granada was only a regional capital for centuries. Gradually the Christian Reconquista moved south, taking Córdoba (1236) and Sevilla (1248). The Moors held Granada until 1492. As you tour their grand palace, remember that while Europe slumbered through the Dark Ages, Moorish magnificence blossomed—busy stucco, plaster "stalactites," colors galore, scalloped windows framing Granada views, exuberant gardens, and water, water everywhere. Water—so rare and precious in most of the Islamic world—was the purest symbol of life to the Moors. The Alhambra is decorated with water: standing still, cascading, masking secret conversations, and drip-dropping playfully.

Getting there: There are three ways to get to the Alhambra.

1. From Plaza Nueva, hike 20 minutes up the street Cuesta de Gomerez. Keep going straight, with the Alhambra high on your left, and follow the street to the ticket pavilion at the far side of the Alhambra, near the Generalife garden.

2. Catch the red minibus marked "Alhambra-Neptuno" from Plaza Nueva (120 ptas, every 15 min).

3. Take a taxi (400 ptas, taxi stand on Plaza Nueva).

Don't drive. If you do, you'll park on the far, far side of the Alhambra, and when you leave, one-way streets will send you into the traffic-clogged center of new Granada.

Cost: While Charles V's Palace is free, the Alcazaba fort, Moorish palace (Palacios Nazaries), and Generalife gardens require a combo ticket that costs 1,000 ptas.

Getting Tickets: There are a number of different ways to snare a ticket. You can buy your ticket at the main Alhambra ticket office (daily 8:30–19:00, Generalife entrance near parking lot). Or you can get a ticket from the BBV Bank in town (Banco Bilbao Vizcaya, Mon–Fri 9:00–14:00, Plaza Isabel la Católica, 125-ptas surcharge) or from any BBV bank in any city in Spain. Or you can reserve by phone (at least 2 days or as much as a year in advance, CC:VM, 125 ptas surcharge, tel. 90-222-4460), pay by credit card, and get a reference number that will allow you to pick up your ticket at any BBV Bank (a minimum of a day before your visit) or at the main Alhambra entrance (at least 2 hours before your visit).

Only 400 visitors per half hour are allowed in the Moorish palace (Palacios Nazaries). Your 30-minute time span is printed on your ticket; it's possible to request a particular half hour when you pay. While you must enter the Palacios Nazaries within this time, once inside you may linger as long as you like. You can visit the rest of the Alhambra before or after your visit to the Palacios Nazaries.

Hours: The Alhambra is open daily from 8:30 to 20:00 (closes in winter at 18:00). The ticket office closes one hour early or when 8,300 tickets have been sold for the day. During peak season and festival times the day's allotment can sell by 13:00 (but on my last visit, I arrived at 18:00 on a mid-July Saturday, went in immediately, and had the normally packed palace all to myself). Avoid arriving as it opens—when countless tour groups also arrive. In peak season, try to snag a ticket in advance (from BBV Bank or by phone; see above), or consider arriving at the Alhambra by 13:00, before tickets are sold out. You may have up to a two- or three-hour wait before your

Alhambra

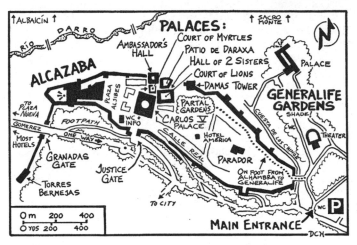

"appointment" to enter the Palacios Nazaries. This time is easily consumed at the fort, garden, museums in Charles V's Palace, or parador bar. While drinks, WCs, and guidebooks ring the Palacios Nazaries, you'll find none inside.

Guidebook: Consider the helpful guidebook *The Alhambra and the Generalife*, available at the souvenir shops across from Charles V's Palace (600 ptas, great layout plan included), or buy it in town and read it the night before. It's easy to get disoriented. Take time to understand the layout and history of this remarkable sight before entering.

Alhambra by moonlight: For maximum palace magic, enjoy a late-night visit (Tue, Thu, and Sat 22:00–23:30; 20:00–22:00 in winter). The late-night visits include only the Moorish palace and not the fort or garden—but hey, the palace is 80 percent of the Alhambra thrills, and by moonlight there's no waiting or obnoxious crowds.

The Alhambra in Four Parts

The Alhambra—not nearly as confusing as it is—consists of four sights: Charles V's Palace (free, Christian Renaissance palace plopped on top of the Alhambra after the reconquest), the Alcazaba (empty old fort), the Palacios Nazaries (exquisite Moorish palace), and the Generalife (garden).

1. Charles V's Palace—It's only natural for a conquering king to build his own palace over his foe's palace—and that's exactly what the Christian king Charles V did. The Alhambra palace wasn't

Palacios Nazaries

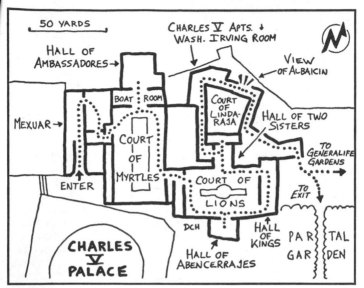

the entrance. The walls, even without their original paint and gilding, are still glorious.

In 1492 two historic events took place in this room. After 700 years the Reconquista was completed as the last Moorish king, Boabdil, signed the terms of his surrender here before packing up and fleeing to Africa. Later, Isabel and Ferdinand received Columbus in this room. Imagine the scene: The king and queen with the greatest minds of the University of Salamanca gathered here to hear Columbus make his case that the world was round—then a still-loony notion that got people burned a few years earlier. Ferdinand and the professors laughed, calling Columbus "mad." But Isabel said *"Sí, señor."* Columbus fell to his knees and promised, "You will be called the Queen of the New World."

Continue deeper into the palace to a court where, 600 years ago, only the royal family and their servants could enter. It's the much-photographed...

Court of the Lions: The Patio de los Leones features a fountain with 12 lions. Why 12? Perhaps because the fountain was a gift from a Jew (representing the 12 tribes of Israel) celebrating good relations with the sultan. Some claim the lions represent the signs of the zodiac or months of the year. During Moorish times, perhaps the fountain functioned as a kind of calendar or even a clock, with only the current lion spouting water. From the center, good enough for Charles, so he built this one—destroying the dramatic Alhambra facade and financing his new palace with a sa on-the-wound tax on Granada's defeated Moorish population. This palace, the most impressive Renaissance building you'll see in Spain, was designed by Pedro Machuca, a devotee of Michelangelo and Raphael. Stand in the circular courtyard then climb the stairs. Imagine being here for one of Charles' bullfights. Inside the palace you'll find two free, but boring, museums: the Museo de Bellas Artes (9:00–20:00, closed Sun afternoon, all day Mon, Tue morning) and the Museo de Alhambra, showing off some of the Alhambra's best Moorish art (Tue–Sat 9:00–14:30).

2. Alcazaba—The fort is the oldest and most ruined part of the Alhambra. What you see is mid-13th century, but there was probably a fort here in Roman times. It's basically a tower offering some exercise and a great city view. From the top find Plaza Nueva, the Albaicín viewpoint, and the mountains. Is anybody skiing today? Look to the south and think of that day in 1492 when the cross and flags of Aragon and Castille were raised on this tower and the fleeing Moorish King Boabdil looked back and wept. His mom chewed him out, saying, "Don't weep like a woman for what you couldn't defend like a man." Much later, Napoleon stationed his troops here, contributing substantially to its ruin when he left. Follow the arrows down and around to the....

3. Palacios Nazaries—During the 30-minute window of time stamped on your ticket, enter the jewel of the Alhambra: the Moorish royal palace. Built mostly in the 14th century, this is our best possible look at the refined and elegant Moorish civilization of Al-Andalus. If you can mentally paint the stucco and imagine a few tapestries, carpets, pillows, and some ivory-studded wooden furniture, the place is much as it was for the Moorish kings. Remember the palace themes: water, no images, "stalactite" ceilings throughout—and no signs telling you where you are.

    Court of Myrtles: Walk through a few administrative rooms (the *mexuar*) until you hit a big rectangular courtyard with a pond lined by a myrtle bush hedge and a fountain at each end. This is the Court of Myrtles (Patio de los Arrayanes).

    Head left (north) from the entry into the long, narrow antechamber to the throne room, called the "Boat Room." While it's understandable that many think this is named for the upside-down hull shape of its fine cedar ceiling, the name is actually a corruption of the Arab word *baraka*, meaning "divine blessing a luck." This was the waiting room for meetings with the sultan, blessings and luck are exactly what you'd need lots of if you had business in the next room. Oh, it's your turn now....

    The fine, stately **Hall of the Ambassadors (Grand Salon Embajadores)** functioned like a throne room. It was here that the sultan received foreign emissaries. The king's throne stood oppo streams went figuratively to the four corners of the earth and literally to various apartments of the royal family. Notice how it looks, with its 124 columns, like the cloister of a Catholic monastery. Six hundred years ago the Muslim Moors could read the Koranic poetry that ornaments this court, and they could understand the symbolism of this lush, enclosed garden (considered the embodiment of paradise or truth). Imagine—they enjoyed this part of the palace even more than we do today.

On the right, off the courtyard, is a square room called the **Hall of the Abencerrajes (Sala de los Abencerrajes)**. According to legend, the father of Boabdil took a new wife and wanted to disinherit the children of his first marriage—one of whom was Boabdil. In order to deny power to Boabdil and his siblings, he killed nearly the entire pro-Boabdil Abencerrage family. The sultan thought this would pave the way for the son of his new wife to be the next sultan. Happily, he stacked 36 Abencerrage heads in the pool under this sumptuous honeycombed stucco ceiling. But his scheme failed, and Boabdil ultimately assumed the throne. Bloody power struggles like this were the norm here in the Alhambra.

The **Hall of the Kings (Sala de los Reyes)** is at the end of the court opposite where you entered. Notice the ceilings of the three chambers branching off this gallery. Paintings on leather depict scenes of the sultan and his family. The center room shows a portrait of the first 10 of the Alhambra's 22 sultans. The scene is a fantasy, since these people lived over a span of many generations. The two end rooms show scenes of princely pastimes, such as hunting and shooting skeet. In a palace otherwise devoid of figures, these offer a rare look at royal life in the palace. The artistry of the paintings is uncertain, perhaps Christian, Moorish, or Xian, dating sometime before 1492.

The next room, the **Hall of the Two Sisters**, named for the two great stone slabs that flank the fountain, has another oh-wow stucco ceiling but no figures—only geometric patterns and stylized Arabic script quoting verses from the Koran.

That's about it for the palace. From here you wander through a few more rooms including one (marked with a large plaque) where Washington Irving wrote *Tales of the Alhambra*. While serving as the U.S. ambassador to Spain in 1829, Irving lived in the Alhambra... and dreamt up his "tales."

Stop at the open-air hallway for the best-in-the-palace view of the labyrinthine Albaicín—the old Moorish town on the opposite hillside. Find the famous viewpoint at the base of the white St. Nicolás church tower breaking the horizon. Creeping into the mountains on the right are the Gypsy neighborhoods of Sacromonte.

Leaving the Palacios Nazaries you walk through a garden and follow signs directing you left to the Generalife or right to the exit.

4. Generalife—On the hillside to the east, the garden with carefully pruned hedges is the Generalife (henneraw-LEEF-ay). This most perfect Arabian garden in Andalucía was the summer home of the Moorish kings, the closest thing on earth to the Koran's description of heaven. If you have a long wait before your entry to the Palacios, tour these gardens first.

Sights—Central Granada

▲Royal Chapel (Capilla Real)—Without a doubt Granada's top Christian sight, this lavish chapel holds the dreams—and bodies—of Queen Isabel and King Ferdinand (300 ptas, Mon–Sat 10:30–13:00, 16:00–19:00, Sun 11:00–13:00, 16:00–19:00; Oct–Mar Mon–Sat 10:30–13:00, 15:30–18:30, closed Sun; entrance on Calle Oficios).

In the lobby notice the painting of Boabdil giving the key of Granada to the conquering King Ferdinand. Boabdil wanted to fall to his knees, but the Spanish king, who had great respect for his Moorish foe, embraced him instead. They fought a long and noble war (for instance, respectfully returning the bodies of dead soldiers). Ferdinand is in red, and Isabel is behind him in white and blue. Behind her (under a black hood) is their daughter Juana. And behind her, wearing a crown, is Juana's husband, Philip the Fair. Philip died young, and for two years Juana kept his casket at her bedside, kissing his embalmed body good night. These four people are buried in this chapel. The painting is flanked by two large portraits of Ferdinand and Isabel.

Isabel decided to make Granada the capital of Spain (and burial place for Spanish royalty) for three reasons: 1) with the conquest of Granada, Christianity had overcome Islam in Europe; 2) her marriage with Ferdinand, followed by the conquest of Granada, had marked the beginning of a united Spain; and 3) Granada had been the departure point for Columbus.

Step into the **chapel**. It's Plateresque Gothic—light and lacy, named for and inspired by the fine silverwork of the Moors. This was the most lavish interior money could buy 500 years ago. Because of its speedy completion, the chapel is an unusually harmonious piece of architecture.

The four **royal tombs** are Renaissance style. Carved in Italy in 1521 out of Carrara marble, they were sent by ship to Spain. The faces—based on death masks—are considered accurate. If you're facing the altar, Ferdinand and Isabel are on the right. (Isabel fans attribute the bigger dent she puts in the pillow to brains.) Philip the Fair and Juana are on the left. (Mounted? No, just holding hands.) Philip was a Habsburg. Their son, Charles V, was a key character in European history, as his coronation merged the Holy Roman Empire (Habsburg domain) with the Spanish empire. Europe's top king, he ruled a vast empire stretching from Budapest to Bolivia (1519–1556).

When the son of Charles V decided to build El Escorial and establish Madrid as the single capital of a single Spain, Granada lost power and importance.

More important, Spain declined. After Charles V, Spain squandered her awesome wealth trying to maintain this impossible empire—not for material riches but to defend the romantic Quixote-esque dream of a Catholic empire ruled by one divinely ordained Catholic monarch against an irrepressible tide of nationalism and Protestantism. Spain's relatively poor modern history can be blamed, in part, by her stubborn unwillingness to accept the end of this "old regime" notion.

Look at the fine carving on the tombs (unfortunately vandalized by Napoleon's troops). It's a humanistic statement with healthy, organic, realistic figures rising above the strict and heavy Gothic past.

From the feet of the marble tombs, step downstairs to see the actual coffins. They are very plain. Isabel was originally buried as a simple monk at the Franciscan monastery (in what is today the Parador at the Alhambra). The fifth coffin (with PM on it) is that of a young Prince Michael, who would have been king of a united Spain and Portugal. A sad—but too-long—story....

The **high altar** is one of the finest Renaissance works in Spain. It's dedicated to John the Baptist and John the Evangelist. (Both Ferdinand's and Isabel's fathers were Johns.) In the center, you can see the Baptist and the Evangelist chatting as if over tapas (an appropriately humanist scene). Scenes from the Baptist's life are on the left: John beheaded after Salome's fine dancing and (below) John baptizing Jesus. Scenes from the Evangelist's life are on the right: John's martyrdom (a failed attempt to boil him alive in oil) and John on Patmos (where he wrote the last book of the Bible, Revelation). John is talking to the eagle that, according to legend, flew him to Heaven.

Anyone who paid for church art got their mug in it. Find Ferdinand and Isabel kneeling in prayer on either far side. The eagle banners around the room are not the aggressive, two-headed, claws-exposed Habsburg eagles but eagles with halos (and crowns for bras). These are symbolic of the eagle that inspired John on Patmos.

The Plateresque (silver-filigree-style) arch leads to a small glass pyramid in the **treasury**. This holds the silver crown of Queen Isabel, ringed by pomegranates (symbolizing Granada), and the sword of Ferdinand. Beside the Plateresque entry arch you'll see an old book. This was the devout Isabel's prayer book, in which she followed the Mass. The book and its sturdy box date from 1496. The fancy box on the other side of the door is the one that Isabel (cash-poor because of her military expenses) filled with jewels and gave Columbus. Columbus sold these to finance his journey. Next, in the corner (and also behind glass), is the cross Cardinal Mendoza carried into the Alhambra on that historic day in 1492. Next, the big silk, silver, and gold tapestry is the altar banner for the mobile campaign chapel of Ferdinand and Isabel, who always traveled with their army. In the next case you'll see the original Christian army flags raised over the Alhambra in 1492.

The room holds the first great art collection ever established by a woman. Queen Isabel amassed more than 200 great paintings. After Napoleon, only 30 remain. Even so, this is a fine collection, all on wood, featuring works by Botticelli, Perugino, the Flemish master Memling, and less-famous Spanish masters.

Finally, at the end of the room, the two carved portraits of Ferdinand and Isabel were the originals from the high altar. Charles V considered them primitive and replaced these with the ones you saw earlier.

Cathedral—The only Renaissance church in Spain, Granada's cathedral is the second-largest in Spain after Sevilla's. Its spacious and bright interior is a refreshing break from the dark Gothic and gilded-lily Baroque of so many Spanish churches. In a modern move back in the 18th century, the choir walls were taken out so that people could be involved in the worship. To make matters even better, an 18th-century bishop ordered the interior painted with lime (for hygienic reasons during a time of disease). The people liked it, and it stayed white. Most of the side chapels are decorated in Baroque style. On the far wall (right of the high altar) is St. James the Moorslayer, with his sword raised high and an armored Moor under his horse's hooves. The Renaissance facade and paintings of the Virgin in the rotunda are by Granada's own Alonso Cano (1601–1661) and can be lit by dropping a coin in the box (300 ptas, Mon–Sat 10:30–13:30, 16:00–19:00, Sun 16:00–19:00; Oct–Mar Mon–Sat 10:30–13:30, closed Sun; entrance off Gran Vía de Colón).

Alcaicería—Originally an Arab silk market, this neighborhood (around the cathedral) still functions as a silk and jewelry market. Ignore the obnoxious Gypsy women giving tourists sprigs of rosemary for good luck. (The flowers they used to give became too expensive. After somehow rerouting the magic power, they now use rosemary, which comes from the parks—for free.) By accepting the sprig you start a relationship. This, while free, leads to palm reading, which isn't.

Explore the mesh of tiny shopping lanes between the cathedral and Calle Reyes Católicos. Go on a photo and sound safari: popcorn machines popping, men selling balloons, leather goods spread out on streets, kids playing soccer, the whirring grind of knife sharpeners in shops, barking dogs, dogged shoeshine boys.

The colorful square behind the cathedral is **Bib-Rambla**. While fine for a coffee and fragrant with flower stalls today, in

Moorish times this was a place of public execution. The small
Mercado Municipal is liveliest on Saturday, spilling out into the
nearby streets (off Plaza Romanilla, best in mornings until 14:00,
closed Sun).

▲**Plaza Isabel la Católica**—Granada's two grand boulevards,
Gran Vía and Reyes Católicos, meet a block off Plaza Nueva at
Plaza Isabel la Católica. Here you'll see a fine statue of Columbus
unfurling a long contract with Isabel. It lists the terms of Columbus'
MCDXCII voyage.

Isabel was driven by her desire to spread Catholicism. Columbus was driven by his desire for money. For adding territory to
Spain's Catholic empire, she promised Columbus the ranks of Admiral of the Oceans and Governor of the New World. To sweeten
the pie, she tossed in 10 percent of all the riches he brought home.
Isabel died thinking Columbus had found India or China. Columbus
died poor and disillusioned.

From here, Reyes Católicos leads to Puerta Real. There
Acera de Darro takes you through modern Granada to the river
via the huge El Corte Inglés department store and lots of modern
commerce.

Paseo de los Tristes—In the cool of the evening, consider strolling the Paseo de los Tristes ("walk of the sad ones"—the route of
funeral processions to the cemetery at the edge of town). Start at
Plaza Nueva. The Church of Santa Anna, which stands at the far
end of the square, was originally a mosque, its tower a minaret.
Notice the ceramic brickwork. This is Mudejar art, the technique
of the Moors used by Christians. Inside you'll see a fine Alhambra-
style cedar ceiling. Follow Carrera del Darro along the River Darro
under the Alhambra. (Nine kilometers upstream, part of the Darro
is diverted to provide water for the Alhambra's many fountains.)
On the left you'll pass the Arab Baths (Tue–Sat 10:00–14:00) and
the Convent de Santa Catalina de Zafra, a home of cloistered nuns
(they worship behind a screen that divides the church's rich interior
in half). On the right, across from the Archeological Museum, is
the Church of San Pedro, the parish church of Sacromonte's Gypsy
community. Within its rich interior is an ornate oxcart used to
carry the Holy Host on the annual pilgrimage to Rocio near Portugal. Finally, you reach the Plaza de los Tristes. Covered with happy
diners, this is a great spot at night, under the floodlit Alhambra.
From here the road arches up (past a rank of "burro taxis" for those
into adventure sports) into Sacromonte. And from here a lane
(called Cuesta de los Chinos or Carretera del Rey Chico) leads up
to the Alhambra "through the back door."

Arab Baths—Consider a visit to the Arab baths at Baños Arabes
Al Andaluz. Popular with local Muslims, the soak and a massage
costs 2,400 ptas (open late, co-ed with swimsuits, just off Plaza
Nueva at Santa Ana 16, tel. 95-822-9978).

Sights—Albaicín

This is the best old Moorish quarter in Spain, with countless colorful corners, flowery patios, and shady lanes to soothe the 20th-century-mangled visitor. Climb high to the San Nicolás church for the best view of the Alhambra. Then wander through the mysterious backstreets.

A handy city minibus threads its way around the Albaicín from Plaza Nueva (4/hrly, makes a circle in 20 minutes; buy ticket from driver for 120 ptas). It gets you scenically and sweatlessly to the St. Nicolás viewpoint. You can also taxi to the St. Nicolás church and explore from there. Consider having your cabbie take you on a Sacromonte detour en route.

If walking up, leave the west end of Plaza Nueva on Calle Elvira then turn right on Calderería Nueva. Follow this stepped street past tapas bars and *teterias* (see "Eating," below) as it goes left around the church, slants, winds, and zigzags up the hill, heading basically straight. (Resist the temptation to turn left on Muladar Sancha.) Near the crest, turn right on Camino Nuevo de San Nicolás, then walk several blocks to the street that curves up left, leading to the steps up to the church's viewpoint.

San Nicolás Viewpoint: For one of Europe's most romantic viewpoints, be here at sunset when the Alhambra turns red and the Albaicín widows share the benches with local lovers and tourists. In 1997 President Clinton made a point to bring his family here—a favorite spot from a trip he made as a student. Many now know this as "The Clinton Mirador."

(If you want a more private mirador, consider Plaza de Carvajales, below San Nicolás. From the top of the teahouse street, at Placeta de la Cruz Verde, jog right then left to a tiny wooded square with grand Alhambra views and local kids rolling joints and playing cards.)

Exploring the Albaicín: From the San Nicolás viewpoint you're at the edge of a neighborhood even people of Granada recognize as a world apart. From the viewpoint turn your back to the Alhambra and walk north (passing the church on your right and the Biblioteca Municipal on your left). A lane leads past a white arch—now a chapel built into the old Moorish wall. At the end of the lane, step down to the right through the 11th-century "New Gate" (Puerta Nueva—older than the Alhambra) and into **Plaza Larga.** In medieval times this tiny square (called "large" because back then it was) was the local marketplace. It still is a busy market each morning, with locals blaring their cheap, pirated cassettes as if to prove there is actually music on them. Casa Pasteles, at the end of the square, serves some of the best coffee and cakes in town. From Plaza Larga, Calle del Agua (named for the public baths that used to line it) shows evidence of the Moorish plumbing system. Back when Europe's streets were filled with muck,

Albaicín Neighborhood

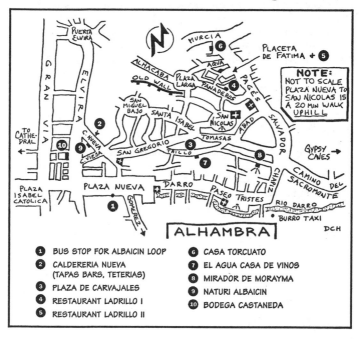

NOTE: NOT TO SCALE PLAZA NUEVA TO SAN NICOLAS IS A 20 MIN WALK UPHILL

- ❶ BUS STOP FOR ALBAICIN LOOP
- ❷ CALDERERIA NUEVA (TAPAS BARS, TETERIAS)
- ❸ PLAZA DE CARVAJALES
- ❹ RESTAURANT LADRILLO I
- ❺ RESTAURANT LADRILLO II
- ❻ CASA TORCUATO
- ❼ EL AGUA CASA DE VINOS
- ❽ MIRADOR DE MORAYMA
- ❾ NATURI ALBAICIN
- ❿ BODEGA CASTANEDA

Granada actually had Roman Empire–style gutters with drains leading to clay and lead pipes.

This is the heart of the Albaicín. Poke into an old church. They're plain by design—to go easy on the Muslim converts who weren't used to being surrounded by images as they worshiped. You'll see lots of real Muslim culture living in the streets, including many recent Spanish converts. Those aren't the Spice Girls, just Gypsy teenagers—as influenced as any teenagers these days by TV.

Sights—Sacromonte and Granada's Gypsies

Spain's Gypsies came from India via Egypt. The Spanish word for Gypsy, *Gitano*, means "Egyptian." They settled mostly in the south, where they found people less racist and more tolerant. Ages ago a Spanish king, exasperated by Gypsy problems, actually declared that these nomads must stay in one place and get a religion—any religion. In most of Spain, Gypsies are more assimilated into the general community, but Granada's Sacromonte district is a large and distinct Gypsy community. Granada's Gypsies arrived in the 16th century and have stuck together ever since.

Local Spaniards, who consider themselves accepting and not racist, claim that in maintaining such a tight community, the Gypsies segregate themselves. The Gypsies call Spaniards *Payo* ("whites").

Sacromonte is served by one main street. Camino del Sacromonte is lined with caves primed for tourists and restaurants ready to fight over the bill. At the beginning of the street, notice the statue of a Gypsy "king"—actually a wise community elder—in traditional attire.

Formerly Europe's most disgusting tourist trap, famous for its cave-dwelling, foot-stomping, flamenco-dancing Gypsies, Sacromonte was dead for years. But it's making a comeback, with more reputable music and dance evenings. You can ask at the TI about flamenco (and personal safety), but I'd save flamenco for Sevilla.

Sights—Near Granada

Carthusian Monastery (La Cartuja)—A church with an interior that looks as if it squirted out of a can of whipped cream, La Cartuja is nicknamed the "Christian Alhambra" for its elaborate white Baroque stucco work. In the rooms just off the cloister, notice the gruesome paintings of martyrs placidly meeting their grisly fate. It's located a mile out of town on the way to Madrid—go north on Gran Vía and follow the signs or take bus #8 from Gran Vía (300 ptas, daily 10:00–13:00, 16:00–20:00, shorter hours Sun morning and Oct–Mar).

Sleeping in Granada
(160 ptas = about $1)

Sleep Code: **S** = Single, **D** = Double/Twin, **T** = Triple, **Q** = Quad, **b** = bathroom, **t** = toilet only, **s** = shower only, **CC** = Credit Card (Visa, MasterCard, Amex), **SE** = Speaks English, **NSE** = No English. Breakfast and the 7 percent IVA tax are not included.

In July and August, when the streets are littered with sunstroke victims, rooms are plentiful. Hotels get booked up fast September through November. Call ahead. Except for the Alhambra listings, all recommended hotels are within a five-minute walk of Plaza Nueva. While almost none of the hotels have their own parking facilities, all can direct you to a garage.

Hotels on or near Plaza Nueva
(zip code: 18009)

Hotel Residencia Macia, right on the colorful Plaza Nueva, is a clean, modern, classy, and hotelesque place. Three-quarters of its 44 rooms have air-conditioning, and all have a TV and a phone. Choose between an on-the-square view or a quiet interior room (Sb-6,375 ptas, Db-9,600 ptas, Tb-13,440 ptas, 1,000 ptas less without air-con, show this book upon arrival to get a 10 percent discount, good buffet breakfast for 700 ptas, CC:VMA, elevator,

Plaza Nueva 4, tel. 95-822-7536, fax 95-822-7533, e-mail: maciaplaza@maciahoteles.com, SE).

Hotel Anacapri is a bright, cool, marble oasis with modern rooms and a quiet lounge (Sb-8,000–10,000 ptas, Db-12,000–14,000 ptas, CC:VMA, elevator, air-con, 2 blocks toward Gran Vía from Plaza Nueva at Calle Joaquin Costa 7, tel. 95-822-7477, fax 95-822-8909, e-mail: acapri@batch-pc.es, SE).

Palacio de Santa Ines is a plush and mysterious old palace buried in the Moorish quarter four blocks from Plaza Nueva. The five doubles and five Alhambra-view suites surround a peaceful Mudejar courtyard. Just like they advertise, you get 20th-century comfort in 16th-century ambience—and just like you might expect, they can be real snobs (Db-13,750–16,500 ptas, Db suite-20,000–30,000 ptas, CC:VMA, air-con, from Plaza Nueva walk up Carrera del Darro, left on Cuesta Santa Ines to #9, tel. 95-822-2362, fax 95-822-2465, NSE).

Hotel Gran Vía, right on Granada's main drag, has Euro-modern business-class rooms and easy garage parking for 1,400 ptas per day (Db-10,500–12,000 ptas, CC:VMA, 5-minute walk from Plaza Nueva, Gran Vía de Colón 25, tel. 95-828-5464, fax 95-828-5591, e-mail: granvia@maciahoteles.com, SE).

Cheaper Places on or near Plaza Nueva
(zip code: 18009)
Most of these are on Cuesta de Gomerez, the street leading from Plaza Nueva up to the Alhambra.

Hostal Landazuri, run by friendly, English-speaking Matilda Landazuri and her son Manolo, is ramshackle but lovingly decorated and homey. It has a great roof garden with an Alhambra view and a hardworking, helpful management (S-2,200 ptas, Sb-3,700 ptas, D-3,200 ptas, Db-4,000 ptas, T-4,200 ptas, Tb-5,200 ptas, simple 225-ptas breakfast or their hearty 650-ptas English breakfast, Cuesta de Gomerez 24, tel. & fax 95-822-1406). The Landazuris also run a good, cheap café.

Hostal Residencia Britz is a simple, no-nonsense place located right on Plaza Nueva. It has an elevator and some questionable beds (S-2,300 ptas, Sb-4,500 ptas, D-3,700 ptas, Db-5,200 ptas, coin-op washing machine, CC:VM, Plaza Nueva y Gomerez 1, tel. & fax 95-822-3652, NSE).

Hostal Navarro Ramos is shiny and well assembled but has almost no warmth or character (15 rooms, S-1,650 ptas, D-2,600 ptas, Db-4,000 ptas, Tb-5,300 ptas, Cuesta de Gomerez 21, tel. 95-825-0555, NSE).

Hostal Viena, run by English-speaking Austrian Irene ("ee-RAY-nay"), is on a quieter side street with basic backpacker-type rooms (S-2,500 ptas, Sb-3,500 ptas, D-3,500–4,000 ptas, Db-5,000 ptas, larger rooms for families and groups, CC:VM,

Hospital de Santa Ana 2, 10 meters off Cuesta de Gomerez, tel. & fax 95-822-1859, e-mail: austria@arrakis.es). Irene also manages the similar **Hotel Austria** nearby.

Hostal Gomerez is run by English-speaking Sigfrido Sanchez de León de Torres (who will explain to you how Spanish surnames work if you've got the time). Clean and basic and listed in nearly every country's student-travel guidebook, this is a fine cheapie (S-1,600 ptas, D-2,700 ptas, T-3,700 ptas, Q-4,200 ptas, laundry service, Cuesta de Gomerez 10, one floor up, tel. 95-822-4437).

Pension Venecia is a perfect student pension run by kind Mary Carmen and Sergio. Rooms are basic, clean, and tastefully decorated (S-1,800 ptas, D-3,000 ptas, T-4,500 ptas, Cuesta de Gomerez 2, 2nd floor, CC:VM, tel. 95-822-3987, NSE).

Sleeping near Plaza Carmen
Two blocks from the TI is the pleasant Plaza Carmen and the beginning of Calle Navas, a pedestrian street offering several good values.

Hotel Residencia Lisboa, which overlooks Plaza Carmen opposite Granada's city hall, offers 28 well-maintained, spacious rooms with firm beds and friendly, helpful owners but no public rooms (D-3,900 ptas, Db-5,600 ptas, includes tax, CC:VM, elevator, Plaza de Carmen 27, tel. 95-822-1413, fax 95-822-1487).

Hotel Navas, a block down Calle Navas, is a modern, well-run, business-class hotel with spacious, stately rooms (Db-11,500 ptas, breakfast buffet-800 ptas, CC:VMA, air-con, Calle Navas 24, tel. 95-822-5959, fax 95-822-7523, e-mail: alixares@jet.es, SE).

Hotel Nizza, another block down Calle Navas, is youthful and easygoing, with flood-stained ceilings and well-worn rooms but lots of character (Sb-4,000 ptas, D-4,500 ptas, Db-6,000 ptas, CC:VM, a cheery breakfast room, Calle Navas 16, tel. 95-822-5430, fax 95-822-5427).

Sleeping near the Cathedral
Hotel Los Tilos offers comfortable rooms on the charming, traffic-free Bib-Rambla square behind the cathedral. Some rooms have balconies, and everyone's welcome to the fourth-floor view terrace overlooking a great café, shopping, and people-watching neighborhood (Sb-5,145 ptas, Db-7,875 ptas, Tb-10,630 ptas, 20 percent discount with this book and cash, breakfast buffet-650 ptas or free in winter, CC:VM, some air-con rooms, elevator, Plaza Bib-Rambla 4, tel. 95-826-6712, fax 95-826-6801, friendly Jose-Maria SE).

Sleeping across the River
The monkish **Monasterio de los Basilios** has a hotel that shares a courtyard with a parochial school and offers quiet, spare rooms with public parking nearby. It's a 15-minute walk from Plaza Nueva through the heart of Granada's commercial district

(Db-8,500 ptas, CC:VMA, Pasco de los Basilios 2, 18008 Granada, tel. & fax 95-881-7401, e-mail: basilios@maciahoteles.com, SE).

Sleeping near the Alhambra
(zip code: 18009)

If you want to stay on or bordering the Alhambra grounds, three popular options are a kilometer up the hill from Plaza Nueva. The first two—famous, overpriced, and often booked up—are actually within the Alhambra grounds.

Parador Nacional San Francisco, offering 36 air-conditioned rooms in a converted 15th-century convent, is called Spain's premier parador (Sb-23,600–26,400 ptas, Db-29,500–33,000 ptas, breakfast-1,600 ptas, free parking, CC:VMA, Real de la Alhambra, tel. 95-822-1440, fax 95-822-2264, SE). You must book ahead to spend the night in this lavishly located, stodgy, classy, and historic place. Any peasant, however, can drop in for coffee or a drink.

Next to the parador, the small **Hotel America** rents 13 rooms. It's cozy, elegant, and snooty (Sb-10,000 ptas, Db-16,000 ptas, Tb-23,000 ptas, includes breakfast and tax, CC:VMA, closed Nov–Mar, tel. 95-822-7471, fax 95-822-7470, e-mail: hamerica @moebius.es, SE). Book three to four months in advance.

The stately old **Hotel Washington Irving** is pleasant, spacious, and charmingly rundown. Not quite as romantically located, it offers the best reasonable beds in this prestigious neighborhood (Sb-10,000 ptas, Db-16,000 ptas, Tb or Qb-18,200 ptas, buffet breakfast-1,350 ptas, CC:VMA, elevator, Paseo del Generalife 2, tel. 95-822-7550, fax 95-822-7559, SE).

Eating in Granada

Traditionally, Granada bars serve a tapa plate free with any beer or wine ordered. Two well-chosen beers can actually end up being a light meal. In search of a memory? A local tradition, *tortilla Sacromonte*, is a spicy omelet with pig's brain and other organs.

In the Albaicín: The most interesting meals hide out deep in the Albaicín quarter. From the San Nicolás viewpoint, find Plaza Larga (ask any local or follow directions above, in "Sights—Albaicín"). Plaza Larga is within two blocks of the first three listings.

For fish, consider **El Ladrillo**, with outdoor tables on a peaceful square (Placeta de Fatima, just off Calle Pages), or **Ladrillo II**, with indoor dining and a more extensive menu (Calle Panaderos 35, tel. 95-829-2651). They each serve a popular *barca* (1200-ptas "boatload" of mixed fried fish), a fishy feast that stuffs two to the gills. The smaller *canoa*, for 800 ptas, fills one adequately. (A *canoa* and a salad feed two well.) Each restaurant is open daily (lunch from 13:00, dinner from 20:00). For fewer tourists, fewer fish, more village atmosphere, and great inexpensive food, eat at **Casa Torcuato** (closed Sun, 2 blocks beyond Plaza Larga on Placeta de Carniceros).

For a more romantic, candlelit setting with Alhambra views, splurge at **El Agua Casa de Vinos** (2,500-ptas 3-course meals—most with cheese fondue, daily from 20:00, also Wed–Sun 13:30–16:00, Placeta Aljibe de Trillo 7, halfway up Albaicín hill, below San Nicolás viewpoint, reservations necessary, tel. 95-822-4356).

Mirador de Morayma, with a similarly intimate, garden-view-mansion ambience, also requires reservations (3,000-ptas meals, Calle Pianista Garcia Carrillo 2, tel. 95-822-8290).

The Albaicín is peppered with lively tapas bars (as is Calle Elvira near Plaza Nueva).

Hippie Options on Calle Calderería Nueva: From Plaza Nueva walk two blocks down Calle Elvira and turn right onto the wonderfully hip and Arabic-feeling Calderería Nueva, which leads uphill into the Albaicín. The street is lined with trendy *teterías*. These small tea shops, open all day, are good places to linger and chat. Some are conservative and unmemorable, and others are filled with incense, beaded cushions, live African music, and effervescent young hippies. They sell light meals and a worldwide range of teas. The plush **Kasbah** has good (canned) music.

Naturi Albaicín is a great vegetarian place with 1,000-ptas three-course meals featuring classy couscous (Calle Calderería Nueva 10, tel. 95-822-0627). Wafting up to the end of the tea-house street you'll find **Bar Restaurant Las Cuevas**—its rickety tables spilling onto the street—serving salads, pizzas, tapas, and wine to a fun family/bohemian crowd. (Peek at the old-time Gypsy photos on the wall inside.)

Other Options: The cheap and easy **Bodega Castaneda** serves a fine *ensalada de casa* and baked potatoes with a fun variety of toppings (on Calle Elvira, a block off the west end of Plaza Nueva). For people-watching ambience, consider the many restaurants on Plaza Nueva, Bib-Rambla, or Plaza de los Tristes.

Transportation Connections—Granada

By train to: Barcelona (2/day, 12 hrs, handy night train), **Madrid** (3/day, 6–9 hrs, 1 night-train; or go via Córdoba and catch the AVE train), **Toledo** (3/day, 9 hrs, transfer in Alcázar, 1 night-train), **Algeciras** (3/day, 5 hrs, possible transfer in Antequera), **Ronda** (3/day, 3 hrs), **Sevilla** (4/day, 3 hrs, transfer in Bobadilla; also 10 buses/day, 3 hrs), **Córdoba** (1/day, 4 hrs, transfer in Bobadilla; also 6 buses/day, 3 hrs), **Málaga** (3/day, 3.5 hrs, transfer in Bobadilla; also hrly buses, 2 hrs). Granada train information: tel. 95-827-1272.

By bus to: Nerja (2/day, 2 hrs, more frequent with transfer in Motril), **Sevilla** (10 buses/day, 3 hrs; plus trains, above), **Córdoba** (6 buses/day, 3 hrs; plus trains above), **Málaga** (hrly, 2 hrs; plus trains, above), **Algeciras** (6/day, 4.5 hrs), **La Línea/Gibraltar** (2/day, 5 hrs). Bus information: tel. 95-818-5480.

SEVILLA

This is the flamboyant city of Carmen and Don Juan, where bull-fighting is still politically correct and where little girls still dream of growing up to become flamenco dancers. While Granada has the great Alhambra, and Córdoba the remarkable Mezquita, Sevilla has a soul. It's a great-to-be-alive-in kind of place.

Sevilla, the gateway to the New World, boomed when Spain did. Explorers such as Amerigo Vespucci and Ferdinand Magellan sailed from its great river harbor, and local artists such as Velázquez, Murillo, and Zurbarán made it a cultural center. Sevilla's Golden Age, with its New World riches, ended when the harbor silted up and the Spanish empire crumbled.

Today Spain's fourth-largest city (pop. 700,000) is Andalu-cía's leading city, buzzing with festivals, life, color, and castanets. James Michener wrote, "Sevilla doesn't *have* ambience, it *is* ambience." Sevilla has its share of impressive sights, but the real magic is the city itself, with its tangled Jewish Quarter, riveting flamenco shows, thriving bars, and teeming evening paseo.

Planning Your Time

If ever there was a big Spanish city to linger in, it's Sevilla. With three weeks in Iberia, spend two nights and a day in Sevilla. On a shorter trip, at least zip down here via the slick AVE train for a day trip from Madrid.

The sights—the cathedral and the Alcázar (about three hours) and a wander through the Santa Cruz district (an hour)—are few and simple for a city of this size. You could spend half a day tour-ing its other sights (described below). An evening is essential for the paseo and a flamenco show. Sevilla's Alcázar is closed on Monday. Bullfights are on most Sundays, April through October.

Córdoba (described at the end of this chapter) is worth a
short stopover if you're taking the AVE.

Orientation

For the tourist, this big city is small. Sevilla's major sights, including the lively Santa Cruz district and the Alcázar, surround the
cathedral. The central boulevard, Avenida de la Constitución (with
TI, banks, and a post office), zips right past the cathedral to Plaza
Nueva (the shopping district). Nearly everything is within easy
walking distance. Taxis are reasonable (400 ptas minimum),
friendly, and easy. The horse-and-buggy rides cost 4,000 to 5,000
ptas for a 60-minute clip-clop.

Tourist Information

Handy TIs are in the center and at the train station. The central
TI is a block toward the river from the cathedral (Mon–Fri 9:00–
19:00, Sat 10:00–14:00, 15:00–19:00, Sun 10:00–14:00, Avenida de
la Constitución 21, tel. 95-422-1404). Ask for the fine city map
(far better than the one in the promo city magazine); a current
listing of sights, hours, and prices; a schedule of bullfights; and
ideas for evening fun. The free monthly events guide, *El Giraldillo*,
in nearly readable Spanish, covers cultural events in all of
Andalucía with a focus on Sevilla. If heading south, ask for the
"Route of the White Towns" brochure and a Jerez map (100 ptas
each). If arriving by bus or train, you'll find helpful TIs in or near
your station (see "Arrival," below).

Arrival in Sevilla

By Train: Trains arrive at the sublime Santa Justa station (banks,
ATMs, TI, luggage storage). The town center, marked by the
ornate Giralda Cathedral bell tower (visible from the front of the
station), is a 30-minute walk, 700-ptas taxi ride, or short bus ride
away. Bus #32 takes you to Plaza de la Encarnación in the center;
pay the driver 125 ptas as you board.

By Bus: Sevilla's two major bus stations have information
offices, cafés, and luggage storage. The decaying station at Prado
de San Sebastian covers Andalucía. To get downtown from the
station, turn right on the major street Carlos V, then right again
on Avenida de la Constitución (10-minute walk).

The modern and well-equipped bus station at Plaza de Armas
(near the river, opposite EXPO '92 site) serves southwest Spain and
Portugal. To get downtown from this station, head toward the
angled brick apartment building and cross the busy Boulevard
Expiración. Go a half-block up Calle Arjona to the stop for bus #C4,
which goes into town (125 ptas, payable on bus; get off at Puerta de
Jerez, near main TI). Another TI is two blocks from this bus stop
at Calle Arjona #28 (near Isabel II Bridge, daily 8:00–20:30, tel.

Sevilla

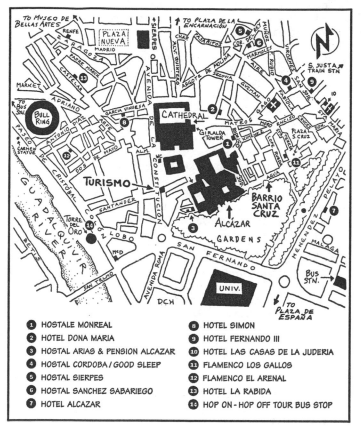

- **1** HOSTALE MONREAL
- **2** HOTEL DONA MARIA
- **3** HOSTAL ARIAS & PENSION ALCAZAR
- **4** HOSTAL CORDOBA / GOOD SLEEP
- **5** HOSTAL SIERPES
- **6** HOSTAL SANCHEZ SABARIEGO
- **7** HOTEL ALCAZAR
- **8** HOTEL SIMON
- **9** HOTEL FERNANDO III
- **10** HOTEL LAS CASAS DE LA JUDERIA
- **11** FLAMENCO LOS GALLOS
- **12** FLAMENCO EL ARENAL
- **13** HOTEL LA RABIDA
- **14** HOP ON - HOP OFF TOUR BUS STOP

95-450-5600). From here you can catch bus #C4 or walk 15 minutes into the center (following map from TI).

By Car: Driving in Sevilla is difficult and parking can be risky. I'd pay to park in a garage. To enter Sevilla, follow signs to Centro Ciudad (city center) and drive along the river. If you need a brief place to park (to get set up), find a place near the cathedral and tower (leave your partner in the car). Paseo de Cristobal Colón has free street parking but is particularly theft-prone in the summer. Self-appointed traffic wardens try to overcharge tourists. Locals pay no more than 100 ptas for their "help." Ideally, get parking advice in advance from your hotel and drive directly to their recommended spot.

Helpful Hints

Telephone: A telephone office, Locutorio Público, has metered phone booths—the cost is slightly more expensive than calls made with Spanish phone cards, but you get a quiet setting with a seat (Mon–Fri 10:00–14:00, 17:00–21:00, Sat 10:00–14:00, in the passage at Sierpes 11, near the intersection with Calle de Rafael Padura, tel. 95-422-6800).

Post Office: The post office is on Avenida de la Constitución 32, across from the cathedral (Mon–Fri 8:30–20:30, Sat 9:30–14:00).

Train Tickets: The downtown RENFE office gives out train schedules and sells train tickets (Mon–Fri 9:00–13:15, 16:00–19:00, CC:VMA, Calle Zaragoza 29, tel. 95-421-7998, NSE). Many travel agencies sell train tickets for the same price as the train station (look for train sticker in agency window). Usit Student Travel is at Mateos Gago 2, just off the cathedral square.

Internet Access: Cibercenter is central (daily 9:00–21:00, just off Reyes Católicos at Julio Cesar 8, tel. 95-422-8899).

Laundromat: Lavanderia Roma offers quick and economical drop-off service (Castela 2, tel. 95-421-0535).

Sights—Sevilla's Cathedral

▲▲**Cathedral and Giralda Tower**—This is the third-largest church in Europe (after the Vatican's St. Peter's and London's St. Paul's) and the largest Gothic church anywhere. When they ripped down a mosque on the site in 1401, the Reconquista Christians bragged, "We'll build a cathedral so huge that anyone who sees it will take us for madmen." They built for 120 years. Even today, the descendants of those madmen proudly display an enlarged photocopy of their *Guinness Book of Records* letter certifying, "The cathedral with the largest area is: Santa Maria de la Sede in Sevilla, 126 meters long, 82 meters wide, and 30 meters high" (700 ptas, Mon–Sat 10:00–17:00, free on Sun 14:00–18:00). Here's a five-stop tour:

1. Cloister: As with most important Spanish churches, this one sits upon the ruins of a Moorish mosque. The cloister was the mosque's Court of the Naranjos (Oranges). Twelfth-century Muslims stopped at the fountain in the middle to wash their hands and feet before praying. The mosque was made of bricks; the church was made of stone.

2. Giralda Tower: Formerly a Moorish minaret from which Muslims were called to prayer, it became the cathedral's bell tower after the Reconquista. Notice the beautiful Moorish simplicity as you climb to its top, 100 yards up, for a grand city view. The spiraling ramp is designed to accommodate riders on horseback, so find the entrance (just inside the church on the left, same hours and ticket as cathedral) and gallop up the 34 ramps and orient yourself from this bird's-eye perspective. It's named for the 4,500-pound bronze statue symbolizing Faith that caps it and serves as a weathervane (*giraldillo*).

3. Sanctuary: Hike through the sanctuary. Then sit down in front of the main chapel (*capilla mayor*) in the center. The incredible main altarpiece (*retablo mayor*) has 4,000 pounds of gold (imported in Spain's post-1492 "free trade" era). Sixty feet tall, with 36 scenes from the life of Jesus, it's composed of 1,500 figures.

4. Tomb of Columbus: Opposite the entry you'll see four kings carrying the tomb of Christopher Columbus. His pallbearers are the kings of Castille, Aragon, Leon, and Navarra (identify them by their team shirts).

5. Treasury: The treasury (*tesoro*) is scattered in several rooms at the exit. Find the Corona de la Virgen de los Reyes, Spain's most valuable crown, with 11,000 precious stones and the world's largest pearl made into the torso of an angel. You'll also see lots of relics (thorns, chunks of the cross, splinters from the Last Supper table), and some of the lavish Corpus Christi festival parade regalia.

Across the street from the exit, you might pop into the Monastero de la Encarnación where cloistered nuns sell pastries from a blind lazy Susan (just inside the door at #3).

Sights—Sevilla

▲**Alcázar**—The Alcazar was originally a 10th-century palace built for the governors of the local Moorish state. But what you see today is an extensive 14th-century remodel job, done by Moorish workmen (Mudejar) for the Christian King Pedro I. Pedro was nicknamed either "the Cruel" or "the Just," depending on which end of his sword you were on.

The Alcázar is a thought-provoking glimpse of a graceful Al-Andalus (Moorish) world that might have survived its Castilian conquerors—but didn't. But I have a tough time hanging any specific history on it. The throne room (#7, Salon de Embajadores) is most impressive. Sit here for a while and freeload off passing tours. The floor plan is intentionally confusing, part of the style designed to make experiencing the place more exciting and surprising.

With a grand collection of royal courts, halls, patios, and apartments, it's been a Spanish royal residence for 600 years (and maintains that function today). The upper floors are more European-style palatial. Seek out the Grand Hall, with its fine tapestries celebrating Emperor Charles V's 1535 victory in Tunis over the Turks. Trace your itinerary on the south-up tapestry map of Iberia and Northern Africa.

The garden is full of tropical flowers, wild cats, cool fountains, and hot tourists (700 ptas, Tue–Sat 9:30–19:00, Sun 9:00–17:00, off-season 9:30–17:00, closed Mon, tel. 95-450-2323). The 400-ptas audio guide (the only such sightseeing aid I encountered in Spain) is tempting and tries hard. But sorry, there's no way to make this palace worth a flowery hour of hard-to-follow commentary.

Archivo de Indias, the archive of the documents of the discovery and conquest of the New World, could be fascinating, but little of importance is on display (old maps of Havana) and there's not a word of English (free, Mon–Fri 10:00–13:00, closed Sat–Sun, in the Lonja Palace, across the street from the Alcázar).

▲▲**Barrio de Santa Cruz**—Even if this old Jewish Quarter is a little overrestored, this classy maze of lanes too narrow for cars, whitewashed houses with wrought-iron latticework, and *azulejo*-tile-covered patios is a great refuge from the summer heat and bustle of Sevilla. Get lost among tourist shops, small hotels, flamenco bars, and peaceful squares. Even with the TI's helpful Barrio de Santa Cruz map (an inset on the city map), you'll get lost—which is the idea anyway. Locals are kind in giving directions.

Hospital de la Caridad—Between the river and the cathedral is the charity hospital founded by the original Don Juan. One of history's great hedonists, his party was crashed by a vision that tuned him on to his own mortality. He paid for the construction of this hospital for the poor and joined the Brotherhood of Charity. Peek into the fine courtyard. On the left, the chapel has some gruesome art (above both doors) illustrating that death is the great equalizer and an altar sweet as only a Spaniard could enjoy (400 ptas, Mon–Sat 9:00–13:30, 15:30–18:30, Sun 9:00–13:00, tel. 95-422-3232).

Torre del Oro/Naval Museum—Sevilla's historic riverside "gold tower" is named for the golden tiles that once covered it—not for all the New World booty that landed here. Since the 13th century it has been part of the city's fortifications, with a heavy chain draped across the river to protect the harbor. Today it houses a mediocre little naval museum with lots of charts showing various knots, models of ships, dried fish, and an interesting mural of Sevilla in 1740 (100 ptas, free Tue, Tue–Fri 10:00–14:00, Sat–Sun 11:00–14:00, closed Mon). Two competing city bus tours leave from the curb near this tower. You'll see the buses parked.

University—Today's university was yesterday's *fabrica de tabacos* (cigar factory), which employed 10,000 young female *cigareras*—including Bizet's Carmen. When built, it was the second-largest building in Spain, after El Escorial. Wander through its halls as you walk to the Plaza de España. The university's bustling café is a good place for cheap tapas, beer, wine, and conversation (Mon–Fri 8:00–21:00, Sat 9:00–13:00, closed Sun).

▲**Plaza de España**—The square, the surrounding buildings, and the nearby María Luisa Park are the remains of a 1929 fair that crashed with the U.S. stock market. This delightful area, the epitome of World's Fair–style building, is great for people watching (especially at early-evening paseo time). Stroll through the park and along the canal. Check out the *azulejo* tiles (a trademark of Sevilla) that show historic scenes and maps from every corner of Spain. Climb to one of the balconies for a fine overview.

▲**Museo de Bellas Artes**—Spain's second-best collection of paintings (after Madrid's Prado) has 50 Murillos and works by Zurbarán, El Greco, and Velázquez (250 ptas, Wed–Sat 9:00–20:00, Sun 9:00–15:00, Tue 15:00–20:00, closed Mon, Plaza Museo 9, tel. 95-422-0790).

▲**Basilica Macarena**—This altarpiece statue of the Weeping Virgin (Virgen de la Macarena), complete with crystal teardrops, is the darling of Sevilla's Holy Week processions. She's beautiful (and her weeping can be contagious). Tour the exhibits behind the altar and go upstairs for a closer peek at Mary. The church is free, but the museum costs 300 ptas (daily 9:00–13:00, 17:00–21:00, long walk or taxi to Puerta Macarena or take bus #C4 from Puerta Jerez).

▲**Bullfights**—Spain's most artistic and traditional bullfighting is done in Sevilla's Plaza de Toros, with fights on most Sundays, April through October. Serious fights with adult matadors—called *corrida de toros*—are in April and October. Summer fights are usually *novillada*, with teenage novices doing the killing. (*Corrida de toros* seats range from 3,000–13,000 ptas; *novillada* seats are half that; get information at a TI, your hotel, or tel. 95-422-8229.) You can follow a two-language, 20-minute guided tour through the strangely quiet and empty arena, its museum, and the chapel where the matador prays before the fight (400 ptas, daily 9:30–14:00, 15:00–18:00; 10:00–15:00 on fight days). See the Appendix for more on the dubious "art" of bullfighting.

Across Paseo de Cristobal Colón from the bullring, note the statue of **Carmen**. This beautiful girl from the cigar factory was the inspiration for Bizet's famous opera.

Nightlife

▲▲**Evening Paseo**—Sevilla is meant for strolling. The areas along either side of the river between the San Telmo and Isabel II bridges (Paseo de Cristobal Colón and Triana district; see "Eating," below), around Plaza Nueva, at Plaza de España, and throughout Barrio de Santa Cruz thrive every nonwinter evening. Spend some time rafting through this sea of humanity. Savor the view of floodlit Sevilla by night from the far side of the river.

▲▲**Flamenco**—This music and dance art form has its roots in th Gypsy and Moorish cultures. Even at a packaged "Flamenco Evening," sparks fly. The men do most of the flamboyant machine-gun footwork. The women concentrate on graceful tur and a smooth, shuffling step. Watch the musicians. Flamenco guitarists, with their lightning finger-roll strums, are among th best in the world. The intricate rhythms are set by castanets o the hand-clapping (called *palmas*) of those who aren't dancing the moment. In the raspy-voiced wails of the singers you'll he echoes of the Muslim call to prayer.

Like jazz, flamenco thrives on improvisation. Also like j

good flamenco is more than just technical proficiency. A singer or dancer with "soul" is said to have *duende*. Flamenco is a happening, with bystanders clapping along and egging on the dancers with whoops and shouts. Get into it.

For a tourist-oriented flamenco show, your hotel can get you nightclub show tickets. **Los Gallos** gives nightly shows at 21:00 and 23:30 (3,000-ptas tickets include one drink, manager Nuria promises goosebumps and a 10 percent discount to those with this book, Plaza de Santa Cruz 11, tel. 95-421-6981, reservations by fax: 95-421-3436). **El Arenal** also does a good show (4,100 ptas, shows at 21:30 and 23:30, near bullring at Calle Rodo 7, tel. 95-421-6492). **El Patio Sevillano** is more of a variety show (shows at 19:30 and 22:00; next to bullring at Paseo de Cristobal Colón, tel. 95-421-4120). These prepackaged shows can be a bit sterile, and an audience of tourists doesn't help. But I find both Los Gallos and El Arenal professional and riveting. El Arenal may have a slight edge on talent, but Los Gallos has a more intimate setting, with soft rather than hard chairs—and it's cheaper.

The best flamenco erupts spontaneously in bars throughout the old town after midnight. Just follow your ears as you wander down Calle Betis, leading off the Plaza de Cuba across the bridge. The **Lo Nuestro** and **Rejoneo** bars are local favorites for impromptu flamenco (at Calle Betis 30 and 32).

In the Barrio Santa Cruz, a mix of students and tourists gathers in **La Carboneria** to hear free flamenco every Thursday after 23:00 (Levies 10, unsigned door, music only, no dancing).

Shopping

The popular pedestrian street **Calle Sierpes** and the smaller lanes around it near the Plaza Nueva are packed with people and shops. The street ends up at Sevilla's top department store, El Corte Inglés. While small shops close between 13:00 and 16:00 or 17:00, El Corte Inglés stays open (and air-conditioned) right through the siesta. It has a supermarket downstairs and a good but expensive restaurant (Mon–Sat 10:00–21:30, closed Sun). **Flea markets** hop on Thursday on Calle La Feria and Sunday along Alameda de Hércules.

Sleeping in Sevilla
(160 ptas = about $1, zip code: 41004)
Sleep Code: **S** = Single, **D** = Double/Twin, **T** = Triple, **Q** = Quad, **b** = bathroom, **t** = toilet only, **s** = shower only, **CC** = Credit Card (Visa, MasterCard, Amex), **SE** = Speaks English, **NSE** = No English.

Sevilla has plenty of $30 to $50 double rooms. All of my listings are centrally located and within a five-minute walk of the cathedral. The first ones are near the charming but touristy Santa Cruz neighborhood. The last group is just as central but closer to the river, across the boulevard and in a more workaday, less touristy zone.

Room rates jump way up during the two Sevilla fiestas (roughly the week before Easter and a week or so after Easter). In general, the busiest and most expensive months are April, May, September, and October. Hotels put rooms on the discounted push list in June, July, and August. Prices rarely include the 7 percent IVA tax. A price range indicates low- to high-season prices (but I have not listed festival prices). Hoteliers speak enough English. The small, family *pensiónes* don't hold reservations as reliably as normal big hotels. Skip ground-floor rooms (because of noise) and ask for upper floors (*piso alto*).

Sleeping near the Santa Cruz Neighborhood

Off Calle Santa Maria la Blanca: The **Hostal Córdoba** has 12 tidy, quiet, air-conditioned rooms, solid modern furniture, and a showpiece plant-filled courtyard (S-3,000–4,000 ptas, Sb-4,000–5,000 ptas, D-5,000–6,000 ptas, Db-6,000–7,000 ptas, a tiny lane off Calle Santa Maria la Blanca, Farnesio 12, tel. 95-422-7498, SE).

Hostal Good Sleep is a homey, backpacker-type place filled with caged birds, family ambience, and 20 neon-lit and cheaply furnished rooms (S-1,800 ptas, D-3,500 ptas, Db-4,000, T-5,000 ptas, Tb-5,000 ptas, prices vary with demand, CC:VM, laundry service, fans in rooms, birds sleep but wake early, welcoming rooftop terrace for picnicking and socializing, next to Hostal Córdoba at Farnesio 8, tel. 95-421-7492, friendly Sr. Rene speaks English).

Off Plaza Santa Maria: The **Hotel Las Casas de la Juderia**, also off Plaza Santa Maria, has quiet, elegant rooms and suites tastefully decorated with hardwood floors and a Spanish flair; the rooms surround a peaceful courtyard. This is a romantic splurge and a fine value (Sb-10,500–12,500 ptas, Db-15,000–18,000 ptas, Db suite-17,500–21,000 ptas, Qb suite-25,000–29,000 ptas, low prices are for Jul–Aug, CC:VMA, air-con, elevator, Callejon de Dos Hermanas 7, tel. 95-441-5150, fax 95-442-2170, e-mail: juderia@zoom.es, SE).

Hotel Fernando III is cavernous, comfortable, modern, and popular with groups, with uniformly big and well-hung rooms (Db-16,500 ptas, CC:VMA, nearly all with twin beds, air-con, rooftop pool, garage, elevator, San Jose 21, just off Plaza Santa Maria, tel. 95-421-7307, fax 95-422-0246, SE).

On Corral del Rey: Walking from the cathedral square straight up Argote de Molina (for 200 yards) you come to **Hostal Sierpes,** a sprawling, 40-room place with fine lounges and a big, cool, airy courtyard. Rooms are small and basic but air-conditioned, with shiny new bathrooms. It's reportedly unreliable for reservations. When you arrive, show this book to the hard-working manager, Quintin, or his equally serious son, Melquiades, for a 15 percent discount (Sb-4,000 ptas, Db-7,000 ptas, quieter rooms upstairs, CC:VMA, Corral del Rey 22, tel. 95-422-4948, fax 95-421-2107, SE).

Across the street, **Hostal Sanchez Sabariego** is a cozier, 10-room place with a folksy garden courtyard. The higher floors are most peaceful (S-3,000 ptas, Db-6,000–7,000 ptas, prices are soft, but you should establish them clearly in writing, Corral del Rey 23, tel. 95-421-4470, SE).

Near Old Bus Station: The **Hotel Alcázar**, on the big and busy Menendez y Pelayo boulevard, is air-conditioned, with lavish, shiny public areas and everything you'd find in a modern, big-city American hotel (Sb-10,350 ptas, Db-14,700 ptas, discounted when slow, includes breakfast, CC:VMA, Menendez y Pelayo 10, tel. 95-441-2011, fax 95-442-1659, SE). Ask for a quiet room off the street.

Sleeping near the Alcázar

In a quiet eddy of lanes behind the tourist office, **Hostal Arias** is cool, clean, and no-nonsense. Its 15 rooms are air-conditioned and comfortable, except for the dark #24 (Sb-5,000 ptas, Db-6,600 ptas, Tb-8,500 ptas, CC:VMA, Calle Mariana de Pineda 9, tel. 95-422-6840, fax 95-421-8389, www.col.com/arias, manager Manuel Reina SE). Around the corner, most of **Pensión Alcázar's** eight pleasant rooms have air-conditioning; top-floor rooms have only ceiling fans but include a fine large terrace (Db-6,000 ptas, extra bed-1,000 ptas, unpredictable management, Dean Miranda 12, tel. 95-422-8457, SE).

Hotel Residencia Doña María tries to be elegant but is just big and stuffy. Facing the cathedral on Plaza Vírgen de los Reyes, it brags that it's "very modern but furnished in an ancient style," with four-poster beds, armoires, and a rooftop swimming pool with a view of Giralda Tower. It is comfortable and has the best location in town (Sb-8,000–11,000 ptas, Db-13,500–18,500 ptas, rip-off 1,500-ptas breakfast, prices go through the roof for festivals, suites are marginally better for an extra 2,000 ptas, CC:VMA, elevator, Don Remondo 19, tel. 95-422-4990, fax 95-421-9546, SE).

Hostal Monreal disguises its basic (sometimes dingy) rooms with a relaxing, cheery courtyard and tiled hallways that give you the sensation of climbing through a complex and colorful tile tree house (S-2,500 ptas, D-4,000 ptas, Db-7,000 ptas, extra bed-40 percent more, CC:VM, some air-con, sun terrace, some balconies, from cathedral take first right off Mateos Gago to Rodrigo Caro 8, tel. 95-421-4166, NSE).

Sleeping West of Avenida de la Constitución

Hotel Simón is a classic 18th-century mansion with a faded-elegant courtyard. The air-conditioned rooms vary in quality, and many are decorated with period furniture under high ceilings. On weekends, avoid rooms on the noisy street. The staff is pleasant and helpful (Sb-6,500–7,500 ptas, Db-8,500–11,500 ptas, add 3,000 ptas for 3rd person, add 4,000 ptas for suite, high prices are only for Apr–May, CC:VMA, a block west of Avenida de la Constitución and the cathedral at Calle García de Vinuesa 19, tel. 95-422-6660, fax 95-456-2241, SE).

Hostal Guadalquiver is sleepable, with seven plain rooms (Db-6,000 ptas, Tb-8,000 ptas, air-con, Garcia de Vinuesa 21, next to Hotel Simón, tel. 95-421-7760, fax 95-421-4404).

Hotel La Rabida has 100 basic rooms surrounding a spacious atrium lobby and delightful garden courtyard, a classy breakfast room, elevators, and an indifferent staff (Sb-6,100 ptas, Db-9,300 ptas, CC:VMA, 10 percent discount with this book, Castelar 24, tel. 95-422-0960, fax 95-422-4375, http://sol.com/hotel-rabida, SE). From Avenida de la Constitución, go down Calle García de Vinuesa and turn right on Calle Castelar.

Eating in Sevilla

Eating across the River

The bridge, Puente Isabel II, leads across the river to my favorite cluster of fish restaurants. Near the yellow bridge tower, **Kiosco de las Flores** is famous for its fish (Tue–Sun 12:00–16:00, 20:00–24:00, closed Mon). For better prices, go a block beyond the bridge to **Los Dos Hermanos** (San Jacinto 3, around the corner from Banco Santander). This is the Triana District. From here, Calle Pureza leads to tapas bars and spontaneous flamenco in the wee hours (see "Flamenco," above).

For a riverside restaurant dinner, consider **Río Grande** (on Calle Betis near Puente San Telmo) or eat the same thing—with the same view but fewer tablecloths—next door at **El Puerto** for half the price (closed Mon).

Eating in the Cathedral/Santa Cruz Area

Plenty of atmospheric-but-touristy restaurants fill the old quarter near the cathedral. Tourist-friendly places line Alvarez Quintero, a street running north from the cathedral.

For tapas, the Barrio de Santa Cruz is trendy, touristic, and *romántico*. From the cathedral, walk up Mateos Gago a few blocks and melt into the narrow lanes on your right. You're likely to enjoy some live music. Consider **Cervecería Giralda** (Mateos Gago 1), **Bodega Belmonte** (Mateos Gago 24), or **Casa Roman** (La Plaza de los Venerables).

Eating along Calle García de Vinuesa

This street (across from the cathedral, over Avenida de la Constitución, near three recommended hotels) is lined with decent tapas places. On the corner, the slick and chrome **Horno San**

Buenaventura is handy for coffee, tapas, and dessert (tapas are posted on the pillar). Farther down the street you'll find **La Gitana Taverna la Andaluza**, a rustic wine bar with good tapas; a **fried fish joint** (*pescado frito*) that also sells homemade potato chips; and **Bodegas Diaz Salazar**, lined with serious kegs of wine and locals. At the end of the street, **Meson Sevilla Jabugo** is fine for breakfast, coffee, and tapas (Calle Castelar 1). More restaurants and tapas bars and a recommended flamenco bar (**El Arenal** at Calle Rodo 7) are in the streets just beyond.

Picnickers forage at the covered fish-and-produce **Mercado del Arenal** (with a small café/bar for breakfast inside, Mon–Sat 9:00–13:00, closed Sun, on Calle Pastor y Landero at Calle Arenal, just beyond bullring).

Transportation Connections—Sevilla

To: Madrid (16 trains/day, 3.25 hrs; 2.5 hrs by AVE, 1,500 ptas reservation fee with railpass; 10 buses/day for 2,700 ptas), **Córdoba** (15 trains/day, 1.5 hrs; 50 min by AVE; 10 buses/day, 2 hrs), **Málaga** (5 trains/day, 3 hrs; 10 buses/day, 4 hrs), **Ronda** (3 trains/day, 3 hrs, change at Bobadilla; 5 buses/day, 3 hrs), **Tarifa** (4 buses/day, 3 hrs), **La Línea/Gibraltar** (4 buses/day, 4 hrs), **Granada** (4 trains/day, 4 hrs; 8 buses/day, 4 hrs), Arcos (2 buses/day, 2 hrs), **Jerez** (7 buses/day, 2 hrs), **Barcelona** (4 trains/day, 10–12 hrs), **Algeciras** (3 trains/day, 5 hrs, change at Bobadilla; 10 buses/day, 4 hrs), **Lisbon** (1 bus/day in summer, 4 buses/week in winter, 8 hrs, 4,500 ptas; or AVE to Madrid and night train). Train information: tel. 95-454-0202 (rarely answered). Bus information: tel. 95-490-8040.

For driving ideas south into Andalucía and west into Portugal's Algarve, see those chapters.

From Sevilla to Portugal's Algarve

To Tavira by bus: 2 buses/day, 3.5 hrs (from Sevilla's Plaza de Armas station), easy transfer in Huelva; 1 direct bus runs 4 mornings/week, 3 hrs, no transfer.

To Lagos by bus/train: The direct bus between Lagos and Sevilla is a godsend (1/day except Mon, 5 hrs, 2,600 ptas). The bus departs from Sevilla's Plaza de Armas bus station and arrives at the Lagos bus station, with stops at Algarve towns such as Tavira. From Lagos catch a one-hour bus to Salema.

Other than the direct bus, it's a long day of bus, ferry, and train rides: Sevilla–Ayamonte bus (4/day from Plaza de Armas station, 2.5 hrs) to Ayamonte at the border, ferry to Vila Real in Portugal (17/day, 15 min), train to Lagos (3/day, more with transfer in Tunes, 4 hrs). Get an early start.

Taking the train from Sevilla to the Algarve is slower and requires a transfer to a bus at Huelva (Sevilla–Huelva: 4 trains/day, 90 min; Huelva–Ayamonte: 6 buses/day, 1 hr). The Sevilla–

Ayamonte bus (4/day) is preferable, cheap, direct, and less hassle. In Vila Real the train station, the buses, and the ferry dock are clustered together. Saturdays and Sundays are dead in Vila Real. Ayamonte is much livelier and tourist-friendly by comparison.

CÓRDOBA

Córdoba is one of Spain's three big Moorish cities. Even though it was the center of Moorish civilization in Spain for 300 years (and an important Roman city), Sevilla and Granada are far more interesting. Córdoba has a famous mosque surrounded by the colorful Jewish quarter, and that's it.

The **Mezquita** (meh-SKEET-ah) was the largest Islamic mosque in its day. Today you can wander past its ramshackle "patio of oranges" and into the cavernous 1,200-year-old building. Grab the English pamphlet at the door (which predictably describes the church history much better than the mosque's). The interior is a moody world of 800 rose- and blue-marble columns and as many Moorish arches. If a guide told me I was in the basement of something important, I'd believe him. The center was gutted to make room for an also-huge Renaissance cathedral (800 ptas, Mon–Sat 10:00–19:00, Sun 14:00–19:00). The mosque is near the TI (Mon–Fri 9:30–20:00, Sat 10:00–20:00, Sun 10:00–14:00, tel. 95-747-1235). The TI also has a handy kiosk at the train station (with a room-finding service).

From the station to the mosque it's a 400-ptas taxi ride or a pleasant 30-minute walk (left on Avenida de America, right on Avenida del Gran Capitan, which becomes a pedestrian zone; when it ends ask someone "*¿Dónde está Mezquita?*" and you'll be directed downhill through the whitewashed old Jewish Quarter).

Sleeping and Eating in Córdoba: Two comfortable, air-conditioned, and expensive hotels are located within a five-minute walk of the station. **Hotel Gran Capitan** is closer (Db-15,625–18,750 ptas, Avenida de America 5, tel. 95-747-0250). **Hotel Sol los Gallos** is cheaper and has a pool (Db-11,650 ptas, Avenida de Medina Azahara 7, tel. 95-723-5500). For food, try **Taverna Salinas** (Tendidores 3, near mosque).

Transportation Connections—Córdoba

Now that Córdoba is on the slick AVE train line, it's an easy stopover between **Madrid** and **Sevilla** (15 trains/day, about an hour from each city, reservations required on all AVE trains).

By bus to: Granada (9/day, 3 hrs), **Málaga** (5/day, 3 hrs), **Algeciras** (2/day, 6 hrs).

ANDALUCÍA'S
WHITE HILL TOWNS

Just as the American image of Germany is Bavaria, the Yankee dream of Spain is Andalucía. This is the home of bullfights, flamenco, gazpacho, pristine-if-dusty whitewashed hill towns, and glamorous Mediterranean resorts. The big cities of Andalucía (Granada, Sevilla, and Córdoba) and the Costa del Sol are covered in separate chapters. This chapter explores its hill-town highlights.

The Route of the White Towns, Andalucía's charm bracelet of cute towns, gives you wonderfully untouched Spanish culture. Spend a night in the romantic queen of the white towns, Arcos de la Frontera. Towns with "de la Frontera" in their names were established on the front line of the centuries-long fight to recapture Spain from the Muslims, who were slowly pushed back into Africa. The hill towns, no longer strategic, no longer on any frontier, are now just passing time peacefully. Join them. Nearby, the city of Jerez is worth a peek for its famous horses in action and a sherry bodega tour.

Planning Your Time
While the towns can be (and often are) accessed from the Costa del Sol resorts via Ronda, Arcos makes the best home base. Arcos, near Jerez and close to interesting smaller towns, is conveniently situated halfway between Sevilla and Tarifa.

On a three-week Iberian vacation, the region is worth two nights and two days sandwiched between Sevilla and Tarifa. Spend both those nights in Arcos. See Jerez (horses and sherry) on your way in or out, spend a day hopping from town to town (Grazalema and Zahara, at a minimum) in the more remote interior, and enjoy Arcos early and late in the day.

Without a car you might keep things simple and focus only

Andalucía

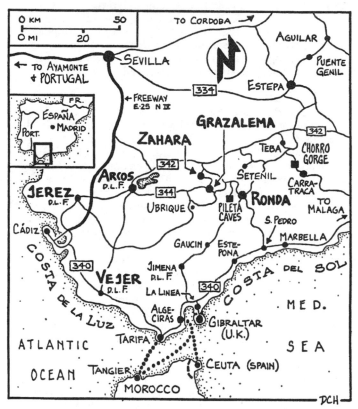

O KM 50 / O MI 20

TO CORDOBA →

TO AYAMONTE & PORTUGAL ←

SEVILLA

AGUILAR

PUENTE GENIL

ESTEPA

← FREEWAY E·25 N II

334

ESPAÑA · MADRID / PORT. / FR.

GRAZALEMA

342

ZAHARA

TEBA

CHORRO GORGE

342

ARCOS D.L.F.

SETENIL

CARRA-TRACA

344

RONDA

TO MALAGA →

UBRIQUE

PILETA CAVES

JEREZ D.L.F.

S. PEDRO

CÁDIZ

MARBELLA

GAUCIN

ESTE-PONA

COSTA DE LA LUZ

340

VEJER D.L.F.

JIMENA D.L.F.

COSTA DEL SOL

LA LINEA

340

MED.

ALGE-CIRAS

GIBRALTAR (U.K.)

ATLANTIC

TARIFA

SEA

OCEAN

TANGIER

CEUTA (SPAIN)

MOROCCO

DCH

on Arcos and Jerez (both well served by public buses). Spring and fall are high season throughout this area. In summer you'll find empty hotels and no crowds.

ARCOS DE LA FRONTERA

Arcos, smothering its hilltop and tumbling down all sides like an oversized blanket, is larger than the other Andalusian hill towns but equally atmospheric. The old center is a labyrinthine wonderland, a photographer's feast. Viewpoint-hop through town. Feel the wind funnel through the narrow streets as cars inch around tight corners. Join the kids' soccer game on the churchyard patio.

There are two towns: the fairy-tale old town and the fun-loving lower or new town. Check out the pleasant evening paseo and café scene, best at Plaza España and the adjacent Paseo Andalucía, the base of the hill where the new and old towns meet. Enjoy the moonlit view from the main square in the old town.

Though it tries, Arcos doesn't have much to offer other than its basic whitewashed self. The locally-produced English guide-book on Arcos waxes poetic and at length about very little. Since the church is open until early evening and the town market is open in the morning, you can arrive late and leave early.

Orientation

Tourist Information: The TI, on the main square across from the parador, is helpful and loaded with information, including bus schedules (Mon–Sat 10:00–14:00, 17:30–19:30, Sun 10:30–13:30, shorter hours in winter, Plaza del Cabildo, tel. 95-670-2264).

Walking Tours: In summer the TI organizes two different one-hour walking tours: "Old Town" and "Patios of Arcos." They leave from the main square, are given in Spanish and/or English, and cost 400 ptas. Old-town walks include the church and general history (10:30 and 17:00). Patio walks get you into private courtyards and cover lifestyles (12:00 and 18:30). On Sunday they do only one tour (at 12:30, a combo of both). Groups can hire a private guide for any walk any time (6,000 ptas).

Arrival in Arcos: The bus station is on Calle Corregidores. To get to the old town, catch a bus marked "*Centro*" (2/hrly, 105 ptas); hop a taxi (400 ptas); or take a 15-minute uphill walk. As you leave the station, turn left on Corregidores, angle left uphill, cross the four-way intersection, angle right uphill, and take Muñoz Vazquez up into town. Go up the stairs by the church to the main square and TI.

Helpful Hints: Arcos' little post office is a few doors away from Hotel Los Olivos (Mon–Fri 8:30–14:30, Sat 9:30–13:00, Paseo Boliches 26). Parking is available in Arcos' main square (ticket from machine 110 ptas/hr, only necessary 9:30–14:00 and 18:00–21:00, can get half-price ticket from old-town hotels, free Sat afternoon and all day Sun).

Self-Guided Tour of the Old Town

Avoid this walk during the midday siesta.

1. Plaza del Cabildo: Stand at the viewpoint opposite the church on the town's main square. Survey the square, which in the old days doubled as a bullring: On your right is the parador, a former palace of the governor. On your left is the **city hall** (with the TI), below the 11th-century Moorish **castle** where Ferdinand and Isabel met to plan the Reconquista (closed to the public). Directly in front is the Church of Santa Maria. Notice the fine but unfin-ished **church bell tower**. The old one fell in the earthquake of 1755 (famous for destroying Lisbon). The new Baroque replace-ment was intended to be the tallest in Andalucía after Sevilla's—

Arcos de la Frontera

but money ran out. It looks like someone lives on an upper floor. They do. You can go through the brown door on the right and climb up to a living room hung with bell-ringing ropes and ask the church guardian if you can go to the top of the tower. He may give you the key (tip 100 ptas per person), or he may say "scram."

Enjoy the square's viewpoint. The people of Arcos boast that only they see the backs of the birds as they fly. Ponder the parador's erosion concerns, orderly orange groves, flower-filled greenhouses, and fine views toward Morocco. Belly up to the railing and look down—the town's suicide departure point.

2. Inside the Church of Santa Maria: After Arcos was retaken from the Moors in the 13th century, this church was built—atop a mosque. The fine Renaissance **high altar** covers up a Muslim prayer niche surviving from the older mosque. The altar shows

God with a globe in his hand on top and scenes from the life of
Jesus on the right and from Mary's on the left. While most of the
architecture is Gothic, the elaborate **chapels** are decorated
Baroque and rococo. The ornate statues are used in the Holy Week
processions. In the choir notice the historic **organ** (1,500 pipes,
from 1789). Sniff out the "incorruptible body" of St. Felix
(a third-century martyr). Rome sent it in 1764 after recognizing
this church as the most important in Arcos. Study the finely carved
stalls and, if you're tired, flip up a seat to see how priests used to
rest and "stand" at the same time. In the back of the church, under
a huge fresco of St. Christopher (carrying his staff and baby Jesus),
is a giant votive candle from 1767 (150 ptas, Mon–Fri 10:00–13:00,
15:30–18:30, Sat 10:00–13:00, closed Sun).

3. Church Exterior: Circle clockwise around the church. Down
four steps find the third-century **Roman votive altar** with a carving of the palm tree of life. While the Romans didn't build this
high, they did have a town and temple below Arcos. This was
found in the foundation of the old Moorish mosque that stood
here before the first church was built.

Down a few more steps you come to the **main entrance**
(west portal) of the church—open only for worship on Sundays.
This is a fine example of Plateresque Gothic (Spain's last and most
ornate kind of Gothic), not counting the minaret incorporated into
the wall. In the pavement notice the 15th-century **magic circle**:
12 red and 12 white stones—the white ones with various constella-
tions marked. When a child came to the church to be baptized, the
parents would stop here first for a good Christian exorcism. The
exorcist would stand inside the protective circle and cleanse the
baby of any evil spirits. While locals no longer use this (and a
modern rain drain now marks the center), Sufis from a sect of
Islam still come here in a kind of magical pilgrimage.

Continue around the church to the intersection below the
flying buttresses. These buttresses were built to shore up the
church when it was wounded by an earthquake in 1699. Thanks to
this, the church survived the bigger earthquake of 1755. Look at
the arches supporting the houses downhill on the left. All over
town, arches support earthquake-damaged structures. The spiky
security grill over the window above protected cloistered nuns
when this building was a convent. Sr. Gonzalez Oca's tiny barbershop at the corner has some exciting posters of bulls running
Pamplona-style through the streets of Arcos during Holy Week—
an American from the nearby Navy base at Rota was killed here by
a bull in 1994. (Sr. Gonzalez Oca is happy to show off his posters;
drop in and say, "*Hola.*" Need a haircut? 800 ptas.) Continuing
along under the buttresses, notice the scratches of innumerable
car mirrors on each wall (and be glad you're walking).

4. From the Church to the Market: Completing your circle around the church, turn left under more earthquake-damaged arches and walk down the bright white Calle Escribanos. From now until the end of this walk you're going basically straight until you come to the town's second big church (St. Peter's). After a block you hit Plaza Boticas. At the end of the street on your left is the finest restaurant in town (El Convento—see "Eating," below). On your right is the last remaining **convent** in Arcos. Notice the no-nunsense window grills above, with tiny peepholes for the cloistered nuns. Step into the lobby under the fine portico to find a one-way mirror and a blind spinning cupboard. Push the buzzer and one of the eight sisters inside will spin some boxes of freshly-baked cookies for you to consider buying (600 ptas). If you ask for *magdalenas*, bags of cupcakes will swing around (250 ptas). These are traditional goodies made from completely natural ingredients (daily 8:30–14:30, 17:00–19:00). Buy some cupcakes to support their church work and give them to kids as you complete your walk.

The covered **market** (*mercado*) at the bottom of the plaza resides in an unfinished church. Notice the half-a-church wall at the entry. This was being built for the Jesuits, but construction stopped in 1767 when King Charles III, tired of the Jesuit appetite for politics, expelled the order from Spain. (Jesuits encountered no such tough treatment in South America.) The market is closed on Sunday and on Monday—when you rest on Sunday there's no produce, fish, or meat ready for Monday. Poke inside (public WC).

5. From the Market to the Church of St. Peter: Continue straight (passing the market on your right) down Calle Boticas. Peek into private **patios**. These wonderful, cool-tiled courtyards filled with plants, pools, furniture, and happy family activities are typical of Arcos (and featured on the TI's "Patios" walks).

Look for Las Doce Campanas bakery, which sells traditional *sultana* cookies. These big, dry macaroons (named for sultans) go back to Moorish times. At the next corner, squint back above the bakery to the corner of the tiled rooftop. The tiny mask was placed here to scare evil spirits from the house. This is Arcos' last surviving mask from a tradition that lasted until the mid-19th century.

At the next intersection notice the **ancient columns** on each corner. All over town these columns, many actually Roman (appropriated from their ancient settlement at the foot of the hill), were put up to protect buildings from reckless donkey carts.

As you walk down the next block, notice that the walls are scooped out on either side of the windows—a reminder of the days when women stayed inside but wanted the best possible view of any people action in the streets.

At the old facade of San Miguel, duck right into the first of two **courtyards**. Retired men hang out here and play poker and dominoes. See the historic photos on the walls of the second courtyard.

Just beyond is Arcos' second church, **St. Peter's**. It really is the second church, having had an extended battle with Santa Maria for papal recognition as the leading church in Arcos. When the pope finally recognized Santa Maria, parishioners from St. Peter's even changed their prayers. Rather than say "Maria," they prayed "Saint Peter, mother of God."

In the cool of the evening, the tiny **square** in front of the church—about the only flat piece of pavement around—serves as the old-town soccer field for neighborhood kids. Until a few years ago this church also had a resident bellman—notice the cozy balcony halfway up. He was a basket maker and a colorful character—famous for bringing a donkey into his quarters that grew too big to get back out. Finally, he had no choice but to kill and eat the donkey.

Twenty yards beyond the church is a fine **gallery**, Galería de Arte San Pedro, featuring painting, pottery, and artisans in action.

From St. Peter's church, circle down and around back to the main square, wandering the tiny neighborhood lanes, peeking into patios, kicking a few soccer balls, and enjoying the views.

Nightlife

New Town Evening Action—The newer part of Arcos has a modern charm, as all the generations are out enjoying life in the cool of the evening around Plaza Andalucía (a 10-minute walk from the old town). There are several fine tapas bars around the square and a good Egyptian restaurant if you're ready for something different (see "Eating," below). The big park below the square (Recinto Ferial) is the late-night fun zone—the *carpas* (tents) fill with merrymakers, especially on weekends, when the scene includes open-air tapas bars, disco music, and dancing. There are free live concerts on Friday evenings throughout the summer.

Flamenco—On Plaza Cananeo in the old town, amateur flamenco sizzles on Thursday evening (free, from 22:00 July–August).

Sleeping in Arcos
(160 ptas = about $1, zip code: 11630)

Sleep Code: **S** = Single, **D** = Double/Twin, **T** = Triple, **Q** = Quad, **b** = bathroom, **t** = toilet only, **s** = shower only, **CC** = Credit Card (Visa, MasterCard, Amex), **SE** = Speaks English, **NSE** = No English. A price range reflects off-season to peak-season prices. Breakfast isn't included, nor is the 7 percent IVA tax.

Hotel El Convento, deep in the old town just beyond the parador, is the best value in town. Run by a hardworking family, this cozy, newly renovated hotel offers 11 fine rooms—all with great views, half with view balconies. In 1998 I enjoyed a big party with most of Arcos' big shots present as they dedicated a fine room with a grand-view balcony to "Rick Steves Periodista Turistico" (all rooms Db-10,000 ptas plus tax, 3rd person or balcony-2,000 ptas extra, CC:VMA, Maldonado 2, tel. 95-670-2333, fax 95-670-4128,

Estefania SE). Enjoy a bird-watching breakfast on their view terrace with all of Andalucía spreading beyond your *café con leche*. The family also runs a good restaurant (see "Eating," below).

Parador de Arcos de la Frontera is royally located, recently refurbished, and, for all its elegance, reasonably priced. If you're going to experience a parador (and you can't get into El Convento), this might be the one (Sb-13,000 ptas, Db-17,500 ptas, 1,000 ptas more with a terrace—well worthwhile if you're into relaxing, CC:VMA, elevator, air-con, minibars, free parking, etc., Plaza del Cabildo, tel. 95-670-0500, fax 95-670-1116, www.parador.es, SE).

Hotel Los Olivos is a bright, cool, and airy new place with a fine courtyard, roof garden, bar, view, friendly English-speaking folks, and easy 700-ptas/day parking. This is a poor-man's parador (Sb-5,000 ptas, Db-9,000 ptas, 3rd person-2,000 ptas, tax not included, 10 percent discount for readers of this book, CC:VMA, San Miguel 2, tel. 95-670-0811, fax 95-670-2018, Raquel SE).

Hotel La Fonda is a great traditional Spanish inn with all the rooms off one grand hall (Db-7,000 ptas, no breakfast, across from Egyptian restaurant at Calle Corredera 83, tel. 95-670-0057).

Hotel Marques de Torresoto is a restored 17th-century palace with 15 classy rooms (few views), a peaceful courtyard, and a view terrace (Sb-6,800 ptas, Db-9,100 ptas, Db with salon-11,200 ptas, air-con, CC:VMA, across from Restaurante El Convento, Marques de Torresoto 4, tel. 95-670-0717, fax 95-670-4205, SE).

Hostal San Marcos offers four air-conditioned rooms above a neat little bar in the heart of the old town and a great sun terrace (Db-4,000 ptas, Tb-5,000 ptas, including tax, Marques de Torresoto 6, tel. 95-670-0721, Loli NSE).

Hostal Callejon de las Monjas offers the closest thing to budget beds in the old town but is on a noisy street behind the Church of Santa Maria. The simple rooms are decent and clean and have fans (Sb-3,000 ptas, D-3,500 ptas, Db-4,500 ptas, CC:V, Dean Espinosa 4, tel. 95-670-2302, NSE). Friendly Sr. Gonzalez Oca runs a tiny barbershop in the foyer and a restaurant in the cellar.

If for some reason you want to sleep on the big, noisy road at the Jerez edge of town, two fine hotels nestle between truck stops on A-382: **Hostal Málaga** is surprisingly nice, with 15 clean, attractive rooms and a breezy two-level roof garden (Sb-2,500–3,000 ptas, Db-4,500–5,000 ptas, air-con, TV, parking-500 ptas/day; CC:VMA, Ponce de Leon 5, tel. & fax 95-670-2010, NSE). **Hostal Voy-Voy** is next door (Sb-2,500–3,000 ptas, Db-5,000–6,000 ptas, attached restaurant, CC:VMA, Ponce de Leon 9, tel. 95-670-1412, NSE).

Eating in Arcos

The parador is very expensive, though a costly drink on its million-dollar-view terrace can be a good value. **Restaurante El Convento** has a wonderful atmosphere and is graciously run by

Señora María Moreno-Moreno and her husband, Señor Roldan (daily 13:00–16:00, 19:00–22:30, near the parador at Marques Torresoto 7, reservations necessary, tel. 95-670-3222). The food is the best of traditional local cuisine and well worth the splurge. The hearty 3,000-ptas menu of the day includes a fine red house wine and circular bread sticks (*picos de Arcos*), a local specialty. Many readers report this to be the best meal of their trip.

The *típico* **Alcaravan** is two blocks off Plaza Cabildo under the castle. You can enjoy your tapas on its classy patio or inside what was actually the dungeon of the castle (closed Mon, Calle Nueva 1).

Los Faraones serves good Egyptian cuisine in the new town near the paseo zone of Plaza Andalucía (1,500 ptas, Tue–Sun from 20:00, closed Mon, Debajo del Corral 8, tel. 95-670-0612, Hussein SE).

Transportation Connections—Arcos
By bus to: Jerez (hrly, 30 min), **Ronda** (4/day, 2 hrs), **Cadiz** (9/day, 2 hrs), **Sevilla** (2/day, 2.5 hrs). From Jerez there are hourly connections to Sevilla. Two bus companies share the Arcos bus station. Their Jerez offices keep longer hours and know the Arcos schedules (Jerez tel. 95-634-2174 or 95-634-7844—make it clear you're in Arcos).

MORE ANDALUSIAN HILL TOWNS: THE ROUTE OF THE PUEBLOS BLANCOS
There are plenty of undiscovered and interesting hill towns to explore. About half the towns I visited were memorable. Unfortunately, public transportation is frustrating; I'd do these towns only by car. Good information on the area is rare. Fortunately, a good map, the tourist brochure (pick it up in Sevilla), and a spirit of adventure work fine. Along with Arcos, here are my favorite white villages.

▲▲**Zahara**—This tiny town with a tingly setting under a Moorish castle (worth the climb) has a spectacular view. While the big church, facing the town square, is considered one of the richest in the area, the smaller church has the most loved statue. The Virgin of Dolores is Zahara's answer to Sevilla's Virgin of Marcarena (and is similarly paraded through town during Holy Week). Zahara is a fine overnight stop for those who want to hear only the sounds of wind, birds, and elderly footsteps on ancient cobbles. (TI open daily 9:00–14:00, plus Fri–Sat 16:00–18:00 as well, tel. 95-612-3114.)

▲**Zahara Castle**—During Moorish times Zahara lay within the fortified castle walls above today's town. It was considered the gateway to Granada and a strategic stronghold for the Moors by the Christian forces of the Reconquista. Locals tell of the Spanish conquest of the Moors' castle as if it happened yesterday: After the Spanish failed several times to seize the castle, a clever Spanish soldier noticed that the Moorish sentinel would check to see if any attackers were hiding behind a particular section of the wall by tossing a rock to set the pigeons to flight. If they flew, the sentinel figured there was no danger. One night a Spaniard hid there with a bag of pigeons and let them fly when the sentinel tossed his rock. Seeing the birds fly, the guard assumed he was clear to enjoy a snooze. The clever Spaniard then scaled the wall and opened the door to let his troops in, and the castle was conquered. That was in 1482. Ten years later Granada fell, the Muslims were back in Africa, and the Reconquista was completed. Today the castle is little more than an evocative ruin (always open, free) offering a commanding view. The lake is actually a reservoir. Before 1991 the valley had only a tiny stream.

Sleeping and Eating in Zahara: The **Hostal Marques de Zahara** is the best central hotel and a good value, with 10 comfortable rooms gathered around a cool, quiet courtyard and mother cooking traditional specialties in the restaurant (Sb-3,950 ptas, Db-5,350 ptas, breakfast-500 ptas, CC:VM, San Juan 3, 11688 Zahara, tel. & fax 95-612-3061, Santiago SE). Sr. Manolo Tardio runs **Meson Los Estribos**, a fine little restaurant across from the church, and rents an apartment (Db-4,000 ptas, CC:VMA, tel. 95-612-3145). **Pensión Los Tadeos** is a simple, blocky place just outside of town by the municipal swimming pool (*piscina*) offering basic rooms with great views (S-1,500 ptas, D-3,000 ptas, Paseo de la Fuente, tel. 95-612-3086, family Ruix NSE).

▲**Grazalema**—Another postcard-pretty hill town, Grazalema offers a royal balcony for a memorable picnic, a square where you can watch old-timers playing cards, and plenty of quiet, whitewashed streets to explore. Plaza de Andalucía, a block off the view terrace, has several decent little bars and restaurants and a popular candy store. Grazalema, situated on a west-facing slope of the mountains, catches clouds and is famous as the rainiest place in Spain—but I've had only blue skies on every visit (TI open Tue–Sun 10:00–14:00, 18:00–20:00, closed Mon, tel. 95-613-2225).

Sleeping in Grazalema: The **Casa de las Piedras** has 30 comfortable rooms just a block up from the town center—ask for a room in their new wing (S-1,500 ptas, Sb-3,600 ptas, D-3,000 ptas, Db-4,900 ptas, T-4,000 ptas, Tb-5,900 ptas, breakfast-250 ptas, Calle Las Piedras 32, 11610 Grazalema, tel. 95-613-2014, NSE). **Villa Turistica Grazalema** is a big, popular, happy place for locals enjoying their national park. It has apartments and regular hotel rooms, with balconies on the first floor or opening onto the swimming pool garden on the ground floor (Db-7,365 plus tax, extra person-1,545 ptas, apartments-8,800 ptas, CC:VM, game rooms, restaurant, half-mile outside town, tel. 95-613-2136, fax 95-613-2213).

JEREZ

Jerez, with nearly 200,000 people, is your typical big-city mix of industry, garbage, car bandits, and dusty concrete suburbs, but it has two claims to touristic fame: horses and sherry.

Jerez is ideal for a noontime (or midday) visit on a weekday. See the famous horses, sip some sherry, wander through the old quarter, and swagger out.

Orientation

Tourist Information: The helpful TI gives out free maps and info on the sights (Mon–Fri 9:00–14:00, 17:00–20:00, Sat 10:00–14:00, 17:00–19:00, closed Sun, Calle Larga 39, tel. 95-633-1150).

Arrival in Jerez: The bus station (at Calle Cartuja and Madre de Dios) has a simple baggage checkroom (if it looks closed, knock on the window). *Consigna* is the Spanish word for "baggage check." The train station, a block away, has lockers that take tokens; buy a 400-ptas token (*ficha*) at the ticket window.

Exit the bus station farthest from the WCs and turn left. The center of town and the TI are a 20-minute walk away. At the five-way intersection angle right on Honda; then, at the fountain, make a sharp left on the pedestrian street, Calle Larga, to reach the TI.

If you're arriving by train, angle right as you leave the station. Cross the intersection. The bus station is on your left. Continue straight, following directions from the bus station (above). Taxis from the station to the horses cost about 500 ptas.

Sights—Jerez

▲▲**Royal Andalusian School of Equestrian Art**—If you're into horses, this is a must. Even if you're not, this is horse art like you've never seen. The school does its Horse Symphony show at noon every Thursday and from March through October on Tuesday as well (1,500–2,500 ptas, cash only, reservations tel. 95-631-9635 or 95-631-1111, fax 95-630-9954, call for current schedule). This is an equestrian ballet with choreography, purely Spanish music, and cos-tumes from the 19th century. The stern horsemen and their talented and obedient steeds prance, jump, and do-si-do in time to the music, to the delight of an arena filled with mostly local horse aficionados. Training sessions, open to the public on Monday, Wednesday, and Friday from 11:00 to 13:00, offer a 600-ptas sneak preview. Practice sessions can be exciting or dull, depending on what the trainers are working on. If you call ahead you can arrange a private guide (free, tips accepted) or join an existing tour to see the stables, horses, tack room, and horse health center. Sip sherry in the arena's bar to com-plete this Jerez experience. If you're driving, follow signs from the center of Jerez to Real Escuela Andaluza de Arte Ecuestre (street parking). Otherwise it's a 30-minute walk from the train station, a 10-minute walk from the TI, or a short taxi ride.

mamalon

Jerez

▲▲**Sherry bodega tours**—Spain produces more than 10 million gallons per year of this fortified wine, ranging in taste from *fino* (dry) to *amontillado* (medium) to *oloroso* (sweet). The name *sherry* comes from English attempts to pronounce Jerez. While traditionally the drink of England's aristocracy, today it's more popular with Germans. Your tourist map of Jerez is speckled with wine barrels. Each of these barrels is a sherry bodega that offers tours and tasting.

Sandeman Sherry Tour: Just over a fence from the horse school is the venerable Sandeman Bodega (which has been producing sherry since 1790 and is the longtime choice of English royalty). This tour is the aficionado's choice for its knowledgeable guides and their quality explanations of the process (500 ptas, tours Mon–Fri 10:00–16:00 on the hour, Sat 10:00–14:00, bottling finishes at 14:00; the finale is a chance to taste three varieties; tel. 95-630-1100 for English tour times and to reserve a place; fax 95-630-2626).

Harvey's Bristol Creme: Their English/German tours (weekdays at 10:30 and 12:00 or by arrangement) aren't substantial but include a 10-minute video and all the sherry you like in the tasting room (500 ptas, Calle Pintor Munoz Cebrian, reservations recommended, tel. 95-634-6004).

Gonzalez Byas: The makers of the famous Tío Pepe offer a tourist-friendly tour with more pretense and less actual sherry making on display (it's done in a new, enormous plant outside of town). Gonzalez Byas is the only bodega that offers daily tours (900 ptas on weekdays, 1,000 ptas on weekends, open year-round, Manuel Maria Gonzalez 12, tel. 95-635-7000 or 95-635-7016). Gonzales Byas is Disneyfying their tours, and schedules change frequently—call for the latest.

The very local **Taberna La Sureña,** across the street from Gonzalez Byas and the Alcazar, serves sherry made by the family of Christo on tap in a 100-year-old hole-in-the-wall wine-bar (daily 9:00–16:00, 19:00–24:00, Puerto 7, tel. 95-631-4180).

Alcazar—This gutted castle looks tempting, but don't bother. The 200-pta entry fee doesn't even include the ramparts. Its underground parking is convenient for those touring Gonzalez Byas Bodega (150 ptas/hr).

Transportation Connections—Jerez

Jerez's bus station is shared by four bus companies, each with its own schedules, some specializing in certain destinations, others sharing popular destinations such as Sevilla and Algeciras. Shop around for the best departure time. By car it's a zippy 30 minutes from Jerez to Arcos.

By bus to: Tarifa (3/day, 3 hrs), **Algeciras** (8/day, 2.5 hrs), **Cadiz** (10/day, 50 min), **Arcos** (hrly, 30 min), **Ronda** (5/day, 2.5 hrs), **Sevilla** (10/day, 90 min), **Málaga** (1/day, 5 hrs), **Córdoba** (1/day, 3.5 hrs), **Madrid** (6/day, 7 hrs).

By train to: Cadiz (2/hr, 50 min), **Sevilla** (12/day, 1 hr), **Madrid** (2/day, 4 hrs), **Barcelona** (3/day, 12 hrs).

Drivers' note: In Jerez, blue-line zones require prepaid parking tickets on your dash on weekdays from 9:00 to 13:30 and 17:00 to 20:00 and on Saturday from 9:00 to 14:00; Sundays and July and August afternoons are free. Otherwise there's the handy underground parking lot near the Alcazar.

MEDINA SIDONIA

(For drivers between Tarifa and Arcos)

This place has no TI (read "no tourists"). It is whitewashed as can be surrounding its church and castle-ruin-topped hill. Give it a quick look. Signs to Vejer and then Centro Urbano route you through the middle to Plaza de España—great for a coffee stop. Or, if it's lunchtime, consider buying a picnic, as all the necessary shops are nearby and the plaza benches afford a fine workaday view of a perfectly untouristy Andalusian town at play.

You can drive from here up to the church (Plazuela de la Yglesia Mayor), where, for a tip, the man will show you around. Even without a tip you can climb yet another belfry for yet another vast Andalusian view. The castle ruins just aren't worth the trouble.

VEJER DE LA FRONTERA

(For drivers between Tarifa and Arcos)

Vejer, south of Jerez and just 20 miles north of Tarifa, will lure all but the very jaded off the highway. Vejer's strong Moorish roots give it a distinct Moroccan (or Greek island) flavor—you know, black-clad women whitewashing their homes and lanes that can't decide if they're roads or stairways. Only a few years ago women wore veils. The town has no real sights (other than its women's faces), no TI, and very little tourism, but it makes for a pleasant stop.

The coast near Vejer is lonely, with fine but windswept beaches. It's popular with windsurfers and sand flies. The Battle of Trafalgar was fought just off Cabo de Trafalgar (a nondescript lighthouse today). I drove the circle so that you need not.

A newcomer on Andalucía's tourist map, the old town of Vejer has only two hotels. **Convento de San Francisco** is a poorman's parador in a classy refurbished convent (Sb-6,800 ptas, Db-9,065 ptas, breakfast-525 ptas, prices bargainable in off-season, CC:VMA, La Plazuela, 11150 Vejer, tel. 95-645-1001, fax 95-645-1004, SE). They have the rare but unnecessary Vejer town map. A much better value is the clean and charming **Hostal La Posada** (S-2,000 ptas, Db-4,000 ptas, cheaper off-season, Los Remedios 21, tel. 95-645-0258, NSE). Both are at the entrance to the old town, at the top of the switchbacks past the town's lone traffic cop.

RONDA

With 40,000 people, Ronda is one of the largest white towns; and with its gorge-straddling setting, it's one of the most spectacular. While it can be crowded with day-trippers, nights are peaceful. And since it's served by train and bus, Ronda makes a relaxing break for nondrivers traveling between Granada, Sevilla, and Córdoba.

Ronda's main attractions are its gorge-spanning bridges, the oldest bullring in Spain, and an interesting old town. Spaniards know it as the cradle of modern bullfighting and the romantic home of old-time banditos. Its cliffside setting is as dramatic today as it was practical yesterday: For the Moors it provided a tough bastion, taken by the Spaniards only in 1485, seven years before Granada fell. To 19th-century bandits it was a Bolivia without the boat ride.

Ronda's breathtaking ravine divides the town's labyrinthine old Moorish quarter and its new, noisier, and more sprawling Mercadillo quarter. A massive-yet-graceful 18th-century bridge connects these two neighborhoods. Most things of touristic importance (TI, post office, hotels, and bullring) are clustered within a few

Ronda

200 YARDS

SOUTH

TO COSTA DEL SOL, MALAGA

CITY WALL

SANTA MARIA LA MAYOR

MONDRAGON PALACE

ARMIÑAN

⑩

MOORISH QUARTER

ARAB BRIDGE

ARMIÑAN

TENORIO

PUENTE NUEVO

⑫

⑬ ⑪

GUADALEVIN RIVER

PARA-DOR

PEÑAS

CANTOS

LOS REMEDIOS

LA

VILLA

⑧

⑦

PLAZA ESPAÑA

PLAZA C.ABELA

NUEVA

⑥

ℹ

MERCA-DILLO

⑭

CORTES

NARANJA

ESPINEL

VIRGEN

PLAZA DE TOROS

QUARTER

ALAMEDA

RAMON

ALMENDRA

SOUVIRON

MOLINO

②

③

⑤

⑩

POZO

PLAZA MERCED

MONTEREJAS

MADRID

SAN JOSE

DR. FLEMING

⑨

TO TRAIN STATION

ANDALUCIA

BUS STATION

TO SEVILLA, ARCOS & PILETA CAVES

① ROYAL	⑦ VIRGIN DEL ROCIO	⑫ CASA DEL MARQUES DE SALVATIERRA
② RONDA SOL	⑧ DON MIGUEL	⑬ PUENTE VIEJO
③ BIARRITZ	⑨ REINA VICTORIA	⑭ HOSTAL SAN FRANCISCO
⑤ EL TAJO	⑩ MUSEO DEL BANDOLERO	
⑥ LA ESPANOLA	⑪ CASA DEL REY MORO	

blocks of the bridge. While day-trippers from the touristy Costa del Sol clog the streets during the day, locals retake the town in the early evening. The paseo scene happens in the new town, on Ronda's major pedestrian street, Carrera Espinel.

Orientation

Tourist Information: The TI is on the main square, Plaza España, opposite the bridge (Mon–Fri 9:00–19:00, Sat–Sun 10:00–14:00, shorter hours off-season, tel. 95-287-1272). Get their free Ronda map and a listing of the latest museum hours; consider buying maps to Granada or Sevilla (100 ptas each). While the town has precious little organized for tourism, you may see the tiny Tajotur bus parked in front of the TI gathering tourists for a drive outside of town to the most scenic places from which to view the gorge and bridge (1,000 ptas, 45 min, no narration, goes when four show up).

Arrival in Ronda: The train station is a 15-minute walk from the center. Turn right out of the station on Avenida Andalucía, turn left at the roundabout (the bus station is on your right), and then walk four blocks and you'll cross Calle Almendra (where several recommended hotels are located). At the pedestrian street (Carrera Espinel, a few blocks farther) turn right to reach the TI. From the bus station, cross the roundabout and follow directions above.

Drivers coming up from the coast catch C339 at San Pedro de Alcantara and wind 30 miles into the mountains. The handiest place to park is the underground lot at Plaza del Socorro (one block from the bullring, 150 ptas/hr, 1,800 ptas/24 hrs).

Sights—Ronda

▲▲▲**The Gorge and New Bridge**—Ronda's main bridge, called Puente Nuevo (New Bridge), mightily spans the gorge. A bridge was built here in 1735 but fell after six years. This one was built from 1751 to 1793. The ravine, called El Tajo—360 feet down and 200 feet wide—divides Ronda into the whitewashed old Moorish town (called La Cuidad) and the new town (El Mercadillo), which was built after the Christian reconquest in 1485. Look down... carefully. The architect fell to his death while inspecting it, and hundreds from both sides were thrown off this bridge during Spain's brutal civil war.

You can see the foundations of the original bridge (and a great view of the New Bridge) from the park named Vista Panoramica Jardines Ciudad de Cuenca. From Plaza España walk down Calle Villanueva and turn right on Calle Los Remedios at the sign.

▲▲**Bullfighting Ring**—Ronda is the birthplace of modern bullfighting, and this ring is the first great Spanish bullring. In the early 1700s Francisco Romero established the rules of modern bullfighting and introduced the scarlet cape, held unfurled with a stick. His son Juan further developed the ritual or sport, and his grandson Pedro was one of the first great matadors (killing nearly 6,000 bulls in his career).

To see the **museum**, buy tickets from the shop to the right of the bullring's central door. You get to walk across the actual arena, with plenty of time to play "*toro*" surrounded by 5,000 empty seats. The arena was built in 1784. Notice the 176 classy Tuscan columns. With your back to the entry you can see the Spanish flag where the dignitaries sit (near the gate where the bull enters). On the left is the place for the band—in the case of a small town like Ronda, a high-school band. *Sol* means "sun" (cheap seats) and *sombra* means "shade." Straight ahead, where the horses drag out the dead bull after each fight, is the gate leading to the museum. The tiny museum—with not a word of English information available—is a shrine to bullfighting and the historic Romero family. You'll see stuffed heads (of bulls), photos, artwork, posters, and costumes (400 ptas, daily 10:00–20:00, closes off-season at 19:00, on the main drag in the new town, two blocks up from the bridge and TI).

Bullfights are scheduled for the first weekend of September and occur occasionally in spring and summer. The Alameda del Tajo park, a block away, is a fine place for people watching or a snooze in the shade.

Santa Maria la Mayor Cathedral—This 15th-century church shares a fine parklike square with orange trees and the city hall. Its Renaissance bell tower still has parts of the old minaret. It was built on and around the remains of Moorish Ronda's main mosque (which was itself built on the site of a temple to Julius Caesar). Partially destroyed by an earthquake, the reconstruction of the church resulted in the Moorish/Gothic/Renaissance/Baroque fusion (or confusion) you see today. Enjoy the bright frescoes and elaborately carved choir and altar. The treasury displays vestments that look curiously like matadors' brocaded outfits (200 ptas, daily 10:00–19:00, closes off-season at 18:00, in the old town).

Mondragon Palace (Palacio de Mondragon)—This beautiful Moorish building was built in the 14th century, possibly as the residence of Moorish kings, and lovingly restored in the 16th. It houses an enjoyable prehistory museum, with exhibits on Neolithic toolmaking and early metallurgy (many captions in English). Even if you have no interest in your ancestors, this is worth it for the architecture alone (250 ptas, Mon–Fri 10:00–19:00, Sat–Sun 10:00–15:00, on Plaza Mondragon in the old town). Linger in the two small view gardens, especially the shady one. Wander out to the nearby Plaza de Maria Auxiliadora for more views.

Museo del Bandolero—This tiny museum, while not as intriguing as it sounds, is an interesting assembly of *bandito* photos, guns, clothing, and knickknacks. The Jesse Jameses of Andalucía called this remote area home, and brief but helpful English descriptions make this a fun detour. One brand of romantic bandits were those who fought Napoleon's army—often more effectively than the regular Spanish troops (300 ptas, daily 10:00–20:00, across the main street below the Church of Santa Maria at Calle Arminan 65, tel. 95-287-7785).

Parador National de Ronda—Walk around and through this newest of Spain's fabled *paradores*. The views from the walkway just below the outdoor terrace are magnificent. Anyone is welcome at the cafés, but you have to be a guest to use the pool.

Walk through Old Town—From the New Bridge you can descend into a world of whitewashed houses, tiny grilled balconies, and winding lanes—the old town. The romantic-sounding but not very interesting **Casa del Rey Moro** (600 ptas, daily 10:00–19:00) offers no *casa*, just a fine old garden combining Muslim, Hispanic, and French traditions and "the Mine," an exhausting series of 365 stairs (like climbing down and then up a 20-story building) leading to the floor of the gorge. This zigzag staircase was cut into the wall of the gorge by the Moors in the 14th century. They used Spanish slaves to haul water to the thirsty town.

Fifty meters downhill from Casa del Rey Moro is **Casa del Marques de Salvatierra**, a much more interesting sight. With the "distribution" following the Reconquista here in 1485, the Spanish king gave this fine house to the Salvatierra family. It's been in their hands ever since. The facade is rich in colonial symbolism from Spanish America. Note the pre-Columbian-looking characters flanking the balcony above the door below the family coat of arms. The interior gives a good look at how Andalucía's rural nobility lived in the 18th century. You visit only with a tour, a low-energy 20-minute ramble with a few words of Spanish to guide you, departing probably at the top and bottom of each hour (400 ptas, Fri–Wed 11:00–14:00, 16:00–19:00, closed Thu).

Continuing downhill you come to **Puente Viejo** (Old Bridge), built in 1616 upon the ruins of a Roman bridge. From here look down to see the old Puente Arabe, originally built by the Moors. Far to the right you can glimpse some of the surviving highly fortified old Moorish city walls. Crossing the bridge you see stairs on the right leading scenically along the gorge back to the New Bridge via a fine viewpoint. Straight ahead bubbles the welcoming "Eight Springs" fountain.

Near Ronda: Pileta Caves

The Pileta Caves (Cuevas de la Pileta) are about the best look a tourist can get at prehistoric cave painting. The caves and their stalagmites, bones, and 20,000-year-old paintings, are 22 kilometers from Ronda, past the town of Benoajan at the end of the road.

Farmer Jose Pullon, whose grandfather discovered the caves, and his family live down the hill from the caves. He leads groups through on one-hour tours (700 ptas, daily 10:00–13:00, 16:00–18:00, closes off-season at 17:00, closing times indicate last entrance, tel. 95-216-7343). Sr. Pullon is a master at hurdling the language barrier. As you walk, he'll spend over an hour pointing out lots of black, ochre, and red drawings (five times as old as the Egyptian pyramids) and some weirdly recognizable natural formations, such as "the Michelin man" and a Christmas tree. The famous caves at Altamira are closed, so if you want to see Neolithic paintings in Spain, this is it.

While possible without wheels (taking the Ronda–Benoajan bus or train and a two-hour, five-kilometer uphill hike), I wouldn't bother. By car it's easy. Leave Ronda on the highway to Sevilla (C339), exit after a few kilometers left toward Benoajan, and then follow the signs, bearing right just before Benoajan, up to the dramatic dead end. Leave nothing of value in your car. Nearby Montejaque has a great outdoor restaurant, La Casita.

Sleeping in Ronda
(160 ptas = $1, zip code: 29400)

Ronda has plenty of reasonably priced, uninspired, decent-value accommodations. It's crowded only during Holy Week (the week before Easter) and through September. My recommendations are in the new town, a short walk from the New Bridge and a 10-minute walk from the train station. (The exceptions are Hostal Andalucía, across from the station, and Reina Victoria, at the edge of town—and the gorge.) In the cheaper places, ask for a room with a *ventana* (window) to avoid the few interior rooms. Breakfast and the 7 percent IVA tax are usually not included.

Hotel La Española is perfectly located on a pedestrian street just off Plaza España around the corner from the TI. Each of its 18 rooms is newly remodeled and comfy, with air-conditioning and modern bathrooms (Sb-6,000 ptas, Db-11,000 ptas, big Db suite-13,500 ptas, includes breakfast but not tax, José Aparicio 3, tel. 95-287-1051, fax 95-287-8001, NSE).

Hotel Royal has clean, boring rooms—many on a busy street. Ask for a *tranquilo* room in the back (Sb-3,500 ptas, Db-5,700 ptas, CC:VMA, air-con, 42 Virgen de la Paz, three blocks off Plaza España, tel. 95-287-1141, fax 95-287-8132, some English spoken).

The friendly **Hostal Ronda Sol** has a homey atmosphere with cheap but monkish rooms (S-1,700 ptas, D-2,800 ptas, Almendra 11, tel. 95-287-4497, NSE). Next door, and run by the same man, **Hostal Biarritz** offers similar rooms, some with private baths (S-1,700 ptas, D-2,800 ptas, Db-3,500 ptas, Almendra 7, tel. 95-287-2910, NSE).

The 65-room **Hotel El Tajo** has pleasant, quiet rooms once you get past the tacky Moorish decoration in the foyer (Sb-4,000 ptas, Db-7,000 ptas, parking-1,000 ptas/day, CC:VMA, air-con, Calle Cruz Verde 7, a half-block off the pedestrian street, tel. 95-287-4040, fax 95-287-5099, SE).

Hostal Virgin del Rocio, spotless and central, won't overwhelm you with friendliness (Db-5,500–7,000 ptas, breakfast-300 ptas, Calle Nueva 18, near Plaza España, tel. & fax 95-287-7425).

Hostal San Francisco offers 15 small, humble rooms a block off the main pedestrian street in the town center (Db-4,000 ptas, includes tax, CC:VM, Maria Cabrera 18, tel. & fax 95-287-3299).

Hostal Andalucía, a plain but clean place with 11 comfortable rooms and a low metabolism, is immediately across the street from the train station (Sb-2,700 ptas, Db-4,500 ptas, air-con, Martinez Astein 19, tel. & fax 95-287-5450, Sra. Campos Garcia NSE).

Splurges: Ronda offers three tempting splurges. The gorge-facing **Don Miguel** is just left of the bridge. Many of its red-tiled and comfortable rooms have gorgeous views and view balconies—at no extra cost—but street rooms come with a little noise (Sb-6,000 ptas, Db-9,500 ptas, cheaper off-season, breakfast-450 ptas, parking garage a block away-750 ptas/day, CC:VMA, air-con, elevator, Calle Villanueva 8, tel. 95-287-7722, fax 95-287-8377, SE).

You can't miss the striking **Parador de Ronda** on Plaza España. It's an impressive integration of stone, glass, and marble. All rooms have hardwood floors and fantastic view balconies (ask about family-friendly duplexes) and are surprisingly reasonable There's also with a pool overlooking the bridge (Sb-12,000–14,800 ptas, Db-15,000–18,500 ptas, breakfast-1,300 ptas, garage-1,200 ptas, CC:VMA, Plaza España, tel. 95-287-7500, fax 95-287-8188, SE). Consider at least a drink on the terrace.

The royal **Reina Victoria**, hanging over the gorge at the edge of town, has a great view—Hemingway loved it—but you'll pay for it (Sb-11,000 ptas, Db-17,600 ptas, CC:VMA, air-con, elevator, Jerez 25, tel. 95-287-1240, fax 95-287-1075, SE).

Eating in Ronda

Dodge the tourist traps. They say the best meal in Ronda is at the **parador** (*muy* elegant, figure 3,500 ptas). **Plaza del Socorro**, a block in front of the bullring, is a wonderful local scene, where families enjoy the square and its restaurants. Take a paseo with the locals down pedestrian-only Carrera Espinel and choose a place with tables spilling out into the action. The best view-drinks in town are sipped on the terraces of the **Don Miguel Hotel** or the parador.

Restaurant Pedro Romero, assuming a shrine to bullfighting draped in *el toro* memorabilia doesn't ruin your appetite, gets good reviews (2,000 ptas meals, nightly from 20:00, air-con, across the street from bullring at Calle Virgen de la Paz 18).

Restaurant "Casa Santa Pola" serves unmemorable but cheap *típico* food with friendly service, gorge views, and a great Moorish cliffside ambience (3-course dinners 1,300 ptas, daily 19:00–23:30, crossing New Bridge, take first the left downhill and you'll see the sign, Calle Santo Domingo).

Transportation Connections—Ronda

By bus to: Arcos (4/day, 2 hrs), **Benoajan** (2/day, 30 min), **Jerez** (5/day, 3 hrs), **Grazalema** (2/day, 1 hr), **Zahara** (1/day, weekdays only, 1 hr), **La Línea** (1/day, weekdays only, 3 hrs), **Sevilla** (5/day, 2.5 hrs; see trains below), **Málaga** (10/day, 3 hrs; access other Costa del Sol points from Málaga), **Marbella** (6/day, 75 min), **Fuengirola** (5/day, 2 hrs), **Nerja** (4 hrs, transfer in Málaga; can take train or bus Ronda–Málaga). There's no efficient way to call "the bus company" because there are four sharing the same station. It's best to just drop by and compare schedules.

By train to: Algeciras (5/day, 2 hrs) **Bobadilla** (4/day, 1 hr), **Málaga** (4/day, 2.5 hrs, transfer in Bobadilla), **Sevilla** (3/day, 3.5 hrs, transfer in Bobadilla), **Granada** (3/day, 3.5 hrs, transfer in Bobadilla), **Córdoba** (4/day, 3.5 hrs, transfer in Bobadilla), **Madrid** (4/day, 5 hrs, 1 direct night train—23:20–8:40). It's a sleepy station serving only 11 trains a day. Transfers are a snap and time-coordinated in Bobadilla; with four trains arriving and departing simultaneously, double-check that you've jumped on the right one. Ronda train information: station tel. 95-287-1673, RENFE office tel. 95-287-1662.

Route Tips for Drivers—Andalucía

Sevilla to Arcos: The remote hill towns of Andalucía are a joy to tour by car with Michelin map #446 or any other good map. Drivers can zip south on N-IV from Sevilla along the river, following signs to Cádiz. Take the fast toll freeway (blue signs, E5, A4). The toll-free N-IV is curvy and dangerous. About halfway to Jerez, at Las Cabezas, take C343 to Villamartin. From there, circle scenically (and clockwise) through the thick of the Pueblos Blancos—Zahara and Grazalema—to Arcos.

It's about two hours from Sevilla to Zahara. You'll find decent but winding roads and sparse traffic. It gets worse if you take the tortuous series of switchbacks over the 4,500-foot summit of Puerto de Las Palomas on the direct but difficult road from Zahara to Grazalema. Remember to refer to your "Ruta de Pueblos Blancos" pamphlet.

Traffic flows through old Arcos only from west to east (coming from the east, circle south under town). The TI, my recommended hotels, and parking (Paseo Andalucía) are all in the west. Driving in Arcos is like threading needles. But if your car is small and the town seems quiet enough, follow signs to the parador, where you'll find the only old-town car park.

Arcos to Tarifa (80 miles): Drive from Arcos to Jerez in 30 minutes. If you're going to Tarifa, take the tiny A393 road at the Jerez edge of Arcos toward Paterna and Vejer. Later you'll pick up signs to Medina Sidonia and then to Vejer and Tarifa.

COSTA DEL SOL: SPAIN'S SOUTH COAST

It's so bad, it's interesting. To northern Europeans the sun is a drug, and this is their needle. Anything resembling a quaint fishing village has been bikini-strangled and Nivea-creamed. Oblivious to the concrete, pollution, ridiculous prices, and traffic jams, tourists lie on the beach like game hens on skewers—cooking, rolling, and sweating under the sun.

Where Europe's most popular beach isn't crowded by highrise hotels, most of it's in a freeway choke hold. Wonderfully undeveloped beaches between Tarifa and Cádiz and east of Alveria are ignored, while lemmings make the scene where the coastal waters are so polluted that hotels are required to provide swimming pools. It's a fascinating study in human nature.

Laugh with Ronald McDonald at the car-jammed resorts. But if you want a place to stay and play in the sun, unroll your beach towel at Nerja.

You're surprisingly close to jolly olde England. The land of tea and scones, fish and chips, pubs and bobbies awaits you—in Gibraltar. And beyond "The Rock," the whitewashed port of Tarifa, the least-developed piece of Spain's generally overdeveloped south coast, provides an enjoyable springboard for a quick trip into Morocco (next chapter).

Planning Your Time

My opinions on the "Costa del Turismo" are valid for peak season. If you're there during a quieter time and you like the ambience of a beach resort, it can be a pleasant stop. Off-season it can be neutron-bomb quiet.

The whole 150-mile-long coastline takes four hours to drive or six hours by bus. You can resort-hop by bus across the entire

Costa del Sol

Costa del Sol and reach Nerja for dinner. If you want to party on the beach, it can take as much time as Mazatlán.

NERJA

Somehow Nerja, while cashing in on the fun-in-the-sun culture, has actually kept much of its quiet, Old World charm. It has good beaches, a fun evening paseo that culminates in the proud Balcony of Europe terrace, enough pastry shops and nightlife, and locals who get more excited about their many festivals than the tourists do. For a taste of the British expatriate scene, pick up the monthly *Street Wise* magazine or tune in to Coastline Radio at 97.7 FM. The weekly market is colorful, lively, and fun (Tue 9:30–14:00, along Calle Antonio Fernandiz at the edge of town).

Orientation

Tourist Information: The helpful, English-speaking TI has town maps, bus schedules, and tips on beaches and side trips (Mon–Fri 10:00–14:00, 17:30–20:30, Sat 10:00–13:00, closed Sun, Puerta del Mar 2, just off the Balcony of Europe, tel. 95-252-1531). Ask for the TI's free *Sierra de Nerja* brochure. Nerja taxis charge a set 600-ptas fee (e.g., to Burriana beach). A goofy little tourist train does its 30-minute loop twice an hour (350 ptas, 10:30–24:00).

Sights—Nerja

▲▲**Balcony of Europe (Balcón de Europa)**—This promenade on a bluff over the beach is the center of the town's paseo. It overlooks miles of coastline as well as a few little coves and caves below.

Beaches—Nerja has several good beaches. The sandiest (and most

Nerja

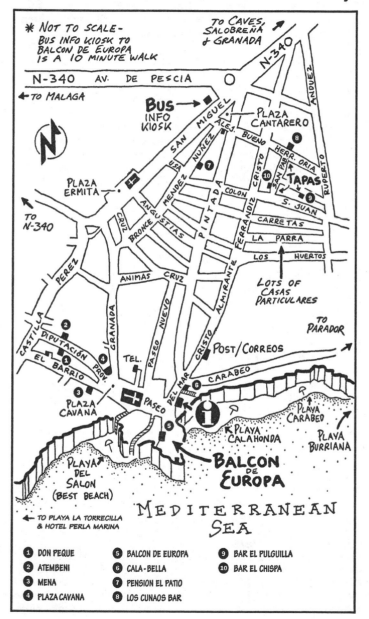

* NOT TO SCALE -
BUS INFO KIOSK TO
BALCON DE EUROPA
IS A 10 MINUTE WALK

N-340   AV. DE PESCIA

← TO MALAGA

TO CAVES,
SALOBREÑA
& GRANADA

N-340

ANDUEZ

BUS
INFO
KIOSK

PLAZA
CANTARERO

SAN MIGUEL

ALEJ.

BUENO

CRISTO

HERR. ORIA

SAN PAB.

RUPERTO

TAPAS

PLAZA
ERMITA

NUÑEZ

USA

MENDEZ

ANGUSTIAS

PINTADA

COLON

FERRANDIZ

S. JUAN

TO
N-340

CRUZ

BRONCE

CARRETAS

LA PARRA

LOS   HUERTOS

PEREZ

ANIMAS

CRUZ

ALMIRANTE

LOTS OF
CASAS
PARTICULARES

CASTILLA

DIPUTACIÓN

GRANADA

PASEO NUEVO

CRISTO

TO
PARADOR

EL BARRIO

PROV.

TEL.

DEL MAR

POST/CORREOS

CARABEO

PLAZA
CAVANA

PASEO

PLAYA
CARABEO

PLAYA
CALAHONDA

PLAYA
BURRIANA

BALCON
DE
EUROPA

PLAYA
DEL
SALON
(BEST BEACH)

← TO PLAYA LA TORRECILLA
& HOTEL PERLA MARINA

MEDITERRANEAN
SEA

❶ DON PEQUE
❷ ATEMBENI
❸ MENA
❹ PLAZA CAVANA

❺ BALCON DE EUROPA
❻ CALA-BELLA
❼ PENSION EL PATIO
❽ LOS CUNAOS BAR

❾ BAR EL PULGUILLA
❿ BAR EL CHISPA

crowded) is down the walkway to the right of the Restaurante Marissal, just off the Balcony of Europe. The pebblier beach, full of fun pathways, crags, and crannies (head down through the arch to the right of the TI office), has a trail leading east to a bigger beach, Playa de Burriana. This is Nerja's leading beach, with all the jet-ski, paddleboat, and entertainment options. Playa de la Torrecilla, a 10-minute walk west of the Balcony of Europe, is the cleanest. All have showers, bars, restaurants, and beach chairs (300–400 ptas/day). Beware of red flags on the beach, which indicate when seas are too rough for safe swimming.

▲**Caves of Nerja (Cuevas de Nerja)**—These caves, four kilometers east of Nerja, have the most impressive array of stalactites and stalagmites I've seen anywhere in Europe, with huge caverns filled with expertly backlit formations and appropriate music. The visit is a 30-minute unguided ramble deep into the mountain, up and down lots of dark stairs congested with Spanish families. At the end you reach the Hall of the Cataclysm, where you'll circle what, according to Guinness, is the world's largest stalactite-made column. Then you hike out. Someone figured that it took one trillion drops to make the column (650 ptas, daily 10:00–14:00, 16:00–20:00, closes off-season at 18:30, tel. 95-252-9520). To get to the caves, catch a bus from the Nerja bus stop on Avenida de Pescia (100 ptas, 16/day, 15 min).

Frigiliani—This picture-perfect whitewashed village, only six kilometers from Nerja, is easy by bus or car. It's a worthwhile detour from the beach, particularly if you don't have time for the Pueblos Blancos hill towns.

Sleeping in Nerja
(160 ptas = about $1, zip code: 29780)
Sleep Code: **S** = Single, **D** = Double/Twin, **T** = Triple, **Q** = Quad, **b** = bathroom, **t** = toilet only, **s** = shower only, **CC** = Credit Card (Visa, MasterCard, Amex), **SE** = Speaks English, **NSE** = No English spoken.

The entire Costa del Sol is crowded during August and Holy Week (when prices are at their highest). The season is basically mid-July through mid-September, prime time for Spanish workers to hit the beaches. Any other time of year you'll find Nerja has plenty of comfy, low-rise, easygoing, resort-type hotels and rooms. Room rates are three-tiered, with the highest being only for August or, at most, July through September.

Sleeping in Hotels
Hotel Plaza Cavana overlooks a plaza lily-padded with cafés. If you like a central location, marble floors, modern furnishings, an elevator, and a small rooftop swimming pool, dive in (Sb-7,500–10,500 ptas, Db-9,500–14,500 ptas, extra bed-3,000 ptas, some view rooms, air-con, your car can ride an elevator into the basement for

1,000 ptas/day, 2 blocks from Balcón de Europa at Plaza Cavana 10, tel. 95-252-4000, fax 95-252-4008, SE).

The best place in town is **Balcón de Europa,** right on the water and on the square, with the prestigious address Balcón de Europa 1. With all the modern comforts and an elevator down to your own private beach, you'll feel like you own the town. Suites all have a sea-view balcony. Half the regular rooms come with a sea view (Sb-7,900–12,350 ptas, Db-11,900–17,100 ptas, add about 4,000 ptas for a suite, 3rd person pays 3,000 ptas, air-con, elevator, parking-900 ptas/day, CC:VMA, tel. 95-252-0800, fax 95-252-4490, SE).

Hotel Perla Marina is a big, modern, splashy place with sprawling public rooms, no soul, and plenty of fun-in-the-sun package groups. It's right on a fine beach a 15-minute walk from the center. Most of its 100 rooms overlook the sea. If you're here for the beach, not the town, this place is ideal (Sb-6,000, 7,000, or 8,500 ptas, Db-9,500, 12,000, or 14,000 ptas, suites for 3,000 ptas extra, breakfast and tax extra, CC:VMA, air-con, elevator, grassy backyard faces the surf, free on-street parking, Calle Merida 7, tel. 95-252-3350, fax 95-252-4083, SE). **Hotel Riu Monica,** next door, is much bigger, classier, and twice as expensive (tel. 95-252-1100).

Nerja's **parador,** housed in a new office-type building rather than a castle, lacks character. The spacious, suite-like rooms are pricey (Sb-12,000–15,200 ptas, Db-15,000–19,500 ptas, CC:VMA, air-con, free parking, swimming pool, 15-minute walk from town center, Almuñecar 8, tel. 95-252-0050, fax 95-252-1997, SE).

Sleeping in Cheaper Hostals

The new **Hostal Marissal,** just next door to the fancy Balcón de Europa hotel, has 14 modern, spacious rooms, four with small view balconies directly above the Balcón (Db-4,500–7,000 ptas, CC:VM, air con, Balcón de Europa 3, reception at café, tel. & fax 95-252-0199, SE).

Hostal Residencia Don Peque, also in the center, has tastefully decorated rooms, all with balconies. Front rooms over the noisy street have air-conditioning (Db-4,000–5,800 ptas, CC:VM, Diputación 13, tel. 95-252-1318, some English spoken).

Hostal Atembeni, across the street from Don Peque, is more basic (Sb-2,400–4,300 ptas, Db-3,500–5,300 ptas, ceiling fans, no air-con, CC:VMA, Diputación 12, tel. 95-252-1341, some English spoken).

Hostal Residencia Mena is erratically run but has homey rooms and a breezy garden (Sb-2,000–3,500 ptas, Db-3,500–5,500 ptas, street noise, El Barrio 15, tel. 95-252-0541, fax 95-252-1764, NSE).

Pensión El Patio is clean, homey, and really local—worth the communication struggles (Db-3,500, 4,000, or 5,000 ptas, Tb-4,500–7,000 ptas, Mendez Nuñez 12, tel. 95-252-2930, NSE). It's in the residential section three blocks from the Nerja bus stop, near the corner of Calle America and Mendez Nuñez. The kids of the family always seem to be dressed up and heading off to some festival, dance, or concert. If no one answers, ask at the nearby fruit shop.

Your cheapest and often most interesting bet may be a room in a private home (*casa particular*). Walk around the residential streets within about six blocks of Calle La Parra or on Calle Nueva with your rucksack. Ask around.

Eating in Nerja

There are three Nerjas: the private domain of the giant beachside hotels; the central zone packed with fun-loving expatriates and tourists enjoying great food with trilingual menus; and the back streets, where local life goes on as if there were no tomorrow (or tourists). The whole old town around the Balcony of Europe sizzles with decent restaurants. It makes no sense for me to recommend one over the others. Wander around and see who's eating best.

Farther inland, prices go down and locals fill the bars and tables. A 10-minute hike uphill takes you into the residential thick of things, where the sea views come thumbtacked to the walls. These three great places cluster within two blocks of each other around Herrera Oria (see map). Each specializes in seafood and is fine for a sit-down meal or a stop on a tapas crawl. Remember that tapas are snack-size portions. To turn tapas into more of a meal, ask for a *ración* or two.

Los Cunaos is most fun late in the evening, when families munch tapas, men watch soccer on TV, women chat, and stray kids wander around like it's home (good seafood and prices, Herrera Oria 19, tel. 95-252-1107).

El Pulguilla specializes in seafood, with clams so fresh they squirt (Bolivia 1, tel. 95-252-1384).

El Chispa is similarly big on seafood, with an informal restaurant terrace in the back (San Pedro 12, tel. 95-252-3697).

If you're out late, consider **Bar El Molino** for folk singing after 23:00. It's a bit touristy but worth the effort (Calle San Jose 4).

Transportation Connections—Nerja

The Nerja bus station is actually just a bus stop on Avenida de Pescia with an info booth (daily 8:00–14:00, 15:00–20:00, helpful schedules posted on booth, tel. 95-252-1504).

By bus to: Nerja Caves (16/day, 15 min), **Málaga** (14/day, 90 min), **Granada** (2/day, more frequent with Motril transfer, 2–3 hrs), **Córdoba** (2/day, 4 hrs), **Sevilla** (3/day, 4 hrs).

Transportation Connections—Málaga

The nearest train station to Nerja is an hourly 90-minute bus ride away in Málaga.

From **Málaga by train to: Ronda** (3/day, 2.5 hrs, transfer in Bobadilla), **Madrid** (7/day, 4.5 hrs on Talgo train), **Córdoba** (6/day, 2 hrs on Talgo), **Granada** (3/day, 3–4 hrs, transfer in Bobadilla), **Sevilla** (2/day, 3 hrs), **Barcelona** (3/day, 14 hrs).

Buses: Málaga's bus station, a block from the train station, has a helpful information office with an invaluable listing combining all the schedules offered by the different bus companies (on Paseo de los Tilos, tel. 95-235-0061).

By **bus to: Algeciras** (12/day, 3 hrs), **Nerja** (14/day, 90 min), **Ronda** (4/day, 2.5 hrs), **La Línea** (5/day, 3 hrs), **Sevilla** (10/day, 3 hrs), **Granada** (14/day, 2 hrs), **Córdoba** (4/day, 3 hrs), **Madrid** (12/day, 7 hrs).

Sights—From Nerja to Gibraltar

Buses take five hours to make the Nerja–Gibraltar trip. They leave nearly hourly and stop at each town mentioned.

Fuengirola/Torremolinos—The most built-up part of the region, where those most determined to be envied settle down, is a bizarre world of Scandinavian package tours, flashing lights, pink flamenco, multilingual menus, and all-night happiness. Fuengirola is like a Spanish Mazatlán with a few less-pretentious, older, budget hotels between the main drag and the beach. The water here is clean and the nightlife fun and easy. James Michener's idyllic Torremolinos has been strip-mauled and parking-metered.

Marbella—This is the most polished and posh of the Costa del Sol's resorts. Look for the *"Turismo"* sign to the right as you enter the center of town. Cross the main street at the signal closest to the *turismo* and walk up to the old city's pedestrian section, veering right. While the high-priced boutiques, immaculate streets, and beautifully landscaped squares are testimony to Marbella's arrival on the world-class-resort scene, cheap accommodations can still be found in old Marbella. Have a *café con leche* on the beautiful Plaza de Naranjas before wandering back down to new Marbella and the high-rise beachfront apartment buildings. Check out the beautiful beach scene before leaving. Marbella is an easy stop on the Algeciras–Málaga bus route (as you exit the bus station, take a left to reach the center of town).

San Pedro de Alcantara—This town's relatively undeveloped sandy beach is popular with young travelers. San Pedro's neighbor, Puerto Banus, is "where the world casts anchor." This luxurious jet-set port, complete with casino, is a strange mix of Rolls-Royces, yuppies, boutiques, rich Arabs, and budget browsers.

GIBRALTAR

One of the last bits of the empire upon which the sun never sat, Gibraltar is a fun mix of Anglican propriety, "God Save the Queen" tattoos, military memories, and tourist shops. The British soldiers you'll see are enjoying this cushy assignment in the Mediterranean sun as a reward for enduring and surviving an assignment in another remnant of the British Empire: Northern Ireland. While things are cheaper in pounds, your Spanish money works as well as your English words here.

The 30,000 Gibraltarians have a mixed and interesting heritage. The Llanitos (yah-nee-tohs), as they call themselves, speak a Creole-like Spanglish. They are a fun-loving and tolerant mix of British, Spanish, Genoese, Maltese, Portuguese, and Moroccan.

You'll need your passport to cross the border (and you may still be able to charm an official into stamping it—ask or you'll get just a wave-through). Make Gibraltar a day trip; rooms are expensive.

Planning Your Time
For the best day in Gibraltar, consider this plan: Walk across the border, catch bus #3, and ride it to the end, following a self-guided tour (see below). Catch bus #3 back to the cable-car station, ride to the top, and then walk down via O'Hara's Battery, St. Michael's Cave, and the monkeys. From there catch the cable car back into town. Spend your remaining free time in town before returning to Spain.

Orientation
(tel. code: 9567 from Spain, or 350 international)
Tourist Information: The main TI is at the Duke of Kent House on Cathedral Square, a few blocks from the town center (bus #3 stops here, Mon–Fri 9:00–17:30, tel. 9567/74950). Other TIs are on Main Street (also open Sat–Sun 10:00–16:00, inside the House of Assembly, tel. 9567/74982) and at customs where you cross the border. The TI can arrange extensive WWII tunnel and cave tours.

Helpful Hints: A Checkout supermarket is on Main Street, off Cathedral Square, next to Marks & Spencer (Mon–Sat 8:30–20:00, Sun 10:00–19:00). Fruit stands bustle at the Market Place (Mon–Sat 9:00–15:00, north end of Main Street). Café Cyberworld has Internet access for a pricey £4.50/hr (daily 12:00–24:00, 14–16 Queensway, in Ocean Heights Gallery, tel. 9567/51416). To telephone Gibraltar from Spain, dial 9567 followed by the five-digit local number.

Arrival in Gibraltar
By Bus: Spain's La Línea bus station is a five-minute walk from the Gibraltar border. If you're day-tripping to Gibraltar it's easy to store luggage in the lockers at the La Línea bus station or the Algeciras train station.

From the La Línea bus station it's a five-minute walk to the border (flash your passport) and then a 30-minute walk into downtown Gibraltar (straight across the runway and up Winston

Gibraltar

SPAIN

TO ALGECIRAS & TARIFA

CUSTOMS

AIRSTRIP

DEVIL'S TOWER ROAD

COACH PARK

STADIUM

CASEMENTS SQUARE

B.K.

MAIN ST

MOORISH CASTLE

SIEGE TUNNELS

HARBOUR

TOWN

MUSEUM

CATALAN BAY

QUEENS WAY

CABLE CAR

CATCHMENT BASIN

CITY WALLS

APE'S DEN

ST MICHAEL'S ROAD

ST. MICHAEL'S CAVE

N

EUROPA ROAD

300 YARDS

TO AFRICA MILES

EUROPA POINT

Churchill Avenue, angling right at the Shell station on Smith Dor-rien Avenue). Otherwise you can take the #3 minibus to the TI at Cathedral Square (or continue on the self-guided tour, below) or the double-decker bus #9 to the beginning of Main Street (100 ptas or 40 pence, every 15 min).

By Car: After taking the La Línea-Gibraltar exit off the main Costa del Sol road, continue in the left lane all the way through La Línea, passing the *Aduana* (customs), to the Gibraltar border. Because of long lines at the border, avoid driving into Gibraltar. Park in Spain instead and walk in. Here's how: At the border, con artists—dressed as traffic cops—will direct you here or there as if the law were on their side. Ignore them. Turning left at the "P" signs takes you into palm-lined blue-lined streets (120 ptas/hr, 680 ptas/day from meter, bring 100 pta coins, leave ticket on dash, Sun free). To save money, turn right at the first intersection and park on the street (give brown-uniformed guard 100 ptas/day). Parking directly across from the border is technically free, but you're wise to pay a vigilante for safety.

If you insist on driving into Gibraltar, there are plenty of parking lots (like the huge one near the cable car), but be prepared for a 90-minute wait both ways at the border.

Tours of Gibraltar

By Minibus: Organized tours such as Blands, Exchange, and Parodytour have predictable set fees (around £10–12) regardless of the number of people on the tour. Travel Exchange offers four-hour tours of the Rock (£10, Mon at 14:00, Thomas Cook, tel. 9567/76151).

By Taxi: You'll find lots of aggressive cabbies at the border who'd love to give you a tour. For those with more money than time, this can be a good value (as low as £10 per person if the taxi is packed) for a ride up the Rock to the Apes' Den and St. Michael's Cave (90 min)—but not all taxis go to the very top of the Rock, so ask. More people in a taxi means a lower cost per person; try to buddy up with other travelers.

The Quick, Cheap, Bus #3 Self-Guided Orientation Tour

At the border, pick up a map at the customs TI. Then walk straight ahead for 200 meters to the bus stop on the right. Catch minibus #3 (4/hrly, pay driver 100 ptas), grab a seat, and enjoy the ride.

You enter Gibraltar by crossing an **airstrip**. Forty times a week, the entry road into Gibraltar is closed to allow airplanes to land or take off. (You can fly to London for about $130.) The airstrip, originally a sports stadium, was filled in with stones excavated from the 34 miles of military tunnels in the Rock. This airstrip was a vital lifeline in the days when

Spain and Britain were quarreling over Gibraltar and the border was closed.

Just after the airstrip, the bus passes a road leading left (which heads clockwise around the Rock to the town of Catalan Bay, peaceful beaches, and the huge mountainside rainwater "catchment" wall). As you pass apartments on the left, find the **Moorish castle** above (now a prison; only the tower is open to the public).

Over the bridge and on the right after the next stop you'll see **World War I memorials**. The first is the American War Memorial, built in 1932 to commemorate American sailors based here in World War I. Farther along you'll see 18th-century cannons and a memorial to Gibraltarians who died in that same war.

Passing the Natwest House office tower on the left, you'll see the **synagogue**. In the 19th century half of Gibraltar was Jewish. The Jewish community now numbers 600.

Zigzagging past cute **Cathedral Square** (TI) and the Moorish-looking Anglican church, you reach Main Street. On the left, polished cannons protect the sentry house. Across the street the stately brick residence has housed the British governor since 1728.

The bus stops before the old **Charles V wall**. The wall was built in response to a 1552 raid in which the pirate Barbarossa stole 70 Gibraltarians into slavery.

Passing under the wall, on the left, you'll see the **Trafalgar cemetery**. Buried here are the British sailors who died defeating the French off the coast of Portugal's Cape Trafalgar in 1805.

The next stop is at the big parking lot for the **gondola** to the top of the Rock. You can get off now or later, on the ride back into town.

Heading uphill out of town you pass the big ugly casino and the path leading up the Rock (a 2.5-hour hike). Soon you'll see the "Mount," the residence of the admiral in command of the British fleet stationed here.

Rolling through a posh residential neighborhood, a curvy road leads past Gibraltar's **hospital** (on right), which, apparently, is not that great. Seriously ill people travel three hours by ambulance to Cadiz in Spain or are flown to England for treatment.

Reaching the end of the Rock you pass modern apartments and the new mosque. The lighthouse marks the windy Europa Point—end of the line. Buses retrace the route you just traveled, departing about every 15 minutes (check schedule before exploring farther).

The **Europa Point**, up the mound from the bus stop and tourist shop (on right), is an observation post. A plaque here identifies the mountains of Morocco 15 miles across the straits. The light of the lighthouse (from 1841, closed to visitors) can be seen from Morocco.

The **King Fahad Mosque**, a gift from the Saudi Sultan, was completed in 1997. Gibraltar's 300 Muslims worship here each Friday. Here—as across the straits in Morocco—five times a day the imam sings the call to prayer. Visitors (without shoes) are welcome (daily 17:00–18:00).

Sights—Gibraltar's Upper Rock Nature Reserve

▲▲▲**The Rock**—The real highlight is the spectacular Rock itself. From the south end of Main Street, catch the cable car to the top (1,000 ptas/£3.65 one way, 1,300 ptas/£4.90 round-trip, Mon–Sat 9:30–17:15, 6/hrly, closed Sun and when it's windy). The cable car drops you at a slick **restaurant/view terrace** at the very top of the Rock, from which you can explore old ramparts and drool at the 360-degree view of Morocco, the Straits of Gibraltar, Algeciras and its bay, and the twinkling Costa del Sol arcing eastward. Below you stretches the giant water "catchment system" that the British built to catch rainwater in the not-so-distant past, when Spain allowed neither water nor tourists to cross its disputed border. The views are especially crisp on brisk off-season days.

Buying a one-way ticket up saves a little money and gives you a chance to hike down to all of the sites. Allow 90 minutes to hike down—or up to 2.5 hours if you stop at the following six sights in the Upper Rock Nature Reserve, which you'll see in order as you descend from the top of the Rock.

With a round-trip ticket, your best strategy is to take the cable car up, hike downhill to St. Michael's Cave and the Apes' Den, and then take the cable car down into town from the Apes' Den, skipping the other sights. Why hike at all, you ask? Because you'd miss St. Michael's Cave if you relied solely on the cable car.

All of the Upper Rock Nature Reserve are open daily 9:30–18:30, with the exception of O'Hara's Battery (see listing below). O'Hara's Battery, St. Michael's Cave, and the Apes' Den are free with your cable-car ticket. A pass for admission to the other sites is 1,400 ptas/£5 (or 1,000 ptas/£4 with your cable-car ticket).

▲▲**O'Hara's Battery**—At 426 meters, this is the highest point on the Rock. While some taxi tours don't come here, you can hike here in 20 minutes from the top of the cable-car lift. A 28-ton, 9-inch gun sits on the summit where a Moorish lookout post once stood. It was built after World War I, and the last test was fired in 1974; locals are glad it's been mothballed. During test firings, if locals didn't open their windows to allow air to move freely after the concussion, their windows would shatter. Thirty-four miles of tunnels, like the tiny bit you see here, honeycomb this strategic rock. During World War II it was thought that an entire garrison could survive six months with the provisions stored in this underground base

(Mon–Sat 10:00–17:30, closed Sun; from the cable-car stop walk 10 minutes down and then 10 minutes up). As you explore the mountain, you may see iron rings. These anchored pulleys used to haul up guns such as the huge one at O'Hara's Battery.

▲**St. Michael's Cave**—Studded with stalagmites and stalactites, eerily lit and echoing with classical music, this cave is dramatic, corny, and slippery when wet. Considered a one-star sight since Neolithic times, these were alluded to in ancient Greek legends—when the Rock was one of the Pillars of Hercules, marking the end of the world, and the caves were believed to be the Gates of Hades. In our century they were prepared (but never used) as a World War II hospital and are now just another tourist site with an auditorium for musical events. Notice the polished cross section of a stalagmite showing weirdly beautiful rings similar to a tree's. Spelunkers who'd enjoy a three-hour subterranean hike through the lower cave can make arrangements in advance at the TI (£5 per person).

Apes' Den—This small zoo without bars gives you a chance for a close encounter with some of the famous (and very jaded) apes of Gibraltar. Keep your distance from the apes and beware of their kleptomaniac tendencies. The man at the little booth posts a record of the names of all the apes. If there's no ape action, wait for a banana-toting taxi tour to stop by and stir some up. (The cable car stops here.)

▲**Siege Tunnels**—Also called the Upper Galleries, these chilly tunnels were blasted out of the rock by the Brits during the Spanish and French siege of 1779–1783. Hokey but fun dioramas help recapture a time when Brits were known more for conquests than for crumpets. The tunnels are at the northern end of the Rock, about a mile from the Apes' Den (at the fork in the road, follow the sign for "All Directions").

Gibraltar, A City Under Siege **Exhibition**—A spin-off of the siege tunnels, this excuse for a museum gives you a look at life during the siege. It's worth a stop only if you already bought a combo ticket (just downhill from Siege Tunnels).

Moorish Castle—Actually more tower than castle, this building offers a tiny museum of Moorish remnants and carpets. The original castle was built by the Moorish Tarik-ibn-Zeyad in 711, but his name lasted longer than the castle; Gibel-Tarik (or Tarik's Hill) became Gibraltar. The tower marks the end of the Upper Rock Nature Reserve. Head downhill to reach the lower town and Main Street.

Sights—Lower Gibraltar

Gibraltar Museum—Built atop a Moorish bath, this museum in Gibraltar's lower town tells the story of a rock that has been fought over for centuries. Highlights are a 15-minute history film and the cavelike room that features prehistoric remains and artifacts (oddly hidden away in a room off the art gallery). The first Neanderthal skull was actually found in Gibraltar in 1848, though no one realized its significance until a similar skull found years later in Germany's Neanderthal Valley was correctly identified, stealing the name, claim, and fame from Gibraltar (530 ptas/£2, Mon–Fri 10:00–18:00, Sat 10:00–14:00, closed Sun, on Bomb House Lane off Main Street, ignore misleading "closed" entrance).

▲Catalan Bay—Gibraltar's tiny second town originated as a settlement of Italian shipwrights whose responsibility was keeping the royal ships in good shape. Today it's just a huddle of apartments around a cute little Catholic church, the best beach on the Rock (fully equipped), and more than enough fish-and-chips joints. Catch bus #4A from opposite the Governor's Residence or the roundabout near the airport.

Sleeping in Gibraltar
(£1 = about $1.70, tel. code: 9567 from Spain, or 350 international, zip code: 29780)
Sleep Code: **S** = Single, **D** = Double/Twin, **T** = Triple, **Q** = Quad, **b** = bathroom, **t** = toilet only, **s** = shower only, **CC** = Credit Card (Visa, MasterCard, Amex), **SE** = Speaks English, **NSE** = No English spoken.

Cannon Hotel is a friendly B&B run by gregarious Swedish sailors who settled in Gibraltar. Centrally located on a quiet street a block off Cathedral Square, the Cannon offers the best value accommodations (D-£34.50, Db-£44.50, includes English breakfast, 9 Cannon Lane, tel. 9567/51711, fax 9567/51789, www.cannonhotel.gi).

Bristol Hotel offers dark, dumpy rooms in a central location at a premium price (Db-£61–66, breakfast-£5, 10 Cathedral Square, tel. 9567/76800, e-mail: bristhtl@gbnet.gi).

Queen's Hotel has reasonable rates and free parking nearby plus special rates for young travelers, but it's noisy and lacks character (student S-£14, student D-£20, Db-£40, across from cable-car station and a few blocks from city center, 1 Boyd Street, tel. 9567/74000, fax 9567/40030).

Transportation Connections—Gibraltar
If you're leaving Gibraltar without a car, you must walk (five minutes) from Gibraltar's border into Spain to reach La Línea, the nearest bus station. The region's main transportation hub is Algeciras, with lots of train, bus, and ferry connections. (For Algeciras connections, see "Tarifa," below.)

La Línea by bus to: Algeciras (2/hrly, 45 min), **Tarifa** (8/day, 1 hr), **Málaga** (4/day, 3 hrs), **Granada** (2/day, 5 hrs).

TARIFA

Europe's most southerly town is a pleasant alternative to gritty, noisy Algeciras. It's an Arabic-looking town with a lovely beach, an old castle, restaurants swimming in fresh seafood, inexpensive places to sleep, enough windsurfers to sink a ship, and, best of all, hassle-free boats to Morocco.

As I stood on the town promenade under the castle, looking out at almost-touchable Morocco across the Straits of Gibraltar, I regretted only that I didn't have this book to steer me clear of wretched Algeciras on earlier trips. Tarifa, with usually daily one-hour trips to Tangier, is the best jumping-off point for a Moroccan side trip.

Tarifa has no blockbuster sights (and is pretty dead off-season), but it's a town where you just feel good to be on vacation.

Orientation

Tourist Information: The TI is on Paseo Alameda (Mon–Fri 11:00–14:00, 18:00–20:00, less off-season, tel. 95-668-0993).

Arrival in Tarifa: The bus station (just a ticket office) is at Batalla de Salado 19 (Mon–Fri 7:15–11:00, 15:00–19:00, Sat–Sun 15:00–20:00, tel. 95-668-4038). When you get off the bus, orient yourself by facing the old-town gate. The recommended hotels in the old town are through the gate; the hotels in the newer part of town are a couple of blocks behind you.

Ferry to Morocco: *If you're going to Morocco, call to make sure the boat is running* (Tarifa travel agencies: Marruecotur, tel. 95-668-1821 and Tour Africa at the boat dock, tel. 95-668-4325). Get your boat ticket as soon as possible—there's only one ferry a day, and it does sell out. Prices are the same in the many travel agencies and hotels, so you might book ahead or stop by the first agency you see when you get to town. The going rate is 7,000 ptas for a round-trip all-day tour or 5,600 ptas for a round-trip without a tour. See the Morocco chapter for more information.

Sights—Tarifa

Castle of Guzman El Bueno—This castle was named after a 13th-century Christian general who gained fame in a sad show of courage while fighting the Moors. Holding Guzman's son hostage, the Moors demanded he surrender the castle or they'd kill the boy. Guzman refused, even throwing his own knife down from the ramparts. It was used on his son's throat. Ultimately, the Moors withdrew to Africa, and Guzman was a hero. *Bueno.* The castle itself is a concrete hulk in a vacant lot, interesting only for the harbor views from the ramparts (200 ptas, Tue–Sun 10:00–14:00, 17:00–19:00, Sun 16:00–19:00, closed Mon).

Church of St. Matthew—Tarifa's main church faces its main drag. Most nights it seems life squirts from the church out the front door

Tarifa

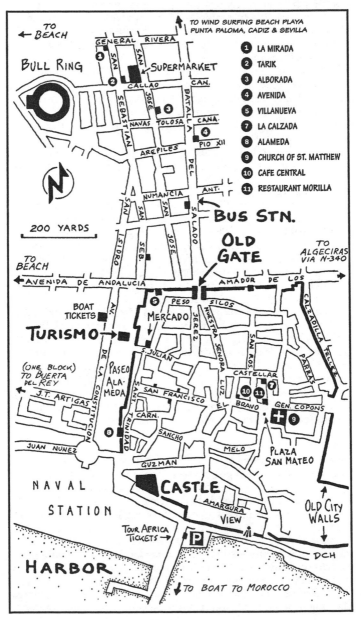

TO
← BEACH

TO WIND SURFING BEACH PLAYA
PUNTA PALOMA, CADIZ & SEVILLA

GENERAL RIVERA

BULL RING

① SupERMARKET

② CALLAO

③

NAVAS TOLOSA

AREPILES

N

200 YARDS

NUMANCIA

BUS STN.

OLD
GATE

TO BEACH

AVENIDA DE ANDALUCIA

AMADOR DE LOS

TO
ALGECIRAS
VIA N-340

BOAT
TICKETS

⑤   PESO   SILOS

MERCADO

TURISMO →

S. JULIAN

(ONE BLOCK)
TO BUERTA
DEL REY

PASEO
ALA-
MEDA

J.T. ARTIGAS

SAN FRANCISCO

CARN.

⑩ ⑪ ⑦

CASTELLAR

GEN. COPONS

EL BRAVO

⑨

JUAN NUÑEZ

⑧

SANCHO

GUZMAN

MELO

PLAZA
SAN MATEO

N A V A L

CASTLE

S T A T I O N

AMARGURA

OLD CITY
WALLS

TOUR AFRICA
TICKETS →

VIEW

P

DCH

HARBOR

↓ TO BOAT TO MOROCCO

① LA MIRADA
② TARIK
③ ALBORADA
④ AVENIDA
⑤ VILLANUEVA
⑦ LA CALZADA
⑧ ALAMEDA
⑨ CHURCH OF ST. MATTHEW
⑩ CAFE CENTRAL
⑪ RESTAURANT MORILLA

and into the fun-loving Calle El Bravo. Wander inside (English leaflets inside on the right).

1. Find the tiny (one-foot-square) piece of **ancient tombstone** in the wall just before the transept on the right side. Probably the most important historic item in town, it proves there was a functioning church here during Visigothic times, before the Moorish conquest. The tombstone reads, in a kind of Latin Spanish, "Flaviano lived as a Christian for 50 years, a little more or less. In death he received forgiveness as a servant of God on March 30, 674. May he rest in peace." If that gets you in the mood to light a candle, switch on an electronic "candle" for 25 ptas on your left.

2. Step into the transept beyond the candles. The centerpiece of the **altar** is a boy Jesus. By Andalusian tradition he used to be naked, but these days he's clothed with outfits that vary with the Church calendar. On the right is a fine 17th-century statue of the "Virgin [protector] of the Fishermen."

3. A statue of **St. James the Moorslayer** (missing his sword) is on the right side wall of the main central altar. Since the days of the Reconquista, James has been Spain's patron saint.

4. The side altar on the left harbors several **statues** that go on parade through town during Holy Week. The **Captive Christ** (with hands bound) goes back to the days when Christians were held captive by Moors.

5. Circling around to the left side you'll find a side door, the **"door of pardons."** For a long time, Tarifa was a dangerous place—on the edge of the Reconquista. To encourage people to live here, the Church offered a huge amount of forgiveness to anyone who lived in Tarifa for a year. One year and one day after moving to Tarifa, they would have the privilege of passing through this special "door of pardons," and a Mass of thanksgiving would be held in that person's honor.

Bullfighting—Tarifa has a third-rate bullring where novices botch fights most Saturdays through the summer. The ring is a short walk from the town. You'll see posters everywhere.

Whale Watching—An eco-tourism organization, FIRMM, offers daily whale- and dolphin-watching excursions in the Strait of Gibraltar (4,500 ptas per person, Pedro Cortés 3 next to Café Central, reserve ahead, tel. & fax 95-662-7008).

▲**Windsurfing**—**Playa Punta Paloma** is a vast, sandy beach about eight kilometers northwest of town. On windy summer days the sea is littered with sprinting windsurfers and the beach with a couple hundred vans and fun-mobiles from northern Europe. Under mountain ridges lined with modern energy-generating windmills, it's a fascinating scene. Drive down the sandy road and stroll along the beach. You'll find a cabana-type hamlet with rental gear, beachwear shops, a bar, and a hip, healthy restaurant with great lunch salads.

Sleeping in Tarifa
(160 ptas = about $1, zip code: 11380)

The first four listings (listed in the order you'll see them if you drive in from Sevilla) are right off the main drag—Batalla del Salado—with easy parking, in the modern, plain part of town. To reach these hotels if arriving by bus, turn left out of the station ticket office and head away from the old-city center. The rest are inside or border the old town. Room rates vary with the season (three tiers vary but are, roughly: high—always August, as much as July–September; mid—spring and fall; and low—winter). Breakfast and a 7 percent tax are extra. There's a handy laundry service (drop off and pick up later) at the big Consum supermarket on Calle San José near the recommended hotels in the newer part of town.

Hotel La Mirada is shiny new, with modern rooms, some of which come with sea views (Sb-3,000, 4,000, or 5,000 ptas, Db-5,000, 6,000, or 7,500 ptas, extra bed-1,000 ptas, breakfast-350 ptas, elevator, great views from large terrace, attached restaurant, CC:VMA, Calle San Sebastián 41, tel. 95-668-4427, fax 95-668-1162, some English spoken). It's two blocks to the right of the main drag and about five blocks away from the old town.

The 10-room motel-style **Hostal Tarik** is clean and pleasant but short on windows (Db-4,500–7,500 ptas, Tb-5,500–9,000 ptas, CC:VMA, Calle San Sebastián 32, tel. 95-668-0648, SE). Surrounded by warehouses, it's one block toward the town center from Hotel La Mirada.

Hostal Alborada is a squeaky-clean place with an attractive courtyard. It's a couple of blocks closer to the old town on a plain street (Sb-2,600, 3,500, or 4,800 ptas, Db-4,000, 5,500, or 7,000 ptas, Tb-5,500–7,000 ptas, high season is Jul–Sept, get your price and then show this book for a 10 percent discount, CC:VM, Calle San José 52, tel. 95-668-1140, fax 95-668-1935, www .hotelalborada.com, fun-loving Rafael Mesa Rodriguez and Juaquina speak only a little English).

The family-run **Hostal Avenida** has 11 tidy, comfy rooms and a pretty courtyard, but it's on a busy street leading into town. Ask for one of the four *tranquilo* rooms off the street (Sb-2,500–4,000 ptas, Db-3,500–6,000 ptas, Tb-5,000–8,000 ptas, Calle Pío XII, just off the main drag, tel. 95-668-4818, Maria NSE).

Hostal Villanueva is your best budget bet. It's friendly, though no English is spoken, and includes a great terrace overlooking the old town. It's on a busy street, and the quiet rooms in the back come with the best views (Sb-2,000–2,500 ptas, Db-3,500–5,500 ptas, extra bed-1,500 ptas, some more expensive new rooms, breakfast-300 ptas, attached restaurant, Avenida de Andalucía 11, just west of the old-town gate, tel. 95-668-4149).

The following are inside the old city: **Hostal La Calzada** has eight well-appointed, quiet, and airy rooms right in the noisy-at-night, old-town thick of things (Db-4,500–7,000 ptas, Tb-5,500–8,000 ptas, closed Oct–Mar, CC:VMA, Calle Justino Pertinez 3, veer left and down from the old-town gate, tel. 95-668-0366 or 95-668-1492, NSE).

Hostal Alameda glistens with pristine marble floors and pastels. It overlooks a square where the local children play (Db-4,000–6,000 ptas, Tb-6,000–8,000 ptas, breakfast-450 ptas, CC:VM, Paseo Alameda 4, tel. 95-668-1181, some English spoken). Its 11 bright rooms are above its restaurant (great gazpacho).

La Casa Amarilla (The Yellow House) offers posh apartments with modern décor and minikitchens (Db-7,000–8,000 ptas, across the street from Café Central, Calle Sancho IV El Bravo #9, tel. 95-668-1993, fax 95-668-0590, www.tarifa.netlacasamarilla.

Eating in Tarifa

You'll find good tapas throughout the old town. **Café Central** is the happening place nearly any time of day (all tapas are priced at 150 ptas—go to the bar and point; great and ingenious 600-pta salads—study the menu; healthy fruit drinks are impressively therapeutic; off Plaza San Mateo). Across the street is a *panadería* offering tasty, cheap sandwiches. Next door, in front of the church, **Restaurant Morilla** serves good local-style food and paella on the town's prime piece of people-watching real estate (long hours, every day, Calle Sancho IV El Bravo, tel. 95-668-1757).

From Café Central follow the cars 100 meters to the first corner on the left to reach **Bar El Frances** for its fine tapas (generally 125 ptas), especially snails (*caracoles*, June–mid-July only). The nearby **Cafe Bar los Melli** is family friendly and serves a good chorizo sandwich. **Bar El Pasillo**, next to Melli, has tapas.

From Melli you can circle around toward the church past some very gritty and colorful tapas bars. Just to the seaside of the church you'll see the mysterious **Casino Tarifeno**. This is an old boys' social club "for members only" but offers a big, musty Andalusian welcome to visiting tourists—even women. Wander through. There's a bar with tapas, a TV room, a card room, and a lounge.

From the town center, walk the narrow Calle San Francisco to survey a number of good restaurants, such as the classy, quiet **Guzman El Bueno** and the cheap and easy **Pizzeria La Capricciosa**.

The street Buerta del Rey, a family scene at night, is punctuated with snack bars. Stop by the *heladeria* for ice cream or **La Dulce Campesina** for tasty pastries and coffee.

Confiteria la Tarifeña serves tasty pastry, including super flan (at the top of Calle Nuestra Sra. De la Luz, near the arch).

Picnics: Try a grocery, the mercado municipal (Mon–Sat 8:00–14:00, closed Sun, in old town), or **Consum supermarket** (Mon–Sat 9:00–14:00, 17:30–21:30, closed Sun, simple cafeteria; at Callao and San José, near the hotels in the new town).

Transportation Connections—Tarifa

By bus to: La Línea and Gibraltar (6/day, 1 hr, 440 ptas; 1st departure at 10:30, last return at 20:00), **Jerez** (3/day, 2 hrs), **Sevilla** (4/day, 3 hrs, 2,050 ptas), **Málaga** (3/day, 4 hrs), **Algeciras** (10/day, 30 min), **Huelva** (1/day, 5 hrs), **Cadiz** (8/day, 2 hrs). Bus information: tel. 95-668-4038.

Transportation Connections—Algeciras

Algeciras is only worth leaving. Use it as a transfer point—and then only if necessary. The train station is four blocks inland on the far side of Hotel Octavio (up Juan de la Cierva). Head toward the sea for the bus station and TI: The Comes bus station, which offers frequent service to La Línea and Tarifa, is a half-block away from the train station (next to Hotel Octavio), and the TI is a couple of blocks down on the same street (Mon–Fri 9:00–14:00, Juan de la Cierva, 2 blocks before the port, tel. 95-657-2636). The many travel agencies along the waterfront all sell ferry tickets and accept credit cards (for ferries to Morocco, see Morocco chapter). The Bus Málaga station is on the waterfront, kitty-corner from the port (11 buses/day to Málaga, 3 hrs, Virgen Carmen 15).

By bus to: La Línea/Gibraltar (2/hrly, 45 min), **Tarifa** (10/day, 30 min), **Jerez** (4/day, 2.5 hrs), **Sevilla** (4/day, 3.5 hrs), **Granada** (3/day, 5 hrs), **Málaga** (11/day, 3 hrs), **Madrid** (2/day, 12 hrs).

By train to: Ronda (4/day, 2 hrs), **Málaga** (3/day, 4 hrs, transfer in Bobadilla), **Granada** (3/day, 5 hrs, transfer in Bobadilla), **Sevilla** (3/day, 5 hrs, transfer in Bobadilla). All four rides are scenic, and the mountainous trip to Málaga via Bobadilla is one of Spain's most scenic train rides. There are also two trains each night to Madrid (12 hrs).

Route Tips for Drivers

Tarifa to Gibraltar (45 min): It's a short and scenic drive, passing a silvery-white forest of windmills, from peaceful Tarifa past Algeciras to La Línea (the Spanish town bordering Gibraltar). Passing Algeciras, continue in the direction of Estepona. At San Roque take the La Línea-Gibraltar exit.

Gibraltar to Nerja (130 miles): Barring traffic problems, the trip along the Costa del Sol is smooth and easy by car—much of it on new highways. Just follow the coastal highway east. After Málaga follow signs to Almería and Motril.

Nerja to Granada (80 miles, 90 min, 100 views): Drive along the coast to Salobrena, catching E103 north for about 40 miles to Granada. While scenic side trips may beckon, don't arrive late in Granada without a firm reservation.

MOROCCO

Go to Africa. As you step off the boat you realize that the hour-long crossing has taken you farther culturally than did the trip from the United States to Iberia. Morocco needs no museums; its sights are living in the streets. The one-day excursions (usually daily, year-round) from Tarifa are well organized and reliable, and given the steep price of the boat passage alone, the tour package is a good value for those who can spare only a day for Morocco.

Morocco in a Day?

There are many ways to experience Morocco, and a day in Tangier is probably the worst. But all you need is a passport (no visa or shots required), and if all you have is a day, this is a real and worthwhile adventure. Tangier is the Tijuana of Morocco, and everyone there seems to be expecting you.

The tours organized in Tarifa charge 7,000 ptas (call ahead to make sure boats are running—see "Ferry Connections from Spain" below) and give you a round-trip crossing, a good guide to meet you at the harbor in Tangier and hustle you through the hustlers and onto your bus, and a bus tour. The latter includes a city tour, a trip to the desolate Atlantic Coast for some rugged African scenery, the famous ride-a-camel stop, a walk through the *medina* (market) with a too-thorough look at a sales-starved carpet shop, and a big lunch in a palatial Moroccan setting with live music.

Sound cheesy? It is. But no amount of packaging can gloss over how exotic and different this culture really is. This kind of cultural voyeurism is almost embarrassing, but it's nonstop action and more memorable than another day in Spain. The shopping is—Moroccan. Bargain hard!

The day trip is so tightly organized you'll have hardly any time

Morocco

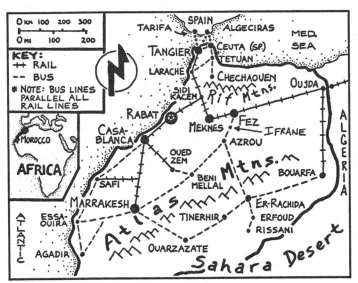

alone in Tangier. For many people, that's just fine. Some, however, spend a night there and return the next day. Ask about the two-day, 12,500-ptas tour at the tourist office in Tarifa. (See "Ferry Connections," below, for travel agencies.) You can buy and sell dirhams at the Bank of Morocco branch in the Algeciras terminal. But for a short one-day trip, there's no need to change money. Everyone you meet will be happy to take your pesetas or dollars.

Extended Tour of Morocco

Morocco gets much better as you go deeper into the interior. The country is incredibly rich in cultural thrills—but you'll pay a price in hassles and headaches. It's a package deal, and if danger's your business, it's a great option.

To get a fair look at Morocco, you must get past the hustlers and con artists of the north coast (Tangier, Tétouan). It takes a minimum of four or five days to make a worthwhile visit—ideally seven or eight. Plan at least two nights in either Fès or Marrakech. A trip over the Atlas Mountains gives you an exciting look at Saharan Morocco. If you need a vacation from your vacation, check into one of the idyllic Atlantic beach resorts on the south coast. Above all, get past the northern day-trip-from-Spain, take-a-snapshot-on-a-camel fringe. Oops, that's us. Oh, well.

If you're relying on public transportation for your extended tour, sail to Tangier, blast your way through customs, listen to no hustler who tells you there's no way out until tomorrow, and hop into a Petit Taxi for the Morora train station four kilometers away (15 dirhams, or $1.50). From there, just set your sights on Rabat, a dignified, European-type town with fewer hustlers, and make it your get-acquainted stop in Morocco. Trains go farther south from Rabat.

If you're driving a car, sail from Algeciras to Ceuta, a Spanish possession. Crossing the border is a bit unnerving, since you'll be jumped through several bureaucratic hoops. You'll go through customs, buy Moroccan insurance for your car (cheap and easy), and feel at the mercy of a bristly bunch of shady-looking people you'd rather not be at the mercy of. Most cars are shepherded through by a guy who will expect a tip. Relax and let him grease those customs wheels. He's worth it. As soon as possible, hit the road and drive to Chefchaouen, the best first stop for those with their own wheels.

Orientation (Mental)

Thrills: Morocco is culture shock—both bad and good. It makes Spain and Portugal look meek and mild. You'll encounter oppressive friendliness, the Arabic language, squiggly writing, the Islamic faith, and ancient cities. It is a photographer's delight, very cheap, and comes with plenty of hotels, surprisingly easy transportation, and a variety of terrain, from Swiss-like mountain resorts to fairy-tale mud-brick oasis towns to luxuriously natural beaches to bustling desert markets.

Spills: Many travelers are overwhelmed by its intensity, poverty, aggressive beggars, brutal heat, and slick con men. Most of the English-speaking Moroccans that the tourist meets are hustlers. Most visitors have some intestinal problems. Most women are harassed on the streets by horny but generally harmless men. Things don't work smoothly. In fact, compared to Morocco, Spain resembles Sweden for efficiency. People don't see the world through the same filters we do, and some very good parents proudly name their sons Saddam. This is Islam.

Leave busy itineraries and split-second timing in Europe. Morocco must be taken on its own terms. In Morocco things go smoothly only "*Inshallah*"—if God so wills.

Helpful Hints

Friday: Friday is the Muslim day of rest, when most of the country (except Tangier) closes down.

Money: Change money only at banks, or even easier, at ATMs (available at most major banks), all of which have uniform rates. The black market is dangerous. Change only what you need and keep the bank receipt to reconvert if necessary. Don't leave the country with Moroccan money. (If you do, the Bank of Morocco branch in Algeciras may buy it back from you.)

Health: Morocco is much more hazardous to your health than Spain or Portugal. Eat in clean—not cheap—places. Peel fruit, eat only cooked vegetables, and drink reliably bottled water (Sidi Harazem or Sidi Ali). When you do get diarrhea, and you should plan on it, adjust your diet (small and bland meals, no milk or grease) or fast for a day but make sure you replenish lost fluids. Relax; most diarrhea is not serious, just an adjustment that will run its course.

Arabic Numerals

0	•	SIFR
1	١	WAAHID
2	٢	ITNEEN
3	٣	TALAATA
4	٤	ARBA'A
5	٥	KHAMSA
6	٦	SITTA
7	٧	SAB'A
8	٨	TAMANYA
9	٩	TIS'A
10	١٠	'ASHRA

Information: For an extended trip, bring travel information from home or Spain. The guides published by Lonely Planet, Rough Guide, and Let's Go (*Let's Go: Spain and Portugal* includes Morocco) are good. The green *Michelin Morocco* guidebook is worthwhile (if you read French). Buy the best map you can find locally—names are always changing, and it's helpful to have towns, roads, and place-names written in Arabic.

Language: The Arabic squiggle-script, its many difficult sounds, and the fact that French is Morocco's second language make communication tricky for English-speaking travelers. A little French goes a long way, but learn a few words in Arabic. Have your first local friend help you pronounce *min fadlik* ("please"; meen FAD-leek), *shókran* ("thank you"; SHOW-kron), *ismahli* ("excuse me"; ees-MAY-lee), *yeh* ("yes"; EE-yuh), *lah* ("no"; lah), and *maa salama* ("good-bye"; mah sah-LEM-ah). In markets, I sing "la la la la la" to my opponents. *Lah shókran* means "No, thank you." Listen carefully and write new words phonetically. Bring an Arabic phrase book. Make a point of learning the local number symbols; they are not like ours (which we call "Arabic").

Keeping your bearings: Navigate the labyrinthine *medinas* by altitude, gates, and famous mosques or buildings. Write down what gate you came in so you can enjoy being lost—temporarily. *Souk* is Arabic for a particular *medina* "department" (such as leather, yarn, or metalwork).

Hustlers: While Moroccans are some of Africa's wealthiest people, you are still incredibly rich to them. This imbalance causes predictable problems. Wear your money belt. Assume con artists are more clever than you. Haggle when appropriate (prices skyrocket for tourists). You'll attract hustlers like flies at every famous tourist sight. They'll lie to you, get you lost, blackmail you, and pester the heck out of you. Never leave your car or baggage where you can't get back to it without your "guide." Anything you buy in their company gets them a 20 percent commission. Normally locals, shopkeepers, and police will come to your rescue when the hustlers' heat becomes unbearable. I usually hire a guide, since it's helpful to have a translator, and once you're "taken," the rest seem to leave you alone.

Marijuana: In Morocco marijuana (*kif*) is as illegal as it is popular, as many Westerners in local jails would love to remind you. Some dealers who sell it cheap make their profit after you get arrested. Cars and buses are stopped and checked by police routinely throughout Morocco—especially in the north and in the Chefchaouen region, which is Morocco's *kif* capital.

Getting around Morocco: Moroccan trains are quite good. Second class is cheap and comfortable. Buses connect all smaller towns quite well. By car, Morocco is easy, but drive defensively and never rely on the oncoming driver's skill. Night driving is dangerous. Pay a guard to watch your car overnight.

TANGIER
Tangier is split into two. The new town has the TI and fancy hotels. The old town has the *medina* (market), the Kasbah (with its palace), cheap hotels, decrepit homes, and 2,000 wannabe guides. The twisty, hilly streets of the old town are caged within a wall accessible by keyhole gates. The big square, Grand Socco, is the link between the old and new parts of town.

Orientation (tel. code: 9)
Many assume they'll be lost in Tangier—because it's in Africa. This makes no sense. The town is laid out very simply. From the boat dock you'll see the old town—circled by its medieval wall—on the right (behind Hotel Continental). The new town sprawls past the industrial port zone to the left. Nothing mentioned in this chapter is more than a 15-minute walk from the port. Petit Taxis are a godsend for the hot and tired tourist. Use them generously and go ahead and just pay double the meter for any ride (10 dirhams = about $1).

Planning Your Time
Consider hiring a guide at the port (see "Guides," below). If you're a shopper, head straight for the market. Otherwise, head to the TI for a map and advice (Mon–Sat 8:30–12:00, 14:30–18:30, Boulevard Pasteur 29, tel. 94-80-50). From there you can walk to the Grand Socco and market. Or, for the more complete tour, catch a taxi to the Place de la Kasbah at the top of the old town

and work your way downhill to the port, seeing these attractions in this order: Start at the Museum of the Kasbah, then wander through the fortress (Dar el-Makhzem) and the Old American Legation Museum, and shop through the Petit Socco. Walk out of the old town into the noisy Grand Socco. From there, catch a taxi to the beach (Place el Cano) and sightsee along the beach and then along Avenue d'Espagne back to the port.

From Tarifa to Tangier

Departing Tarifa: At the Tarifa port, bring or buy your boat ticket (if you're doing Tangier on your own). If you're taking a tour, bring the tour voucher you bought at the travel agency to the boat office and get your ticket. If you have confirmed your boat's departure time carefully the night before, there's no reason to show up more than 15 minutes before departure.

On the boat: If you're on your own and plan to stay only one day, do what you can to get your ticket stamped twice (*"Entree"* and *"Sortie"*) by the Moroccan customs man. (Those taking the tour get this done automatically.) If you manage this, show your ticket—not your passport—upon arrival and departure in Morocco and you'll save 30 minutes of messing around as you leave Tangier. If, on the other hand, you plan to stay longer than a day in Morocco (or you want the option to stay longer than a day), make sure your passport is stamped only once (*"Entree"*). The boat has a gruesome cafeteria bar, plenty of WCs, stuffy indoor chairs, and grand top-deck views. Carefully confirm the time your return boat departs from Tangier. The time difference between the countries can be up to two hours.

Arriving in Tangier: If you're on a tour, just follow your leader. Note that your leader meets you in Tangier after you get off the boat from Spain (not in Spain when you board). In Tangier you'll be corralled at the gangplank onto your waiting tour bus.

Independent travelers will take a five-minute walk from the boat, through customs, and out of the port. Taxis at the port are more expensive. Ask the cost before taking one. The big yellow Port de Tanger gateway defines the end of the port area and the start of the city. Leave mental bread crumbs so you can find your way back to your boat. It will just stay put all day. Just outside the port gate on the busy traffic circle you'll find plenty of fair, metered Petit Taxis along with a line of decent fish restaurants, the boulevard arcing along the beach into the new town, and stairs leading up into the old town (on the right). Catch a taxi to the TI.

Guides

If you're on your own, you'll be fighting off "guides" all day. In order to have your own translator and a shield from less scrupulous touts that hit up tourists constantly throughout the old town,

Tangier

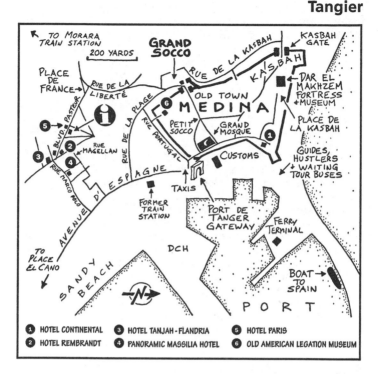

TO MORARA
TRAIN STATION
200 YARDS
GRAND SOCCO
KASBAH GATE
RUE DE LA KASBAH
KASBAH
PLACE DE FRANCE
RUE DE LA LIBERTÉ
DAR EL MAKHZEM FORTRESS + MUSEUM
OLD TOWN M E D I N A
PLACE DE LA KASBAH
RUE DE LA PLAGE
RUE PORTUGAL
PETIT SOCCO
GRAND MOSQUE
GUIDES, HUSTLERS + WAITING TOUR BUSES
BLVD. PASTEUR
RUE MAGELLAN
CUSTOMS
RUE MARCO POLO
AVENUE D' ESPAGNE
TAXIS
FORMER TRAIN STATION
PORT DE TANGER GATEWAY
FERRY TERMINAL
TO PLACE EL CANO
SANDY BEACH
DCH
N
BOAT TO SPAIN
P O R T

1 HOTEL CONTINENTAL	**3** HOTEL TANJAH - FLANDRIA	**5** HOTEL PARIS
2 HOTEL REMBRANDT	**4** PANORAMIC MASSILIA HOTEL	**6** OLD AMERICAN LEGATION MUSEUM

I recommend hiring a guide. Stress your interest in the people and culture rather than shopping. Guides, hoping to get a huge commission from your purchases, can cleverly turn your Tangier day into a Marco Polo equivalent of the Shopping Channel.

I've had good luck with the private guides who meet the boat. These hardworking, English-speaking, and licensed guides offer their services for the day for 2,000 ptas. The TI also has official guides (half-day for $15, 2,000 ptas, or 120 dirhams).

If you don't want a guide, ask directions of people who can't leave what they're doing (such as the only clerk in a shop) or of women who aren't near men. Ask "Kasbah?" or wherever you want to go, and you'll get pointed in the right direction. Fewer hustlers are in the new (but less interesting) part of town.

Sights—Tangier

Kasbah—This is the fortress atop old Tangier. You'll find a history museum in a former palace on Place de la Kasbah (10 dirhams, Wed–Mon 8:00–15:00, closed Tue) and a colorful gauntlet of Kodak moments waiting to ambush tour groups as they wander through: snake charmers, squawky dance troupes, and colorful water vendors. Before descending out of the Kasbah, don't miss the ocean viewpoint, the Mosque de la Kasbah, and Dar el-Makhzen, the fortress of the pasha of Tangier.

The *Medina* and Petit Socco—From the Kasbah, a maze of winding lanes and tiny alleys weave through the old-town market area. Petit Socco, a little square in the old town, is lined with tea shops. A casual first-time visitor cannot stay oriented. I just wander, knowing that if I keep going downhill, I'll eventually pop out at the port; if I veer to the right while going downhill, I'll come to a gate leading into the modern town probably via the Grand Socco, the big and noisy market square. The *medina* is filthy and reportedly dangerous after dark. Plain-clothed tourist police are stationed throughout, making sure you are safe as you wander.

Tangier American Legation Museum—Morocco was the first country to recognize the United States as an independent country. This building, given to the United States by the sultan of Morocco, became the American government's first foreign possession. It served as our embassy or consulate from 1821 to 1956, is still owned by the United States, and is the only U.S. national historic landmark overseas. Today this 19th-century mansion is a strangely peaceful oasis within Tangier's intense *medina*. It offers a warm welcome and lots of interesting paintings. It's a reminder of how long the United States and Morocco have had good relations (free, donations accepted, Mon–Fri 10:00–13:00, 15:00–17:00, Rue America 8, tel. 93-53-17).

Grand Socco—This big square is a transportation hub. From here, a gate leads into the old town *medina*; Rue de la Kasbah leads uphill along the old wall to Port de la Kasbah (a gate leading into the Kasbah); Rue de la Liberte leads to Place de France and Boulevard Pasteur (TI and recommended hotels); and Rue de la Plage leads to the train station, the port, and the beach.

Tangier Beach—This fine, white-sand crescent beach, stretching eastward from the port, is lined by fun eateries and packed with locals doing what people around the world do at the beach—with a few variations: You'll see lazy camels and people, young and old, covered in hot sand to combat rheumatism.

Sleeping in Tangier
(10 dirhams = about $1, tel. code: 9)
Sleep Code: **S** = Single, **D** = Double/Twin, **T** = Triple,
Q = Quad, **b** = bathroom, **t** = toilet only, **s** = shower only,
CC = Credit Card (Visa, MasterCard, Amex), **SE** = Speaks English, **NSE** = No English.

These hotels are centrally located, near the TI and American Express (Boulevard Pasteur 54), and within walking distance of the market. The first two are four-star hotels. To reserve from Spain, dial 00 (Spain's international access code), 212 (Morocco's country code), 9 (Tangier's city code), then the local number. July through mid-September is high season, when rooms may be a bit more expensive and a reservation is wise.

Hotel Rembrandt, with a restaurant, a bar, and a swimming pool surrounded by a great grassy garden, has 75 clean, comfortable rooms, some with views (Sb-431 dirhams, Db-499 dirhams, elevator, CC:VMA, tel. 93-78-70 or 33-33-14, fax 93-04-43, SE). Across the street, **Hotel Tanjah-Flandria** is more formal, stuffy, and comfortable but soulless, no fun, and a lesser value (Sb-630 dirhams, Db-774 dirhams, restaurant, elevator, air-con, rooftop terrace, small pool, CC:VMA, tel. 93-32-79, fax 93-43-47, SE).

Hotel Continental, the Humphrey Bogart option, is a grand old place sprawling along the old town. It overlooks the port, with lavish, evocative public spaces, a chandeliered breakfast room, and 70 spacious bedrooms with rough hardwood floors. Jimmy, who runs the place with a Moroccan flair, says he offers everything but Viagra. When I said "I'm from Seattle," he said, "206." Test him. He knows your area code (Db-260 dirhams, includes tax and breakfast, Dar Baroud 36, tel. 93-10-24, fax 93-11-43, SE).

Panoramic Massilia Hotel, an elegant old house, is on a quiet street two blocks off the beach and a block below Hotel Rembrandt near the TI. The rooms are ramshackle, but the location and price are right (Db-150 dirhams, Tb-200 dirhams, includes breakfast, Rue Targha 11, tel. & fax 93-50-15).

Hotel Paris, across from the TI, is noisy, dingy, and friendly. Ask for a room in the back—and a mop. (Sb-224 dirhams, Db-260 dirhams, Boulevard Pasteur 42, tel. 93-18-77; the helpful and informative manager, Abdullatif, SE.)

Ferry Connections from Spain

Boats run daily year-round. Some Spanish hotels also sell the tours (same price as travel agencies). In summer Tangier is two hours earlier than Tarifa (one hour in winter). Confirm the local time of departure. For each departure you'll go through two different passport stamping lines (unless you managed to get your ticket prestamped; see "From Tarifa to Tangier" section, above). Plan on spending one hour of your day in lines. Departing from Spain, passports are checked on the boat.

Tarifa to Tangier: There's a daily one-hour crossing every morning around 10:00 (without a tour, it's 5,600 ptas round-trip, passengers only, free parking at Tarifa boat dock). Tour options cost 7,000 ptas for one day, 12,500 ptas for two days (includes crossing). Two-day tours are the same as the one-day tour, but you just go to a fancy hotel (with dinner) rather than the boat at 15:00 and catch the same boat 24 unstructured hours later.

Departtures from Tarifa would be earlier if it weren't for the need to wait for the mobs from Costa del Sol resorts. While waiting in line, psychoanalyze the difference between travelers staying in Tarifa and group tourists from Málaga.

You'll leave Tarifa at 10:00 and return by 18:00. Note that returns on Friday tours are delayed four hours, which for some means being bored and killing time at the port and for others means getting lots more time for exploring Tangier. If considering Friday, also remember that it is the Muslim Sabbath, which means there will be less business action in the streets.

Sailing to Tangier takes 90 minutes; coming back takes one hour. (The Straits of Gibraltar are a busy two-lane shipping highway. To cross it, Africa-bound boats are required to jog far to the west before cutting back to Tangier.)

Get the local times straight: Morocco is two hours earlier than Spain (one hour in winter). I'd keep my watch on Spanish time and get my departure times clear in Spanish time. Boats are most crowded on Tuesday, Wednesday, and Thursday, when the Costa del Sol groups come en masse and can book up the boat entirely in August. Only about seven crossings a year are canceled because of storms (mostly in winter), but if you're going to Tarifa for the sole purpose of catching the boat to Morocco, call one of the travel agencies below to make sure the boats are running.

Get your ticket any way you like. Many hotels and travel agencies sell the same boat tickets and tours for the same price. The major travel agencies in Tarifa are Marruecotur and Tour Africa. Marruecotur has a handy office across from the Tarifa TI on Avenue di Constitutión (daily 8:30–21:00, in-person bookings only, tel. 95-668-1214) and another office at Batalla de Salado 57 (Mon–Sat 8:30–20:00, Sun 8:30–13:00, shorter hours off-season, CC:VMA, tel. 95-668-1821, fax 95-668-0256, e-mail: mctotravel@hotmail.com). Tour Africa is at the far end of the dock (daily 8:00–13:00, 17:00–20:00, shorter hours at whim, GAT 143, CC:VMA, tel. 95-668-4325, fax 95-668-4835). You rarely need to book more than a day in advance, even during peak season.

Algeciras to: Tangier (5 ferries/day, 1/hrly in summer, 2.5 hrs, 3,200 ptas each way, 9,300 ptas for a car; plus 1 hydrofoil/day, 1 hr, 3,800 ptas), **Ceuta** (7 ferries/day, 1/hrly in summer, 90 min, 1,800 ptas each way, 8,223 ptas for a car; plus 12 hydrofoils/day, 35 min, 2,900 ptas each way). **Ceuta**, an uninteresting Spanish possession in North Africa, is the best car-entry point but is not for those relying on public transport. From Ceuta, drive into Morocco. For more info on ferry schedules, call the Algeciras TI (Mon–Fri 9:00–14:00, tel. 95-657-2636). Moroccans clog the Algeciras port, especially in July and August, making Tarifa a relatively relaxing and easygoing option.

Sights—Moroccan Towns

▲▲**Chefchaouen**—Just two hours by bus or car from Tétouan, this is the first pleasant town beyond the Tijuana-type north coast. Monday and Thursday are colorful market days. Stay in the classy old **Hotel Chaouen** on Plaza el-Makhzen. This former Spanish parador faces the old town and offers fine meals and a refuge from hustlers. Wander deep into the whitewashed old town from here.

▲▲**Rabat**—Morocco's capital and most European city, Rabat is the most comfortable and least stressful place to start your North African trip. You'll find a colorful market (in the old neighboring town of Salé), bits of Islamic architecture (Mausoleum of Mohammed V), the king's palace, mellow hustlers, and fine hotels.

▲▲▲**Fès**—More than just a funny hat that tipsy Shriners wear, Fès is Morocco's religious and artistic center, bustling with craftsmen, pilgrims, shoppers, and shops. Like most large Moroccan cities, it has a distinct new town from the French colonial period and an exotic—and stressful—old Arabic town, where you'll find the *medina*. The Fès marketplace is Morocco's best.

▲▲▲**Marrakech**—Morocco's gateway to the south, this market city is a constant folk festival bustling with djellaba-clad Berber tribespeople and a colorful center where the desert, mountain, and coastal regions merge. The new city has the train station, and the main boulevard (Mohammed V) is lined with banks, airline offices, a post office, a tourist office, and comfortable hotels. The old city features the mazelike *medina* and the huge Djemaa el-Fna, a square seething with people—a 43-ring Moroccan circus.

▲▲▲**Over the Atlas Mountains**—Extend your Moroccan trip several days by heading south over the Atlas Mountains. Take a bus from Marrakech to Ouarzazate (short stop) and then to Tinerhir (great oasis town, comfy hotel, overnight stop). The next day go to Er Rachidia and take the overnight bus to Fès.

By car, drive from Fès south, staying in the small mountain town of Ifrane, and then continue deep into the desert country past Er Rachidia and on to Rissani (market days: Sun, Tue, and Thu). Explore nearby mud-brick towns still living in the Middle Ages. Hire a guide to drive you past where the road stops and head cross-country to an oasis village (Merzouga) where you can climb a sand dune and watch the sun rise over the vastness of Africa. Only a sea of sand separates you from Timbuktu.

Transportation Connections—Morocco

All train traffic comes and goes from the suburban Morora station (both downtown stations have been closed). The Morora station is four kilometers from the city center and a short Petit Taxi ride away (15 dirhams, $1.50). Upon your return, catch the bus, which meets every train arrival and takes passengers all the way to the port for 2.5 dirhams. (The bus also goes from downtown 1 hr before each departure but is not worth the trouble.)

From Tangier by train to: Rabat (4/day, 6 hrs), **Casablanca** (5/day, 6 hrs), **Marrakech** (5/day, 10 hrs), **Fès** (2/day, 6 hrs), **Ceuta and Tétouan** (hrly buses, 1 hr).

From Fès to: Casablanca (8/day, 5 hrs), **Marrakech** (4/day, 9 hrs), **Rabat** (7/day, 4 hrs), **Meknes** (10/day, 1 hr), **Tangier** (5/day, 5 hrs).

From Rabat to: Casablanca (12/day, 90 min), **Fès** (6 buses/day, 5.5 hrs), **Tétouan** (2 buses/day, 4 hrs).

From Casablanca to: Marrakech (6/day, 5 hrs).

From Marrakech to: Meknes (4/day, 10 hrs), **Ouarzazate** (4 buses/day, 4 hrs).

By Plane: Flights within Morocco are convenient and cheap (around $60).

LISBON

Lisbon is a ramshackle but charming mix of now and then. Old wooden trolleys shiver up and down its hills, bird-stained statues mark grand squares, taxis rattle and screech through cobbled lanes, and well-worn people sip coffee in Art Nouveau cafés.

Lisbon, like Portugal in general, is underrated. The country seems somewhere just beyond Europe. The pace of life is noticeably slower than in Spain. Roads are rutted. Prices are cheaper. While the unification of Europe is bringing sweeping changes, the traditional economy is based on fishing, cork, wine, and textiles. Be sure to balance your look at Iberia with enough Portugal.

While Lisbon's history goes back to the Romans and Moors, its glory days were the 15th and 16th centuries, when explorers such as Vasco da Gama opened new trade routes around Africa to India, making Lisbon one of Europe's richest cities. (These days, in the wake of the 500th anniversary of his 1498 voyage, da Gama has a higher profile.) Portugal's "Age of Discovery" fueled an economic boom, which fueled the flamboyant art boom called the Manueline period—named after King Manuel I (ruled1495–1521). In the early 18th century, the gold and diamonds of Brazil, one of Portugal's colonies, made Lisbon even wealthier.

Then, on All Saints' Day in 1755, while most of the population was in church, the city was hit by a tremendous earthquake. Candles quivered as far away as Ireland. Lisbon was dead center. Two-thirds of the city was leveled. Fires started by the many church candles raged through the city, and a huge tidal wave blasted the waterfront. Of Lisbon's 270,000 people, 30,000 were killed.

Under the energetic and eventually dictatorial leadership of Prime Minister Marques de Pombal—who had the new city

Lisbon

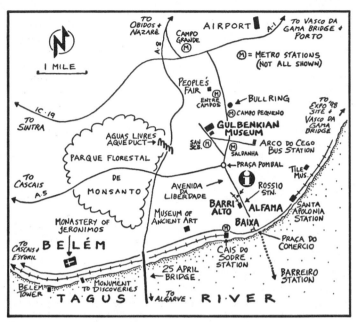

planned within a month of the quake—Lisbon was rebuilt in a
progressive grid plan, with broad boulevards and square squares.
Remnants of pre-earthquake Lisbon charm survive in Belém, the
Alfama, and the Baírro Alto district.

The heritage of Portugal's Age of Discovery was a vast
colonial empire. Except for Macao and the few islands off the
Atlantic coast, the last bits of the empire disappeared with the
1974 revolution, which delivered Portugal from the right-wing
Salazar dictatorship. Emigrants from former colonies such as
Mozambique and Angola have added diversity and flavor to the
city, making it more likely that you'll hear African music than Portuguese fados these days.

But Lisbon's heritage survives. The city seems better
organized, cleaner, and more prosperous and people-friendly
than ever. With its elegant outdoor cafés, exciting art, entertaining museums, a hill-capping castle, the saltiest sailors' quarter
in Europe, and the boost given the city after hosting the
1998 World's Fair, Lisbon is a world-class city. And with
some of Europe's lowest prices, enjoying Lisbon is easy on
the budget.

Planning Your Time

With three weeks in Iberia, Lisbon is worth two days.

Day 1: Start by touring Castle São Jorge, at the top of the Alfama, and surveying the city from its viewpoint. Hike down to another fine viewpoint, Miradouro de Santa Luzia, and descend into the Alfama. Explore. Back in the Baixa (bai-shah; "lower city"), have lunch on or near Rua Augusta and walk to the funicular near Praça dos Restauradores. Start the described walk through the Baírro Alto with a ride up the funicular. Take a joyride on trolley #28. If it's not later than 14:00, art lovers can Metro or taxi to the Gulbenkian Museum. Consider dinner at a fado show in the Baírro Alto. If one of your nights is a summer Thursday, consider a bullfight.

Day 2: Trolley to Belém and tour the Tower, Monastery, and Coach Museum (note: most of Belém's sights are closed Monday). Have lunch in Belém. You could catch the train or drive to Sintra to tour the Pena Palace and explore the ruined Moorish castle. If you're itchy for the beach, drive four hours from Sintra to the Algarve.

A third day could easily be spent at the Museum of Ancient Art and browsing through the Rossio, Baírro Alto, and Alfama neighborhoods.

The side trip to Sintra is time-consuming and rushes Lisbon. If you'd appreciate more time to absorb the ambience of the city, spend a full two days in Lisbon and do the Sintra side trip on a third day (but not Monday, when Sintra's Pena Palace is closed).

Orientation

Greater Lisbon has around 3 million people and some frightening sprawl, but for the visitor, Lisbon can be a delightful small-town series of parks, boulevards, and squares bunny-hopping between two hills down to the waterfront. The main boulevard, Avenida da Liberdade, goes from the high-rent district downhill, ending at the grand square called Praça dos Restauradores. From here the Baixa—the post-earthquake, grid-planned lower town, with three fine squares—leads to the riverfront. Rua Augusta is the grand pedestrian promenade running through the Baixa to the river.

Most travelers focus on the three characteristic neighborhoods that line the downtown harborfront: Baixa (flat, in the middle), the Baírro Alto (literally "high town," Lisbon's "Latin Quarter" on a hill to the west), and the tangled, medieval Alfama (topped by the castle on the hill to the east).

From ye olde Lisbon, Avenida da Liberdade storms into the no-nonsense real world, where you find the airport, bullring, popular fairgrounds, Edward VII Park, and breezy botanical gardens.

Tourist Information

Lisbon's city TI is in the peach-colored Palacio Foz at the bottom of Praça dos Restauradores (daily 9:00–18:00, 21-346-3314).

The national TI for Portugal is in the same office (daily 9:00–20:00, tel. 21-346-3658). The free city map lists all museums and has a helpful inset of the town center. The free biweekly *Follow Me Lisboa* is better than the TI's *Cultural Agenda*. The Falk Map, sold for 1,200$ at bookstores (*livrerias*), is excellent. Each summer cheery little "Ask Me about Lisbon" info booths, staffed by tourism students, pop up all over town (less busy and jaded, actually eager to help you enjoy their town). The city has no regular walking tours, but for a private guide you can call the Guides' Union (13,000$/4 hrs, 24,000$/full-day, tel. 21-346-7170). Angela da Silva is a good local guide (tel. 21-479-3597, cellular tel. 96-605-9518).

Arrival in Lisbon

By Train: Lisbon has four train stations—Santa Apolonia (to Spain and most points north), Rossio (for Sintra, Óbidos, and Nazaré), Barreiro (for Algarve), and Cais do Sodre (Cascais and Estoril). If leaving Lisbon by train, see if your train requires a reservation (boxed "R" in timetable).

Santa Apolonia Station covers international trains and nearly all of Portugal (except the south). It's just past the Alfama and includes foreign-currency change machines and good bus connections to the town center (buses #9, #39, #46, and #90 go from station through center, up Avenida da Liberdade). A taxi from Santa Apolonia to any hotel I recommend should cost around 700$. If there's a long taxi-stand lineup, walk a block away and hail one off the street.

Rossio Station is in the town center (within walking distance of most of my hotel listings) and handles trains from Sintra (and Óbidos and Nazaré, with transfers at Cacém). It has a handy all-Portugal train information office on the ground floor (Mon–Fri 9:15–13:00, 14:00–18:30).

Barreiro Station, a 30-minute ferry ride across the Tagus River (Rio Tejo) from Praça do Comércio, is for trains to the Algarve and points south (the 170$ ferry ticket is generally sold to you with a train ticket).

Caís do Sodre Station handles the 40-minute rides to Cascais and Estoril.

By Bus: Lisbon's bus station is at Arco do Cego (200 meters from Metro: Saldanha, tel. 21-354-5439).

By Plane: Lisbon's easy-to-manage airport is eight kilometers northeast of downtown, with a 24-hour bank, ATMs, a tourist office, reasonable taxi service (1,800$ to center), good city bus connections into town (#44 and #45, 160$), and an airport bus.

The Aero-Bus #91 runs from the airport to Restauradores, Rossio, and Praça do Comércio (450$, 3/hrly, 30 min, 7:00–21:00, buy ticket on bus). Your ticket is actually a one-day Lisbon transit pass that covers bus, tram, and elevator rides. If you fly in on TAP

Central Lisbon

1. Hotel Lisboa Tejo
2. Albergaria Insulana
3. Pensao Aljubarrota
4. Hotel Metropole
5. Pensao Geres
6. Pensao 13 da Sorte
7. Hotel Lisboa Plaza & Ibis
8. Residencial Nova Silva
9. Residencial Camoes
10. Hotel Suisso Atlantico
11. Residencial Florescente
12. Canto Camoes Fado
13. La Brasileira & Metro
14. Tours depart from here

airline, show your ticket at the TAP welcome desk on the arrivals level to get a free one-way voucher for the Aero-Bus (TAP tel. 21-841-6990). A Lisbon transit pass (sold in one-day and three-day versions) covers the Aero-Bus trip to the airport if you're flying out of Lisbon. (Airport information: tel. 21-841-3500; flight info: tel. 21-841-3700.)

Getting around Lisbon

By Metro: Lisbon's simple, fast subway is handy for trips to the Gulbenkian Museum, the fairgrounds, bullfights, the Colombo mall, the Expo '98 site, and the long-distance bus station. Bring change for the machines, as many stations are not staffed (100$

per ride or 250$ all day). Remember to stamp your ticket in the machine. Metro stops are marked with a red "M." *Saida* means exit.

By Trolley, Funicular, and Elevator: For fun and practical public transport, use the trolley, the funicular, and the Eiffelesque elevator (might be closed in 2000; otherwise, tickets at the door, going every few minutes) that connect the lower and upper towns. One ride costs 160$ (no transfers). The 450$ day pass and the 1,060$ three-day transit pass cover all public transportation (including the extensive city bus system) except for the Metro.

The 160$ Bilhete Unico de Coroa gives you two trips on the trolley, bus, or elevator for the cost of one. Buy these tickets at green-and-yellow Carris booths (on Praça Figueira or at the base of the Santa Justa elevator—up a few stairs and behind the elevator).

By Taxi: Lisbon cabbies are good-humored and abundant, and they use their meters. Rides start at 280$, and you can go anywhere in the center for under 500$. Especially if there are two of you, Lisbon cabs are a great, cheap time saver. For an average trip, couples save less than a dollar by taking public transport and spend an extra 20 minutes to get there—bad economics. If time is limited, taxi everywhere.

Helpful Hints

Bullfights take place most summer Thursdays in Lisbon and most Sundays nearby. Tuesdays and Saturdays are flea-market days in the Alfama.

Museums: Most museums are free on Sunday until 14:00 and closed all day Monday (a good day to explore Lisbon's neighborhoods or Sintra's Moorish ruins).

LisboaCard: This card covers all public transportation (including the Metro), allowing free entrance to most museums and discounts on others, plus discounts on city tours. If you plan to museum-hop, the card is a good value, particularly for a day in Belém (covers your transportation and every worthwhile sight in Belém). Don't use one on a Monday, when virtually all sights are closed, or on a Sunday, when many sights are free until 14:00 (24-hour card/1,900$; 48-hour card/3,100$; 72-hour card/4,000$; includes excellent explanatory guidebook). Buy it at the city TI (in Palacio Foz at Praça do Restauradores). You can choose what date and time you want it to "start."

Pedestrian Warning: Sidewalks are narrow, and drivers are daring; cross streets with care. Avoid nighttime strolls through the seedy area near Rossio station and San Vincente Church.

Language: Remember to try to start conversations in Portuguese (see "Survival Phrases," near the back of this book). Fortunately, many people in the tourist trade speak some English. Otherwise, try Portuguese, French, or Spanish, in that order. Lisbon comes with some tricky pronunciations. Locals call their city

Lisboa (LEEZH-bo-ah) and their river the Tejo (TAY-zhoo).
Squares are major navigation points and are called *praça* (PRA-sah).

Time Zone Change: Portuguese time is usually one hour
earlier than Spanish time.

Banking: ATMs are the way to go, giving more escudos
per dollar all over Lisbon. Banks offer fine rates but high fees to
change checks or cash. Shop around and minimize trips to the
bank by changing large amounts (bank hours are generally
Mon–Fri 8:30–15:00). American Express cashes any kind of
traveler's check at a decent rate without a commission, but the
office is not central (Mon–Fri 9:30–13:00, 14:30–18:30, in Top
Tours office at Avenida Duque de Loule 108, Metro: Rotunda,
tel. 21-315-5885). Automatic bill-changing machines are available
and seductive, offering fair rates but high fees.

Post Office and Telephones: The post office, at Praça dos
Restauradores 58, has easy-to-use metered phones (Mon–Fri
8:00–22:00, Sat–Sun 9:00–18:00). The telephone center, on the
northwest corner of Rossio Square, sells phone cards and also has
metered phone booths (daily 8:00–23:00, accepts credit cards).

Internet Access: Ciber Ciado is at Largo de Picadero in the
Baírro Alto (600$/hr).

Do-It-Yourself Walking Tours

▲▲**The Baírro Alto and Chiado Stroll**—This colorful upper-city
walk starts at the funicular and ends with the elevator (might be
closed in 2000), each a funky 160$ experience in itself. Leave the
lower town on the funicular, called Elevator da Gloria, near the
obelisk at Praça dos Restauradores. (Notice the plaque inside near
the ceiling from the car's 100th birthday in 1985.) Leaving the
funicular on top, turn right to enjoy the city view from Miradouro
de São Pedro Alcantara (San Pedro Park belvedere). Wander over to
the tile map, which helps guide you through the view, stretching
from the castle birthplace of Lisbon on the right to the towers of
the new city in the distance on the left. The centerpiece of the park
is a statue honoring a 19th-century local writer. This district is
famous for its writers, poets, and bohemians.

If you're into port (the fortified wine that takes its name from
the city of Oporto), you'll find the world's greatest selection
directly across the street from the lift at **Solar do Vinho do Porto**
(run by the Port Wine Institute, Mon–Fri 10:00–23:30, less on
Sat, closed Sun, Rua São Pedro de Alcantara 45). In a plush,
air-conditioned living room you can, for 200$ to 3,000$ per glass
(poured by an English-speaking bartender), taste any of 300
different ports—though you may want to try only 150 or so and
save the rest for the next night. Fans of port describe it as "a
liquid symphony playing on the palate."

Follow the main street (Rua São Pedro de Alcantara) downhill

Pombal's Lisbon

After the earthquake of 1755, Prime Minister Marques de Pombal rebuilt much of Lisbon. He had served as a diplomat in London where he picked up some city-planning ideas—considered pretty wild by 18th-century Lisbon.

Avenida da Liberdade is the tree-lined grand boulevard of Lisbon, connecting the old town near the river (where most of the sightseeing action is) with the newer upper town. Before the great earthquake this was a royal promenade. After 1755 it was the grand boulevard of Pombal's new Lisbon—originally limited to the aristocracy. The present street, built in the 1880s and inspired by Paris' Champs-Élysées, is lined with banks, airline offices, nondescript office buildings . . . and eight noisy lanes of traffic. The grand "rotunda"—as the roundabout formally known as Praça Marques de Pombal is called—tops off the Avenida da Liberdade with a commanding statue of Pombal, decorated with allegorical symbols of his impressive accomplishments. (A single-minded dictator can do a lot in 27 years.) Beyond that stretches the fine Edward VII Park. The 20-minute downhill walk from the Rotunda (Metro: Rotunda) along the half-mile length of the avenue to the old town is enjoyable.

Praça dos Restauradores is the monumental square at the lower end of Avenida da Liberdade. Its centerpiece, an obelisk, celebrates the restoration of Portuguese independence from Spain in 1640. (In 1580 the Portuguese king died without a direct heir. The closest heir was Philip II of Spain—yuck.

a couple of blocks; it turns into the Rua Misericordia. The grid plan of streets to your right is 16th-century Renaissance town planning—predating the earthquake and grid plan of the lower town by two centuries.

São Roque Church is on your left at Largo Trindade Coelho (8:00–17:00). It looks like just another church, but wander slowly under its flat, painted ceiling and notice the rich side chapels. The highlight is the Chapel of St. John the Baptist (left of altar, gold and blue), which looks like it came right out of the Vatican. It did. Made in Rome out of the most precious materials, it was the site of one papal mass; then it was shipped to Lisbon—probably the most costly chapel per square inch ever constructed. Notice the beautiful mosaic floor and the three paintings that are actually intricate mosaics—a Vatican specialty (designed to avoid damage from candle smoke that would darken paintings). The São Roque Museum, with some

He became Philip I of Portugal, ushering in an unhappy 60 years when three Spanish Philips ruled Portugal.) Within a few meters of the obelisk is Lisbon's oldest hotel (Avenida Palace), Rossio train station, TI, bullfight ticket kiosk, a funicular which climbs to the high town, a huge underground parking lot, and a Metro station.

Baixa, between Avenida da Liberdade and the harbor, is the flat, lower city. The grid plan (with many streets named for the crafts and shops historically found there) and most of the five-story facades are Pombal's from just after 1755. Baixa's pedestrian streets, inviting cafés, bustling shops, and elegant old storefronts give the district a certain magnetism. I find myself doing laps in a people-watching stupor. The mosaic-decorated Rua Augusta (with the grand arch near the river framing the equestrian statue of King José I) has a delightful strolling ambience—reminding many of Barcelona's Ramblas.

The Baixa has three great squares, each ornamented with a statue of a Portuguese king. **Rossio** and **Figueira** squares—congested with buses, subways, taxis, and pigeons leaving in all directions—stand side-by-side at the top. Rossio, which is Portuguese for "Plaza Mayor" (main square), has been the center of Lisbon since medieval times. **Praça do Comércio** borders the Baixa at the riverfront. Nicknamed "Palace Square" by locals, for 400 pre-earthquake years it was the site of Portugal's royal palace. It's ringed by government ministries and is the departure point for city tours and the boat across the Tagus. The statue is of King José I, the man who put Pombal to work rebuilding the city.

impressive old paintings and church riches (150$, Tue–Sun 10:00–17:00, closed Mon) is not as interesting as the church itself.

After a visit with the poor pigeon-drenched man in the church square (TI and WC), continue downhill along Rua Misericordia into the more elegant shopping district called the **Chiado** (SHEE-ah-doo).

When you reach Praça Luis de Camões (named after Portugal's best-loved poet), turn left to a small square (Largo Chiado) past **A Brasileira café** and the classy Rua Garrett. The statue is of a famous local poet (Fernando Pessoa) who was a regular at Brasileira. Coffeehouse aficionados enjoy this grand old café, which reeks with smoke and the 1930s (open daily). Drop in for a *bica* (Lisbon slang for an espresso) and a *pastel de Belém* (140$ cream cake—a local specialty).

Browse downhill for two blocks on Rua Garrett, peeking into the classy shops. Notice the lamps with the symbol of Lisbon: a ship, or caravel—carrying the remains of St. Anthony—guarded by two ravens. This street was one of Lisbon's best shopping streets before the fire of 1988.

At Calle Sacramento, go left uphill to another pleasant square, Largo dos Carmo, with the ruins of the **Convento do Carmo** (if it's open, pop in to see the elegant, earthquake-ruined Gothic arches for free or pay 300$ to get all the way in and see the museum, Mon–Sat 10:00–17:30, closed Sun).

Trolley tracks lead from the square past the church to the Santa Justa elevator. At the elevator, climb the spiral stairs one floor to the small observatory deck or to the top of this Eiffelian pimple for a great view café (daily, English spoken, reasonable coffee, expensive eats). The elevator (built by a pupil of Eiffel) takes you down into the Baixa.

▲▲▲**Alfama Stroll**—Europe's most colorful sailors' quarter goes back to Visigothic days. It was a rich district during the Arabic period and finally the home of Lisbon's fisherfolk (and of the poet Luis de Camões, who wrote, "our lips meet easily high across the narrow street"). The tangled street plan is one of the few aspects of Lisbon to survive the 1755 earthquake, helping make the Alfama a cobbled playground of Old World color. A visit is best during the busy midmorning market time or in the late afternoon/early evening, when the streets teem with locals.

Consider riding a taxi or bus #37 from Praça Figueira to the castle—the highest point in town—and walking from there down to the Alfama viewpoint and into the Alfama.

Start at **Castle São Jorge**. Lisbon's castle is boring as far as castles go. But it's the birthplace of the city, it offers a fine view, and it's free (open daily until sunset). Straddle a cannon, enjoy the view and park, and wander the sterile ramparts if you like. Within the castle, **Olisiponia** (the Roman name for Lisbon) is a high-tech syrupy multimedia presentation offering a sweeping video overview of the city's history in English (600$, daily 10:00–17:30).

It's a five-minute walk downhill to another great Alfama viewpoint, at **Largo Santa Luzia**. (This square is a stop for trolleys #12 and #28; some prefer to start their Alfama exploration here and take the steep but worthwhile 10-minute uphill hike to the castle.) Admire the panoramic view from the square's small terrace, Miradouro de Santa Luzia, where old-timers play cards in the shade of the bougainvillea amid lots of tiles. Probably the most scenic cup of coffee in town is enjoyed from the nearby Cerca Moura bar/café terrace (after 11:30, Largo das Portas do Sol 4).

The **Museum of Decorative Arts**, next to the Cerca Moura bar, offers a unique (but nearly meaningless with its lack of decent English descriptions) stroll through aristocratic households richly decorated in 16th- to 19th-century styles (800$, Tue–Sun 10:00–17:00, closed Mon, Largo das Portas do Sol 2, tel. 21-886-2183).

From the Largo das Portas do Sol (Cerca Moura bar), stairs lead deep into the Alfama. To descend from the viewpoint: behind the Santa Luzia church, take Rua Norberto de Araujo down a few stairs and go left under the arch and you'll hook up with Beco Santa Helena, an alley of steps leading downhill.

The Alfama's urban jungle roads are squeezed into tangled, confusing alleys; bent houses comfort each other in their romantic shabbiness; and the air drips with laundry and the smell of clams and raw fish. Get lost. Poke aimlessly, sample ample grapes, peek through windows, buy a fish. Don't miss Rua de São Pedro, the liveliest street around. On Tuesday and Saturday mornings the fun Feira da Ladra flea market rages on Campo de Santa Clara (a 20-minute walk; worth it only if it's flea-market day).

Tours—Lisbon

▲▲**Ride a Trolley**—Lisbon's vintage trolleys, most from the 1920s, shake and shiver all over town, somehow safely weaving within inches of parked cars, climbing steep hills, and offering sightseers breezy views of the city. Line #28 is a Rice-A-Roni Lisbon joyride. Tram #28 stops from west to east include Estrela (the 18th-century late-Baroque Estrela Basilica and Estrela Park—cozy neighborhood scene with pond-side café and a "garden library kiosk"), the top of the Bica funicular (drops steeply through a rough-and-tumble neighborhood to the riverfront), Chiado square (Lisbon's café and "Latin Quarter"), Baixa (on Rua da Conceicão between Augusta and Prata), the cathedral (*sè*), the Alfama viewpoint (Santa Luzia belvedere), Portas do Sol, Santa Clara Church (flea market), and the pleasant and untouristy Graca district. Just pay the conductor as you board, sit down, and catch the pensioners as they lurch at each stop. For a quicker circular Alfama trolley ride, catch #12 on Praça da Figueira (departs every few minutes, 20-minute circle, driver can tell you when to get out for the viewpoint near the castle—about three-quarters through the ride).
City Bus Tours—Two tours give tired tourists a lazy overview of the city. Neither is great, but both are handy, daily, and inexpensive. **Tagus Tour** lets you hop on and off their topless double-decker buses (2,000$, hrly beginning at 11:00 May–Sept, 90-minute tour covers the town and Belém, taped, English, Portuguese, and French). On the **Hills Tour** you follow the rails on restored turn-of-the-century trams through the Alfama and Baírro Alto (2,800$; live, trilingual guide; 4 or 5 departures daily in summer, less off-season). While the ride is scenic, the information is sparse. Both leave from the Praça do Comércio (tel. 21-363-2021).

Sights—Lisbon

▲▲▲**Gulbenkian Museum**—This is the best of Lisbon's 40 museums. Gulbenkian, an Armenian oil tycoon, gave his art collection (or "harem," as he called it) to Portugal in gratitude for the hospitable asylum granted him during World War II. This great collection, spanning 2,000 years and housed in a classy modern building, offers the most purely enjoyable museum experience in Iberia. It's cool, uncrowded, gorgeously lit, and easy to grasp, displaying only a few select and exquisite works from each epoch.

Savor details as you stroll chronologically through the ages past the delicate Egyptian, vivid Greek (fascinating coins), and exotic Oriental sections and the well-furnished Louis land. There are masterpieces by Rembrandt, Rubens, Renoir, Rodin, and artists whose names start with other letters. The nubile finale is a dark room filled with Art Nouveau jewelry by the French designer Rene Lalique (500$, free Sun, Tue 14:00–18:00, Wed–Sun 10:00–18:00, closed Mon, pleasant gardens, good air-con cafeteria, take Metro from Rossio to São Sebastião and walk 200 meters, or 500$ taxi from downtown, Berna 45, tel. 21-793-5131).

▲▲**Museum of Ancient Art (Museu Nacional de Arte Antiga)**—This is the country's best for Portuguese paintings from her glory days, the 15th and 16th centuries. (Most of these works were gathered in Lisbon after the dissolution of the abbeys and convents in 1834.) You'll also find the great European masters—such as Bosch, Jan van Eyck, and Raphael—and rich furniture, all in a grand palace. Highlights include the *Temptations of St. Anthony* (a three-paneled altarpiece fantasy by Bosch, c. 1500); *St. Jerome* (by Dürer); the *Adoration of St. Vincent* (a many-paneled altarpiece by the late-15th-century Portuguese master Nuno Goncalves, showing everyone from royalty to sailors and beggars surrounding Portugal's patron saint); and the curious Namban screens (16th-century Japanese depictions of Portuguese traders in Japan). The museum has a good cafeteria, with seating in a shaded garden overlooking the river (500$, Tue 14:00–18:00, Wed–Sun 10:00–18:00, closed Mon, tram #15, bus #40, or #60 from Praça Figueira, Rua das Janeles Verdes 9, tel. 21-397-6002).

▲**National Tile Museum (Museu Nacional do Azulejo)**—This museum, filling the Convento da Madre de Deus, features piles of tiles, which, as you've probably noticed, are an art form in Portugal. The presentation is very low tech, but the church is sumptuous, and the tile panorama of pre-earthquake Lisbon (upstairs) is fascinating (350$, Tue 14:00–18:00, Wed–Sun 10:00–18:00, closed Mon, 10 minutes on bus #105 from Praça Figueira, Rua da Madre de Deus 4, tel. 21-814-7747).

Cathedral (Sè)—Just a few blocks east of Praça do Comércio, it's not much on the inside, but its fortresslike exterior is a textbook example of a stark and powerful Romanesque fortress of God. Started in 1150, after the Christians reconquered Lisbon from the Islamic Moors, its crenellated towers made a powerful statement: The Reconquista was here to stay. St. Anthony—the patron saint of Portugal but known to most of us as the saint in charge of helping you find lost things—is buried in the church. In the 12th century his remains were brought to Lisbon on a ship, as the legend goes, guarded by two sacred black ravens...the symbol of the city. The **cloisters** are peaceful and an archaeological work in progress—uncovering Roman ruins (100$). The humble **treasury** shows off relics of St. Anthony but is worthwhile only if you want to support the church and climb some stairs (400$).

Expo '98 Grounds and Aquarium—Lisbon celebrated the 500th anniversary of Vasco da Gama's voyage to India by hosting Expo '98. The theme was "The Ocean and the Seas," with an emphasis on the importance of healthy, clean waters in our environment. The riverside fairgrounds are east of the Santa Apolonia train station in an area suddenly revitalized with luxury condos and crowd-pleasing terraces and restaurants. Ride the Metro to the last stop (Oriente—meaning east end of town) to join the riverside promenade and visit Europe's biggest aquarium.

Vasco da Gama Bridge—The second-longest bridge in Europe (14 km) was opened in 1998 to connect the Expo grounds with the south side of the Tagus and to alleviate the traffic jams on Lisbon's only other bridge over the river. As the 25th of April Bridge (see below) was modeled after the Golden Gate bridge in San Francisco (same company built it and was paid off by years of tolls), this new Vasco da Gama Bridge was designed with engineering help from the people building the new San Francisco Bay Bridge.

▲25th of April Bridge—At a mile long, this is one of the longest suspension bridges in the world. Built in 1966, it was originally named for the dictator Salazar but was renamed for the date of Portugal's 1974 revolution and freedom. For over 30 years locals could show their political colors by choosing what name to use. While conservatives called it the Salazar Bridge, liberals called it the 25th of April Bridge. Those who preferred to keep their politics private simply called it "the bridge over the river." Now, with the opening of the second bridge over the Tagus in 1998, everyone has to choose a name...and show their politics.

Cristo Rei—A huge statue of Christ (à la Rio de Janeiro)—with outstretched arms, symbolically blessing the city—overlooks Lisbon from across the Tagus River. It was built as a thanks to God, funded by Lisboetas grateful that Portugal stayed out of World War II. While it's designed to be seen from a distance, a lift takes visitors to the top for a great view (250$, daily 9:00–18:00). Catch the ferry from downtown Lisbon (6/hrly, from Praça do Comércio) to Cacilhas then take a bus marked "Cristo Rei" (4/hrly, from ferry dock). Because of bridge tolls, taxis to or from the site are expensive. For drivers, the most efficient visit is a quick stop on your way south to the Algarve.

Sights—Lisbon's Belém District

Three miles from downtown Lisbon, the Belém District is a
sprawling pincushion of important sights from Portugal's Golden
Age, when Vasco da Gama and company made it Europe's richest
power. Belém was the send-off point for voyages from the Age of
Discovery. Sailors would stay and pray here before embarking.
The tower would welcome them home. For some reason, the
grand buildings of Belém survived the great 1755 earthquake.
Consequently, this is the only place to experience the grandeur of
pre-earthquake Lisbon. Safety-conscious royalty lived here after
the earthquake, and the modern-day president of Portugal has his
house here today. To celebrate the 300th anniversary of independence from Spain, a grand exhibition was held here in 1940,
resulting in the fine parks, fountains, and monument.

While the monastery is great, Belém's several museums are
somewhere between good and mediocre, depending upon your
interests. Belém's sights are closed on Monday, except for the
Coach Museum, which closes on Tuesday instead.

Get to Belém by taxi (800$ from downtown), bus (#27, #28,
#29, #43, #49, and #51), or the sleek new tram #15 from Praça da
Figueira (buy 160$ tickets from machine onboard, no change).
The first stop is the Coach Museum; the second is the monastery.
Consider doing Belém in this order: the Coach Museum, pastry
and coffee break, Monastery of Jerónimos, (Maritime Museum if
interested), Monument to the Discoveries, Belém Tower.

▲▲**Coach Museum (Museu dos Coches)**—In 1905 the Queen of
Portugal decided to use the palace's riding-school building to pre-
serve this fine collection of royal coaches. Claiming to be the most
visited sight in Portugal, it is impressive, with more than 70 dazzling
carriages (well-described in English). The oldest is the crude and
simple coach used by King (of Spain and Portugal) Philip II to shuttle between Madrid and Lisbon around 1600. Imagine how slow and
rough the ride would be with bad roads and no suspension. Study
the evolution of suspension and the highly symbolic ornamentation
of the coaches. The newly restored "Ocean Coach" has figures symbolizing the Atlantic and Indian Oceans holding hands, in recognition of Portugal's mastery of the sea (450$, free Sun until 14:00,
Wed–Mon 10:00–17:30, closed Tue, tel. 21-361-0850).

Rua de Belém leads from the coach museum and the monastery past the guarded entry to Portugal's presidential palace,
some fine pre-earthquake buildings, and a famous pastry shop.
This shop, **Casa Pasties de Belém** (Rua de Belém 88), is the
birthplace of the wonderful cream tart called *pastel del Nata*
throughout Portugal. In Lisbon they're called *pastel del Belém*.
Since 1837 locals have come here to get them warm out of the
oven. Sit down and order one with a *café com leite*. Sprinkle on the
cinnamon and powdered sugar.

Belém

▲▲▲**Monastery of Jerónimos**—This is Portugal's most exciting building. King Manuel (who ruled from 1495) had this giant church and its cloisters built (starting in 1501) with "pepper money"—a 5 percent tax on spices brought back from India—as a thanks for the discoveries. Sailors would spend their last night here in prayer before embarking on their frightening voyages.

1. South portal: The ornate south portal, facing the street, is a great example of the Manueline style. Manueline—like Spain's Plateresque but with motifs from the sea—bridged Gothic and Renaissance. Henry the Navigator stands in the middle of the door with his patron saint, St. Jerome (with the lion), up in the tympanum. This door is only used when mass lets out.

2. Church interior: The interior is best viewed from the high altar in the middle. Look back down the nave to see how Manueline is a transition between Gothic and Renaissance. While in Gothic architecture huge columns break the interior into a nave with low-ceilinged ambulatories on either side, here the slender palm-tree-like columns don't break the interior space, and the ceiling is all one height. Find some of the Manueline motifs from the sea: the shells providing ceilings for the niches, the ropelike arches, the ships, coral, and seaweed. It is, after all, the sea that brought Portugal its 16th-century wealth and power and made this art possible.

3. Front of church: Now turn 180 degrees toward the front and see how the rest of the church is Renaissance. Everything but a cupola and the stained glass (replacement glass is from 1940) survived the earthquake. In the apse lions support two kings and two queens (King Manuel I is front left).

4. Tombs: The rear of the nave (near the entry) sports two memorial tombs. Closest to the street is the one for Portugal's much-loved poet, Camões (he's buried elsewhere). Vasco da Gama might be buried in the other. Check out its richly symbolic carving: The proud sailboat is a Portuguese caravel (a technological marvel in its day, with a sail that could pivot to catch the wind effiiciently). The sphere is a common Manueline symbol. Some say the diagonal slash is symbolic of the unwritten pact and ambition of Spain and Portugal to split the world evenly. Even the ceiling—a Boy Scout handbook of rope and knots—comes with a whiff of the sea.

   5. Cloisters: Leave the church (turn right, buy a ticket) and enter the cloisters. These cloisters, my favorite in all of Europe, are the architectural highlight of Belém. The lacy lower arcade is textbook Manueline; the simpler top floor is Renaissance. Study the carvings. The 12 doors lead to confessionals in the church. Traditionally girls put their right hand on the left paw of St. Jerome's lion (in the corner of the courtyard) and were married within six months. Upstairs you'll find better views and the bookshop (church free, 400$ for cloisters, Tue–Sun 10:00–17:00, closed Mon; women's WC upstairs, men's downstairs).

Maritime Museum (Museu de Marinha)—If you're interested in the ships and navigational tools of Portugal's Age of Discovery, this museum, which fills the east wing of the monastery, is worth a look. Sailors love it (500$, Tue–Sun 10:00–18:00, closed Mon, Praça do Império).

▲**Monument to the Discoveries**—This giant riverside monument was built in 1960 to honor Prince Henry the Navigator on the 500th anniversary of his death. Huge statues of Henry, Magellan, Vasco da Gama, and other heroes of Portugal's Age of Discovery line the giant concrete prow of a caravel. Note the marble map chronicling Portugal's empire building (on the ground in front). Follow the years as Portuguese explorers gradually worked their way around Africa. In 1999 Portugal granted Macau its independence, leaving only the Azores and Madeira (whose original inhabitants were Portuguese) as Portuguese possessions. Inside the monument, a TV plays footage of the 1940 Expo, and you can ride a lift to a fine view (330$, Tue–Sun 9:30–18:30, closed Mon, tel. 21-362-0034).

▲**Belém Tower**—The only purely Manueline building in Portugal (built 1515–1520), this tower protected Lisbon's harbor and today symbolizes the voyages that made Lisbon powerful. This was the last sight sailors saw as they left and the first when they returned loaded with gold, spices, and social diseases. When the tower was built, the river went nearly to the walls of the monastery and the tower was midriver. Its interior is pretty bare, but the view from its top is fine (400$, Tue–Sun 10:00–17:00, closed Mon, tel. 21-362-0034). The floatplane on a pedestal is a monument to the first flight across the South Atlantic (Portugal to Brazil) in 1922. The original plane is across the street in the Maritime Museum.

Popular Art Museum (Museu de Arte Popular)—This museum

takes you through Portugal's folk art one province at a time, providing a sneak preview of what you'll see throughout the country (300$, Tue–Sun 10:00–12:30, 14:00–17:00, closed Mon, between the monument and the tower on Avenida Brasilia).

Shopping

Flea Market—On Tuesday and Saturday, the Feira da Ladra flea market hops in the Alfama on Campo de Santa Clara.

Colombo Shopping Mall—While Lisbon offers decaying but still elegant department stores, a teeming flea market, and classy specialty shops, nothing is as impressive as the enormous Centro Colombo, the largest shopping center in Spain and Portugal. More than 400 shops, 10 cinemas, 60 restaurants, and a health club sit atop Europe's biggest underground car park and under a vast and entertaining play center (daily until midnight, pick up a map at the info desk, Metro: Colegio Militar takes you right there, tel. 21-711-3636).

Nightlife

Nightlife in the Baixa seems to be little more than loitering prostitutes and litter stirred by the wind. But head up into the Baírro Alto and you'll find plenty of action. The Jardím do São Pedro is normally festive and the Rua Diario de Noticias is lined with busy bars.

▲**Fado**—Fado is the folk music of Lisbon's back streets. Since the mid-1800s it's been the Lisbon blues—mournfully beautiful, haunting ballads about lost sailors, broken hearts, and sad romance. To the lilting accompaniment of the Portuguese *guitarra* (like a 12-string mandolin), the singer longs for what's been lost.

These days, the fado songs come with a new casualty—a tourist's budget. Fado has become one of Lisbon's favorite late-night tourist traps, but it can still be a great experience. The Alfama has a few famous touristy fado bars, but the Baírro Alto is better (and safer late at night). Wander around Rua Diario de Noticias and neighboring streets either for a late dinner (after 22:00) or later for just drinks and music. Homemade "fado tonight" signs in Portuguese are good news, but even a restaurant filled with tourists can come with good food and fine fado. Prices for a fado performance vary greatly. Many have a steep cover charge, while others have a minimum purchase. Any place a hotel sends you to has a bloated price for the kickback.

Canto do Camões is my favorite, run by friendly Gabriel (2,000$ minimum, 3,900$ menu, Travessa da Espera 38, call ahead to reserve—ask for Mr. Rick's table, tel. 21-346-5464, e-mail: cantodocamoes@ip.pt). The meal is punctuated with sets of three fado songs with different singers. For a snack, a good vintage Porto goes nicely with a plate of *queso de cera* (sheep cheese) and pancetta (salt-cured ham). Relax, spend some time, make eye contact with the singer. Let the music and wine work together.

▲▲▲**Portuguese Bullfight**—If you always felt sorry for the bull, this is Toro's Revenge—in a Portuguese bullfight, the matador is brutalized along with the bull. After an exciting equestrian prelude in which the horseman (*cavaleiro*) skillfully plants barbs in the bull's back while trying to avoid the padded horns, a colorfully clad eight-man team (suicide squad called a *forcado*) enters the ring and lines up single file facing the bull. The leader prompts the bull to charge and then braces himself for a collision that can be heard all the way up in the cheap seats. As he hangs onto the bull's head, his buddies then pile on, trying to wrestle the bull to a standstill. Finally, one guy hangs on to el toro's tail and "water-skis" behind him. Unlike at the Spanish *corrida*, the bull is not killed in front of the crowd at the Portuguese *tourada* (but it is killed later).

You'll most likely see a bullfight in Lisbon or Estoril or on the Algarve (Easter–Oct, flyers at TI). In Lisbon's Campo Pequeno, fights are on Thursday at 22:00 mid-June through September. Tickets cost 1,000$ to 10,000$. The ring is small. There are no bad seats. To sit nearly at ringside, try the cheapest *bancada* seats, on the generally half-empty and unmonitored main floor.

Note: Half the fights are simply Spanish-type *corridas* without the killing. For the real slam-bam Portuguese-style fight, confirm that there will be *grupo de forcados*. Tickets are nearly always available at the door (no surcharge, tel. 21-793-2143 to confirm). For an 11 percent surcharge you can buy them at the green ABEP kiosk above Lisbon's central TI (bottom of Praça dos Restauradores).

▲**People's Fair (Feira Popular)**—Consider spending a lowbrow evening at Lisbon's Feira Popular, which bustles on weekends with Portuguese families at play. Pay the entry fee then enjoy rides, munchies, people watching, and music—basic Portuguese fun. Have dinner among the chattering families, with endless food and wine paraded frantically in every direction. Fried ducks drip, barbecues spit, and dogs squirt the legs of chairs while, somehow, local lovers ignore everything but each other's eyes. (300$, nightly 19:00–24:00 May–Sept, on Avenida da República at Metro: Entre-Campos.)

Movies—Lisbon reels with theaters, and, unlike in Spain, most films are in the original language with subtitles. Many of Lisbon's theaters are classy, complete with assigned seats and ushers, and the normally cheap tickets go for half-price on Monday. Check the cinema listings in the monthly magazine *Lisboaem* (free at TI).

Sleeping in Lisbon
(190$ = about $1)
Sleep Code: **S** = Single, **D** = Double/Twin, **T** = Triple, **Q** = Quad, **b** = bathroom, **t** = toilet only, **s** = shower only, **CC** = Credit Card (Visa, MasterCard, Amex), **SE** = Speaks English, **NSE** = No English. Breakfast is usually included.

With the exception of a few splurges, rooms downtown feel like Lisbon does downtown: tired and well worn. To sleep in a well-located place with local character, you'll be climbing dark stairways into a world of cracked plaster, taped handwritten signs, dingy carpets, cramped and confusing floor plans, and ramshackle plumbing. If you're on a tight budget, arrive without a reservation and bargain. While old Lisbon seems a little sleazy at night, with normal discretion my listings are safe.

Singles cost nearly the same as doubles. As in France, bathtubs and twin beds can cost more than showers and double beds. Addresses like 26-3 stand for street #26, third floor (which is fourth floor in American terms). Never judge a place by its entryway.

Sleeping Downtown in Baixa
(zip code: 1100)

Central as can be, this area bustles with lots of shops, traffic, people, buskers, pedestrian areas, and urban intensity.

Near Praça da Figueira: The **Lisboa Tejo** is an oasis, newly and tastefully refurbished, with 58 comfortable rooms and an attentive and welcoming staff (Sb-14,000–16,000$, Db-16,000–18,000$, prices vary according to room size, includes huge buffet breakfast, 8 percent discount with this book, air-con, CC:VMA, Poço do Borratém 4, from southeast corner of Praça da Figueira, walk one block down Rua Dos Condes de Monsanto and turn left, tel. 21-886-6182, fax 21-886-5163, SE). Manolo Carrera is proud of his historic fountain and wine shop.

On Rua da Assunção: The **Albergaria Residencial Insulana**, on a pedestrian street, is very professional, with 32 quiet and comfortable—if a bit smoky—rooms (Sb-9,000$, Db-10,000$, Tb-14,000$, includes continental breakfast, CC:VMA, elevator, air-con, Rua da Assunção 52, tel. & fax 21-342-3131, SE).

Pensão Aljubarrota is a fine value if you can handle the long climb up four floors, claustrophobic hallways, and the black-vinyl flooring. Once you're on top it's a happy world of small rustically furnished rooms with cute take-my-photo balconies from which to survey the Rua Augusta scene (S-3,500–4,500$, D-5,800–7,000$, Ds-7,000–8,500$, T-8,100–10,800$, 10 percent discount with cash and this book, includes breakfast, all but singles have balconies, CC:VM, priority given for stays of 2 or more nights, Rua da Assunção 53-4, tel. & fax 21-346-0112, Italian Pino and lovely Rita SE).

On or near Rossio Square: The **Hotel Metropole**, right on Rossio Square, offers 1920s-style elegance and 36 big, beautiful rooms, some of which overlook the square (Sb-16,900–21,100$, Db-18,800–23,200$, extra bed-5,000$, includes breakfast, CC:VMA, air-con, elevator, double-paned windows, spacious bathrooms, Rossio 30, tel. 21-346-9164, fax 21-346-9166, SE).

Pensão Residencial Gerês, a good budget bet downtown,

has bright, basic, cozy rooms with older plumbing. Recently remodeled, it lacks the dingy smokiness that pervades Lisbon's cheaper hotels (S-6,500$, Sb-8,000$, D-8,000$, Db-10,000$, T-9,500$, Tb-12,000$, Qb-14,000$, 10 percent discount for cash with this book, CC:VMA, Calçada do Garcia 6, uphill a block off the northeast corner of Rossio, tel. 21-881-0497, fax 21-888-2006, Nogueira family speaks some English).

Near Praça dos Restauradores: The **Hotel Suisso Atlantico** is formal, hotelish, and stuffy, but it's a functional hotel with a practical location (Sb-7,900$, Db-10,000$, Tb-11,800$, includes breakfast, CC:VMA, no fans or air-con, Rua da Gloria 3-19, 1250 Lisbon, behind funicular station, on a quiet street near a peep show 1 block off Praça dos Restauradores, tel. 21-346-1713, fax 21-346-9013, SE).

Residencial Florescente rents 72 rooms on a thriving pedestrian street a block off Praça dos Restauradores. It's a slumber mill, but rooms are clean, and some are nearly charming (S-4,000$, Ss-5,000$, Sb-7,000$, D-5,000$, Ds-6,000$, Db-8,000$, no breakfast, most Db with air-con, CC:VMA, Rua Portas S. Antão 99, 1150 Lisbon, tel. 21-346-3517, fax 21-342-7733, SE).

Sleeping Uptown along Avenida da Liberdade
These listings are a 10-minute walk or short Metro ride from the center.

Pensão Residencial 13 da Sorte, a simple but cheery place, has full bathrooms in each of its 22 rooms and bright tiles throughout (Sb-6,500$, Db-8,000$, Tb-9,500$, no breakfast, CC:VM, elevator, just off Avenida da Liberdade near the Spanish Embassy at Rua do Salitre 13, 1250 Lisbon, 50 meters from Metro: Avenida, tel. 21-353-9746, fax 21-353-1851, Alexandra SE).

Hotel Lisboa Plaza, a four-star gem, is by far my classiest Lisbon recommendation. It's a spacious and plush mix of traditional style with bright-pastel modern elegance, and offers a warm welcome without the stuffiness you'd expect in this price range (Db-30,000–34,000$, CC:VMA, air-con, well-located on a quiet street off busy Avenida da Liberdade, a block from Metro: Avenida at Travessa do Salitre 7, 1250 Lisboa, tel. 21-346-3922, fax 21-347-1630, e-mail: plaza.hotels@mail.telepac.pt).

Sleeping in Baírro Alto
(zip code: 1200)
Just west of downtown, this area is a bit seedy but full of ambience, good bars, local fado clubs, music, and markets. The area may not feel comfortable for women alone at night, but the hotels themselves are safe.

Residencial Nova Silva is a quiet, ramshackle place on the crest of the Baírro Alto overlooking the river. The five borderline dumpy rooms with grand little river-view balconies give you

bird noises rather than traffic noises (priority for longer stays).
It's three blocks from the heart of Chiado on the scenic #28 tram
line and has the easiest street parking (12 hrs/1,200$) of all my
listings (S-4,500$, Ss-5,000$, Sb-6,000$, D-5,000$, Ds-5,500$,
Db-6,000–6,500$, T-7,500$, Ts-7,000$, Tb-8,500$, breakfast-
400$, no elevator, lots of stairs, Rua Victor Cordón 11, tel. &
fax 21-342-4371, Fatima SE).

Residencial Camões lies right in the seedy thick of the
Baírro Alto but offers sleepable rooms. Street-side rooms have
balconies and noise (S-3,500$, D-7,000$, Db-8,500$, includes
breakfast, Travessa Poco da Cidade 38, 1 block south of São
Roque Church and to the west, tel. 21-346-7510, fax 21-346-4048,
some English spoken).

Sleeping away from the Center
Hotel Ibis Lisboa-Centro is big, concrete, modern, and practical
in a soulless area far from the center but near a Metro station.
It offers plain, modern comforts and no stress for a good price
(Db-9,100$, without breakfast, CC:VMA, air-con, next to Novotel
and Metro: Palhava, Avenida Jose Malhoa, tel. 21-727-3181,
fax 21-727-3287, SE). Forgive me.

Eating in Lisbon

Eating in the Alfama
This gritty chunk of pre-earthquake Lisbon is full of interesting
eateries, especially along Rua San Pedro and on Largo de São
Miguel. Eat fast, cheap, and healthy at **Comidas de Santiago**, a
little salad bar with great gazpacho (choose 2 salads on a small plate
for 530$ or 4 on a big plate for 860$, open from 11:00, 1 block
uphill from Santa Luzia viewpoint terrace, Largo do Contador
Mor 21, tel. 21-887-5805).

For a seafood feast, consider dining high in the Alfama at the
Farol de Santa Luzia restaurant (2,600$ fixed-price *menu turistico*,
closed Sun, Largo Santa Luzia 5, across from Santa Luzia viewpoint terrace, no sign but many window decals, tel. 21-886-3884).

For cheap and colorful dinners, walk past Portas do Sol and
follow the trolley tracks along Rua da São Tome to a square called
Largo Rodrigues Freitas, where **Nossa Churrasqueira** is busy
feeding chicken to finger-lickin' locals on rickety tables and
meager budgets (closed Mon).

Arco Do Castello, an Indo-Portuguese restaurant, dishes up
delicious fish and shrimp curries from Goa, a former Portuguese
colony in India. A complete meal for two costs around 5,000$. Top
it off with a shot of the Goan firewater, *feni*, made from cashews
(just across from ramp leading into castle, tel. 21-887-6598).

While in the Alfama, brighten a few dark bars. Have an

aperitif, taste the *branco seco* (local dry white wine). Make a friend, pet a chicken, read the graffiti, and pick at the humanity ground between the cobbles.

Eating in Baírro Alto

Lisbon's "high town" is full of small, fun, and cheap places. Fishermen's bars abound. Just off São Roque's Square you'll find two fine eateries: the very simple and cheap **Casa Trans-Montana** (closed Sun, down the steps of Calcada do Duque at #43) and the bright and touristy **Cervejaría da Trindade**, a Portuguese-style beer hall covered with historic tiles and full of seafood (3,000$ meals, good *bacalhau*—cod, daily 12:00–24:00, CC:VMA, 1 block down from São Roque at Rua Nova da Trindade 20C, tel. 21-342-3506). You'll find many less-touched restaurants deeper into the Baírro Alto on the other (west) side of Rua Misericordia.

Eating in Rossio and Beyond

In Rossio: For cod and vegetables prepared faster than a Big Mac and served with more energy than a soccer team, stand or sit at **Restaurant Beira-Gare** (a greasy spoon in front of Rossio train station at the end of Rua 1 de Dezembro, Mon–Sat 6:00–24:00, closed Sun). To get a house-special pork sandwich, ask for a *bifane no pão*. Farther down the same street is **Celeiro**, a handy and bigger-than-it-looks supermarket (Mon–Fri 8:30–20:00, Sat 9:00–18:00, closed Sun, Rua 1 de Dezembro 67-83). Across the street at #65 (same hours), Celeiro runs a **health-food store** with a bleak but healthy cafeteria in its basement. The Rossio's Rua dos Correeiros is lined with competitive local cafés.

The "eating lane" is a galaxy of eateries with small zoos hanging from their windows for you to choose from (opposite Rossio station, just off Praça dos Restauradores down Rua do Jardím do Regedor and Rua das Portas de St. Antão). The seafood is among Lisbon's best. **Restaurant da Casa do Alentejo**, part of a cultural and social center for people from the traditional southern province of Portugal living in Lisbon, fills an old ballroom and specializes in dry and salty meat and potatoes—Alentejo cuisine (3-course 2,500$ menu, open from 19:30, Rua das Portas de St. Antao 58).

On Praça da Figueria: Casas Suissa is a bright, modern, air-conditioned place popular with locals because it's classy but affordable (cheap at the bar, reasonable at tables, good salads and fruit cups, 7:00–22:00, entries on both Praça da Figueria and Rossio squares). For a gritty snack, stand with the locals at **Pastelaria Tentacão** and munch a *prato do dia* (daily specials, all under 1,000$, daily 7:00–22:00, east side of Praça Figueria). The house specialty to try—or avoid—is *leitão*, a suckling pig sandwich. Pick up the tally sheet as you enter, eat what you like, and turn it in to pay up as you leave. A few doors down, **Mercado da Figueira** is a great grocery.

Eating Elsewhere in Lisbon

Up Avenida da Liberdade: **Cerevejaria Ribadouro** is popular with locals for seafood. The menu is simple, with many items listed at per-kilo prices. The waiter will explain the price per portion (3,000$ meals, Avenida da Liberdade 155, at intersection with Rua do Salitre, Metro: Avenida, tel. 21-354-9411).

At **Feira Popular:** For a chance to go purely local, join hundreds of Portuguese families having salad, fries, chicken, and wine at the **Feira Popular** (nightly from 19:00 May–Sept, Avenida da República, Metro: Entre-Campos).

Drinks

Ginjinha (zheen-zheen-yah) is the diminutive name for a favorite Lisbon drink. *Ginjinha* is a sweet liquor made from the sour cherry-like *ginja* berry, sugar, and schnapps. It's sold for 150$ a shot in funky old hole-in-the-wall shops throughout town. The only choices are with or without berries (*com* or *sem fruta*) and *gelada* (if you want it from a chilled bottle out of the fridge—very nice). In Portugal, when someone is impressed by the taste of something, they say, "*Sabe melhor que nem ginjas*" ("It tastes even better than *ginja*").

Transportation Connections—Lisbon

Remember to reserve ahead if your train requires a reservation.

By train to: Madrid (1/day, overnight 21:56–8:35), **Paris** (1/day, 17:56–15:00, 21 hrs), **Évora** (5/day, 2 hrs), **Lagos** (5/day, 3.5 hrs, overnight possible, likely transfer in Tunes), **Faro** (2 fast trains/day, 3.5 hrs), **Coimbra** (17/day, 2 hrs), **Nazaré Valado** (4/day, 2.5 hrs), **Sintra and Cascais** (4/hrly, 45 min). Train information: tel. 21-888-4025.

To Salema: Both bus and train take about five hours from Lisbon to Lagos. Trains from Lisbon to the south coast leave from the Barreiro station across the Tagus from downtown. Boats shuttle train travelers from Praça do Comércio to the Barreiro train station, with several departures each hour (175$, 30-min ride, note that schedule times listed are often when the boat sails, not when train departs). The 23:10-to-6:28 night train, while no fun, allows you to enjoy the entire day on the Algarve.

By bus to: Coimbra (12/day, 2.5 hrs, 1,450$), **Nazaré** (6/day, 2 hrs), **Fatima** (9/day, 1.5 hrs), **Alcobaça** (5/day, 2 hrs), **Évora** (12/day, 2 hrs), **Lagos** (8/day, 5 hrs, 2,400$, easier than the train, must book ahead, get details at TI). Buses leave from Lisbon's Arco do Cego bus station (Metro: Saldanha, tel. 21-354-5439). Intercentro Lines' buses to Spain leave from the same station (tel. 21-315-9277).

Driving in Lisbon

Driving in Lisbon is big-city crazy. If you enter from the north, a series of boulevards takes you into the center. Navigate by following signs to Centro, Avenida da República, Praça dos Marques de Pombal, Avenida da Liberdade, Praça dos Restauradores, Rossio, and Praça do Comércio. Consider hiring a taxi (cheap) to lead you to your hotel.

There are many safe underground pay parking lots (follow the blue "P" signs), but they get more expensive by the hour and can cost you 4,000$ per day or more. The one under Praça dos Restauradores (under the obelisk, next to the TI, 250$ first hour, 5,900$/day) is within a five-minute walk of most of my recommended hotels. The one at Praça Marquis de Pombal is less expensive. (For ideas on the drive south to the Algarve, see the Algarve chapter.)

NEAR LISBON: SINTRA, CABO DA ROCA, CASCAIS, ESTORIL, AND ÉVORA

For centuries, Portugal's aristocracy considered Sintra the natural escape from Lisbon. Now tourists do, too. Climb through the Versailles of Portuga, the Pena Palace; romp along the ruined ramparts of a deserted Moorish castle on a neighboring hilltop; and explore the rugged and picturesque westernmost tip of Portugal at Cabo da Roca. You can also mix and mingle with the jet set (or at least press your nose against their windows) at the resort towns of Cascais or Estoril.

If you're heading south, you might venture inland to historic Évora, exploring dusty droves of olive groves and scruffy seas of peeled cork trees along the way.

Planning Your Time

While Évora is a stop on the way to Portugal's south coast, the other sights combine to make a fine day trip from Lisbon. Remember that there are two bullrings out here, and it's more likely that your schedule will hit a fight here than in Lisbon. If this is the case, plan accordingly.

Without a car I'd skip Cabo da Roca and do Sintra, Cascais, and Belém as individual side trips from Lisbon.

By car, the 70-mile circular excursion (Lisbon–Belém–Sintra–Cabo da Roca–Cascais–Lisbon) makes for a fine day. Traffic congestion around Sintra can mess up your schedule. Follow the coast from Praça do Comércio west, under the bridge to Belém. Continue west to just before Cascais, where Sintra (11 km) is signposted. Sintra itself is far easier by train than by car from Lisbon.

Drivers who are eager for beach time can leave Lisbon, do the Sintra circle, and drive directly to the Algarve that evening (4 hrs from Lisbon). From Sintra/Cascais, get on the freeway into Lisbon and exit at the Sul Ponte A2 sign, which takes you over the 25th of April Bridge and south on A2.

Sights near Lisbon

SINTRA

For centuries, Sintra—just 12 miles north of Lisbon—was the summer escape of Portugal's kings. Those with money and a desire to be close to royalty built their palaces in lush gardens in the same neighborhood. Byron called this bundle of royal fancies and aristocratic dreams a "glorious Eden," and today it's mobbed with tourists. You can easily spend a day in this lush playground of castles, palaces, sweeping coastal views, and exotic gardens.

Tourist Information: The helpful TI, a block off the town's main square, can provide a map and directions to the castles and can arrange *quartos* (rooms in private homes) for overnighters (daily 9:00–20:00, less off-season, tel. 21-923-1157). Their free map is a virtual Sintra guide packed with travel and sightseeing information. There is also a small TI at the train station.

Planning Your Time

A full day from Lisbon might go like this: Catch early Lisbon–Sintra train (4/hrly from Rossio station, 45 min). Visit Sintra's new modern art museum (near train station). Catch bus to main square and TI, visit National Palace, and buy picnic lunch (fine ready-made "club" sandwiches at the bar 20 meters below the London-style phone booth on the main square). Catch 500$ shuttle bus #434 up to Pena Palace. Lunch in Pena Gardens. Tour

Sintra

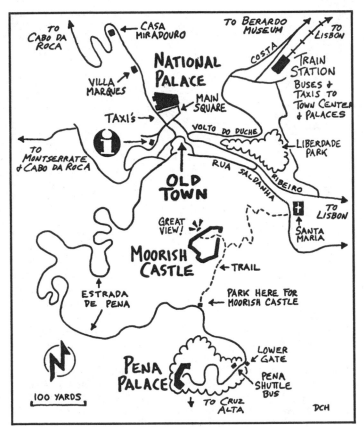

palace. Walk down to the Moorish castle and explore. Hike from the Moorish castle into town (30-minute steep, wooded path; fork in path leads down from within the castle grounds—see map at entry turnstile). Catch train back to Lisbon (before or after dinner in Sintra). Note that the Pena Palace is closed Monday, the Sintra Museum of Modern Art is closed Monday and Tuesday, and the National Palace is closed Wednesday.

Getting around Sintra

Cars are the curse of Sintra. Traffic and parking can be terrible. But public transportation puts the glorious back into Byron's Eden. Across the street from Sintra's train station, bus #434 loops together all the important stops: old town/TI/National Palace; Moorish Ruins; Pena Palace; and back to the station (3/hrly, 2/hrly in winter, 500$ tickets good for 24 hours, buy from driver). It's a pleasant and level 10-minute walk from the station to the old town/TI/National Palace. Taxis don't use a meter but have set fares (e.g., from town center or train station to Pena Palace-1,200$). If you decide (probably regrettably) to drive to the sights, you'll take a one-way winding loop and be encouraged to park "as soon as you can" or risk having to drive the huge loop again.

Sights—Sintra

National Palace (Palacio Nacional)—While going back to Moorish times, most of what you'll see is from the 15th-century reign of João I and later Manueline work. While echoing with Portuguese history and intrigue, the castle is most interesting for Portugal's finest collection of 500-year-old *azulejos* (tiles), its armory, and its fine furnishings (400$, Thu–Tue 10:00–12:30, 14:00–16:30, closed Wed; it's the Madonna bra building, a 10-minute walk from the train station).

▲▲**Pena Palace (Palacio de Pena)**—This magical hilltop palace sits high above Sintra, a steep 15-minute hike above the ruined Moorish castle. Portugal's German-born Prince Ferdinand hired a German architect to build him a fantasy castle, mixing elements of German and Portuguese style. He got a crazy neo-fortified casserole of Gothic, Arabic, Moorish, Disney, Renaissance, and Manueline architectural bits and decorative pieces. (The statue on the nearby ridge is of the architect.) Built in the 1840s, the palace is well-preserved and feels as if it's the day after the royal family fled Portugal in 1910 (during a popular revolt making way for today's modern republic). This gives the place a charming intimacy rare in palace-going. English descriptions throughout give meaning to the rooms (400$, Tue–Sun 10:00–18:00, closed Mon, closes at 16:30 off-season). For a spectacular view of Lisbon and the Tagus River, hike for 15 minutes from the palace to the Chapel of Santa Eufemia.

▲▲**Moorish Castle (Castelo dos Mouros)**—These 1,000-year-old Moorish castle ruins, lost in an enchanted forest and alive with winds of the past, are a castle lover's dream come true and a great place for a picnic with a panoramic Atlantic view. While built by the Moors, the castle was taken by Christian forces in 1147. What you'll climb on today, while dramatic, was much restored in the 19th century. To get from Sintra to the ruins, hike two miles, taxi, or ride bus #434—see "Getting around Sintra," above. The ruins are free (daily 10:00–19:30, closes at 17:00 off-season).

▲**Sintra Museum of Modern Art: The Berardo Collection**—Everyone's raving about Sintra's new private modern art gallery, which is arguably the best in Iberia. The art is presented chronologically and grouped by style in hopes of giving the novice

a better grip on post-1945 art (600$, Wed–Sun 10:00–18:00, closed Mon and Tue, 500 meters from the train station, in Sintra's former casino on Avenida Heliodoro Salgado, tel. 21-924-8170).
Monserrate—Just outside of Sintra is the wonderful garden of Monserrate. If you like tropical plants and exotic landscaping, a visit is time and money well spent (free, daily 10:00–17:15, less in winter). Some say that the Pena Palace Park (below the palace) is just as good as the more famous Monserrate.

Sleeping and Eating in Sintra
(190$ = about $1)
Casa Miradouro is a beautifully restored mansion from 1890. With six spacious and stylish rooms, an elegant lounge, castle and sea views, and a stay-awhile garden, it's a worthy splurge. The place is graciously run by Frederic, who speaks English with a Swiss accent (Sb-11,000–16,800$, Db-13,500–19,800$, highest prices mid-Jul–Sept, CC:VM, easy free street parking, Rua Sotto Major 55, from the National Palace go past Hotel Tivoli Sintra and 400 meters down the hill, tel. 21-923-5900, fax 21-924-1836).

Vila Marques, another elegant old mansion, is funkier, with an eccentric flair, fine rooms, and a great garden. It's 100 meters behind Hotel Tivoli and 200 meters from the National Palace (D-8,000$, D/twin-9,000$, no sinks in rooms, Rua Sotto Mayor 1, tel. 21-923-0027, Sra. Marques NSE and does not accept reservations).

In Sintra, the hardworking, tourist-friendly **Restaurant Regional de Sintra** feeds locals and tourists well (2,000$ dinners, 12:00–22:30, 200 meters from train station at Travessa do Municipio 2, tel. 21-923-4444).

Transportation Connections—Sintra
A slick commuter train connects **central Lisbon** (Rossio Station) with Sintra's new town, called **Estefania** (4/hrly, 45 min). Buses connecting Sintra and **Cascais** (1-hr trip, bus stop is across the street from the Sintra train station) stop at Cabo da Roca.

CABO DA ROCA
Wind-beaten, tourist-infested Cabo da Roca is the westernmost point in Europe. It has a fun little shop, a café, and a tiny TI that sells a cool "proof of being here" diploma (500$, daily 9:00–20:00). Nearby, on the road to Cascais, you'll pass a good beach for wind, waves, sand, and the chance to be the last person in Europe to see the sun set.

CASCAIS AND ESTORIL
Before the rise of the Algarve, these towns were the haunt of Portugal's rich and beautiful. Today they are quietly elegant, with noble old buildings, beachfront promenades, a bullring, a casino,

and more fame than they deserve. Cascais is the more enjoyable of the two; it's not as rich and stuffy and has a cozy touch of fishing village, great seafood, and a younger, less pretentious atmosphere. Both are an easy day trip from Lisbon (4 trains/hrly, 40 min from Lisbon's Caís do Sodre station).

For a Swim
The water at Cascais isn't very clean, and the Lisbon city beach at Costa da Caparica is good but crowded. For the best swimming, drive (public transport is difficult) 30 miles south to the golden beaches, shell-shaped bay, restaurants, and warm, clean water at Port Portinho da Arrabida. Or, better yet, head south to the Algarve.

ÉVORA
Deep in the heart of Portugal, in the barren, arid plains of the southern province of Alentejo, Évora has been a cultural oasis for 2,000 years. With a beautifully untouched provincial atmosphere, fascinating whitewashed old town, plenty of museums, a cathedral, and even a Roman temple, Évora stands proudly amid groves of cork and olive trees.

The **major sights** (Roman temple of Diana, early Gothic cathedral, archbishop's palace, and a luxurious *pousada* in a former monastery) crowd close together at the town's highest point. Osteophiles eat up the macabre "House of Bones" chapel at the Church of St. Francis, lined with the bones of 5,000 monks. A subtler but still-powerful charm is contained within the town's medieval wall. Find it by losing yourself in the quiet lanes of Évora's far corners.

The **TI** is on the central square, Praça do Giraldo 73 (Mon–Fri 9:00–19:00, Sat–Sun 9:00–12:30, 14:00–17:00, tel. 26-670-2671).

For budget sleeping and eating, look around the square. Evora has one of Portugal's most luxurious *pousadas* (the stuffy **Convento dos Loios**, Db-25,000–30,000$, CC:VM, air-con, across from Roman temple, tel. 26-670-7051, fax 26-670-7248, SE). **Residencia Riviera** is a better value (Db-10,500$, CC:VMA, air-con, Rue 5 di Octobro, tel. 26-670-3304, fax 26-670-0467). On the square, the **Solar de Monfalim** is a great traditional splurge (tel. 26-675-0000, fax 26-674-2367, www.monfalimtur.pt). I ate well for a moderate price at **O Fialho** (closed Mon, Travessa Mascarhenas 14). For very local atmosphere, eat at the **"Restaurant"** just off the Praça at Rua Romano Romalha 11.

Three trains and three buses connect Évora daily with Lisbon (3 hrs). One daily bus connects Évora and Lagos/Algarve (5 hrs).

THE ALGARVE

The Algarve has long been known as Europe's last undiscovered tourist frontier. But that "jumbo shrimp" statement contradicts itself. The Algarve is well discovered, and if you go to the places featured in tour brochures, you'll find it much like Spain's Costa del Sol—paved, packed, and pretty stressful. But there are a few great beach towns left, mostly on the western tip, and this part of the Algarve is the south coast of any sun worshiper's dreams.

For some rigorous rest and intensive relaxation in a village where the tourists and the fishermen sport the same stubble, make sunny Salema your Algarve hideaway. It's just you, a beach full of garishly painted boats, your wrinkled landlady, and a few other globetrotting experts in lethargy. Nearby sights include Cape Sagres (Europe's "Land's End" and home of Henry the Navigator's famous navigation school) and the jet-setty resort of Lagos. Or you could just work on a tan and see how slow you can get your pulse in sleepy Salema. If not now, when? If not you, who?

Planning Your Time

The Algarve is your vacation from your vacation. How much time it deserves depends upon how much time you have and how much time you need to recharge your solar batteries. On a three-week Iberian blitz, I'd give it three nights and two days. After a full day of sightseeing in Lisbon, I'd push it by driving four hours around dinnertime to gain an entirely free beach day. With two days, I'd spend one enjoying side trips to Cape Sagres and Lagos and another just lingering in Salema. Plan on an entire day to get from Salema to Sevilla (with a break in Tavira). With more time, I'd spend it in Salema. Eat all dinners in Salema unless you're fighting bulls in Lagos. The only other Algarve stop to consider is Tavira.

The Algarve

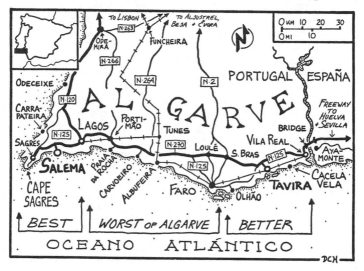

Getting around the Algarve

Trains and buses connect the main towns along the south coast (except on weekends, when service gets skimpy). Trains run nearly hourly between Lagos and the Spanish border, and buses take you west from Lagos, where trains don't go. A new highway makes driving—barring traffic problems—quick and easy. (See "Transportation Connections" at the end of this chapter.)

SALEMA

One bit of old Algarve magic still glitters quietly in the sun— Salema. It's at the end of a small road just off the main drag between the big city of Lagos and the rugged southwest tip of Europe, Cape Sagres. This simple fishing village, quietly discovered by British and German tourists, has a few hotels, time-share condos up the road, some hippies' bars with rock music, English and German menus, a classic beach, and endless sun.

Salema Beach Bum's Quickie Tour

Salema has a split personality: the whitewashed old town for locals, the other half built for tourists. Locals and tourists pursue a policy of peaceful coexistence. Tourists laze in the sun while locals grab the shade.

Market action: Salema's flatbed truck market rolls in most mornings—one truck each for fish, fruit, and vegetables and a five-and-dime truck for clothing and other odds and ends. The *1812 Overture* horn of the fish truck wakes you at 8:00. The bakery trailer sells delightful fresh bread and "store-bought" sweet rolls each morning (about 8:00–10:00). And afternoons around 14:00 the red mobile post office stops by.

Fishing scene: Salema is still a fishing village. While the fishermen's hut no longer hosts a fish auction, you'll still see the old-timers enjoying its shade, oblivious to the tourists, mending their nets and arm wrestling the octopus. In the calm of summer, boats are left out on buoys. In the winter, the community-subsidized tractor earns its keep by hauling the boats ashore. (In pretractor days, such boat hauling was a 10-man chore.) The pottery jars stacked everywhere are octopus traps. These are tied about a meter apart in long lines and dropped offshore. Octopi, thinking these would make a cozy place to set an ambush, climb in and get ambushed. When the fishermen hoist them in, they hang on, unaware they've made their final mistake. Unwritten tradition allocates different chunks of undersea territory to each Salema family.

Beach scene: Locals, knowing their tourist-based economy sits on a foundation of sand, hope and pray that sand returns after being washed away each winter. Some winters turn the beach into a pile of rocks. In Portugal, restaurateurs are allowed to build a temporary, summer-only, on-the-beach restaurant if they provide a lifeguard and run the green/yellow/red warning-flag system (red means dangerous). All over the country you'll see lonely beaches with solitary temporary structures housing such beach restaurants. The Atlantico Restaurant got permission to dominate Salema's beach by providing a lifeguard through the summer. And, as is often the case, they've quietly evolved from a temporary to a permanent business. Beach towns must also provide public showers and toilets, such as Salema's Balneario Municiple (daily 14:00–19:00, showers 150$, run by Manuela). The fountain in front of it is a reminder of the old days. When water to the village was cut off, this was always open.

On the west end of the beach, you can climb over the rocks past tiny tide pools to the secluded Figuera Beach. While the old days of black widows chasing topless Nordic women off the beach are gone, nudism is still risqué today. Over the rocks and beyond the view of prying eyes, Germans grin and bare it.

Community development: The whole peninsula has been declared a natural park, and further development is forbidden. Salema will live with past mistakes, such as the huge hotel in the town center that pulled some mysterious strings to go two stories over the height limit. Up the street is a huge community of Club Med–type vacationers who rarely leave their air-conditioned bars and swimming pools. Across the highway, a mile or two inland is an even bigger golfing resort (worth exploring by car). Just off the beach is a tiny strip mall with a souvenir shop (Rosa's shop is

Salema

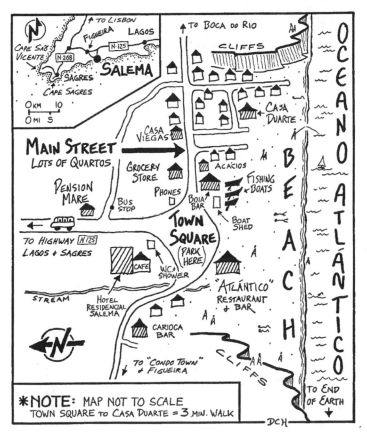

silly with ceramics), a fine grocery store, and a pastry shop with the best coffee in town.

Coastal boat tours: Local English-speaking guide Sebastian offers a two-hour scenic cruise along the coast. He gives a light commentary on the geology and the plant and bird life as he motors halfway to Cape Sagres and back. Trips include nipping into some cool blue natural caves. Morning trips are best for bird-watching. Kicking back and watching the cliffs glide by, I felt like I was scanning a superrelaxing gallery of natural art. Consider being dropped at Figueira Beach just before returning to Salema (say, "Nice to see you" to the nude Germans; it's a 20-minute walk home to Salema—bring shoes, a picnic, and extra water). Easygoing and gentle Sebastian charges little more than what it costs to run his small boat (2,500$ per person, daily 10:30 and 13:30 Jun–Sept, 2–5 passengers, tel. 28-269-5458 or ask for Sebastian at the beach-side fishermen's hut or at Pensión Mare).

Salema after dark: Salema has three late-night bars—each worth a visit. Consider a Salema pub crawl. *Armarguinha* is a sweet and likeable almond drink you might try. The **Boia Bar** offers beachfront drinks and music. Guillermo Duarte's **Atabua Bar** is the liveliest, with the youngest crowd (20:00–02:00 or later, across the street, famous sangria). Ze runs the **Carioca Bar** on the street leading up to condo city. The Carioca is also a restaurant, but Ze's Louis Armstrong laugh is at its anarchist best when the eating's done and the drinking gets going.

Travel agency: Horizonte Travel Agency changes money at fair rates; posts bus schedules; sells long-distance bus tickets (e.g., to Lisbon); rents cars, mopeds, and mountain bikes; books flights and hotels; offers apartment rentals in Salema; and runs all-day jeep tours to the nature park on the southwest coast (Mon–Sat 9:30–20:00, Sun 10:00–14:00; Oct–June Mon–Sat 9:30–19:00, closed Sun, CC:VMA, Salema Beach Club, 5-minute walk from the beach, turn right at phone booth, tel. & fax 28-269-5920; e-mail: horizonte .passeios.turis@mail.telepac.pt, Andrea Fernandes SE).

Sleeping in Salema
(190$ = about $1, zip code: 8650)
Sleep Code: **S** = Single, **D** = Double/Twin, **T** = Triple, **Q** = Quad, **b** = bathroom, **t** = toilet only, **s** = shower only, **CC** = Credit Card (Visa, MasterCard, Amex), **SE** = Speaks English, **NSE** = No English. When a price range is given, the lowest is the winter rate and the highest is the peak-season summer rate.

Salema is crowded in July, August, and September. The town has three streets, five restaurants, several bars, a lane full of fisher-folk who happily rent out rooms to foreign guests, and a circle of modern condo-type hotels, apartments, and villas up the hillside. Parking is free and easy on the street (beware of the no-parking signs near the bus stop).

For maximum comfort there's no need to look beyond John's Pensión Mare. For economy and experience, go for the *quartos* (rooms rented out of private homes).

Pensiónes and Hotels
Pensión Mare, a blue-and-white building looking over the village above the main road into town, is the best good, normal hotel value in Salema (Sb-5,000–6,000$, Db-7,000–9,000$, Tb-9,500–11,500$, includes good breakfast, 10 percent discount with this book and cash if arranged in advance, CC:VMA, guests-only laundry service for 500$ a kilo, Praia de Salema, Vila do Bispo,

Algarve, tel. 28-269-5165, fax 28-269-5846, www.algarve.co.uk).
An easygoing Englishman, John, runs this place, offering six comfortable rooms, two fully equipped apartments, and a tidy paradise.
He speaks English better than I do and will hold rooms with a
phone call and a credit card. John also rents a gem of a fisherman's
cottage on the "*quartos* street" for 14,000$.

Hotel Residencial Salema, the oversized hotel towering
crudely above everything else in town, is a good value if you simply
want a modern, comfortable room handy to the beach. Its red-tiled
rooms all have air-conditioning, balconies, and partial views
(Sb-6,000–11,000$, Db-7,200–12,900$, 10 percent discount with
this book, extra bed-30 percent more, includes breakfast, CC:VMA,
elevator, changes money, rents cars and mopeds, closed Nov–Mar,
tel. 28-269-5328, fax 28-269-5329, SE).

Estalagem Infante do Mar is a three-star hotel on top of
the cliff. Its rooms are plain but all have balconies, and the views
are spectacular—ask for an upstairs room to get a full sea view
(Sb-5,400–10,500$, Db-6,000–14,000$, extra bed-30 percent more,
includes small breakfast, pool, bar, restaurant, parking, changes
money, has no address except its name, CC:VMA, tel. 28-269-0100,
fax 28-269-0109, SE). It's a stiff 10-minute walk uphill. From the
Hotel Residencial Salema, cross the bridge and then head up.

Casa Saudade, a miniature parador, is a tastefully remodeled
apartment for four with a kitchen, two bedrooms, and two terraces
(15,000$ per day, 3-night minimum stay required, Rua Beco de 1
Maio #9; reserve by calling John of Pensión Mare at tel. 28-269-
5165 or Wilfried at tel. & fax 28-269-5020). The same owner
rents **Casa Alegria,** a colorful apartment with a splash of Santa Fe
and a fantastic view (at the top of the "*quartos* street").

Quartos *and Camping*

Quartos abound along the residential street (running left from the
village center as you face the beach). Ask one of the locals at the
waterfront or ask at the Boia Bar or Mini-Market. Prices vary with
the season (doubles-3,000–6,000$), breakfast is not included, and
credit cards are useless. Many places offer beachfront views. It's
worth paying extra for *com vista* rooms, since the rooms on the
back tend to be dark and musty. Few *quartos*' landladies speak
English, but they're used to dealing with visitors. Many will clean
your laundry for a few escudos. If you're settling in for a while or
are on a tight budget, park your bags and partner at a beachside
bar and survey several places. There are always rooms available
for those dropping in. Especially outside of July and August, prices
can be soft.

Casa Duarte has five pleasant rooms (four with views), a
communal kitchenette, and two terraces (D-4,000–6,500$, tel.
28-269-5206, or their English-speaking daughter Cristina at

28-269-5307; son Romeu, who works at the Mini-Market, speaks English). From "*quartos* street," turn right at the Clube Recreativo and then left on the paved path. Duarte's is #7, the first building on the right. If you buy some *sardinhas fresquinhos* from the fish market in the morning (600$/kilo), Sra. Duarte will teach you how to cook them on her grill for lunch.

The friendly **Acacio family** rents a simple ground-floor Db on the beach and a fine upstairs apartment with kitchenette, balcony, and a great ocean view for two to four people (Db-4,000– 6,000$, Tb/Qb in apartment-9,000–12,000$, on "*quartos* street" at #91, tel. 28-269-5473, Silvina NSE).

Maria Helena and Jorge Ribeiro, a helpful young couple, rent two small and humble doubles and a charming tree-house-type apartment with a kitchen, fine terrace, and view toilet (D-4,500$, apartment-7,000$, Rua dos Pescadores 83, tel. 28-269-5289, SE).

Senhor and Senhora Boto rent two immaculate, comfortable rooms with hillside views (D-3,500–4,000$) and a spacious two-bedroom view-terrace apartment (Db-6,000–7,000$, Tb/Qb-8,000$, great value for up to 4 people). It's at the top of "*quartos* street" at Rua dos Pescadores 4 (walk 5 minutes up, on the left, tel. 28-269-5265, NSE).

Rosa rents a small double with a big terrace for 4,000$ and a comfortable apartment with balcony that can sleep two couples and a small child. This super value at 7,000$ is worth the hike and the two-night minimum stay (near top of hill, Rua dos Pescadoes 18, tel. 28-269-5255, NSE).

Campers (who don't underestimate the high tides) sleep free and easy on the **beach** (public showers available in the town center) or at a well-run **campground** with bungalows half a mile inland, back toward the main road.

Eating in Salema

Fresh seafood, eternally. Salema has six or eight places to eat. Happily, those that face the beach (the three listed below) are the most fun and have the best service, food, and atmosphere.

The **Boia Bar**, at the base of the residential street, has a classy beachfront setting and a knack for doing whitefish just right. Their vegetarian lasagna and salads are popular. And their hearty loss-leader breakfast gives you bacon, eggs, toast, coffee, and fresh-squeezed orange juice for the cost of two glasses of orange juice anywhere else in town.

The **Atlantico** is noisier, big, busy, right on the beach, and especially atmospheric when the electricity goes out and faces flicker around candles. It's run by the Duarte clan, and the service is friendly. Consider taking your dessert wine or coffee to the beach for some stardust.

The intimate **Mira Mar**, farther up the residential street, is run by Mario Furtado and family and the closest thing to a barbecue on the beach. If you like garlic, check out the specials.

If you'd rather share a tiny jazz-filled loft with the town bohemians than see the sea from your dinner table, hike three blocks inland for the best *cataplanas* (lush fish stew) in town at **Ze's Carioca Restaurant**. Ze has developed a secret recipe for this local specialty and promises "If you don't like it, you don't pay." For anything else on the menu, "If you don't pay, we break your fingers." Ze opens when he feels like it.

Need a break from fish? **Carapan Franies**, in the middle of town, serves good pizzas for 800$ to 1,000$.

Entrepreneurial Romeu's **Mini-Market** has all the fixings for a great picnic (fresh fruits, veggies, bread, sheep's cheese, sausage, *vinho verde*) to take with you to a secluded beach or Cape Sagres. Romeu also changes money and gives travel advice.

Drivers who want a classy meal outside of town should consider the elegant **Restaurant Vila Velha** in Sagres or the romantic **Castelejo Restaurante** at Praia do Castelo (see "Cape Sagres," below).

CAPE SAGRES

This rugged southwestern tip of Portugal was the spot closest to the edge of our flat earth in the days before Columbus. Prince Henry the Navigator, determined to broaden Europe's horizons and spread Catholicism, sent sailors ever farther into the unknown. He lived here at his navigators' school, carefully debriefing shipwrecked and frustrated explorers as they washed ashore. (TI tel. 28-262-4873.)

Portugal's "end of the road" is two distinct capes. Windy **Cabo St. Vincent** is actually the most southwestern tip. It has a desolate lighthouse that marks what was even in prehistoric times referred to as "the end of the world" (open to the public 10:00–17:00, snoop around, peek over the far edge). Outside the lighthouse, salt-of-the-earth merchants sell figs, fritters, and sea-worthy sweaters (25$ and up). **Cape Sagres**, with its old fort and Henry the Navigator lore, is the more historic cape (excellent *Age of Exploration* maritime history exhibit for 300$, old church, dramatic views). At either cape, look for daredevil windsurfers and fishermen casting off the cliffs.

Lashed tightly to the windswept landscape is the salty town of Sagres, above a harbor of fishing boats and the lavish **Pousada do Infante**. For a touch of local elegance, pop by the *pousada* for breakfast. For 1,500$ you can sip coffee and nibble on a still-warm croissant while gazing out to where, in the old days, the world dropped right off the table. The classy *pousada*, a reasonable splurge with a magnificent setting (Db-24,600$, 8650 Sagres, tel. 28-262-4222, fax 28-262-4225), offers a warm welcome to anyone ready to pay so much for a continental breakfast.

Restaurant Vila Velha in Sagres is the place to eat if want to dine really well. Owner Luis speaks English and serves traditional cuisine with a candlelit and dressy ambience. While Vila Velha does fine fish, for some the meaty side of its menu offers a needed break from seafood (3,000$ meals, next to *pousada*, reservations are smart, tel. 28-262-4788). Ask Luis for a glass of his homemade—and complimentary—*ginja* after dinner. A stop here makes sense after tripping out to Cape Sagres.

Sagres is a popular gathering place for the backpacking bunch, with plenty of private rooms in the center and a great beach and bar scene. From Salema, Sagres is a 20-minute drive or hitch, a half-hour bus trip (nearly hourly trips from Salema, check return times), or a taxi ride (3,500$ two-hour round-trip includes one hour free in Sagres).

The best secluded beach in the region is **Praia do Castelo**, just north of Cape Sagres (from the town of Vila do Bispo, drive inland and follow the signs for 15 minutes). If you have a car and didn't grow up in Fiji, this really is worth the drive. Overlooking the deserted beach, **Castelejo Restaurante** specializes in seafood *cataplanas*, a hearty stew that feeds two to three people (12 km from Salema at Praia do Castelo, tel. 28-263-9777).

LAGOS

The major town and high-rise resort on the west end of the Algarve was the capital of the Algarve in the 13th and 14th centuries. The first great Portuguese maritime expeditions embarked from here, and the first African slave market in Europe was held here (understandably not advertised by the local TI). The old town, defined by its medieval walls, stretches between Praça Gil Eannes and the fort. It's a whitewashed jumble of pedestrian streets, bars, funky craft shops, outdoor restaurants, and sunburned tourists. The church of San Antonio and the adjoining regional museum (Tue–Sun 9:00–12:30, 14:00–17:00, closed Mon) are worth a look, but the morning fish market at the harbor-front Mercado Municipal is more interesting (produce upstairs). The beaches with the exotic rock formations (of postcard fame) are near the fort.

Lagos has a small, for-tourists bullfight in its dinky ring from June through September on most Saturdays at 18:30. Seats are a steep 4,000$, but the show is a thriller. Signs all along this touristy coastline advertise this *stierkampf*.

Tourist Information: The TI is a six-minute walk from the train or bus stations; take the main road east in the direction of Portimão. The TI is near São João Church (Mon–Sat 9:30–12:30, 14:00–19:00, Sun until 17:30, tel. 28-276-3031). Neither the bus station nor the train station offers luggage storage. If you're continuing on to Sevilla by bus or train, read ahead and don't leave Lagos without schedules.

Sleeping and Eating in Lagos
(190$ = about $1, zip code: 8600)
When a price range is given, the lowest is the winter rate, the highest is the peak-season summer rate. Lagos is enjoyable for a resort its size, but I must remind you that Salema is a village paradise and is only a 20-minute taxi ride (2,500–3,000$, no meter, settle price first) or 60-minute bus ride away.

Casa de São Goncalo de Lagos, a beautifully decorated 18th-century home with a garden, lovely tile work, parquet floors, and elegant furnishings, is a fine value. While the downstairs rooms are relatively plain, upstairs you'll find a plush Old World lounge, a dreamy garden, and classy old rooms with all the comforts (Sb-7,500–10,000$, Db-8,000–18,000$, depending on room and season, includes breakfast, closed Nov–mid-Mar, CC:A, Rua Candido dos Reis 73, on a pedestrian street two blocks from the TI, tel. 28-276-2171, fax 28-276-3927, SE).

If you missed the last bus to Salema (leaves Lagos around 20:00), these places are within 100 meters of the bus station. **Pensão Residencial Solar**, a good budget bet, has simple, clean rooms (Db-8,000–12,000$, includes breakfast, CC:VMA, elevator, Rua Antonio Crisogono dos Santos 60, tel. 28-276-2477, fax 28-276-1784, SE). The big, slick, and sternly run **Albergeria Marino Rio** faces the harbor front and the busy main street. Its modern, air-conditioned rooms come with all the amenities (Db-8,000–16,000$, extra bed 2,160–4,800$, CC:VMA, swimming pool, elevator, Avenida dos Descobrimentos-Apartado 388, tel. 28-276-9859, fax 28-276-9960, SE).

The Club Med–like **youth hostel** is a lively, social, and very cushy experience (dorm bed in quad-2,000$, some D-5,000$, includes breakfast, kitchen facilities, hostel card required, Rua Lancarote de Freitas 50, tel. 28-276-1970).

Transportation Connections— Lagos and Salema
Lagos to: Lisbon (5 trains/day, 5 hrs, possible transfer in Tunes; 4 buses/day, 5 hrs), **Évora** (1 bus/day, 5 hrs), **Vila Real St. Antonio** (3 trains/day, 4 hrs), **Tavira** (7 trains/day, 3.5 hrs, 2 daily express trains do it in 2 hrs). Bus information: tel. 28-276-2944.

Lagos and Salema: Lagos is your Algarve transportation hub and the closest train station to Salema (15 km). Buses go almost hourly between Lagos and Sagres (1-hr ride, last bus departs Lagos around 20:00); about half of them go right into the village of Salema—the others drop you at the top of its dead-end road, a 20-minute walk downhill into the village. From Lagos' train station (ignore the "*quartos* women" who tell you Salema is 60 km away), walk straight out, go through the marina, cross the bridge and then the main boulevard, and walk straight into the bright yellow EVA bus station. Before heading to Salema, pick up return bus schedules and train schedules for your next destination. If you venture into Lagos, buses to Salema (and Sagres) also stop on the waterfront. Allow 2,500$ to 3,000$ for a taxi from Lagos to Salema (settle price first).

Lagos and Sevilla: The direct bus between Lagos and Sevilla is worth every escudo (about 3,200$, 5 hrs, 1/day except Mon Jun–Oct, 1/day Thu–Sun Apr–May). The bus departs from the Lagos bus station and arrives at Sevilla's Plaza de Armas bus station, with stops at Algarve towns such as Tavira.

Unless you take the direct bus, getting to Sevilla is a very long day by bus or by bus and train. From Salema take an early bus to Lagos (I walk up to the main road to catch the Sagres–Lagos express bus). From Lagos you have two options: Take a bus or train to Faro (about 2 hrs either way) and catch the Faro–Sevilla bus (2 buses/day, 5 hrs) or take the train until the last stop in Vila Real de San Antonio (several morning departures, allow 4.5 hours, possible transfer in Tunes or Faro), which connects directly to a river-crossing ferry (200$, 17 boats/day) to the pleasant Spanish border town of Ayamonte. From the Ayamonte dock, walk through the town (angling slightly to the right) and find the bus stop next to the main square (shops take escudos; banks change coins). From Ayamonte to Sevilla, catch a direct bus to Sevilla (4/day, 2.5 hrs) or transfer at Huelva (frequent buses, easy transfer). From Huelva, buses run at least hourly to Sevilla (1 hr), and the new Huelva bus station is heavenly: English information, ATMs, and a bank that changes Portuguese coins and sells phone cards. You could take one of four daily trains to Sevilla from Huelva (2 hrs), but I wouldn't. Bus and train stations are connected by a 15-minute walk along Avenida Italia. Sunday schedules are limited and more frustrating. (See "Transportation Connections" near the end of the Sevilla chapter for more specifics.)

TAVIRA

Straddling a river, with a lively park, chatty locals, and boats sharing its waterfront center, Tavira is a low-rise, easygoing alternative to the other, more aggressive Algarve resorts. It's your best east Algarve stop. Because of Tavira's good train service to the rest of Portugal and handy bus connections to Sevilla (and other destinations), many travelers find it more accessible than Salema.

The many churches and fine bits of Renaissance architecture sprinkled through Tavira remind the wanderer that 500 years ago the town was the largest on the Algarve (with 1,500 dwellings according to a 1530 census) and an important base for Portuguese adventurers in Africa. The silting up of its harbor, a plague, the 1755 earthquake, and the shifting away of its once-upon-a-time lucrative tuna industry left Tavira in a long decline. Today the town relies on tourism.

Tavira

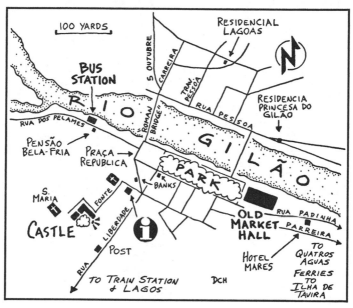

Orientation

Tavira straddles the Rio Gilao three kilometers from the Atlantic. Everything of sightseeing and transportation importance is on the south bank. A clump of historic sights—the ruined castle and main church—fills its tiny fortified hill and tangled Moorish lanes. But today the action is outside the old fortifications along the riverside Praça da Republica and the adjacent shady, fountain- and bench-filled park. The old market hall is beyond the park. And beyond that is the boat to the beach island. The old pedestrian-only "Roman Bridge" leads from Praça da Republica to the north bank (two recommended hotels and most of the evening and restaurant action).

Tavira is on the trans-Algarve train line, with hourly departures both east and west. The train station is a 10-minute walk from the town center: leave the station following the yellow "Turismo" sign and follow this road downhill to the river and Praça da Republica. The new riverside bus station is three blocks from the town center; simply follow the river into town.

Tourist Information: The TI is up the cobbled steps from the inland end of the Praça da Republica (May–Sept daily 9:30–19:00, often closed for lunch and may be closed Sun afternoon, Mon, or after 17:30, depending on staff availability; shorter hours off-season; Rua Galeria 9, tel. 28-132-2511). The TI offers 500$ guided town walks (call for information and reservations).

Sights—Tavira

The TI's fine, free map describes a dozen churches with enthusiasm. But for most tourists, the town's sights can be seen in a few minutes. Uphill from the TI you'll find the ruined **castle**, offering only plush gardens and a fine city view (free, 10:00–19:30). Just beyond the castle ruins is the town's most visit-worthy church, the **Church of Santa Maria**. From there I'd enjoy the riverside park at **Praça da Republica** and the fun architecture of the low-key 18th-century buildings facing the river. After dinner take a stroll along the fish-filled river, with a pause on the pedestrian bridge or in the park if there's any action in the bandstand.

Beaches—The big hit for travelers is Tavira's great beach island, **Ilha da Tavira**. The island is a long, almost treeless sandbar with a campground, several restaurants, and a sprawling beach. A summer-only boat takes bathers painlessly from downtown Tavira to the island (about hourly, 200$ round-trip, departs 200 meters downriver from the former market hall). It's an enjoyable ride even if you just go round-trip without getting out. Or you can bus, taxi, ride a rental bike, or walk three kilometers out of town to Quatro Aguas, where the five-minute ferry shuttles sunbathers to Ilha da Tavira (runs constantly with demand, last trip near midnight in high season to accommodate people dining).

Another fine beach, the **Barril Beach resort**, is just four kilometers from Tavira: walk, rent a bike, or take a city bus to Pedras del Rei and then catch the little train (runs Apr–Sept) or walk 10 minutes any time of the year from the Pedras del Rei bus stop to the resort. Get details at the TI.

Sleeping in Tavira
(190$ = about $1, zip code: 8800)

Residencial Lagoas is spotless, homey, and a block off the river. Friendly, English-speaking Maria offers a communal refrigerator, a rooftop patio with a view made for wine and candles, and laundry washboard privileges (S-3,000$, D-4,500$, Db-6,500$, Tb-8,000$, less off-season, no breakfast, Rua Almirante Candido dos Reis 24, tel. 28-132-2252). Maria also rents several apartments. Cross the Roman footbridge from Praça da República, follow the middle fork on the other side, and turn right where it ends.

The modern, hotelesque **Residencia Princesa do Gilão** offers bright, modern, riverfront rooms, some with balconies and a view (Db-7,000–8,000$, includes breakfast, Rua Borda de Agua de Aguiar 10, cross the Roman bridge and turn right along the river, tel. & fax 28-132-5171, SE).

Pensão-Residencial Bela Fria is a shiny eight-room place with a rooftop sun terrace overlooking the river. Its simple air-conditioned rooms are quiet, modern, and comfortable (Db-4,500–7,500$, 11,000$ in Aug, Rua dos Pelames 1, directly across from the bus station, tel. 28-132-5375, NSE).

For quiet, spacious, comfort, **Rosa's Quartos** are tops. Rosa rents 14 big, new, shiny, marble-paved rooms on a quiet alley (Db-5,000–7,000$, over bridge and through Jardim da Alagoa square to Rua da Porta Nova 4, tel. 28-132-1547, NSE).

For a splurge, consider **Hotel Mare**'s red-tiled and smartly appointed rooms, firm beds, sauna, and rooftop terrace. Some rooms on the second floor have balconies overlooking the river (Db-7,000–12,000$, 16,000$ in Aug, air-con CC:VMA, Rua Jose Pires Padinha, on the TI side of the river just beyond the old market hall, tel. 28-132-5815, fax 28-132-5819, SE).

Eating in Tavira

Tavira is filled with reasonable restaurants. A couple of classy places face the riverbank just beyond the old market hall. A few blocks inland, hole-in-the-wall places offer more fish per dollar.

These places are all within two blocks of the pedestrian Roman bridge, just over the river from the town center. For seafood, I enjoyed the inexpensive and relaxed **Restaurant Bica,** below the Residencial Lagoas (see first hotel listing, above). The **Patio**, on a classy rooftop, is worth the extra escudos. For Italian cuisine, consider **Patrick's Place** (good lasagna) and **Aquasul** (pasta, pizza, and more). From the bridge, if you turn left and go upstream through the tunnel you'll find the rickety riverside tables of the popular **Restaurant O Simão** (cheap, tasty grills). **Anazu Pasteleria** is a popular bar for nursing a late riverside drink or grabbing breakfast (one block to the right of the bridge).

Transportation Connections—Tavira

To: Lisbon (5 trains/day, 5 hrs; 5 buses/day, 5 hrs), **Lagos** (12 trains/day, change in Faro, 2–3.5 hrs), **Sevilla by bus** (2/day, 3.5 hrs, easy transfer in Huelva; 1 direct bus, 2.5 hrs, Tue–Sun May–Oct, less off-season), **Sevilla by train** (go by bus instead). Train info: tel. 28-132-2354, bus info: tel. 28-132-2546.

CACELA VELHA

Just a few miles east of Tavira (one kilometer off the main road), this tiny village sits happily ignored on a hill with its fort, church, one restaurant, a few *quartos*, and a beach, the open sea just over the sandbar, a short row across its lagoon. The restaurant serves a sausage-and-cheese specialty fried at your table. If you're driving, swing by, if only to enjoy the coastal view and imagine how nice the Algarve would be if people like you and me had never discovered it.

Alentejo: Corks and Jokes

Driving from Lisbon to the Algarve, you'll pass through the Alentejo region, known for producing cork. Portugal, the world's leading producer of that wonderful tasteless, odorless seal for wine bottles, produces 30 million corks a day. Driving through the Alentejo region, you'll see vast fields of cork oaks. Every seven to nine years the bark is stripped, leaving a sore red underskin.

The Alentejo region is also known for being extraordinarily traditional. Throughout Europe, what a tourist might see as quaint is seen by city folk as backward. The people of Alentejo are the butt of local jokes. It's said you'll see them riding motorcycles in pajamas . . . so they can better lay into the corners. Many Portuguese call porno flicks "Alentejo karate." I met a sad old guy from Alentejo. When I asked him what was wrong, he explained that he was on the verge of teaching his burro how to live without food . . . but it died. The big event of the millennium in Lisbon is expected to be the arrival of the Alentejanos for Expo '98.

Route Tips for Drivers in the Algarve

Lisbon to Salema (150 miles, 4 hrs): Following the blue "Sul Ponte" signs, drive south over Lisbon's 25th of April Bridge. A short detour just over the bridge takes you to the giant concrete statue of *Cristo Rei* (Christ in Majesty). Continue south past Setubal to the south coast (following signs to Algarve, Vila do Bispo, Sagres, Lagos, and Salema). Just east of Vila do Bispo, you'll hit Figueira and the tiny road to the beach village of Salema. Decent roads, less traffic, and the glory of waking up on the Algarve make doing this drive at night a reasonable option.

Algarve to Sevilla (150 miles): Drive east along the Algarve. In Lagos, park along the waterfront by the fort and the Mobil gas station. From Lagos follow the signs to Faro and then, near Loule, hit the new freeway (direction: España) to Tavira. It's a two-hour drive from Salema to Tavira. Leaving Tavira, follow the signs to Vila Real and España. You'll cross over the new bridge into Spain (where it's one hour later) and glide effortlessly (90 minutes by freeway) into Sevilla. At Sevilla follow the signs to Centro Ciudad ("city center"), drive along the river, and park (at least to get set up) near the cathedral and tower.

CENTRAL PORTUGAL: COIMBRA AND NAZARÉ

While the far north of Portugal has considerable charm, those with limited time enjoy maximum travel thrills on or near the coast of central Portugal. This is an ideal stop if you're coming in from Salamanca or Madrid or are interested in a small-town side trip north from Lisbon.

The college town of Coimbra (three hours north of Lisbon by train, bus, or car) is Portugal's Oxford and its easiest-to-enjoy city. Browse through the historic university, fortresslike cathedral, and lively Old Quarter of what was once Portugal's leading city.

Nazaré, an Atlantic-coast fishing-town-turned-resort, is black-shawl traditional and beach friendly. You'll be greeted by the energetic applause of the surf, widows with rooms to rent, and big plates of steamed shrimp. Have fun in the Portuguese sun in a land of cork groves, eucalyptus trees, ladies in seven petticoats, and men who stow cigarettes and fishhooks in their stocking caps.

Several other worthy sights are within easy day-trip distance of Nazaré. You can drop by the Batalha Monastery, the patriotic pride and architectural joy of Portugal. If the spirit moves you, the pilgrimage site at Fatima is nearby. Alcobaça has Portugal's largest church (and saddest romance). And Portugal's almost edibly cute walled town of Óbidos is just down the road.

Planning Your Time

Few Americans give Portugal much time. Most do Lisbon and the south coast. On a three-week trip through Spain and Portugal, Coimbra and Nazaré each merit a day. There's another day's worth of sightseeing in Batalha, Alcobaça, and Fatima. If you're connecting Salamanca or Madrid with Lisbon, I'd do it this way (for specifics see "Transportation Connections," at the end of this chapter):

By Car
Day 1: Leave Salamanca early, breakfast in Ciudad Rodrigo, early afternoon arrival in Coimbra, tour university and old cathedral.
Day 2: Shop and browse the Old Quarter, lunch at Batalha, tour church, visit Fatima, evening in Nazaré.
Day 3: A 10-mile side trip from Nazaré to Alcobaça (town, monastery, wine museum). Afternoon back in Nazaré with a look at Sitio and beach time. Seafood dinner.
Day 4: Visit Óbidos on your way to Lisbon. Arrive in Lisbon by noon.

By Train
Day 1: The only alternative to the miserable 4:55-to-10:45 Salamanca–Coimbra train connection is spending half of yesterday on a bus. Spend the day seeing Coimbra.
Day 2: Catch morning bus (or train) from Coimbra to Nazaré. Set up and relax in Nazaré, Sitio, and beach. Seafood dinner.
Day 3: Do the triangular loop (Nazaré–Batalha–Alcobaça–Nazaré) by bus.
Day 4: Train into Lisbon.

COIMBRA
Don't be fooled by Coimbra's drab suburbs. Portugal's most important city for 200 years, Coimbra (KWEEM-bra) remains second only to Lisbon culturally and historically. It served as Portugal's leading city while the Moors controlled Lisbon. Only as Portugal's maritime fortunes rose was landlocked Coimbra surpassed by the ports of Lisbon and Porto. Today Coimbra is Portugal's third-largest city (pop. 100,000) and home to its oldest and most prestigious university (founded 1290). When school is in session, Coimbra bustles. During school holidays, it's sleepier. Coimbra's got a great Arab-flavored Old Quarter—a maze of people, narrow streets, and tiny *tascas* (restaurants with just four or five tables).

Orientation
Coimbra is a mini-Lisbon—everything good about urban Portugal without the intensity of a big city. I couldn't design a more enjoyable city for a visit. There's a small-town feeling in the winding streets set on the side of the hill. The high point is the old university. From there, little lanes meander down like a Moroccan *medina* to the main pedestrian street. This street (named Visconde da Luz at the top, turning into Rua de Ferreira Borges halfway down) runs from the square Praça 8 de Maio to the Mondego River, dividing the old town into upper (Alta) and lower (Baixa) parts.

From the Largo da Portagem (main square by the river) everything is within an easy walk. The Old Quarter spreads out like an amphitheater—timeworn houses, shops, and stairways all

Coimbra

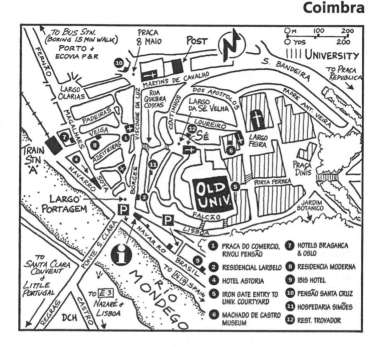

TO BUS STN.
(BORING 15 MIN WALK)
PORTO &
ECOVIA P&R

PRAÇA
8 MAIO

POST

0 M   100   200
0 YDS   200

|||| UNIVERSITY

S. BANDEIRA

TO PRAÇA
REPÚBLICA

FERRAXO

LARGO
OLARIAS

MARTINS DE CAVALHO

RUA
QUEBRA
COSTAS

DOS APOSTOLOS

PADRE ANT. VEIRA

PADEIRAS

VEIGA

MAGALHAES

AZEITEIRAS

NAVARRO

SOTA

BORGES

VISCONDE DA LUZ

COUTINHOS

LARGO
DA SÉ VELHA

LOUREIRO

SÉ

LARGO
FEIRA

PRAÇA
DINIS

TRAIN
STN
"A"

LARGO
PORTAGEM

PORTA FERREA

OLD
UNIV.

JARDIM
BOTÂNICO

FALCÃO

LISBOA

NAVARRO

TO
SANTA CLARA
CONVENT
&
LITTLE
PORTUGAL

PONTE S. CLARA

REGRAS

CASTRO

DCH

TO E.3
NAZARÉ &
LISBOA

BRASIL

TO N.B SPAIN

RIO MONDEGO

① PRAÇA DO COMERCIO,
RIVOLI PENSÃO

② RESIDENCIAL LARBELO

④ HOTEL ASTORIA

⑤ IRON GATE ENTRY TO
UNIV. COURTYARD

⑥ MACHADO DE CASTRO
MUSEUM

⑦ HOTELS BRAGANCA
& OSLO

⑧ RESIDENCIA MODERNA

⑨ IBIS HOTEL

⑩ PENSÃO SANTA CRUZ

⑪ HOSPEDARIA SIMÕES

⑫ REST. TROVADOR

lead up to the university. The best views are looking up from the far end of Santa Clara Bridge and looking down from the observation deck of the university or the arcade in the Machado de Castro Museum. The TI and plenty of good budget rooms are along the river, within four blocks of the train station.

Tourist Information

Pick up a map at the TI at Largo da Portagem (Mon–Fri 9:00–19:00, Sat–Sun 10:00–13:00, 14:30–17:30, less off-season, entrance on Navarro, tel. 23-985-5930). Here you can get all bus schedules and information on sights in central Portugal. Other TIs, with similar hours, are on Praça Dinis and Praça da República (near the university). While there are no regular walking tours, the TI has a list of private guides (15,000$ per half-day, Christina at tel. 23-983-5428 is one of many).

Helpful Hints

The Abreu travel agency sells bus tickets to Salamanca and beyond (Rua da Sota 2, near train station A, tel. 23-982-7011). ATMs and banks (Mon–Fri 8:30–15:00) are plentiful. Avis has an office in

train station A (tel. 23-988-5520 or 23-982-7011), and Hertz is at
Rua João de Ruão 1 (tel. 23-983-7491).

Arrival in Coimbra

By Train: There are two Coimbra train stations, A and B. Major
trains (e.g., from Lisbon and Salamanca) stop only at B (big).
From there, simply hop the three-minute shuttle train to the very
central A station (take the A train; free, included with ticket that
got you to the B train station). Local trains (e.g., to Nazaré) stop
at both stations. Station A has a helpful English-speaking information office (*informações*) tucked away in a waiting room (daily
9:00–13:00, 14:00–18:00, tel. 23-983-4998).

By Bus: The bus station, on Avenida Fernão de Magalhaes
(tel. 23-982-7081), is a boring 15-minute walk from the center.
Exit the bus station to the right and follow the busy street into
town or take a taxi (500$). Local buses are expensive (210$), and
by the time the #5 bus comes along, you could already have
walked downtown. (If you need only bus schedules, the much
more central TI has a folder with all the timetables.)

Do-It-Yourself Orientation Tour of Coimbra's Old Quarter

Coimbra is a delight on foot. You'll find yourself doing laps along
the straight (formerly Roman) pedestrian-only main drag. Do it
once following this quickie tour:

Start at **Santa Clara Bridge**. The bridge has been a key
bridge over the Mondega River since Roman times. For centuries
it had a tollgate (*portagem*). Cross the bridge for a fine Coimbra
view, a lowbrow popular fairground, and free parking.

The square, **Largo da Portagem** (at the end of the bridge on
the Coimbra side), is a great place for a coffee or pastry. Pastelaria
Briosa's pastries are best.

Strolling down the **pedestrian boulevard** you'll pass Pastelaria
Arcadia on the left. Known as the "café of the old ladies," it's
filled with local grandmothers enjoying English-style afternoon tea.
Ignoring the illegal street vendors, find the Camera Municipal (on
the right), with its free, interesting town photo exhibits. Wander
in. Steps lead right under the ancient arched gateway—Arco de
Almedina—into the old city and to the old cathedral and university.
We'll go there later.

Farther along the pedestrian drag, stop at the picturesque
corner just beyond the cafés (where the building comes to a triangular corner). The steep road climbs into Coimbra's historic ghetto
(no Jewish community remains). On the left, stairs lead down into
the pleasant **Praça do Comércio** (shaped like a Roman chariot
racecourse—and likely to have been one 2000 years ago) and the
lower town. Look at your map. The circular street pattern outlines

the wall used by Romans, Visigoths, Moors, and Christians to protect Coimbra. Historically the rich could afford to live within the protective city walls (the "Alta" or high town). Even today, the Baixa, or low town, remains a poorer section, with haggard women hurling buckets of dirty water into the streets, dirty children running barefoot, and drunk men peeing as if you don't exist.

Farther down (on the right) is a photography studio with a display case featuring graduation photos. Check out the students decked out in their traditional university capes (displaying rips on the hem for girlfriends) and color-coded sashes (yellow for medicine, red for law, and so on).

The pedestrian street ends at Praça 8 de Maio with the **Church of Santa Cruz** and its ornate facade. The shiny "necklace" on the angel behind the trumpeter is actually electrified to keep pigeons from dumping their corrosive load on the tender limestone.

People (and pigeons) watch from the terrace of **Café Santa Cruz** (to the right of church). Built as a church but abandoned with the dissolution of the monasteries in 1836 (the women's room is in a confessional), this was the 19th-century haunt of local intellectuals. (There's also a good self-service cafeteria behind the church at Jardim da Manga.)

Backtrack to **Arco de Almedina** (literally "gate to the *medina*") and climb into the old town. If you can't make it to Morocco, this dense jungle of shops and markets may be your next-best bet. Part of the old town wall, this is a double gate with a 90-degree kink in the middle for easier defense. The two square holes in the ceiling, through which boiling oil would be poured, turned attacking Moors into fritters. Shops here show off the fine local blue and white ceramic work (*faiança*).

You're climbing the steep **Rua de Quebra Costas**—"Street of Broken Ribs." At one time this lane had no steps and literally was the street of broken ribs. During a strong rain this becomes a river. A few steps uphill is the old cathedral. Beyond that is the Machado de Castro Museum and the university.

Sights—Coimbra's Old University

Coimbra's 700-year-old university was modeled after Bologna's university (Europe's first, A.D. 1139). It's a stately, three-winged former royal palace (from when Coimbra was the capital), beautifully situated overlooking the city. At first, law, medicine, grammar, and logic were taught. Then, with Portugal's seafaring orientation, astronomy and geometry were added. While Lisbon's university is much larger, Coimbra's is still considered the country's most respected university. Combo tickets for all university sites cost 500$ (daily 9:30–12:00, 14:00–17:00). Consider a taxi ride to the Iron Gate and sightsee Coimbra downhill.

Coimbra's Old University

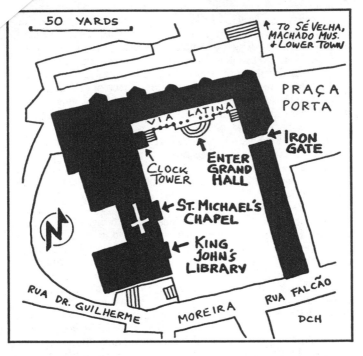

Iron Gate—Find the gate to the old university (on Praça da Porta Ferrea). Before entering, stand with your back to the gate (and the old university) and look across the stark modern square at the fascist architecture of the new university. In what's considered one of the worst cultural crimes in Portuguese history, the dictator Salazar tore down half the old town of Coimbra to build these university halls. Salazar, proud that Portugal was the last European power to hang onto its global empire, wanted a fittingly monumental university here. After all, Salazar—and virtually all people of political importance in Portugal—was educated in Coimbra. If these bold buildings are reminiscent of Mussolini's EUR in Rome, perhaps it's because they were built in part by Italian architects for Portugal's little Mussolini.

OK, now turn and walk through the Iron Gate. Traditionally, freshmen, proudly wearing their black capes for the first time, pass through the Iron Gate to enroll. But to get out they find an Iron Gate gauntlet of butt kicks from upperclassmen. Walk into the...
Old University Courtyard—The statue in the square is of King

John III. While the university was established in 1290, it went back and forth between Lisbon and Coimbra (back then, university students were adults, privileged, and a pain to have in your town). In 1537 John III finally established the school permanently in Coimbra (away from Lisbon). Standing like a good humanist (posing much like England's Renaissance King Henry VIII), John modernized Portugal's education system Renaissance-style. But he also made the university the center of Portugal's Inquisition.

Survey the square with your back to the gate. The dreaded sound of the clock tower's bell—named the "baby goat" for its nagging—called the students to class. On several occasions the clapper has been stolen. No bell ... no class. No class ... big party. A larger bell (the "big goat") rings only on grand and formal occasions.

The university's three important stops all face this square: the Grand Hall (up the grand stairway on the right between you and the clock tower), St. Michael's Chapel (straight ahead, under the arch, then to the left), and King John's Library (across the square, farthest door on left).

The arcaded passageway between the Iron Gate and the clock tower is called Via Latina, from the days when only Latin was allowed in this part of the university. Purchase your tickets at the end of Via Latina immediately under the tower. See the following sights in any order you like.

The Grand Hall (Sala dos Capelos)—Enter from the middle of Via Latina. This is the site of the university's major academic ceremonies, such as exams and graduations. This was originally the throne room of the royal palace. Today the green rector's chair sits thronelike in front. While students in their formal outfits filled the benches, teachers sat along the perimeter, and gloomy portraits of Portuguese kings looked down. Since there is no clapping during these formal rituals, a brass band (on the platform in the back) would punctuate the ceremonies with solemn music. Tourists look down from balconies above the room.

View Catwalk: Continue around the Grand Hall and out onto the narrow observation deck for the best possible views of Coimbra. Scan the old town. Remember, before Salazar's extension of the university, this old town surrounded the university. The Baroque facade breaking the horizon is the "New" Cathedral—from "only" the 16th century. Below that, with the fine arcade, is the Machado de Castro Museum, housed in the former bishop's palace and sitting on a Roman site (see below). And below that, like an armadillo, sits the old cathedral. The noisily painted yellow and blue windows above that are of a *republica*. Traditionally, Coimbra students (from the same distant town) lived together in groups of about a dozen in communal houses called *republicas*. Today *republicas* function as tiny fraternities—some are highly cultured, others are mini-Animal Houses. The Mondego River is the longest entirely Portuguese river. Over the bridge and above the popular fairgrounds is the 17th-century Santa Clara Convent—at 180 meters, the longest building in Coimbra. In 1836 Prime Minister Marquis de Pombal decreed that monasteries and convents were an obstacle to the modern development of Portugal and dissolved them all. Today these are generally museums or abandoned ruins. Pombal was a forceful figure. Not only did he rebuild Lisbon after the earthquake, but he also ended the Inquisition and expelled the Jesuits, who were the intellectual powers behind the Inquisition.

St. Michael's Chapel—This chapel is behind the 16th-century Manueline facade (enter through the next door—once inside, push the door on the left marked "*capela*"). The architecture of the church interior is Manueline (notice the golden "rope" trimming the arch before the altar). The decor is from a later time. I like the slinky 17th-century Adam and Eve tile paintings flanking the rope archway. The tiled walls are decked out in Persian carpet–type designs. The altar is 17th-century Mannerist, with steps unique to Portugal (and her South American colonies) symbolizing the steps the faithful take on their journey to heaven. The 2,100-pipe 18th-century German-built organ is notable for its horizontal "trumpet" pipes. Unique to Iberia, these help the organist perform the allegorical fight between good and evil—with the horizontal pipes trumpeting the arrival of the good guys. Finally, above the loft in the rear are the box seats for the royal family.

The **Museum of Sacred Art** is one glass door away (toward the bookshop, on the left through door marked "Museu de Arte Sacra"). In the stairway, John the Baptist points the way to art that nuns and priests would find fascinating. The museum was created in 1910 to keep the art in Coimbra when the new republic wanted to move all the art to Lisbon.

King John's Library—This grand library displays 30,000 books in 18th-century splendor. The zealous doorkeeper locks the door at every opportunity to keep out humidity. Buzz to get into this temple of thinking. At the "high altar" stands its founder, the Divine Monarch John V. The reading tables inlaid with exotic South American woods (and ornamented with silver ink wells) and the precious wood shelves (with clever hide-away staircases) are reminders that Portugal's wealth was great—and imported. Built Baroque, the interior is all wood. Even the marble is just painted wood. Look for the trompe l'oeil Baroque tricks on the painted ceiling. Gold leaf (from Brazil) is everywhere, and the Chinese themes are pleasantly reminiscent of Portugal's once-vast empire. The books, all from before 1755, are in Latin, Greek, or Hebrew. Imagine being a student in Coimbra 500 years ago. As you leave, watch how the doorman uses the giant key as a hefty doorknob.

More Sights—Coimbra

Machado de Castro Museum—Housed in the old bishop's palace, this museum contains ceramics, 14th- to 16th-century religious sculpture (mostly taken from the dissolved monasteries), and a Roman excavation site.

Upstairs, don't miss the impressive 14th-century *Cristo Negro* carved in wood. Until its restoration a decade ago, this was black from candle soot and considered to be a portrait of a black Christ. Enjoy the views from the top-floor arcade.

The Roman building in the basement provided a level foundation for an ancient Roman forum that stood where the museum does today. Notice the economical "plug-on" Roman busts (from the days when they'd keep the bodies but change the heads according to whoever the latest emperor was). At the entry read the Latin-inscribed Roman stone: bottom line—Aeminiens, referring to the people who lived in Roman Coimbra, then called Aeminium; fifth line—the fourth-century emperor of the day, Constantio; and the second line—a reference perhaps to an early alliance of barbarian tribes from the North Atlantic (250$, Tue–Sun 9:30–12:30, 14:00–17:30, closed Mon, free Sun morning). Visit this before or after the old university, since both are roughly at the same altitude.

Old Cathedral (Sè Velha)—Same old story: Christians push out Moors (1064), tear down their mosque, and build a church. The Arabic script on a few of the stones indicates that rubble from the mosque was used in the construction. The facade of the main entrance even feels Arabic. Notice the crenellations along the roof of this fortresslike Romanesque church; the Moors, while pushed out, were still considered a risk.

The three front altars are each worth a look. The main altar is a fine example of Gothic. The 16th-century chapel to the right is one of the best Renaissance altars in the country. The apostles all look to Jesus as he talks, while musical angels flank the holy host. To the left of the high altar, the Chapel of St. Peter shows Peter being crucified upside down. The fine points of the carving were destroyed by Napoleon's soldiers.

The giant holy water font shells are a 19th-century gift from Ceylon, and the walls are lined with 16th-century tiles from Sevilla.

On the right just before the transept is a murky painting of a queen with a skirt full of roses. She's a local favorite with a sweet legend: Against the wishes of the king, she always gave bread to the poor. One day, when he came home early from a trip, she was busy doling out bread from her skirt. She pulled the material up to hide the bread. When the king asked her what was inside (suspecting bread for the poor), the queen—unable to lie—lowered the material and miraculously it was only roses.

The peaceful cloister (entrance near back of church) is the

oldest Gothic cloister in Portugal. Its decaying walls, neglected courtyard, and overgrown roses offer a fine framed view of the cathedral's grassy dome (church is free, cloisters cost 100$, Mon–Fri 10:00–12:00, 14:00–19:30, may be closed Fri afternoons and off-season, but you're always welcome to drop by during mass: Mon–Sat 19:00 and Sun 11:00).

Little Portugal (Portugal dos Pequenhitos)—This is a children's (or tourist's) look at the great buildings and monuments of Portugal in miniature, scattered through a park a couple of blocks south of town, across the Santa Clara Bridge (800$, daily 10:00–19:00, until 17:00 off-season).

Kayaks and Boats—O Pioneiro takes you from Coimbra to Penacova (25 kilometers away) by minibus and leaves you with a kayak and instructions on getting back. It's a three-hour paddle downstream on the Rio Mondego to Coimbra (3,000$, 10 percent discount with this book, daily Apr–mid-Oct, 1- and 2-person kayaks available, book by phone, meet at park near TI, tel. 23-947-8385 to reserve, best times to phone are 13:00–15:00 and 20:00–22:00, SE). Most people stop to swim or picnic on the way back, so it often turns into an all-day journey. For the first 20 km you'll go with the flow, but you'll get your exercise paddling the last five flat kilometers.

If you'd rather let someone else do the work, O Basofia boats cruise up and down the river daily in summer (1,500$, 3/day, fewer off-season, 75 min, depart from dock across from TI, tel. 23-940-4135).

Sights—Near Coimbra
▲**Conimbriga Roman Ruins**—Portugal's best Roman site is impressive... unless you've been to Rome. Little remains of the city, in part because its inhabitants tore down buildings to throw up a quick defensive wall against an expected barbarian attack. Today this wall cuts crudely through the site. Highlights are the fine mosaics of the Casa dos Fonts (under the protective modern roofing) and a delightful little museum (350$, daily 9:00–13:00, 14:00–20:00; museum opens 1 hour later, closes 2 hours earlier, and is closed all day Mon; ruins close at 18:00 off-season). The ruins are 15 kilometers south of Coimbra on the Lisbon road. On weekdays two buses leave for the ruins each morning from Coimbra's A Station and return late afternoon (255$). Normal buses run twice per hour to Condeixa but leave you a mile from the site. Check bus schedules at the Coimbra TI.

Sleeping in Coimbra
(190$ = about $1, zip code: 3000)
Sleep Code: **S** = Single, **D** = Double/Twin, **T** = Triple, **Q** = Quad, **b** = bathroom, **t** = toilet only, **s** = shower only, **CC** = Credit Card

(Visa, MasterCard, Amex), **SE** = Speaks English, **NSE**
glish. Breakfast isn't included unless noted.

The listings are an easy walk from the central A station
Santa Clara Bridge. For the cheapest rooms, simply walk from
A station a block into the old town and choose one of countless
dormidas (cheap pensions). River views come with traffic noise.

Hotel Astoria gives you the thrill of staying in the city's
finest old hotel for a painless price (Sb-11,000–14,000$, Db-
14,000–17,000$, depending on season, extra bed-3,200$, includes
breakfast, 10 percent discount with this book, CC:VMA, air-con,
elevator, fine Art Deco lounges, plush breakfast room, no parking,
central as can be at Avenida Navarro 21, tel. 23-982-2055, fax 23-
982-2057, SE). Rooms with river views cost nothing extra.

Hotel Oslo rents 33 good business-class rooms a block from
the A station. Rooms are small but hint of Oslo (Sb-6,000–7,000$,
Db-9,000–11,000$, CC:VMA, air-con, free parking, Avenida
Fernão de Magalhaes 25, tel. 23-982-9071, fax 23-982-0614, SE).

Hotel Braganca's ugly lobby disguises clean, comfortable,
but often smoky rooms with modern bathrooms (Sb/shower-
6,000$, Sb/tub-9,500$, Db/shower-9,500$, Db/tub-12,000$,
save money by requesting a shower, or*chuveiro*, includes breakfast,
CC:VMA, air-con, elevator, no parking, Largo das Ameias 10,
tel. 23-982-2171, fax 23-983-6135, SE). Ask to sniff several rooms.
(The manager believes that in 10 years the United States will
grow out of its smoke-free-zones kick.)

Residencial Moderna hides 16 delightful little rooms in a
shopping building overlooking a pedestrian street. Many rooms
come with a balcony (ask *com varanda*) and parquet floors (Db-
5,000–7,000$, 10 percent discount with this book, air-con, a block
from A station, Rua Adelino Veiga 49, 3rd floor, tel. 23-982-5413,
fax 23-982-9508, Fernandes family NSE).

Ibis Hotel is a modern high-rise. Its shipshape little rooms
come with all the comforts and American Motel 6 charm. Well-
located on a riverside park, it's three blocks past the Santa Clara
Bridge and the Old Quarter (Sb/Db-8,000$, Tb-9,000$, breakfast
extra, easy 520$/day parking in basement, elevator, some smoke-
free rooms, Avenida Emidio Navarro, tel. 23-949-1559, fax 23-
949-1773, SE).

Rivoli Pensão offers a fine location three blocks off the river
on lovable Praça do Comércio. While a bit eccentric and minimal,
it's friendly, superclean, and a fine value (S-2,200$, D-5,000$,
Ds-5,500$, Ts-7,000$, no rooms have toilets, Praça do Comércio
27, tel. 23-982-5550, NSE).

Pensão Santa Cruz overlooks the charming and traffic-free
square called Praça 8 de Maio at the end of the pedestrian mall.
It's a homey place, with rooms van Gogh would paint. You'll find
lots of stairs, dim lights, and some balconies worth requesting

)-2,500–4,000$, Db-3,500–5,500$, most expensive Jul–Aug,
prices are soft so ask for relief if you need it, Praça 8 de Maio 21,
3rd floor, tel. & fax 23-982-6197, www.interacesso.pt\~psantacruz,
Walter and Anna SE).

Hospedaria Simões is buried in the heart of the old town, just
below the old cathedral. Run by the Simões family, it offers 18 clean
rooms, but only six have real windows; ask for a *quarto com janela*
(Sb-2,500$, Db-3,500$, Tb-4,500$, Qb-5,600$, piles of stairs, fans,
from Rua Ferreira Borges, go uphill through old gate toward cathedral, take first right, Rua Fernandes Tomas 69, tel. 23-983-4638).

On Largo da Portagem, in front of the bridge, **Residencial
Larbelo** is run-down but likeably mixes frumpiness and former
elegance. The old-fashioned staircase, elegant breakfast room,
and weary management take you to another age (Sb-4,000$, Db-
4,000–6,000$, depending on season and plumbing—shower
cheaper than bath, Largo da Portagem 33, tel. 23-982-9092,
fax 23-982-9094, NSE).

The youth hostel, **Pousada de Juventude**, on the other
side of town in the student area past the Praça da República, is
friendly, clean, well run, and recently remodeled but is no
cheaper than a simple *pensão* (1,700$ beds in 4-bed rooms, closed
12:00–18:00, membership required, Rua Antonio Henriques Seco
14, tel. 23-982-2955, SE).

Eating in Coimbra

Restaurant Trovador, while a bit touristy, serves wonderful food
in a classic and comfortable ambience, with entertaining fado per-
formances nearly nightly after 21:00. It's the place for an old-town
splurge (daily menu 2,500$, Mon–Sat 12:00–15:00, 19:30–22:30,
closed Sun, CC:VM, facing the old cathedral, reservations necessary to eat with the music—ask for a seat with a music view,
tel. 23-982-5475).

Boemia Bar, a happy student place, serves 900$ grilled pork
meals near the old cathedral, behind Restaurant Trovador (Mon–
Sat 19:00–24:00, closed Sun).

Adega Paço do Conde knows how to grill. Choose your
seafood or meat selection from the display case, and it's popped
on the grill. Students and families like this place (800$ meals,
Mon–Sat 10:00–23:00, closed Sun, Rua Paço do Conde 1,
CC:VMA, take the last left off Praça do Comércio, opposite the
church on Adelino Veiga).

For a quick, easy, and cheap meal with locals next to a cool
and peaceful fountain, slide a tray down the counter at **Self-
Service Restaurant Jardim da Manga** (900$ meals, Sun–Fri
8:00–23:00, closed Sat, faces Jardim da Manga, behind Church
of Santa Cruz on Rua Olimpio Nicolau Rui Fernandes).

For an acceptable meal on a great square, eat at **Restaurant**

Praça Velha (don't let the waiters con you, daily 8:00–01:00, Praça do Comércio 72).

The **Santa Cruz Café**, next to the Church of Santa Cruz, is old-world elegant, with outdoor tables offering great people watching over the Praça 8 Maio. The **Italian restaurant** behind the café is popular and open late.

Picnics: Shop at the municipal *mercado* behind the Church of Santa Cruz (Mon–Sat 8:00–14:00, closed Sun) or the supermarket **Minipreço** behind train station A. The well-maintained gardens along the river across from the TI are picnic pleasant.

Transportation Connections—Coimbra

By bus to: Alcobaça (2/day, 90 min, 9:15 and 16:15, 1250$), **Batalha** (3/day, 75 min), **Fatima** (9/day, 1 hr), **Nazaré** (5/day, 1.75 hrs, 1300$), **Lisbon** (17/day, 2.5 hrs), **Évora** (8/day, 8.25 hrs), **Lagos** (7/day, 10 hrs with 1 change). Bus information: tel. 23-985-5270.

By train to: Nazaré/Valado (6/day, 3.5 hours, transfer in Figueira de la Foz, bus is better). Train info: tel. 23-983-4998.

To Salamanca: One train a day drops you in Salamanca at 19:53 in the morning (6-hr trip). The better option is the direct bus (1/day Tue–Sat, 6 hrs, worth the 2,600$ even if you have a railpass, can buy ticket at bus station or at Abreu travel agency, Rua da Sota 2, near train station, tel. 23-982-7011).

NAZARÉ

I got hooked on Nazaré when colorful fishing boats littered its long, sandy beach. Now the boats motor comfortably into a new harbor a 30-minute walk south of town, the beach is littered with frolicking families, and it seems most of Nazaré's 10,000 inhabitants are in the tourist trade. But I still like the place.

Even with its summer crowds, Nazaré is a fun stop offering a surprisingly good look at old Portugal. Somehow the traditions survive, and the locals are able to go about their black-shawl ways. Wander the back streets for a fine look at Portuguese family-in-the-street life. Laundry flaps in the wind, kids play soccer, and fish sizzle over tiny curbside hibachis. Squadrons of sun-dried and salted fish are crucified on nets pulled tightly around wooden frames and left under the midday sun. Locals claim they are delightful—but I don't know. Off-season Nazaré is almost empty of tourists—inexpensive, colorful, and relaxed, with enough salty fishing-village atmosphere to make you pucker.

Nazaré doesn't have any blockbuster sights. The beach, the tasty seafood, and the funicular ride up to Sitio for a great coastal view are the bright lights of my lazy Nazaré memories.

Plan some beach time here. Sharing a bottle of *vinho verde* (a new wine specialty of central Portugal) on the beach at sundown is a good way to wrap up the day.

Nazaré

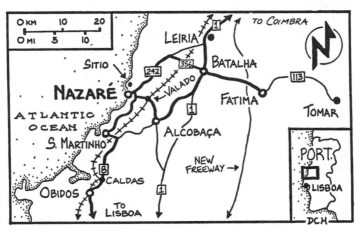

Orientation

Nazaré faces its long beach, stretching from the new harbor
north to the hill-capping old town of Sitio. Leaving the bus station, turn right and walk a block to the waterfront and survey the
town. Scan the cliffs. The funicular climbs to Sitio (the hilltop
part of town). Scan the road kinking toward the sea. The building (on the kink) with the yellow balconies is the Ribamir Hotel,
next to the TI. Just beyond the Ribamir you'll find the main
square (Praça Sousa Oliveira, with banks and ATMs) and most of
my hotel listings.

Sitio, which feels like a totally separate village sitting quietly
atop its cliff, is reached by a frequent funicular (110$). Go up at
least for the spectacular view.

Tourist Information: The TI faces the beach (Jun–Sept
daily 10:00–20:00; Oct–Mar daily 10:00–13:00, 15:00–19:00, tel.
26-256-1194). Ask about summer activities, bullfights in Sitio, folk
dancing at the Casino, fado at Mar Alto, and music on the beach
(22:00, weekends).

Sights—Nazaré

Nazaré Fashions: Seven Petticoats and Black Widows—
Nazaré is famous for its women who wear skirts with seven petticoats. While this is mostly just a creation for the tourists, there is
some basis of truth to the tradition. In the old days, women would
sit on the beach waiting for their fishermen to sail home. To keep
warm during a cold sea wind and stay modestly covered, they'd
wear several dresses in order to fold layers over their heads, backs,

and legs. Even today, older and more traditional women wear short skirts made bulky by several—but not seven—petticoats.

Black outfits are worn by a person in mourning. Traditionally, if your spouse died you wore black for the rest of your life. This tradition is still observed, although in the last generation, widows began remarrying—considered quite racy at first.

The Beach—Since the new harbor was built in 1986, boats are no longer allowed on the beach. Before that they filled the squares in the winter and the beaches in the summer. Today it's the domain of the beach tents—a tradition in Portugal. In Nazaré, the tents are run as a cooperative by the old women you'll see sitting in the shade ready to collect 1,000$ a day. The beaches are groomed and guarded. Flags indicate danger level: red (no one in the water), yellow (wading is safe), green (no problem). If you see a mass of children parading through town down to the beach, they're likely from a huge dorm in town that provides poorer kids from this part of the country with a summer break.

Funicular to Sítio—Nazaré's funicular was built in 1889—the same year as the Eiffel Tower—by the same disciple of Eiffel who built the much-loved elevator in Lisbon. Ride up the lift; it goes every few minutes (110$ each way). Walk to the staggering Nazaré viewpoint behind the station at the top. Sítio feels different. Its people are farmers, not fishing folk.

Activities—Sítio stages Portuguese-style **bullfights** on Saturday nights from July through early September (tickets from 2,000$ at the kiosk in Praça Sousa Oliveira). Sítio's **NorParque** is a family-friendly **water park** with a pool, slides, and Jacuzzi (open Jun–Sept). Fish aficionados might enjoy the **auction** every weekday evening from 17:00 at the harbor (30-minute walk, explain you're a *turista*, bidders have to pay an entrance fee).

A **flea market** pops up near Nazaré's town hall every Friday (9:00–13:00) and the colorful **produce market** bustles daily (8:00–13:00, off-season closed Mon, kitty-corner from the bus station).

Sleeping in Nazaré
(190$ = about $1, zip code: 2450)

You should have no problem finding a room, except in August, when the crowds, temperatures, and prices are all at their highest. You'll find plenty of hustlers meeting each bus and Valado train and waiting along the promenade. Even the normal hotels get into the act during the off-season. I've never arrived in town without a welcoming committee inviting me to sleep in their *quartos* (rooms in private homes).

I list a price range for each hotel: The lowest is for winter, the sky-highest for mid-July through August. In spring and fall expect to pay about midrange. You will save serious money if you arrive with no reservations and bargain. Even the big professional places are down on their knees for 10 months of the year.

Ribamar Hotel Restaurant has a prime location on the waterfront, with an Old World, hotelesque atmosphere, including dark wood and four-poster beds (Sb-4,000–8,000$, Db-6,000–12,000$, prices flexible, includes breakfast, CC:VMA, parking 1,000$, 2,000$ in Aug, TV, some balconies, good restaurant downstairs, Rua Gomes Freiren 9, tel. 26-255-1158, fax 26-256-2224, some English spoken). Look for the yellow awnings and balconies.

Albergaria Mar Bravo is on the corner where the main square meets the waterfront next to Ribamir. Its comfy rooms are modern, bright, and fresh, with air-conditioning and balconies (Sb-8,000–17,000$, Db-12,000–19,500$, depending on view and month, CC:VMA, elevator, Praça Sousa Oliveira 67-A, tel. 26-255-1180, fax 26-255-3979, SE).

Residencial A Cubata, a friendly place on the waterfront on the north end, has small, comfortable rooms (Sb-5,000–10,000$, Db-6,500–15,000$, depends on view and season, includes breakfast, 10 percent discount with this book if you pay cash, CC:VMA, free parking, noisy bar below, Avenida da República 6, tel. 26-256-1706, fax 26-256-1700, not much English). For a peaceful night, forgo the private view balcony, take a back room (and save some money), and enjoy the communal beachfront balcony.

Hotel Mare, just off the Praça Sousa Oliveira, is a big, modern, American-style hotel (Sb-5,750–10,700$, Db-7,500–13,900$, includes breakfast, CC:VMA, all with air-con and balconies, elevator, free parking lot, Rua Mouzinho de Albuquerque 8, tel. 26-256-1122, fax 26-256-1750, SE).

Quartos: I list no dumpy hotels or cheap pensions because the best budget option is *quartos*. Like nowhere else in Iberia, locals renting spare rooms clamor for your business here. Except perhaps for weekends in August, you can stumble into town any day and find countless women hanging out on the street with fine modern rooms to rent. (I promise.) Their rooms are generally better than hotel rooms—for half the cost. Your room is likely to be large and homey, with old-time-elegant furnishings (with no plumbing but plenty of facilities down the hall) and in a quiet neighborhood, six short blocks off the beachfront action. I'd come into town and have fun looking at several places. Hem and haw and the price goes down. **Nazaré Amada** rents four fine rooms (average price for D-5,000$, Rua Adriao Batalha, garage, cellular tel. 96-257-9371, SE).

Eating in Nazaré

In this fishing village even the snacks come from the sea. *Percebes* are local boiled barnacles, sold on the street like munchies. Merchants are happy to demonstrate how to eat them and let you sample one for free. They're great with beer in the bars.

Vinho verde, a northern Portugal specialty, refreshing and a bit like champagne without the bubbles, is a very new wine—picked, made, and drunk within a year. Generally white, cheap, and on every menu, it goes great with shellfish. *Amendoa amarga* is the local amaretto.

Nazaré is a fishing town, so don't order *hamburguesas*. Fresh seafood is great all over town, more expensive (but affordable) along the waterfront, and cheaper in holes-in-the-wall farther inland.

A restaurant lane leads from the town square to the base of the funicular. Among the many hardworking places here, I like **Restaurante Aquario** (Largo das Caldeiras 14).

The family-run **Oficina** serves home-style seafood dishes, not fancy but filling, in a friendly setting that makes you feel like you're eating at someone's kitchen table (daily 12:00–15:00, 19:00–22:00, Rua das Flores 33, off Praça Dr. Manual Arriaga).

Chicken addicts can get roasted chickens to go at **Casa dos Frango** (Praça Dr. Manual Arriaga 20); picnic gatherers should head for the covered *mercado* across from the bus station.

Restaurante O Luis in Sitio serves excellent seafood and local cuisine to an enthusiastic crowd in a cheery atmosphere. While few tourists go here, friendly waiters make you feel very welcome. This place is worth the trouble if you want to eat well in Nazaré: ride the lift up to Sitio, walk five minutes to Praça de Republica and then one block more (2,000$ dinners, nightly 19:00–24:00, R. Teofilo Braga, tel. 26-256-1621).

Transportation Connections—Nazaré

Nazaré's train station is at Valado (three miles toward Alcobaça, connected by semi-regular 200$ buses and reasonable, easy-to-share 1,000$ taxis). To avoid this headache, consider using inter-city buses. If you're heading to Lisbon, trains and buses work equally well. While the train station is three miles from Nazaré and a trip to Lisbon requires a transfer in Cacem, you'll arrive at Lisbon's very central Rossio station (near recommended hotels). Lisbon's bus station is a Metro (or taxi) ride away from the center.

Nazaré/Valado by train to: Coimbra (6/day, 3.5 hrs, change at Foz da Figueira; see bus info below), **Lisbon** (7/day, 3 hrs). Train information: tel. 26-257-7331.

Nazaré by bus to: Alcobaça (stopping at Valado, 13/day, 20 min), **São Martinho** (9/day, 20 min), **Batalha** (8/day, 1 hr, some change at São Jorge), **Óbidos** (6/day, 1 hr; bus is better than train), **Fatima** (3/day, 90 min), **Coimbra** (6/day, 1.75 hrs; bus is better than train), **Lisbon** (5/day, 2 hrs). Buses are scarce on Sunday. Bus information: tel. 26-255-1172.

Day-tripping from Nazaré to: Alcobaça, Batalha, Fatima, or Óbidos: Traveling by bus you can see both Alcobaça and Batalha in one day (but not Sunday, when bus service is sparse). Alcobaça is easy to visit on the way to or from Batalha (and both are connected by bus with Óbidos). Ask at the bus station for schedule information and be flexible. Fatima has the fewest connections and is farthest away. Without a car, for most, Fatima is not worth the trouble. A taxi from Nazaré to Alcobaça costs about 2,000$.

BATALHA

The only reason to stop in the town of Batalha is to see its great monastery. Considered Portugal's greatest architectural achievement and a symbol of its national pride, the Batalha (which means "battle") Monastery was begun in 1388 to thank God for a Portuguese victory that kept it free from Spanish rule (400$, daily 9:00–18:00, until 17:00 off-season, tel. 24-476-5497).

Tourist Information: The TI, located across from the monastery, has free maps and information on buses (daily 10:00–13:00, 15:00–19:00, shorter hours off-season, tel. 24-476-5180). Batalha's market day is Monday morning.

Arrival in Batalha: If you take the bus to Batalha, you'll be dropped off within a block of the monastery and TI. There's no official luggage storage, but you can leave luggage at the monastery's ticket desk while you tour the cloisters.

Sights—Monastery of Santa María

Monastery Exterior—The equestrian statue outside the church is of Nuno Álvares Pereira, who commanded the Portuguese in the battle and masterminded the victory. Before entering the church, study the carving on the west portal (noticing the angels with their modesty wings).

Founder's Chapel—This chapel (near the church entrance) holds several royal tombs, including Henry the Navigator's. Tucked in the wall, Henry wears the church like a crown on his head.

Cloisters—Pay before entering. The greatness of Portugal's Age of Discovery shines brightly in the royal cloisters, which combine the simplicity of Gothic with the elaborate decoration of the Manueline style.

Chapter Room—This is famous for its fine and frighteningly broad vaults. The ceiling was considered so dangerous to build (it collapsed twice) that only prisoners condemned to death were allowed to work on it. Today unknowing tourists are allowed to wander under it. It's the home of Portugal's Tomb of the Unknown Soldier. The adjacent refectory holds a small museum of World War I memorabilia, and the long hall dotted with architectural scraps used to be the monks' dorm.

Keep your ticket, exit the first cloister to a square, follow signs to the right (WC is to the left), and you'll reach the...

Unfinished Chapels—The chapels were started for King Duarte around 1435 to house the tombs of his family and successors.

Never finished, the building—with the best Manueline details you see here—is open to the sky. Across from the elaborate doorway are the tombs of King Duarte and his wife, their recumbent statues hand in hand, blissfully unaware of the work left undone.

Transportation Connections—Batalha

By bus to: Nazaré (6/day, 1 hr), **Alcobaça** (10/day, 30 min), **Fatima** (3/day, 30 min), and **Lisbon** (5/day, 2 hrs). Expect fewer buses on Sunday. By car, Batalha is an easy 10-mile drive from Fatima. You'll see signs from each site to the other.

FATIMA

On May 13, 1917, the Virgin Mary, "a lady brighter than the sun," visited three young shepherds and told them peace was needed. World War I raged on, so on the 13th day of each of the next five months Mary dropped in again to call for peace. On the 13th of October, 70,000 people witnessed the parting of dark storm clouds as the sun wrote "God's fiery signature" across the sky. Now, on the 13th of May, June, July, September, and October and on the 19th of August, thousands of pilgrims gather at the huge neoclassical **basilica of Fatima** (evening torchlit processions for two nights, starting the night before, usually the 12th and 13th). In 1930 the Vatican recognized Fatima as legit, and in 1967, on the 50th anniversary, 1.5 million pilgrims—including the Pope—gathered here. Fatima welcomes guests. (TI tel. 24-953-1139).

The impressive **Basilica do Rosário** stands in front of a mammoth square lined with parks. (Dress modestly to enter the basilica.) Surrounding the square are a variety of hotels, restaurants, and tacky souvenir stands.

Visitors may want to check out two museums (both open daily 9:30–18:30). The **Museo de Cera de Fatima** is a series of rooms telling the story of Fatima one scene at a time with wax figures (700$, English leaflet describes each vignette). The **Museu-Vivo Aparicões**, a low-tech sound and light show, tells the same story (650$, worthless without the English soundtrack playing). While the wax museum is better, both exhibits are pretty cheesy for those who are inclined not to take Fatima seriously.

Apart from the 12th and 13th of most months, cheap hotel rooms abound. Buses go from Fatima to **Batalha** (3/day, 45 min), **Leiria** (15/day 50 min), and **Lisbon** (10/day, 1.5–3 hrs, depending on route); service drops on Sunday.

ALCOBAÇA

This pleasant little town is famous for its church, the biggest in Portugal and one of the most interesting. I find Alcobaça more interesting than Batahla.

Tourist Information: The multilingual TI is across the

square from the church (daily 10:00–13:00, 15:00–19:00; Nov–Apr closes at 18:00 and on Mon, tel. 26-258-2377).

Arrival in Alcobaça: If you arrive by bus, exit right from the station (on Avenida Manuel da Silva Carolino), take the first right, and continue straight (on Avenida dos Combatentes) to the town center and monastery. It's a five-minute walk.

Sights—Alcobaça

▲▲**Cistercian Monastery of Santa María**—This abbey church—the best Gothic building and the largest church in Portugal—is a clean and bright break from the heavier Iberian norm. It was started in 1178 after this area was reconquered from the Moors. It became one of the most powerful abbeys of the Cistercian Order and a cultural center of 13th-century Portugal. The abbey is clean and simple, designed to be filled with hard work, prayer, and total silence. The abbey and cloisters cost 400$ (worthwhile 200$ English leaflet, free info at TI, daily 9:00–19:00, until 17:00 off-season, tel. 26-258-3469).

Nave and Tombs of Dom Pedra and Ines: A long and narrow nave leads to two finely carved Gothic tombs (from 1360) in the transepts. These are of Portugal's most romantic and tragic couple, Dom Pedro (King Peter I) and Dona Inês de Castro. They rest feet-to-feet in each transept so that on Judgment Day they'll rise and immediately see each other again. Pedro, heir to the Portuguese throne, was in love with the Spanish aristocrat Inês. Concerned about Spanish influence, Pedro's father, Alfonso IV, forbade their marriage. You guessed it—they were married secretly. The angry father-in-law, in the interest of Portuguese independence, had Inês murdered. When Pedro became king (1357), he ripped out and ate the hearts of the murderers. And even more interesting, he had Inês' rotten corpse exhumed, crowned it, and made the entire royal court kiss what was left of her hand. Now that's *amore*. The carvings on the tomb are just as special. Like religious alarm clocks, the attending angels are poised to wake the couple on Judgment Day. Study the relief at the feet of Ines: Heaven, Hell, and jack-in-the-box coffins on Judgment day. Napoleon's troops vandalized the tombs.

More Tombs and Relics in the Sacristy: Near the King's tomb, step into the Hall of Tombs for more deceased royalty. Behind the high altar is the sacristy. In the round room decorated with painted wooden sculptures, the little glassed-in hollows in the statues and beams hold relics (tiny bits of bones or clothing) of the monks who died in the monastery.

Cloisters: Pay before entering. Circle the cloister counterclockwise. Cistercian monks built the abbey in 40 years, starting in 1178. They inhabited it until 1834 (when the Portuguese king disbanded all monasteries). Cistercian monks spent most of their lives in silence and were allowed to speak only when given permission by the abbot.

Kitchen: The 18th-century kitchen's giant three-part oven could roast seven oxen simultaneously. The industrious monks rerouted part of the River Alcoa to bring in running water. And how about those hard surfaces?

Refectory or Dining Hall: This is opposite the fountain in the cloister used by the monks to wash up before eating. Imagine the hall filled with monks eating in silence as one reads from the Bible atop the "Readers' Pulpit."

Hall of Kings: Located just before you reenter the nave, this hall features statues of most of Portugal's kings and tiled walls telling the story of the building of the monastery.

▲**Mercado Municipal**—The Old World is housed happily here under huge steel-and-fiberglass domes. Inside, black-clad, dried-apple-faced women choose fish, chicks, birds, and rabbits from their respective death rows. You'll also find figs, melons, bushels of grain, and nuts—it's a caveman's Safeway. Buying a picnic is a perfect excuse to drop in (Mon–Sat 9:00–13:00, closed Sun, best on Mon). It's a five-minute walk from the TI or bus station; ask a local, "*Mercado municipal?*"

▲▲**National Museum of Wine (Museu Nacional do Vinho)**— This museum, a half-mile outside Alcobaça (on the road to Batalha and Leiria, right-hand side), offers a fascinating look at the wine of Portugal (Tue–Sun 9:00–12:30, 14:00–17:30, closed Mon and off-season Sun, tel. 26-258-2222; your car is safer parked inside the gate). Run by a local cooperative winery, the museum teaches you everything you never wanted to know about Portuguese wine in a series of rooms that used to be fermenting vats. With some luck you can get a tour—much more hands-on than French winery tours—through the actual winery. You'll see mountains of centrifuged, strained, and drained grapes—all well on the road to wine. Ask if you can climb to the top of one of 20 half-buried, white, 80,000-gallon tanks, all busy fermenting. Look out. I stuck my head into the manhole-sized top vent, and just as I focused on the rich, bubbling grape stew, I was walloped silly by a wine-vapor punch.

Eating in Alcobaça

Restaurante Coracoes Unidos is a fine, tourist-free restaurant in an old school (near the abbey and across the street from the post office).

Transportation Connections—Alcobaça

By bus to: Lisbon (5/day, 2 hrs), **Nazaré** (12/day, 30 min), **Batalha** (4/day, 30 min), **Fatima** (3/day, 75 min, more frequent with transfer in Batalha). Bus frequency drops on Sunday. A taxi to the Valado train station costs 800$, to Nazaré 1,600$.

ÓBIDOS

This medieval walled town was Portugal's "wedding city"—the perfect gift for a king to give to a queen who has everything. (Beats a toaster.) Today it's preserved in its entirety as a national monument surviving on tourism. Óbidos is crowded all summer, especially in August. Filter out the tourists and see it as you would a beautiful painted tile. It's worth a quick visit.

Postcard perfect, the town sits atop a hill, its 40-foot-high 14th-century wall corralling a bouquet of narrow lanes and flower-bedecked, whitewashed houses. Óbidos is ideal for photographers who want to make Portugal look prettier than it is. Walk around the wall and peek into the castle (now an overly-impressed-with-itself *pousada*, Db-34,000$, CC:VMA, tel. 26-295-9105, fax 26-295-9148).

Wander the back lanes and lose yourself in this lived-in open-air museum of medieval town nonplanning. Study the centuries-old houses and drop by the churches. St. Mary's Church, on the town square, gleams with lovely 17th-century *azulejo* tiles. The small Municipal Museum, also on the square, is not worth the 300$ unless you enjoy stairs, religious art, and Portuguese inscriptions. Outside the town walls are a 16th-century aqueduct, a windmill, and a small produce market.

Óbidos is tough on the average tourist's budget. Pick up your picnic at the small grocery store just inside the main gate (on the street heading downhill), the larger grocery near the TI on Rua Direita, or the tiny market just outside the town wall.

Orientation

Tourist Information: There are two TIs almost next to each other in the middle of town on the main street, Rua Direita. The Região de Turismo do Oeste covers the region, and, a few doors down, the TI specializes in the town (Sun–Fri 9:30–19:00, Sat 9:30–13:00, 14:00–19:00, tel. 26-295-9231).

Arrival in Óbidos: Ideally take a bus to Óbidos and leave by either bus or train. If you arrive at the train station, you're faced with a 20-minute uphill hike into town (a killer with luggage). The bus drops you off much closer (go up the steps and through the archway on the right). While there's no official place to store luggage, the TI will let you leave your bag there.

Sleeping in Óbidos

To enjoy the town without tourists, spend the night. Two reasonable values in this overpriced toy of a town are the hotelesque **Albergaria Rainha Santa Isabel** (Sb-9,500–11,000$, Db-12,500–14,000$, includes breakfast, CC:VMA, air-con, elevator, on the main one-lane drag, Rua Direita, 2510 Óbidos, tel. 26-295-9323, fax 26-295-9115, SE) and **Casa do Poço**, with four dim, clean rooms around a bright courtyard (Db-9,000–14,500$, includes breakfast, Travessa da Mouraria, 2510 Óbidos, in old center near the castle, tel. 26-295-9358, SE).

For less expensive intimacy, try a *quarto*. Signs advertise rooms for rent all over town. **Lelia and Joao Fonseca da Silva** rent two good rooms (D-5,000$, 100 meters in from the town gate on the low road, Rua Josefa d'Obidos, tel. 26-295-9113, NSE).

Transportation Connections—Óbidos
To: Nazaré (5 buses/day, 1 hr), **Lisbon** (3 buses/day, 75 min; 2 trains/day, 2 hrs, transfer in Cacem), **Alcobaça** (6 buses/day, 1 hr), **Batalha** (4 buses/day, 2 hrs). Fewer buses run on Sunday.

Route Tips for Drivers in Central Portugal
Lisbon to Coimbra: This is an easy 2.5-hour straight shot on the slick new Auto-Estrada A1 (toll: 1,800$). You'll pass convenient exits for Fatima and the Roman ruins of Conimbriga along the way. Leave the freeway on the easy-to-miss first Coimbra exit and then follow the "*centro*" signs. Four kilometers after leaving the freeway you'll cross the Mondego River. You can go straight to the Ecovia park-and-ride (cheap parking, two blocks past the bridge, shuttle bus to the town center) or arc right, following Avenida Fernão de Magalhaes directly into town. Most hotels are near the train station and the next bridge—Ponte de Santa Clara. Free parking (safe during the day) is just over the Santa Clara Bridge.

Óbidos to Lisbon: Don't drive into tiny, cobbled Óbidos. Ample tourist parking is provided outside of town. From Óbidos, the slick tollway zips you directly into Lisbon. For arriving and parking in Lisbon, see that chapter. If going to Sintra, follow signs to Cascais as you approach Lisbon.

APPENDIX

Iberian History

The cultural landscape of modern Spain and Portugal was shaped by the various civilizations that settled on the peninsula. Iberia's sunny weather and fertile soil made it a popular place to call home.

The Greeks came to Cadiz around 1100 B.C., followed by the Romans, who occupied the country for almost 1,000 years, until A.D. 400. Long after the empire crumbled, the Roman influence remained, including cultural values, materials, building techniques, and even Roman-style farming equipment, which was used well into the 19th century. And, of course, wine.

Moors (711–1492)

The Moors—North Africans of the Muslim faith who occupied Spain—had the greatest cultural influence on Spanish and Portuguese history. They arrived on the Rock of Gibraltar in A.D. 711 and moved north. In the incredibly short time of seven years, the Moors completely conquered the peninsula.

The Moors established their power and Muslim culture in a subtle way. Non-Muslims were tolerated and often rose to positions of wealth and power; Jewish culture flourished. Rather than brutal subjugation, the Moorish style of conquest was to employ their sophisticated culture to develop whatever they found. For example, they encouraged wine-making, although for religious reasons they themselves weren't allowed to drink alcohol.

The Moors ruled for more than 700 years. Throughout that time, pockets of Christianity remained. Local Christian kings fought against the Moors whenever they could, whittling away at the Muslim empire, gaining more and more land. The last Moorish stronghold, Granada, fell to the Christians in 1492.

The slow, piecemeal process of the Reconquista split the peninsula into the independent states of Portugal and Spain. In 1139 Alfonso Henriques conquered the Moors near present-day Beja in southern Portugal and proclaimed himself king of the area. By 1200 the Christian state of Portugal had the borders it does today, making it the oldest unchanged state in Europe. The rest of the peninsula was a loosely knit collection of smaller kingdoms. Spain's major step toward unity was in 1469, when Fernando II of Aragon married Isabel of Castile. Known as the "Catholic Monarchs," they united the other kingdoms under their rule.

The Golden Age (1500–1700)

The expulsion of the Moors set the stage for the rise of Portugal and Spain as naval powers and colonial superpowers. The Spaniards, fueled by the religious fervor of the Reconquista, were interested in spreading Christianity to the newly discovered New World. Wherever they landed, they tried to Christianize the natives—with the sword, if necessary.

The Portuguese expansion was motivated more by economic concerns. Their excursions overseas were planned, cool, and rational. They colonized the nearby coasts of Africa first, progressing slowly around Africa to Asia and South America.

Through exploration (and exploitation) of the colonies, tremendous quantities of gold came into each country. The aristocracy and the clergy were swimming in money. It was only natural that art and courtly life flourished during this Golden Age.

Slow Decline
The fast money from the colonies kept Spain and Portugal from seeing the dangers at home. Great Britain and the Netherlands also were becoming naval powers, defeating the Spanish Armada in 1588. The Portuguese imported everything, stopped growing their own wheat, and neglected their fields.

During the centuries when science and technology in other European countries developed as never before, Spain and Portugal were preoccupied by their failed colonial politics. In the 18th century Spain was ruled by the French Bourbon family. (This explains the French Baroque architecture that you'll see, such as La Granja near Segovia and the Royal Palace in Madrid.) Endless battles, wars of succession, revolutions, and counterrevolutions weakened the countries. In this chaos there was no chance to develop democratic forms of government. Dictators in both countries made the rich richer and kept the masses underprivileged.

During World War I Portugal fought on the Allied side and Spain stayed neutral. In World War II both countries were neutral, uninterested in foreign policy as long as there was quiet in their own states. In the 1930s Spain suffered a bloody and bitter civil war between fascist and democratic forces. The fascist dictator Francisco Franco prevailed, ruling the country until his death in 1975.

Democracy in Spain and Portugal is still young. After an unbloody revolution, Portugal held democratic elections in 1975. After 41 years of a fascist dictatorship, Spain finally had elections in 1977.

Today socialists are in power in both countries. They've adopted a policy of balance to save the young democracies and fight problems such as unemployment and foreign debts—with moderate success. Spain recently joined the European Union. Today Spain's economy is among the fastest growing in Europe.

Art
The "Big Three" in Spanish painting are El Greco, Velázquez, and Goya.

El Greco (1541–1614) exemplifies the spiritual fervor of much Spanish art. The drama, the surreal colors, and the intentionally unnatural distortion have the intensity of a religious vision.

Diego Velázquez (1599–1660) went to the opposite extreme. His masterful court portraits are studies in realism and cool detachment from his subjects.

Goya (1746–1828) matched Velázquez's technique but not his detachment. He let his liberal tendencies shine through in unflattering portraits of royalty and in emotional scenes of abuse of power. He unleashed his inner passions in the eerie, nightmarish canvases of his last, "dark" stage.

Not quite in the league of the Big Three, Murillo (1617–1682) painted a dreamy world of religious visions. His pastel, soft-focus works of cute baby Jesuses and radiant Virgin Marys helped make Catholic doctrine palatable to the common folk at a time when many were defecting to Protestantism.

You'll also find plenty of foreign art in Spain's museums. During its Golden Age, Spain's wealthy aristocrats bought wagon loads of the most popular art of the time—Italian Renaissance and Baroque works by Titian, Tintoretto, and others. They also loaded up on paintings by Rubens, Bosch, and Brueghel from the Low Countries, which were under Spanish rule.

In this century Pablo Picasso (don't miss his *Guernica* mural in Madrid), Joan Miró, and surrealist Salvador Dalí have made their marks (great museums featuring all three are in or near Barcelona).

Architecture

The two most fertile periods of architectural innovation in Spain and Portugal were during the Moorish occupation and in the Golden Age. Otherwise, Spanish architects have marched obediently behind the rest of Europe.

The Moors brought Middle Eastern styles with them, such as the horseshoe arch, minarets, and floor plans designed for mosques. Islam forbids the sculpting or painting of human or animal figures ("graven images"), so artists expressed their creativity with elaborate geometric patterns. The ornate stucco of Granada's Alhambra, the elaborate arches of Sevilla's Alcázar, and decorative colored tiles are evidence of the Moorish sense of beauty. Islamic and Christian elements were blended in the work of Mozarabic (Christians living under Moorish rule) and Mudejar (Moors living in Spain after the Christian reconquest) artists.

As the Christians slowly reconquered the country, they turned their fervor into stone, building churches both in the heavy, fortress-of-God Romanesque style (Lisbon's cathedral) and in the lighter, heaven-reaching, stained-glass Gothic style (Barcelona, Toledo, Sevilla). Gothic was an import from France, trickling into conservative Spain long after it swept through Europe.

The money reaped and raped from Spain's colonies in the Golden Age spurred new construction. Churches and palaces were built using the solid, geometric style of the Italian Renaissance (El Escorial) and the more ornamented Baroque. Ornamentation reached unprecedented heights in Spain, culminating in the Plateresque style of stonework, so called because it resembles intricate silver filigree work. Portugal's highly ornamented answer to Plateresque is called Manueline. Lisbon's Belém Tower is its best example.

In the 18th and 19th centuries, innovation in both countries died out. Spain's major contribution to modern architecture is the Art Nouveau work of Antonio Gaudí early in this century. Most of his "cake-left-out-in-the-rain" buildings, with asymmetrical designs and sinuous lines, can be found in Barcelona.

Bullfighting—Legitimate Slice of Spain or Cruel Spectacle?

The Spanish bullfight is as much a ritual as it is sport. Not to acknowledge the importance of the bullfight is to censor a venerable part of Spanish culture. But it also makes a spectacle out of the cruel killing of an animal. Should tourists boycott bullfights? I don't know.

Today bullfighting is less popular among locals. If this trend continues, bullfighting may survive more and more as a tourist event. When the day comes that bullfighting is kept alive by our tourist dollars rather than the local culture, then I'll agree with those who say bullfighting is immoral and that tourists shouldn't encourage it by buying tickets. Consider the morality of supporting this gruesome aspect of Spanish culture before buying a ticket. If you do decide to attend a bullfight, here is what you'll see.

While no two bullfights are the same, they unfold along a strict pattern. The ceremony begins punctually with a parade of participants around the ring. Then the trumpet sounds, the "Gate of Fear" opens, and the leading player—*el toro*—thunders in. An angry half-ton animal is an awesome sight, even from the cheap seats.

The fight is divided into three acts. Act 1 is designed to size up the bull and wear him down. The matador (literally "killer"), with help from his assistants, attracts the bull with the shake of the cape, then directs the animal past his body, as close as his bravery allows. The bull sees only things in motion and red. After a few passes the picadors enter, mounted on horseback, to spear the swollen lump of muscle at the back of the bull's neck. This lowers the bull's head and weakens the thrust of his horns. (In the 19th century horses had no protective pads and were often killed.)

In act 2, the matador's assistants (banderilleros) continue to enrage and weaken the bull. The unarmed banderillero charges the charging bull and, leaping acrobatically across its path, plunges brightly colored barbed sticks into the bull's vital neck muscle.

After a short intermission, during which the matador may,

according to tradition, ask permission to kill the bull and dedicate the kill to someone in the crowd, the final, lethal act 3 begins.

The matador tries to dominate and tire the bull with hypnotic cape work. A good pass is when the matador stands completely still while the bull charges past. Then the matador thrusts a sword between the animal's shoulder blades for the kill. A quick kill is not always easy, and the matador may have to make several bloody thrusts before the sword stays in and the bull finally dies. Mules drag the bull out, and his meat is in the market *mañana*. *Rabo del toro* (bull-tail stew) is a delicacy.

Throughout the fight, the crowd shows its approval or impatience. Shouts of "*¡Olé!*" or "*¡Torero!*" mean they like what they see. Whistling or rhythmic hand-clapping greets cowardice and incompetence.

You're not likely to see much human blood spilled. In 200 years of bullfighting in Sevilla, only 30 fighters have died (and only one was actually a matador).

If a bull does kill a fighter, the next matador comes in to kill him. Even the bull's mother is killed, since the evil qualities are assumed to have come from the mother.

After an exceptional fight, the crowd may wave white handkerchiefs to ask that the matador be awarded the bull's ear or tail. A brave bull, though dead, gets a victory lap from the mule team on his way to the slaughterhouse. Then the trumpet sounds, and a new bull barges in to face a fresh matador.

A typical bullfight lasts about three hours and consists of six separate fights—three matadors (each with their own team of picadores and banderilleros) fighting two bulls each. For a closer look at bullfighting by an American aficionado, read Ernest Hemingway's classic *Death in the Afternoon*.

The Portuguese bullfight is different from the Spanish bullfight. For a description, see the Lisbon chapter. In Portugal, the bull is not killed in front of the crowd (but it is killed later).

Fiestas

Iberia has many regional and surprise holidays. Regular nationwide holidays are as follows:

Portugal: January 1, Easter, April 25, May 1, June 10, August 15, October 5, November 1, December 1, December 8, and December 25.

Spain: January 1, January 6, March 19, Good Friday, Easter, May 1, Corpus Christi (early June), June 24, June 29, July 18, July 25, August 15, October 12, November 1, December 8, and December 25.

Spain and Portugal erupt with fiestas and celebrations throughout the year. Semana Santa (Holy Week) fills the week before Easter with processions and festivities all over, but especially in

Sevilla. To run with the bulls, be in Pamplona the second week in July. For more information, call or write to the Spanish or Portuguese National Tourist Offices (see Introduction).

Numbers and Stumblers

- Europeans write a few of their numbers differently than we do: 1 = 1 , 4 = 4 , 7= 7. Learn the difference or miss your train.
- Europeans write dates day/month/year (Christmas is 25/12/00).
- Commas are decimal points, and decimals are commas. A dollar and a half is 1,50. There are 5.280 feet in a mile.
- When pointing, use your whole hand, palm downward.
- When counting with fingers, start with your thumb. If you hold up your first finger to request one item, you'll probably get two.
- What we Americans call the second floor of a building is the first floor in Europe.
- Europeans keep the left "lane" open for passing on escalators and moving sidewalks. Keep to the right.

Let's Talk Telephones

This is a primer on telephoning. For specifics on Spain and Portugal, also see "Telephones" in the Introduction.

Dialing Direct

Calling between Countries: Dial the international access code (of the country you're calling from), then the country code (of the country you're calling), the area code (if it starts with zero, drop the zero), and the local number. Note that Spain and Portugal don't use area codes (see "Europe's Exceptions," below). Also see "International Access Codes" and "Country Codes," below.

    Calling Long Distance within a Country: In most European countries, dial the area code (including its zero), then the local number. In Spain and Portugal all numbers have nine digits and are dialed direct throughout the country.

    Europe's Exceptions: Some countries, such as Spain, Portugal, France, Italy, Norway, and Denmark, do not use area codes. To make an international call to these countries, dial the international access code (usually 00, but 011 in the United States), then the country code, then the local number in its entirety. (OK, so there's one exception; for France, drop the initial zero of the local number.) To make long-distance calls within any of these countries, simply dial the local number.

International Access Codes

When dialing direct, first dial the international access code of the country you're calling from. Virtually all European countries, use "00" (the only exceptions are Finland, 990; Estonia, 800; and Lithuania, 810). For both the United States and Canada, it's "011."

Country Codes

After you've dialed the international access code, dial the code of the country you're calling.

Austria—43	Ireland—353
Belgium—32	Italy—39
Britain—44	Morocco—212
Canada—1	Netherlands—31
Czech Rep.—420	Norway—47
Denmark—45	Portugal—351
Estonia—372	Russia—7
Finland—358	Spain—34
France—33	Sweden—46
Germany—49	Switzerland—41
Greece—30	U.S.A.—1

Dial Away . . .

United States to Spain: 011/34/nine-digit number
United States to Portugal: 011/351/nine-digit number
Spain or Portugal to United States: 00/1/area code/number
Spain to Portugal: 00/351/nine-digit number
Portugal to Spain: 00/34/nine-digit number
Long Distance within Spain or within Portugal: Whether dialing across the street or across the country, you use the same nine-digit number.
Directory Assistance: In Spain, dial 1004 for local numbers and 025 for international numbers (expensive); in Portugal, dial 13. (Note: In Spain a 608 or 609 area code indicates a mobile phone.)

Calling Card Operators

It's cheaper to call direct, but some travelers prefer to use their calling cards (AT&T, MCI, or Sprint).

	AT&T	MCI	Sprint
Spain	900-99-00-11	900-99-00-14	900-99-00-13
Portugal	0800-800-128	0800-800-123	0800-800-187
Morocco	002-110-011	002-110-012	————
Gibraltar	8800	————	————

Metric Conversion (approximate)

1 inch = 25 millimeters	32 degrees F = 0 degrees C
1 foot = 0.3 meter	82 degrees F = about 28 degrees C
1 yard = 0.9 meter	1 ounce = 28 grams
1 mile = 1.6 kilometers	1 kilogram = 2.2 pounds
1 centimeter = 0.4 inch	1 quart = 0.95 liter
1 meter = 39.4 inches	1 square yard = 0.8 square meter
1 kilometer = .62 mile	1 acre = 0.4 hectare

Climate

First line, average daily low temperature; second line, average daily high; third line, days of no rain.

	J	F	M	A	M	J	J	A	S	O	N	D
PORTUGAL	57	50	52	56	60	64	65	62	58	52	48	47
Lagos/	61	63	67	73	77	83	84	80	73	66	62	61
Algarve	19	20	24	27	29	31	31	28	26	22	22	22
Lisbon	47	49	52	56	60	63	64	62	57	52	47	46
	58	61	64	69	75	79	80	76	69	62	57	56
	20	21	23	25	28	30	30	26	24	20	21	22
SPAIN	35	40	44	50	57	62	62	56	48	40	35	33
Madrid	47	51	47	64	71	80	87	86	77	66	54	48
	22	19	20	21	22	24	28	29	24	23	20	22
Barcelona	42	44	47	51	57	63	69	69	65	58	50	44
	56	57	61	64	71	77	81	82	67	61	62	57
	26	21	24	22	23	25	27	26	23	23	23	25
Costa	47	48	51	55	60	66	70	72	68	61	53	48
del Sol	61	62	64	69	74	80	84	85	81	74	67	62
	25	22	23	25	28	29	31	30	28	27	22	25

Basic Spanish Survival Phrases

Hello.	**Hola.**	**oh**-lah
Do you speak English?	**¿Habla usted inglés?**	ah-blah oo-**stehd** een-**glays**
Yes. / No.	**Sí. / No.**	see / noh
I don't speak Spanish.	**No hablo español.**	noh ah-bloh ay-spahn-**yohl**
I'm sorry.	**Lo siento.**	loh see-**ehn**-toh
Please.	**Por favor.**	por fah-**bor**
Thank you.	**Gracias.**	**grah**-thee-ahs
Goodbye.	**Adiós.**	ah-dee-**ohs**
Where is a...?	**¿Donde hay un...?**	**dohn**-day ī oon
...hotel	**...hotel**	oh-**tel**
...youth hostel	**...albergue de juventud**	ahl-**behr**-gay day *h*oo-behn-**tood**
...restaurant	**...restaurante**	ray-stoh-**rahn**-tay
...supermarket	**...supermercado**	soo-pehr-mehr-**kah**-doh
Where is the...?	**¿Dónde está la...?**	**dohn**-day ay-**stah** lah
...train station	**...estación de trenes**	ay-stah-thee-**ohn** day **tray**-nays
...tourist information office	**...Oficina de Turismo**	oh-fee-**thee**-nah day too-**rees**-moh
Where are the toilets?	**¿Dónde están los servicios?**	**dohn**-day ay-**stahn** lohs sehr-**bee**-thee-ohs
men / women	**hombres / mujeres**	**ohm**-brays / moo-*h*eh-rays
How much is it?	**¿Cuánto cuesta?**	**kwahn**-toh **kway**-stah
Write it?	**¿Me lo escribe?**	may loh ay-**skree**-bay
Cheap(er).	**(Más) barato.**	(mahs) bah-**rah**-toh
Is it included?	**¿Está incluido?**	ay-**stah** een-kloo-**ee**-doh
I would like...	**Quería...**	keh-**ree**-ah
We would like...	**Queríamos...**	keh-**ree**-ah-mohs
...a ticket.	**...un billete.**	oon bee-**yeh**-tay
...a room.	**...una habitación.**	**oo**-nah ah-bee-tah-thee-**ohn**
...the bill.	**...la cuenta.**	lah **kwayn**-tah
one	**uno**	**oo**-noh
two	**dos**	dohs
three	**tres**	trays
four	**cuatro**	**kwah**-troh
five	**cinco**	**theen**-koh
six	**seis**	says
seven	**siete**	see-**eh**-tay
eight	**ocho**	**oh**-choh
nine	**nueve**	**nway**-bay
ten	**diez**	dee-**ayth**
At what time?	**¿A qué hora?**	ah kay **oh**-rah
now / later	**ahora / más tarde**	**ah-oh**-rah / mahs **tar**-day
today / tomorrow	**hoy / mañana**	oy / mahn-**yah**-nah

Basic Portuguese Survival Phrases

Hello.	**Olá.**	oh-**lah**
Do you speak English?	**Fala inglês?**	fah-lah een-**glaysh**
Yes. / No.	**Sim. / Não.**	seeng / no<u>w</u>
I'm sorry.	**Desculpe.**	dish-**kool**-peh
Please.	**Por favor.**	poor fah-**vor**
Thank you.	**Obrigado[a].**	oh-bree-**gah**-doo
Goodbye.	**Adeus.**	ah-**deh**-oosh
Where is...?	**Onde é que é...?**	oh<u>n</u>-deh eh keh eh
...a hotel	**...um hotel**	oo<u>n</u> oh-**tehl**
...a youth hostel	**...uma pousada de juventude**	**oo**-mah poh-**zah**-dah deh zhoo-vay<u>n</u>-**too**-deh
...a restaurant	**...um restaurante**	oo<u>n</u> rish-toh-**rahn**-teh
...a supermarket	**...um supermercado**	oo<u>n</u> soo-pehr-mehr-**kah**-doo
...the train station	**...a estação de comboio**	ah ish-tah-**sow** deh koh<u>n</u>-**boy**-yoo
...tourist information	**...a informação turística**	ah een-for-mah-**sow** too-**reesh**-tee-kah
...the toilet	**...a casa de banho**	ah **kah**-zah deh **bahn**-yoo
men / women	**homens / mulheres**	**aw**-may<u>n</u>sh / mool-**yeh**-rish
How much is it?	**Quanto custa?**	**kwahn**-too **koosh**-tah
Cheap(er).	**(Mais) barato.**	(m<u>ī</u>sh) bah-**rah**-too
Is it included?	**Está incluido?**	ish-**tah** een-kloo-**ee**-doo
I would like...	**Gostaria...**	goosh-tah-**ree**-ah
...a ticket.	**...um bilhete.**	oo<u>n</u> beel-**yeh**-teh
...a room.	**...um quarto.**	oo<u>n</u> **kwar**-too
...the bill.	**...a conta.**	ah **kohn**-tah
one	**um**	oo<u>n</u>
two	**dois**	doysh
three	**três**	traysh
four	**quatro**	**kwah**-troo
five	**cinco**	**seeng**-koo
six	**seis**	saysh
seven	**sete**	**seh**-teh
eight	**oito**	**oy**-too
nine	**nove**	**naw**-veh
ten	**dez**	dehsh
At what time?	**A que horas?**	ah keh **aw**-rahsh
now / soon / later	**agora / em breve / mais tarde**	ah-**goh**-rah / ay<u>n</u> **bray**-veh / m<u>ī</u>sh **tar**-deh
Today.	**Hoje.**	**oh**-zheh
Tomorrow.	**Amanhã.**	ah-ming-**yah**

For 336 more pages of survival phrases for your next trip to Iberia, check out *Rick Steves' Spanish & Portuguese Phrase Book and Dictionary.*

Faxing Your Hotel Reservation

Faxing is more accurate and cheaper than telephoning. Use this handy form for your fax (or find it online at www.ricksteves.com /reservation). Photocopy and fax away.

One-Page Fax

To: _____ @ _____
                 hotel   *fax*

From: _____ @ _____
                 name   *fax*

Today's date: ____ /_____ /____
                day *month* *year*

Dear Hotel _____,

Please make this reservation for me:

Name: _____

Total # of people: _____   # of rooms: _____   # of nights: _____

Arriving: ____ /_____ /____ My time of arrival (24-hr clock): _____
          day *month* *year*   (I will telephone if I will be late)

Departing: ____ /_____ /____
           day *month* *year*

Room(s): Single___ Double___ Twin___ Triple___ Quad___

With: Toilet___ Shower___ Bath___ Sink only___

Special needs: View___ Quiet___ Cheapest Room___

Credit card: Visa___ MasterCard___ American Express___

Card #: _____

Expiration date:_____

Name on card: _____

You may charge me for the first night as a deposit. Please fax or mail me confirmation of my reservation, along with the type of room reserved, the price, and whether the price includes breakfast. Thank you.

_____
Signature

_____
Name

_____
Address

_____
City   *State*   *Zip Code*   *Country*

_____
E-mail Address

Road Scholar Feedback for
SPAIN & PORTUGAL 2000

We're all in the same travelers' school of hard knocks. Your feedback helps us improve this guidebook for future travelers. Please fill this out (or use the on-line version at www.ricksteves.com/feedback), attach more info or any tips/favorite discoveries if you like, and send it to us. As thanks for your help, we'll send you our quarterly travel newsletter free for one year. Thanks! Rick

Of the recommended accommodations/restaurants used, which was:

Best _____

      Why? _____

Worst _____

      Why? _____

Of the sights/experiences/destinations recommended by this book, which was:

Most overrated _____

      Why? _____

Most underrated _____

      Why? _____

Best ways to improve this book:

_____

I'd like a free newsletter subscription:

_____ Yes   _____ No   _____ Already on list

_____
Name

_____
Address

_____
City, State, Zip

_____
E-mail Address

Please send to: ETBD, Box 2009, Edmonds, WA 98020

Jubilee 2000—Let's Celebrate the Millennium by Forgiving Third World Debt

Let's ring in the millennium by convincing our government to forgive the debt owed to us by the world's poorest countries. Imagine spending over half your income on interest payments alone. You and I are creditors, and poor countries owe us more than they can pay.

Jubilee 2000 is a worldwide movement of concerned people and groups—religious and secular—working to cancel the international debts of the poorest countries by the year 2000.

Debt ruins people: In the poorest countries, money needed for health care, education, and other vital services is diverted to interest payments.

Mozambique, with a per-capita income of $90 and life expectancy of 40, spends over half its national income on interest. This poverty brings social unrest, civil war, and often costly humanitarian intervention by the United States. To chase export dollars, desperate countries ruin their environment. As deserts grow and rain forests shrink, the world suffers. Of course, the real suffering is among local people born long after some dictator borrowed (and squandered) that money. As interest is paid, entire populations go hungry.

Who owes what and why? Mozambique is one of 41 countries defined by the World Bank as "Heavily Indebted Poor Countries." In total, they owe $200 billion. Because these debts are unlikely to be paid, their market value is only a tenth of the face value (about $20 billion). The United States' share is under $2 billion.

How can debt be canceled? This debt is owed mostly to the United States, Japan, Germany, Britain, and France, either directly or through the World Bank. We can forgive the debt owed directly to us and pay the market value (usually 10 percent) of the debts owed to the World Bank. We have the resources. (Norway, another wealthy creditor nation, just unilaterally forgave its Third World debt.) All the United States needs is the political will...people power.

While many of these poor nations are now democratic, corruption is still a concern. A key to Jubilee 2000 is making certain that debt relief reduces poverty in a way that benefits ordinary people—women, farmers, children, and so on.

Let's celebrate the new millennium by giving poor countries a break. For the sake of peace, fragile young democracies, the environment, and countless real people, forgiving this debt is the right thing for us in the rich world to do.

Tell Washington, D.C.: If our government knows this is what we want, it can happen. Learn more, write letters, lobby legislators, or even start a local Jubilee 2000 campaign. For details, contact Jubilee 2000 (tel. 202/783-3566, www.j2000usa.org). For information on lobbying Congress on J2000, contact Bread for the World (tel. 800/82-BREAD, www.bread.org).

INDEX

Accommodations, *see* Sleeping
Airports: Barcelona, 27; Lisbon, 188–189; Madrid, 50–51
Alcobaça, 247–249
Algarve, 214–228; map, 215
Algeciras, 167, 172
Alhambra, Granada, 102–108
Andalusian white hill towns, 132–152
Arcos de la Frontera, 133–140; eating, 139–140; map, 135; sleeping, 138–139; transportation connections, 140
Art and architecture, 253–255
Ávila, 78

Banking, 4–5
Barcelona, 25–46; eating, 40–43; maps, 26, 31; sleeping, 38–40; transportation connections, 43–44
Batalha, 246–247
Belém, Lisbon, 198–201
Bullfighting, 255–256
Bullfights, 59–60, 147–148, 202, 222

Cabo da Roca, 212
Cacela Velha, 227
Cadaques, 44–45
Cape Sagres, 221–222
Cascais, 212
Caves, near Nerja, 156; prehistoric, 149–150
Ciudad Rodrigo, 84
Climate, 259
Coimbra, 230–241; eating, 240–241; map, 231; sleeping, 238–240; transportation connections, 241
Córdoba, 131
Costa del Sol, 153–172
Costs, trip, 2–3

Dali Museum, Figueres, 44
Don Quixote, 97
Drivers, route tips: Algarve, 228; Andalucía, 144, 152; Central Portugal, 230, 251; Costa del Sol, 172; Gibraltar, 162, 172; Granada, 98, 101–102, 172; Lisbon, 208, 228;

Madrid area, 68, 85, 98; Morocco, 175; Sevilla, 121, 228; South Portugal, 228
Driving, 15–16
E-mail, 17
Eating, 20–22
El Escorial, 70–72
El Greco, 89, 92–93
Estoril, 212
Europe Through the Back Door, 9–10
Évora, 213
Exchange rates, 3

Fado bars, 201–202
Fatima, 247
Feedback, 23; form, 263
Fès, 174, 183
Fiestas, 256–257
Figueres, 44
Flamenco, 125–126
Food, *see* Eating
Fuengirola, 159

Gaudí, 34–36
Gibraltar, 159–166
Granada, 99–118; eating, 117–118; maps, 101, 113; sleeping, 114–117; transportation connections, 118
Grazalema, 141
Guernica, Picasso's, 58
Guidebooks, recommended, 8–9

Henry the Navigator, 200, 221, 246
History, Iberian, 252–253
Holidays, 256–257
Horses, 142

Itinerary priorities, 4, 6, 7

Jerez, 142

La Mancha, 97–98
Lagos, 222–224
Language, 5, 28, 260–261
Lisbon, 185–213; eating, 205–207; maps, 186, 189, 209; sleeping, 203–205; transportation connections, 207–208

Madrid, 47–68; eating, 63–68; maps, 49, 53, 55, 66; sleeping,

60–63; transportation
connections, 68
Mail, 17
Málaga, transportation
connections, 158–159
Maps, general, 10
Marbella, 159
Marijuana, 177
Marrakech, 174, 183
Medina Sidonia, 144–145
Metric conversion, 258
Modernisme, 35
Montserrat, 45–46
Morocco, 173–184

Nazaré, 241–245
Nerja, 154–158

Óbidos, 250–251

Paradores and pousadas, 19
Philosophy, Back Door Travel, 24
Picasso Museum, Barcelona, 32–33
Pileta Caves, 149–150
Portuguese phrases, 261
Prado Museum, Madrid, 57
Puerto Banus, 159
Pueblos Blancos, *see* Andalusian
white hill towns

Rabat, 175, 183
Rates, exchange, 3
Reservations, hotel, 19–20;
fax form, 262
Roast suckling pig, 77, 96
Ronda, 145–152; eating, 151;
sleeping, 150–151

Sagres, Cape, 221–222
Salamanca, 78–84

Salema, 215–221; eating, 220–221;
sleeping, 218–220
San Pedro de Alcantara, 159
Segovia, 73–78
Sevilla, 119–131; eating, 129–130;
map, 121; sleeping, 126–129;
transportation connections, 130
Sherry bodega tours, 143–144
Sightseeing priorities, 4
Sintra, 209–212
Sleep code, 18
Sleeping, general, 17–20; hotel
fax form, 262
Spanish phrases, 260

Tangier, 177–182
Tapas (bar snacks), 21, 43, 64–67
Tarifa, 167–172; eating, 171;
sleeping,170–171
Tavira, 224–227
Telephoning, 16–17, 257–258
Toledo, 86–98; eating, 96–97;
maps, 87, 88; sleeping, 93–96;
transportation connections, 97
Torremolinos, 159
Tourist offices, general, 6, 8; U.S.
branches, 8
Transportation, 10–16; by bus,
13–14; by car, 15–16; by taxi, 14;
by train, 11–13; to Morocco,
173–175, 178, 181–182

Valley of the Fallen, 72–73
Vejer de la Frontera, 145

Weather, 259
When to go, 4

Zahara, 140–141
Zarazuela, 60

Rick Steves' Phrase Books

Unlike other phrase books and dictionaries on the market, my well-tested phrases and key words cover every situation a traveler is likely to encounter. With these books you'll laugh with your cabby, disarm street thieves with insults, and charm new European friends.

Each book in the series is 4" x 6", with maps.

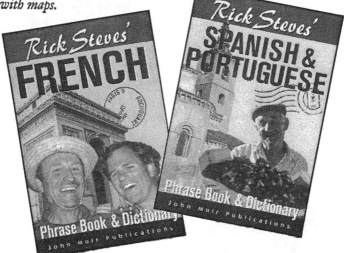

RICK STEVES' FRENCH PHRASE BOOK & DICTIONARY
U.S. $6.95/Canada $10.95

RICK STEVES' GERMAN PHRASE BOOK & DICTIONARY
U.S. $6.95/Canada $10.95

RICK STEVES' ITALIAN PHRASE BOOK & DICTIONARY
U.S. $6.95/Canada $10.95

RICK STEVES' SPANISH & PORTUGUESE PHRASE BOOK & DICTIONARY
U.S. $8.95/Canada $13.95

RICK STEVES' FRENCH, ITALIAN & GERMAN PHRASE BOOK & DICTIONARY
U.S. $8.95/Canada $13.95